D1015489

The Innovative University

The Jossey-Bass Higher and Adult Education Series

The Innovative University

CHANGING THE DNA OF HIGHER EDUCATION FROM THE INSIDE OUT

Clayton M. Christensen and Henry J. Eyring

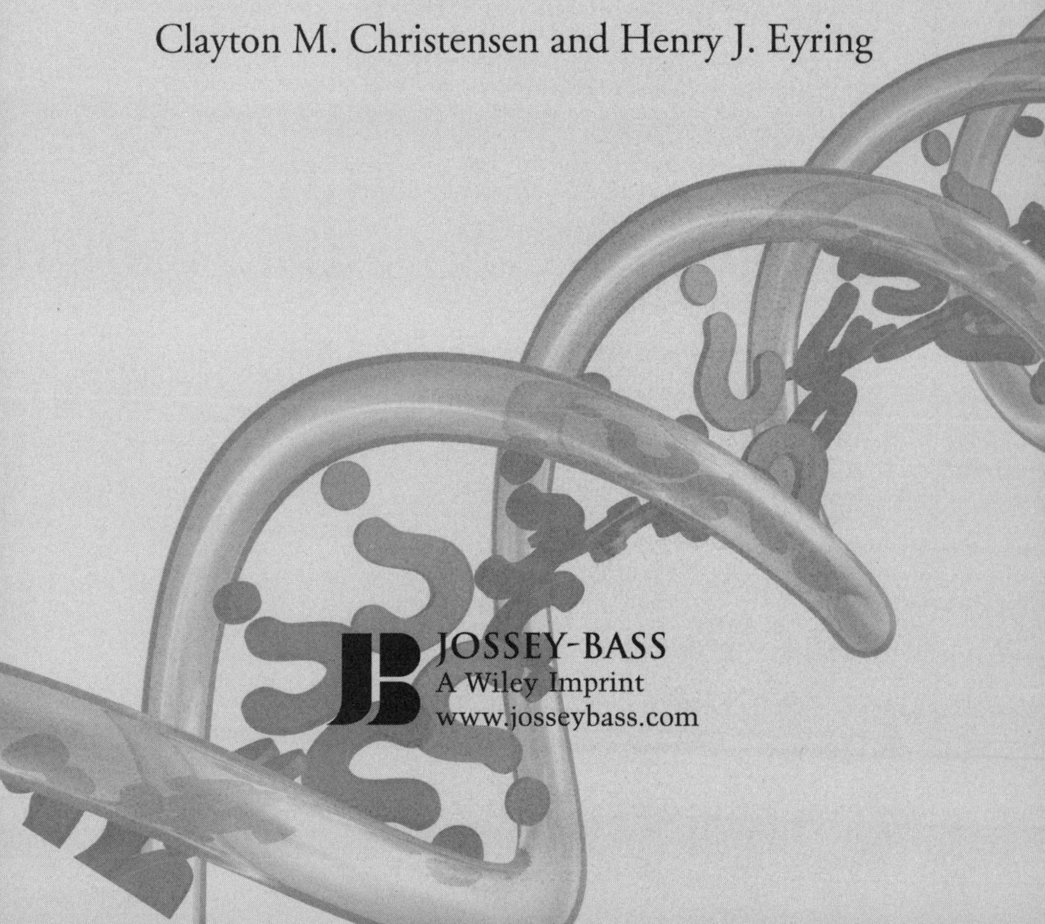

JOSSEY-BASS
A Wiley Imprint
www.josseybass.com

Published by Jossey-Bass
A Wiley Imprint
989 Market Street, San Francisco, CA 94103-1741—www.josseybass.com

Jossey-Bass books and products are available through most bookstores. To contact Jossey-Bass directly call our Customer Care Department within the U.S. at 800-956-7739, outside the U.S. at 317-572-3986, or fax 317-572-4002.

Jossey-Bass also publishes its books in a variety of electronic formats. Some content that appears in print may not be available in electronic books.

Library of Congress Cataloging-in-Publication Data

Christensen, Clayton M.
The innovative university : changing the DNA of higher education from the inside out / Clayton M. Christensen and Henry J. Eyring.
p. cm
Includes index.
ISBN 978-1-118-06348-4 (hardback); 978-1-118-09125-8 (ebk); 978-1-118-09126-5 (ebk); 978-1-118-09127-2 (ebk)
1. Universities and colleges–United States. 2. Educational change–United States. I. Eyring, Henry J. II. Title.
LA227.4.C525 2011
378.73–dc22

2011015805

Printed in the United States of America
FIRST EDITION

HB Printing 10 9 8 7 6 5 4 3 2 1

Contents

Part Three: Ripe for Disruption

Part Four: A New Kind of University

Part Five: Genetic Reengineering

Preface

Because the research and writing of this book began and ended with Henry Eyring, I have written this preface so that our readers might glimpse what a privilege it has been for me to watch Henry's extraordinary mind and his selfless heart at work as we crafted this book.

In 2000, Ricks College, a two-year school in rural southern Idaho, became a four-year school, Brigham Young University (BYU)-Idaho. The creation of BYU-Idaho took almost everyone by surprise. It wasn't just that its sponsor, the Church of Jesus Christ of Latter-day Saints (more commonly known as the Mormon Church) had a policy of preventing "mission creep" at its four institutions of higher learning.[1] At least as surprising as the decision to make Ricks a four-year institution was its unique design. The new university would remain focused on undergraduate instruction: there would be no graduate programs and no traditional research scholarship. One of the most successful junior college athletic programs in the United States would be eliminated.

The university would also pursue new efficiencies. It would operate year-round, and new technologies, especially online learning, would be used to serve more students at lower cost. In becoming a university, the former Ricks College would actually operate more in the spirit of a community college than it had before.

At the time of BYU-Idaho's creation, Henry J. Eyring was at a sister institution, Brigham Young University in Provo, Utah, directing the MBA program at the Marriott School of Management. A graduate of that program, Henry had been hired a few years earlier to help reverse a slide in its *US News & World Report* ranking, which had tied with Penn State for the last place in the top fifty MBA programs. The mandate was to move up quickly. Among other things, that meant becoming more selective in admissions; placing more students in higher-paying jobs; and bolstering the faculty's research and publication quality and quantity in order to enhance the program's reputation in the eyes of other academic leaders. These were crucial initiatives—and expensive ones.

This wasn't the first time Henry had seen the costs of operating at the upper heights of the academic hierarchy, however. As chief financial officer for the Huntsman Cancer Foundation, he approved outlays for medical research facilities and faculty salaries at the University of Utah's Huntsman Cancer Institute. Jon M. Huntsman Sr.'s initial commitments of more than $100 million were just enough to prime a pump that would need continual fueling by other sources, particularly federal research grants.

Thus, in 2000, the design of the new BYU-Idaho riveted Henry's attention. On a higher education landscape where the general goal is to move up notwithstanding the high cost of doing so, here was an institution focused on a relatively lowly niche. When, in 2005, Harvard Business School dean Kim Clark was named president of BYU-Idaho, Henry was among many who wondered whether the institution's strategy would change: Wouldn't an accomplished scholar and fundraiser from the world's preeminent business school attempt to raise the institution's prestige and profile?

In his inauguration address Kim squashed such speculation. As expected, he talked of raising the quality of a BYU-Idaho education. However, Kim projected a decline in the university's operating costs and an expansion of its reach to benefit even students in Africa. He admitted the difficulty of simultaneously raising the school's quality, decreasing its costs, and serving more students. But he spoke optimistically and with the credibility not only of a Harvard Business School dean but also as a distinguished scholar of operations management. Henry, who had met Kim only once, contacted him to learn more about his vision and then jumped at Kim's offer to join the BYU-Idaho team.

Working with Kim and his team proved as stimulating as expected—especially as Henry observed the differences between BYU-Idaho and most other universities. The people weren't fundamentally different: BYU-Idaho faculty members and administrators love learning and helping others learn, but that is true of almost everyone who embarks on an academic career. Somehow, though, the BYU-Idaho environment fostered unusual innovation and learning outcomes. Responding to his musings on these paradoxes one day, Henry's wife Kelly explained the difference with a metaphor: "BYU-Idaho has different DNA."

The metaphor clicked. At the time Henry was reading a book called *Excellence Without a Soul: How a Great University Forgot Education.*[2] Author Harry Lewis, a former dean of Harvard College, begins the book with an overview of Harvard's history. He summarizes innovations that produced institutional features familiar to any college student: merit-based admissions and scholarships; general education and majors; grading curves and honors; intercollegiate athletes and faculty members striving for up-or-out tenure. Reading now with BYU-Idaho's unique traits in mind, Henry recognized Harvard as the source of much of the DNA of traditional universities, from long-established research institutions to up-and-coming regional schools.

The thought occurred to Henry to contrast the differences between the DNA of Harvard and BYU-Idaho by telling their stories from initial founding to the present. The comparison might show how other institutions could change their DNA as BYU-Idaho has done. Kim Clark initially questioned the idea. Given Henry's employment at BYU-Idaho and the fact that his father was president of its forerunner, Ricks College, from 1971 to 1977, there could be accusations of self-serving bias. Kim was also sensitive to the potential inference that BYU-Idaho considers its educational model somehow preferable to Harvard's. A holder of bachelor's, master's, and doctoral degrees from

Harvard, Kim knew that the two institutions are different species and literally incomparable.

Henry argued that that was exactly the point. His zeal for contrasting the DNA of BYU-Idaho and Harvard grew as Kim pointed out the features that make the latter different not only from the former but also from the many institutions that have attempted to copy Harvard. Kim described the intellectual stimulation of the Harvard house environment, with its tutors who showed him how to study more effectively and how to "navigate the system." He told of being mentored by world-class scholars in graduate-level courses that were open to him as an undergraduate student.

Kim, who along with others well acquainted with Harvard, became a key advisor on the writing project, also talked about how much Harvard spends to simultaneously set the worldwide pace for scholarship and create a nurturing environment for all students, including undergraduates. The weight of that financial burden became generally apparent in 2009, as Harvard dealt with the budgetary fallout from a huge endowment loss. Henry realized that one reason other institutions struggle as they attempt to emulate Harvard is that essential elements of the DNA—especially Harvard's unrivaled wealth—are hard to copy.

As Henry studied the Harvard-emulation phenomenon, he recognized some of the pattern of disruptive innovation that I have found in so many industries. The theory of disruptive innovation asserts that in industries from computers to cars to steel those entrants that start at the bottom of their markets, selling simple products to less demanding customers and then improving from that foothold, drive the prior leaders into a disruptive demise. I was wrestling to explain the same issues in higher education, a natural next step after writing a book about disruptive innovation in public education. So when Henry invited me to join him in studying the past and future of higher education, I jumped at the chance.

We concluded that universities are an anomaly that my original framing of disruption could not explain. True, most entrants have indeed entered into the "low end" or "new market" of higher education, often as community colleges. And they have almost uniformly driven up-market to offer bachelor's and advanced degrees in more and more fields—just as the theory would predict. But the demise of the incumbents that characterizes most industries in the late stages of disruption has rarely occurred among colleges and universities. We have had entry, but not exit.

We identified three factors that resolved this anomaly. First, teaching. In the past, teaching was difficult to disrupt because its human qualities couldn't be replicated. In the future, though, teaching *will* be disruptable as online technology improves and shifts the competitive focus from a teacher's credentials or an institution's prestige to what students actually learn.

Second, we observed two distinct groups of college students who have different "jobs-to-be-done." In one group, the campus experience is central to the college experience. For members of this group, the campus experience is hard to disrupt. Because of family and work responsibilities, however, students in the other group don't want to spend time on campus to earn a degree. They want to learn when they have time to learn—often after work, when their children are asleep. New entrants to higher education that focus on these potential students are indeed classic disruptors.

And the third reason why higher education has seen many new entrants but few exits is alumni and state legislators, who are "customers" of their institutions. Their support is typically driven not only by public spiritedness but also by deep personal relationships with faculty members and coaches who profoundly molded their lives. Alumni and state support gives traditional universities and colleges staying power unique to higher education.

These observations supported the finding of other studies that learning occurs best when it involves a blend of online and face-to-face learning, with the latter providing essential intangibles best obtained on a traditional college campus. I believe a more nuanced theory of higher education innovation emerged from our collaboration. The physical campuses and full-time faculty members of traditional universities and colleges can embrace online learning as a sustaining innovation—technology could make them stronger than ever. This is a different situation than the more straightforward dilemma that the newspapers and video rental stores faced when online technology knocked on their doors.

By the summer of 2010, Henry and I had revised the story of Harvard, BYU-Idaho, and disruptive innovation in higher education to the point of apparent diminishing returns. As I said on July 16, "Finishing a book like ours is like playing football on a logarithmic grid: regardless of how hard you work to cross the goal line with a perfect product, you see an eternity of additional work required to get there. At some point, you just have to declare victory, spike the ball and walk off the field." We agreed that Henry would tighten the final part of the manuscript while I wrote a new introduction. Then we would call it good.

Two days later I suffered a stroke as I addressed a church group near MIT. A neurologist in the group recognized the slurring of my speech as a sign of stroke and admitted me to Massachusetts General Hospital, just five minutes away. The stroke rendered me unable to speak and write. Henry's able shoulders therefore had to carry not only his assignments but mine too, while I focused on learning again to speak and write. The delay brought unexpected benefits to the writing project. Most notably, the November 2010 release of a study called *Winning by Degrees: The Strategies of Highly Effective Higher Education Institutions*[3] enriched the manuscript with its descriptions of the innovations of schools other than BYU-Idaho and Harvard. Henry did a magnificent job.

At a time when my persuasive abilities were still limited, Henry and the publishers concluded that our two names would appear alphabetically on the cover—because we both contributed all that we could. Our goal is to inspire today's higher education community to do what it did in the late 1800s, when Harvard and its peers created a new model of higher education. It was a model that built on the best traditions of U.S. and European institutions but added powerful innovations that took them all to greater heights. Along with the Morrill Act, which established the land-grant colleges, the new model dramatically expanded the quality and accessibility of higher learning, helping to fulfill Abraham Lincoln's dream of a "new birth of freedom."

The technologies that now threaten to disrupt traditional universities and colleges can also reinvigorate them to the benefit of so many people. We hope that this book will help—that it will be widely read and debated. Our motive is not pecuniary; our royalties have been assigned to the Innosight Institute, our partner in promoting higher education innovation.

Henry and I love higher education. We appreciate what it has done for us, and we love the people who make it possible. They include not only teachers and administrators but also students and parents and taxpayers. This book is for them, in a spirit of love and hope.

Clayton M. Christensen and
my magnificent partner in this
effort, Henry J. Eyring

Acknowledgments

We are grateful to many people whose support and direction made this book possible. They include the following volunteers who generously read and commented on the manuscript. Each made it better, though none bears any blame for its flaws.

Josh Allen and the students of his BYU-Idaho professional editing class
Scott Anthony
Douglas Anderson
Devan Barker
Ross Baron
Michael Bassis
David Bednar
Susan Bednar
Robert Bird
Derek Bok
Jack Brittain
Molly Corbett Broad
Fenton Broadhead
Merv Brown
Kelly Burgener
Mary Carter
Max Checketts
Kim Clark
Jordan Clements
Hyrum Conrad
Maureen Devlin
Rob Eaton
Jason Earl
Tom Eisenmann
Glenn Embree
Henry B. Eyring
Henry C. Eyring
Matthew Eyring
Mark Fuller
Gordon Gee
Clark Gilbert

Mary Glenn
Jack Harrell
Roger Hoggan
Matt Holland
Steve Hunsaker
John Ivers
Shawn Johansen
Paul Johnson
Todd Kelson
Jorge Klor de Alva
Bruce Kusch
Martha Laboissier
Michael Leavitt
Paul Le Blanc
Nicholas Lemann
Doug Lederman
Harry Lewis
Kent Lundin
Michael Madsen
Scott McKinley
Louis Menand
Joel Meyerson
Todd Nelson
Reed Nielsen
Rulon Nielsen
Jeffrey Olson
Luba Ostashevsky
Ric Page
Greg Palmer
David Peck
Chase Peterson
Richard Pieper
Michael Porter
LaNae Poulter
Stephen Prescott
Martin Raish
Kirk Rawlins
Henry Rosovsky
Cecil Samuelson
Matt Sanders
Len Schlesinger
Rhonda Seamons
Mack Shirley
Steven Snow
Louis Soares
Danny Stern
Richard Tait
John Thomas
Eric Walz
Steve Wheelwright
Alan Young
Michael Young

We received extraordinary professional support in the production of the book. Jesse Wiley correctly described his Jossey-Bass colleague Sheryl Fullerton as "simply perfect for the job" of editing the manuscript. Along with her teammates, Alison Knowles and Joanne Clapp Fullagar, Sheryl exceeded all reasonable expectations of effort and skill.

We are similarly grateful to Danny and Susan Stern and their gifted team at Stern + Associates: Millie Mortan, Laura Moss, Jim Nichols, Adria Tomaszewski, and Ned Ward. Each of them improved the book and played a vital role in publicizing it. The same is true of our Innosight Institute colleague Michael Horn.

We are particularly indebted to Clay's assistant Lisa Stone, who kept the channel of communication between us open as he experienced and miraculously recovered from a severe stroke. Lisa also helped us see the holes in our thinking and made brilliant suggestions for filling them. She is a friend of remarkable dedication, optimism, and talent.

For Christine, who keeps my mind sharp amidst everything else
—Clay Christensen

To Kelly, who suggested the DNA metaphor
— Henry J. Eyring

Introduction

Ripe for Disruption—and Innovation

Just how much trouble is American higher education in, really? The answer may vary greatly depending on your primary source of information. If you rely mainly on the news media and books, things look grim. State legislators seem to be at war with their own public institutions; higher education, the largest discretionary item in the state budget, is on the chopping block. At a national level, the United States appears to be in educational decline relative to countries in which college participation and completion is steadily rising. From campuses come books by university scholars who cite research and personal experience in declaring their institutions to be broken.

If you are the parent of a college student, this disturbing picture finds some support in your personal experience. Notwithstanding all the talk of growing federal financial aid, you may have stretched to the breaking point to send your child to a well-regarded school. Then you receive reports of unavailable courses, inadequate academic counseling, and hard-to-access professors. The learning experience, though it carries a much higher price tag, sounds reminiscent of your own college days, dominated by textbooks, lectures, and multiple choice exams. Other than the increased cost, the only thing that sounds significantly different is the amount of partying going on (though your memory may be selective on that point).

If your student is attending a public institution, progress toward graduation seems haphazard and slow: by the end of what should be your student's junior year there may be no set date for graduation. Your child, in fact, has almost a 50 percent chance of failing to finish at all.[1] (The problem exists at private institutions as well, though not with the same severity.) At graduation there may be no job in his or her field of study. Your debt-laden college graduate may return home from the search with news that good employment requires a master's degree.

If you are a college professor or administrator, you appreciate these views but see things a little differently. You read the papers, and you may have children of your own in college. But you appreciate the paradoxes at the heart of American higher education. For decades, you have heard complaints about its ineffectiveness and high cost, as well as its statistical decline relative to other countries. Yet you know that what Henry Rosovsky, former dean of Harvard's Faculty of Arts and Sciences, wrote in 1990 remains true: "Fully two thirds to three quarters of the best universities are located in the United States."[2] In fact, if anything, the dominance of the American university model has increased since Dean Rosovsky made his declaration. In 2010, the Academic Ranking of World Universities, which measures achievements such as Nobel Prize awards and scholarly publications, listed seventeen U.S. institutions among the top twenty globally; of the top fifty universities, thirty-six were American.[3] Rosovsky's rhetorical follow-up question about U.S. higher education preeminence seems to apply today with the same force it did in 1990: "What sector of our economy and society can make a similar statement?"[4]

As a professor or administrator, you hear complaints that your institution exalts scholarship above teaching as well as the insinuation that your compensation is what makes higher education increasingly more expensive. Yet you know firsthand that tuition is not raised to pay the faculty more—your salary is rising much more slowly than overall institutional costs and tuition prices.[5] And the number of highly paid administrators is small relative to the total operating budget.

Nor are students' preferences ignored. In fact, in large measure it is an obsession with attracting students that drives up the institution's cost. What is most different about today's colleges and universities is not the price of the professoriate and administration but the cost of scholarships and financial aid, physical facilities, Internet access, and intercollegiate athletic teams—all things that matter to students as they choose one school over another. Rankings measure other things of importance to students: student–teacher ratios; graduation rates; student and alumni satisfaction; academic reputation. To a significant degree, colleges and universities have become expensive as a result of attempting to attract the most capable and discerning student-customers, not because of trying to accommodate employees.

As a college or university employee, you also know your own motives. You didn't pay the high price in time and money of getting an advanced degree because of the potential financial rewards. The decision to give a lifetime to higher education was about learning and sharing that learning. It certainly wasn't about giving students the short end of the stick. Notwithstanding the intense pressure on faculty members to publish, nationwide surveys indicate that they value teaching as highly as scholarly research.[6] For every research superstar seeking international acclaim and association only with graduate students, there are many professors who value not only scholarship but also teaching and mentoring undergraduates.[7]

UNIVERSITY VERSUS COLLEGE: WHAT'S IN A NAME?

Throughout this book, sidebars like this one offer commentary and provide examples to clarify the main story. Higher education is a complex world with unique practices and terms, and a bit of explanation and illustration can be helpful even to insiders. For instance, between one-half and two-thirds of the 17.8 million students who were "going to college" in the U.S. in 2006 were actually attending institutions bearing the name *university*. The others were enrolled in a school called by the name *college, institute,* or some similar label.[8]

For our purposes, we simply use the term *university*. Many colleges don't perform all of the functions that universities do, scholarly research and granting Ph.D. degrees being leading examples. But the things that most traditional colleges do, particularly the ways they educate students, have been determined largely by universities. That's true, for example, of the way that college instruction is divided up into semester-long courses. It's also true of the expectation that full-time college professors have advanced degrees. Because of these similarities, we'll find that many of the threats and opportunities facing traditional institutions of higher education are the same for both universities and colleges. Our illustrations of those threats and opportunities include institutions bearing both names, including some community colleges and technical institutes.

Another Lens for Viewing the University

We authors, Clayton and Henry, share all of these views of universities—we read news reports and books about them, we have children at school, and we enjoy working at our respective universities. But we also have another lens for viewing the challenges facing universities. That lens is called the "theory of disruptive innovation." Our purpose in writing this book is to apply this lens to reveal both the serious threats and the great opportunities facing traditional universities. Seen through the lens of disruptive innovation theory, universities are at a critical crossroad. They are both at great risk of competitive disruption and potentially poised for an innovation-fueled renaissance.

The current crisis in today's universities is real, and much of it is of the universities' own making. In the spirit of honoring tradition, universities hang on to past practices to the point of imperiling their futures. When reduced budgets force them to cut costs, they trim but rarely make hard tradeoffs. Nor do they readily reinvent their curricula to better prepare students for the increasing demands of the world of work. Paradoxically, they respond to economic downturn by raising prices. From a market competition standpoint, it is slow institutional suicide. It is as if universities do not care about what is going on around them or how they are perceived.

With traditional universities charging more and seemingly engendering in students fewer of the skills needed to succeed in the global workplace, students, parents, and policymakers are naturally drawn to alternative forms of higher education. For-profit universities and technical institutes, though expensive relative to public institutions and in some cases of dubious quality, are more convenient and more attuned to students' needs, especially the need for marketable skills. Significantly for taxpayers and legislators, they fund their own operations. Given these private sector alternatives, traditional universities seem to deserve no more support or sympathy than tradition-bound steel mills, automakers, or airlines.

But that is not the case. The traditional university is still indispensable. Mastering the challenges and opportunities presented by a fast-paced, global society requires more than just basic technical skill and cognitive competence. Young college students in particular need an environment in which they can not only study but also broaden their horizons and simply "grow up." Though for-profit educators can play important, complementary roles in higher education, the ideal of the traditional university, with its mix of intellectual breadth and depth, its diverse campus social milieu, and its potentially life-changing professors, is needed now more than ever.

Yet to play its indispensable function in the new competitive environment, the typical university must change more quickly and more fundamentally than it has been doing. Invaluable strengths notwithstanding, the way it has historically operated has become too expensive. Its unique design, created by visionary leaders in the late nineteenth and early twentieth centuries, has until recently gone unchallenged and thus largely unaltered. Now innovation is disrupting the status quo. For the first time since the introduction of the printed textbook, there is a new, much less expensive technology for educating students: online learning. Simultaneously, more outcome-oriented accreditation standards have begun to level the competitive playing field; it is no longer as important to evidence educational capacity via brick-and-mortar facilities and Ph.D.-trained faculty as to demonstrate student learning. The combination of disruptive technology and increased focus on educational outcomes opens the door to new forms of competition, particularly from the private sector. This is a situation ripe for disruption, a concept that Clayton researched and wrote about in his book *The Innovator's Dilemma.*[9]

To play its indispensable function in the new competitive environment, the typical university must change more quickly and more fundamentally than it has been doing.

Disruptive Innovation and the University

The theory of disruptive innovation, which we'll apply throughout this book, holds that there are two main types of innovation. The first type, *sustaining innovation*, makes something bigger or better. Examples of sustaining innovations include airplanes that fly farther, computers that process faster, cell phone batteries that last longer, televisions with clearer images, and universities with more college majors and better activity centers. Industry leaders almost always win the battles to create these sustaining innovations, not only because of their financial resources, but also because their expertise in traditional practices gives them an advantage in making things bigger and better.[10]

A *disruptive innovation*, by contrast, disrupts the bigger-and-better cycle by bringing to market a product or service that is not as good as the best traditional offerings but is more affordable and easier to use. Online learning is an example. Particularly in its infancy, when Internet speeds were low and many online courses were simply computer-based versions of traditional lectures and exams, the quality of online learning fell far below that of face-to-face instruction. Only consumers who couldn't attend a class offered at just one place and time, such as working adults, found this new form of education attractive or at least tolerable. For them, the definition of quality was different—a computer-based lecture that you could consume late at night in your own home beat a face-to-face class requiring a commute and a strict schedule.

Disruptive innovation is thus initially a boon to nonconsumers of a product or service. Traditional providers ignore it, assuming that their current clientele won't be interested. But as the disruptive innovation improves—by its own sustaining innovations—it becomes a threat to traditional providers. For example, online course developers not only add features such as video conferencing that make the online course more like a classroom setting, they also create online tutorials and student discussion forums that the traditional face-to-face course doesn't provide. Because the underlying technology offers advantages in cost and ease of use, these quality innovations gradually improve the product to the point that even students at traditional institutions find it appealing.

> *Our duty is to wholly reinvent ourselves. We are America's future—intellectually, socially, culturally.*[11]
>
> —Gordon Gee, president of Ohio State University

Though traditional universities continue to perform the critical, unique functions of discovering and preserving knowledge and of educating students in face-to-face communities of scholars, they also face disruptive innovations that call for reexamination. If they cannot find innovative, less costly ways of performing their uniquely valuable functions, they are doomed to decline, high global and national rankings notwithstanding. Fortunately, such innovation is within their power.

The university's innovations must be informed by self-awareness and by an understanding of history. The typical university and college succeeded in the past by emulating a group of elite research institutions, Harvard University foremost among them.[12] Smaller institutions grew, for example, by adding subjects of study and offering more advanced degrees. For much of the twentieth century, that strategy of emulation proved highly successful. As community and state colleges slowly but steadily made themselves into universities, they brought higher education to the masses and contributed to the advance of knowledge and of social and economic welfare; taxpayers and donors willingly contributed to the cause, inspired by the institutional growth and the benefits that flowed from it.

Now, though, the standard model has become unsustainable. To avoid disruption, institutions of higher education must develop strategies that transcend imitation. They must also master the disruptive technology of online learning and make other innovations. Strategies for doing so are the focus of this book.

Our Purpose and Approach

Charting an effective future course for institutions as venerable and complex as universities requires a thorough understanding not only of the present state of affairs but also of the past. Thus, in this book, we'll study together the evolution of the paradoxical American university. We'll discover why the university is simultaneously world-leading and domestically derided, research driven and student dependent, technologically outdated and socially indispensable.

> *Look to your roots, in order to reclaim your future.*[13]
>
> —Ghanaian proverb, quoted by Mary Sue Coleman, president of University of Michigan

Studying the university's history and confronting these paradoxes will allow us to move beyond the forlorn language of crisis to hopeful and practical strategies for success. We'll see that to survive, established universities will have to break with tradition. But we'll also find that to thrive they must build on what they have always done best. We'll look at more than a dozen institutions that are doing that.

This book is meant to engage all who share an interest in the fate of higher education, which ought to be everyone: students, parents, alumni, employers, taxpayers, legislators, and other policymakers. A particularly important audience, though, is faculty and administrators; they have the power to lead traditional universities and colleges from within, which is the only way it can be done well.

The pages that follow offer insights into the paradoxical behavior of universities and the kind of innovation and change that is necessary to ensure their vitality. In particular, we'll explore the tendency of universities to copy the elite research institutions such as Harvard. Because of Harvard's extraordinary influence, we'll study it in detail in Part II of this book, The Great American University. We'll explore Harvard's evolution over nearly four hundred years and see how it has served as a prototype for other institutions. One can think of it as having established the institutional "DNA," or the fundamental organizational traits, that other universities have copied.

Harvard offers its undergraduate students a vast curriculum spanning the arts and sciences. It also operates more premier professional schools and sets the standard of research excellence in more disciplines than any other institution of higher learning. Harvard incurs tremendous costs in achieving such wide-ranging excellence; its annual operating budget approaches $4 billion.[14] Fortunately, a gargantuan endowment and apparently unlimited demand for its high-priced degrees allow it to bear these expenses, at least in good economic times.

As we'll see in Part III, Ripe for Disruption, the Harvard model, which was not fully understood by the many institutions that have copied it, is now unsustainable for all but a few. Most universities cannot afford to offer so many subjects to such diverse types of students or to require their professors to compete in a world of research scholarship that is becoming increasingly expensive and conceptually narrow. The burden of these choices, adopted by Harvard emulators lacking the financial resources necessary to bear them, have made most American-style universities vulnerable to competitive disruption.

In Part IV, A New Kind of University, we'll encounter an institution, Brigham Young University (BYU)-Idaho, that embodies a different university model. Compared to Harvard, BYU-Idaho hardly makes the traditional higher education map. It is tucked away in rural southeast Idaho and is still in its infancy as a university. Yet BYU-Idaho provides a useful case study because it is a fresh experiment that demonstrates the potential for traditional universities to harness the power of disruptive innovation.

BYU-Idaho's founders created the university in 2000 from a two-year institution, Ricks College, that had few of the traits of the great academic research institutions; these innovators had the opportunity to design a university essentially from scratch. As they did so, they considered the needs of twenty-first-century college students and the strengths and shortcomings of the traditional university model, particularly in light of new learning technologies and their own institutional mission. In the end, BYU-Idaho's designers made unusually focused choices about the range of students to be served and the subjects to be taught. They defined scholarship unusually broadly, to include and even emphasize the scholarship of learning. In effect, they created a new species of university, one genetically different from Harvard.

Neither Harvard nor BYU-Idaho alone is a practical model for most established universities. The one is inimitably prestigious and powerful. The other had unusual starting conditions that allowed a radical redesign. Yet their unique missions and traits notwithstanding, the evolutionary histories of Harvard and BYU-Idaho illustrate the types of strategic choices for traditional universities to consider and provide examples of alternative ways in which they might be made. BYU-Idaho is representative of institutions that are pursuing models that blend the traditional, Harvard-inspired model and the disruptive approach of the purely online educators. In addition to our in-depth study of Harvard and BYU-Idaho, we'll also look at more than a dozen other innovative schools, many profiled in a 2010 McKinsey & Company report, *Winning by Degrees: The Strategies of Highly Productive Higher Education Institutions.*[15]

MCKINSEY'S WINNING BY DEGREES

In 2010, McKinsey & Company, one of the world's largest and most highly regarded consulting companies, undertook a study of U.S. higher education, with financial support from the Bill & Melinda Gates Foundation. McKinsey's goal was to determine whether increased productivity by colleges and universities—without increased spending—could contribute substantially to the nation's higher education needs. The McKinsey team began by quantifying the average cost incurred by all institutions to produce one associate's or bachelor's degree: $56,289 and $74,268, respectively.[16]

The team then identified institutions with significantly lower costs per degree granted. They chose for further study five bachelor's degree-granting universities whose costs ranged from a high of $52,285 to a low of $27,495—roughly one-third to two-thirds less than the average, and in all cases less than the cost of the typical associate's degree. Three of these institutions, Southern New Hampshire University, Indiana Wesleyan University, and BYU-Idaho, are "traditional" private nonprofit schools that deliver the majority of their instruction in face-to-face classrooms. Another institution, Western Governors University, is a highly innovative nonprofit that offers online competency-based instruction; students neither gather in classrooms nor spend a set amount of time studying. The fifth institution, DeVry University, is a private sector company that offers degrees both online and face to face.

McKinsey also looked at two community colleges and a system of state technical institutes. One of the community colleges, Florida's Valencia Community College, grants both associate's degrees and technical certificates; at $22,311 per associate's degree granted, Valencia's cost is only 40 percent of the national average. The other community college, Arizona's Rio Salado College, grants primarily certificates. A pioneer in the use of online learning, it enrolls more online students than any other community college in the nation. The technical institute system, Tennessee Technology Centers, confers technical certificates with markedly higher completion rates than the national average.

In-depth study of these eight institutions led the McKinsey team to conclude that their practices, if broadly applied, would allow the U.S. to match the world's leaders in educational attainment without increased expenditure. We'll explore new university models like the ones profiled by McKinsey in Part V, Genetic Reengineering. We'll see that universities must define themselves in individual terms rather than emulating others. They must become much more affordable, particularly by embracing online learning technology. At the same time, though, they should make the most of their full-time professors and physical campuses, which might be misperceived as a competitive liability in a world of technological disruption. In fact, the university's professors and face-to-face meeting spaces, while expensive, are unique and potentially invaluable. They allow the university to perform functions that other institutions cannot. Among them are the critical jobs of discovering new knowledge, preserving the discoveries of the past, and mentoring the rising generation. Universities that adapt to the new competitive environment, drawing on their historical strengths even as they transcend Harvard imitation and embrace new technologies, can have a bright future.

Our journey through the past, present, and future of higher education begins with Harvard's founding, in the early 1600s. First, though, in Chapter One we return briefly to 2006, a year of portents and warnings.

The Innovative University

PART ONE

Reframing the Higher Education Crisis

Times of terror and deepest misery may be in the offing. But if any happiness at all is to be extracted from that misery, it can only be a spiritual happiness, looking backward toward conservation of the culture of earlier times, looking forward toward serene and stalwart defense of the things of the spirit in an age which otherwise might succumb wholly to material things.[1]

Reverend Father Jacobus
The Glass Bead Game, by Hermann Hesse

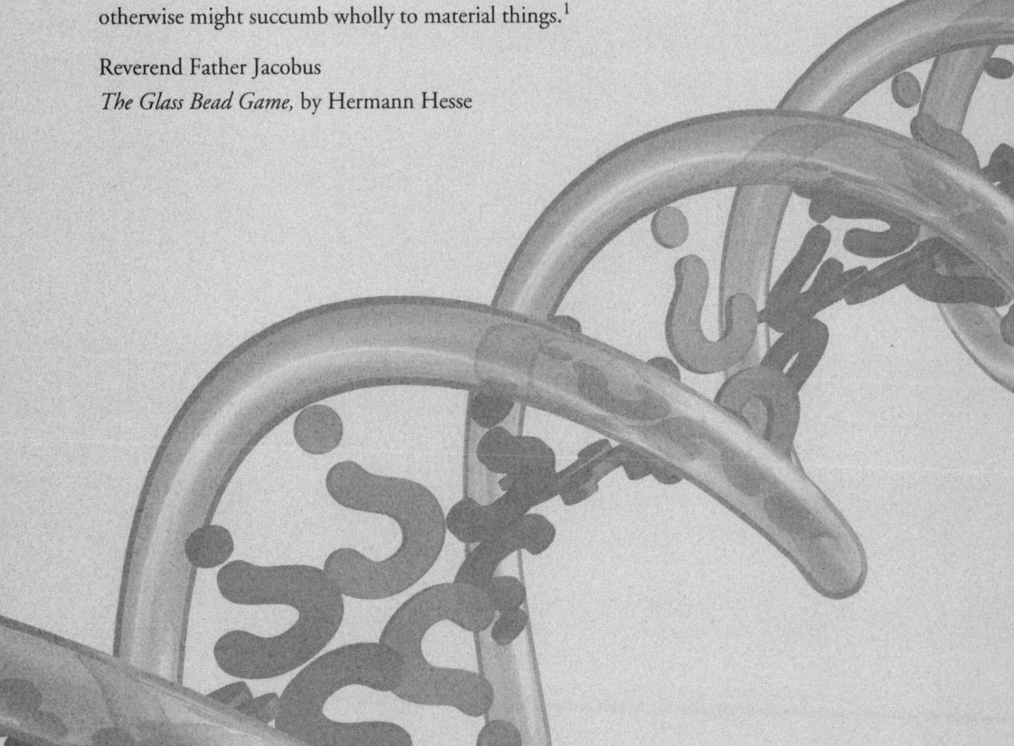

Chapter 1

The Educational Innovator's Dilemma

Threat of Danger, Reasons for Hope

No one could doubt that U.S. Education Secretary Margaret Spellings meant business. In upbraiding the nation's universities and colleges, the 2006 report of her commission on the future of higher education used the language and metaphors of business:

> What we have learned over the last year makes clear that American higher education has become what, in the business world, would be called a mature enterprise: increasingly risk-averse, at times self-satisfied, and unduly expensive. It is an enterprise that has yet to address the fundamental issues of how academic programs and institutions must be transformed to serve the changing educational needs of a knowledge economy. It has yet to successfully confront the impact of globalization, rapidly evolving technologies, an increasingly diverse and aging population, and an evolving marketplace characterized by new needs and paradigms.
>
> History is littered with examples of industries that, at their peril, failed to respond—or even to notice—changes in the world around them, from railroads to steel manufacturers. Without serious self-examination and reform, institutions of higher education risk falling into the same trap, seeing their market share

substantially reduced and their services increasingly characterized by obsolescence.[1]

Not surprisingly, such confrontational, business-oriented language provoked controversy. During its drafting, the Spellings Commission report had been described by one of its own members as "flawed" and "hostile."[2] Higher education officials and lobbyists agreed when they read the official report. Many saw it as a politically motivated attack that overlooked the fundamental mission and spirit of higher education. The report's comparison of higher learning to railway transportation and steel manufacturing was, at the individual level, an inapt analogy: the process of smelting steel offers little insight into the delicate task of molding a mind. And to speak of universities and colleges as having market share is to imply disregard for higher education's noneconomic role in creating knowledge and promoting social well-being.

Yet it was difficult to rebut many of the Spellings Commission report's most serious indictments—that fewer U.S. adults are completing post-high school degrees; that the costs of attending college are rising faster than inflation; that employers report hiring college graduates unprepared for the workplace.[3]

THE GLASS BEAD GAME

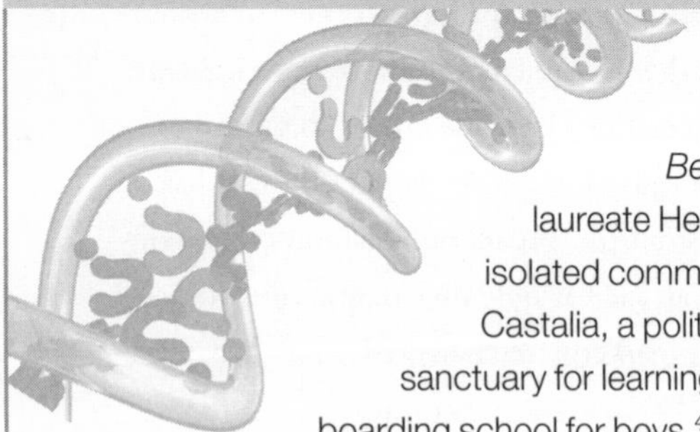

In his novel *Das Glasperlenspiel (The Glass Bead Game)*, Nobel literature laureate Hermann Hesse describes an isolated community of scholars in fictional Castalia, a political province set apart as a sanctuary for learning, where the scholars run a boarding school for boys.[4] For the most elite of these scholars, however, the real interest is an abstract intellectual game that rewards individual contemplation. The Glass Bead Game, which takes years of training to master, is said to have existed from time immemorial. Its procedures and rules are described as a strict "secret language." It forbids "private," value-based judgments, recognizing only "legitimate," objective observations. In the words of Hesse's narrator, "Any enrichment of the language of the Game by addition of new content is subject to the strictest possible control by the directorate of the Game."[5]

Hesse's protagonist, a young student named Joseph Knecht, enjoys the nurturing of scholarly mentors who assume the stature of saints in his eyes; one of the most influential is the kindly, optimistic Father Jacobus. With the help of these mentors, Knecht becomes a master of the Glass Bead Game. It is the highest of intellectual honors. Yet with the passage of time and a growing personal awareness of the turmoil outside of Castalia, Knecht begins to wonder about his institution's role in the world. The questions with which he grapples, and the answers to which he comes, offer insights useful in higher education today. We will revisit Castalia and its Glass Bead Game from time to time throughout this book.

Voices of Warning from Within

The Spellings Commission was not a lone voice of criticism in 2006. That same year two distinguished academics, Derek Bok and Harry Lewis, both of Harvard, published books critical of higher education. Though eschewing—and, in Lewis's case, rejecting—the business terms and competitive logic of the Spellings Commission report, these seasoned academic administrators were no less vocal about the shortcomings of higher education. Bok, a former president of Harvard University, titled his book *Our Underachieving Colleges: A Candid Look at How Much Students Learn and Why They Should Be Learning More.* Lewis, a forty-year veteran and former dean of Harvard College, the sub-unit of the university that serves undergraduate students, detailed its defects in a work called *Excellence Without a Soul: How a Great University Forgot Education.*

Bok's work was the more diplomatic of the two, as befitting a senior Harvard statesman who twice presided over the university. Yet Bok sounded his alarm with language reminiscent of the Spellings

Commission's allusions to market forces. Having summarized the growing threat of global competition, he warned:

> In view of these developments, neither American students nor our universities, nor the nation itself, can afford to take for granted the quality of higher education and the teaching and learning it provides. To be sure, professors and academic leaders must keep proper perspective. It is especially important to bear in mind all the purposes universities serve and to resist efforts to turn them into instruments preoccupied primarily with helping the economy grow. But resisting commercialization cannot become an excuse for resisting change. Rather, universities need to recognize the risks of complacency and use the emerging worldwide challenge as an occasion for a candid reappraisal to discover whether there are ways to lift the performance of our institutions of higher learning to higher levels.[6]

After exploring the important noneconomic purposes of universities and noting the general satisfaction of students and recent graduates, Bok nonetheless leveled an indictment similar to that of the Spellings Commission:

> Despite the favorable opinions of undergraduates and alumni, a closer look at the record . . . shows that colleges and universities, for all the benefits they bring, accomplish far less for their students than they should. Many seniors graduate without being able to write well enough to satisfy their employers. Many cannot reason clearly or perform competently in analyzing complex, nontechnical problems, even though faculties rank critical thinking as the primary goal of a college education.[7]

Harry Lewis likewise pulled few punches in *Excellence Without a Soul.* But in arguing that Harvard had "forgot[ten] education," Lewis took a different tack than Bok. Rather than warning of the forces of global competition, he accused Harvard and its peers of being driven too much by their own competitive ambitions. In particular, he noted how scholarly activity tends to distance professors from the undergraduate teaching and learning process. At the same time, he argued, the desire to attract and satisfy students as though they are mere customers leads to academic coddling, in the form of easy grades and expensive facilities and entertainments, such as intercollegiate athletic teams. In the process, Lewis concluded:

> Universities have forgotten their larger role for college students. . . . Rarely will you hear more than bromides about personal strength, integrity, kindness, cooperation, compassion, and how to leave the world a better place than you found it. The greater the university, the more intent it is on competitive success in the marketplace of faculty, students, and research money. And the less likely it is to talk seriously to students about their development into people of good character who will know that they owe something to society for the privileged education they have received.[8]

Lewis's prescription for solving this problem was for universities to be less businesslike:

> Changing direction requires . . . leadership that views the university idealistically, as something more than a business and something better than a slave to the logic of economic competition.[9]

Pressures from Without

Ironically, Lewis's call for transcending economic competition sounded on the eve of the deepest financial crisis since the Great Depression. By 2009, the universities and colleges that the Spellings Commission had characterized as self-satisfied were struggling to fill budget gaps left by dramatic drops in their endowments and state appropriations. Even mighty Harvard was forced to suspend a major construction project and to lay off staff after its endowment, which had been producing one-third of its operating revenues, shrank from $37 billion to $26 billion.[10] The budget crisis was particularly acute for universities modeled after Harvard, with expensive commitments to graduate schools and research activities spanning a wide array of academic disciplines. Unfortunately, few of these schools enjoyed Harvard's financial clout. Endowment losses and decreases in state funding led inevitably to budget cuts and tuition increases.

Meanwhile, new federal government attention and dollars flowed to public two-year colleges, which were perceived as offering the better near-term investment in economic revival; in the decade before the downturn, their prices increased only one-fifth as fast as those of their four-year counterparts.[11] The enrollments of these two-year colleges swelled, as did those of rapidly proliferating for-profit higher education companies.[12] Many of the for-profits in particular applied the power of online learning technology. Online courses offer the benefits of greater convenience and also lower total cost, as much of a student's expense in getting a traditional higher education is not in tuition but in leaving the workplace and relocating to a residential campus.

Online offerings grew in popularity throughout the decade but especially when times got tough. The downturn that knocked the wind out of the traditional universities billowed the sails of the for-profit educators. The University of Phoenix, for example, recognized revenues of $2.5 billion in 2007; by the end of 2009 that figure had risen to nearly $3.8 billion.[13] In that year it enrolled 355,800 new students, roughly 150,000 more than the total enrollment of the ten campuses of the University of California.[14] Investigations of student-recruiting abuses and proposals to tighten regulatory standards slowed the for-profits, but it would be unwise to dismiss the disruptive power of their educational model, especially the use of online learning technology.

A PRIVATE SECTOR EDUCATIONAL INNOVATOR

In 1912 the thirty-six-year-old German immigrant and self-taught engineer Herman DeVry introduced a cutting-edge silent movie projector for the classroom; he called it a "theater in a suitcase."[15] The company that DeVry created to make the projectors found its biggest markets in schools and churches. In 1925 he opened the DeVry Summer School of Visual Instruction in Chicago, to which he invited educators and religious leaders, to explore the potential of motion pictures in classroom instruction.[16]

In 1931 DeVry created what would later become DeVry University. Initially a training school for electrical and motion picture technicians, the institution granted its first associate's degree, in electronic engineering technology, in 1957; it introduced a bachelor's degree in that same field in 1969.[17]

By 2010, regionally accredited DeVry University operated 90 campuses and served more than 80,000 students, many of them via online technology partly descended from Herman DeVry's early educational movies. DeVry students can earn technical certificates as well as associate's, bachelor's, and master's degrees, in fields ranging from technology to business management and health care. Courses are offered face to face, online, and in hybrid form. A trimester system allows bachelor's degree-seekers to graduate in three calendar years.

In 2010 McKinsey & Company found that DeVry was 50 percent more efficient in administrative functions than typical universities, thanks to a high degree of process automation and operations management training—for example, the person responsible for financial aid was a Six Sigma Black Belt, the highest level of certification in a business management system designed to improve the quality of process by identifying and removing the causes of defects and minimizing process variability. DeVry also saves money by eschewing nonacademic functions such as food services and athletics. Quality is monitored through rigorous learning outcomes measurement and via a "Net Promoter Score, the percentage of students and employees who would recommend the institution to a friend."[18]

In most industries, technology-enabled competition is deemed healthy and vital. Accustomed to a hyper-competitive modern world, we expect even the largest and most prestigious companies to be continually challenged by nimbler, more creative upstarts. Economists teach that disruptive innovation by newcomers and creative destruction of entrenched incumbents leads to better products and services.[19] When a century-old auto company, airline, investment bank, or newspaper files for bankruptcy or disappears altogether, we regret the attendant human suffering but count the loss as the price of progress, knowing that without competitive innovation and destruction we would enjoy a standard of living no better than our great-grandparents did.

Higher education, though, has been different. Large universities rarely cease to operate. Nor are the prestigious ones quickly overtaken. Part of the reason is a dearth of disruptive competition. The most innovative would-be competitors, for-profit education companies, find great success among working adults, many of whom care more about the content and convenience of their education than the label on it. But many young college students still seek the assurance of traditional university names and the benefits of campus life. Because of loyal support from this large group of higher education customers, the incumbents have felt little pressure from the for-profits' use of potentially disruptive online technology.

Meanwhile, the terms of competition among traditional institutions, the public and private not-for-profit universities, have been set primarily by those at the top. The strategy of most schools is one of imitation, not innovation.[20] Little-known and smaller institutions try to move up in the ranks by adding students, majors, and graduate programs, so as to look more like the large universities. They also task their faculty with research responsibilities. In the process the emulators incur new costs and thus must raise tuition. This blunts the price advantage that they began with. They are stuck in a dangerous competitive middle ground, neither highest in quality nor lowest in cost. The great schools, rather than being discomfited by the imitation, seem all the more desirable because of it.

The terms of competition among traditional institutions, the public and private not-for-profit universities, have been set primarily by those at the top.

THE CARNEGIE CLASSIFICATION SYSTEM, OR "THE CARNEGIE LADDER"

The inclination to become more Harvard-like has been reinforced for the past four decades by something colloquially known as "the Carnegie ladder." The Carnegie Commission on Higher Education was created in 1967 by the Carnegie Foundation for the Advancement of Teaching, established by Andrew Carnegie in 1905.

To guide its work in aiding different types of institutions, the Carnegie Commission produced a classification system that listed first four types of doctoral degree-granting institutions, ordered according to their emphasis on research and doctoral programs. Next came two tiers of "Comprehensive Colleges," ranked by their breadth of disciplines and number of degrees granted. A third group, "Liberal Arts Colleges," were divided into two camps according to student selectivity. Below them came "All Two-Year Colleges and Institutes," as well as "Professional Schools and Other Specialized Institutions."[21]

The Carnegie Commission's intent was to segregate the schools so that unique policies could be crafted to support each type in its unique educational mission; the commission saw the diversity of U.S. higher education as an asset to be preserved and enhanced, given the diverse needs of the huge population of post-high school students. However, the classification put all of the most prestigious schools into two categories: doctoral institutions with a heavy emphasis on research (elite private and public universities) and highly selective private liberal arts colleges such as Williams and Amherst. These represented the top rungs on what became known as the "Carnegie ladder."

The unintended effect was to create a widely accepted scorecard for Harvard emulation, or "Carnegie climbing." What had been a matter of general academic ambition became an intense competition with real financial ramifications, as noted in a 2005 Carnegie Foundation report:

Foundations sometimes use the classification as an eligibility criterion for grant programs; some states use the classification (or a derivative system) in their funding formulas; and in its annual college rankings, *U.S. News & World Report* bases its comparison groups on categories of the classification. With each of these, an institution can have a very tangible interest in maintaining or changing its classification, and the stakes can be high.[22]

The Educational Innovator's Dilemma

In their defense, the institutions that emulate Harvard and strive to climb the Carnegie ladder are doing just as conventional business logic dictates—trying to give customers what they want. The great universities such as Harvard inspire not just administrators, faculty, and alumni at other schools. They also excite the most elite prospective students, who want to win admission to the most Harvard-like institution they can. Thus, less prestigious schools emulate Harvard's essential features, such as graduate programs and expert faculty researchers and research facilities. They also give students costly noneducational amenities such as intercollegiate athletic teams, which Harvard no longer supports at the level of the most competitive schools.

The result of this competition-by-imitation is to solidify past educational practice among traditional universities, making them increasingly more expensive but not fundamentally better from a learning standpoint. The great-grandparents of today's students would easily recognize the essential elements of modern higher education. Though the students are more diverse, the shape of classrooms, the style of instruction, and the subjects of study are all remarkably true to their century-old antecedents. Great-grandpa and Grandma would likewise recognize the three schools atop *U.S. News*'s 2010 college rankings: Harvard, Princeton, and Yale. In fact, asked to guess, they'd probably have picked just those three.

Only the costs of a higher education, one can argue, have kept pace with the times. In the ten years after 1997, the inflation-adjusted cost of a year of college at the average public university rose by 30 percent, while the earning power of a bachelor's degree remained roughly the same.[23] Cost increases derive partly from higher faculty salaries, but more from activities unrelated to classroom instruction. Scientific research, competitive athletics, and student amenities require both large operating outlays and the construction of high-tech laboratories, football stadiums, and activity centers. As a result, the cost of higher education grows faster than faculty salaries or other instruction-related costs.[24]

The problem is not unique to higher education. In fact, in products ranging from computers to breakfast cereals, history reveals a pattern of innovation that ultimately exceeds customers' needs. Hoping to get an edge on their competitors, companies offer new features, such as faster processing speeds in a computer or increased vitamin fortification in cereals. These enhancements are sustaining innovations rather than reinventions: the product becomes better while its basic design and uses remain the same.

The catch, as Clayton Christensen has shown in *The Innovator's Dilemma*, is that these performance enhancements at some point exceed even the most demanding customers' performance needs

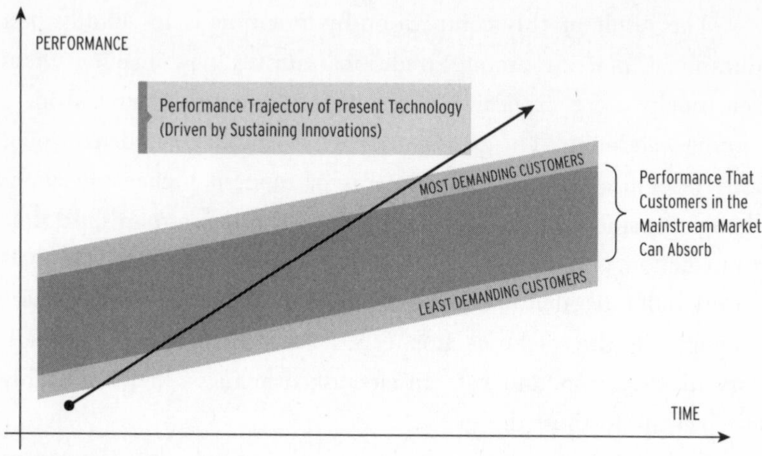

FIGURE 1.1 The Path of Sustaining Innovation.

(see Figure 1.1). The producer is incurring greater costs and thus must raise prices. That leaves the typical purchaser of a $5,000 laptop or a $5 box of cereal paying more than they want to, given what they actually need.

Universities tend to innovate and set prices in similar ways. Those in a particular tier attempt to match one another's services; the ambitious ones also emulate the more prestigious institutions above them. To offset the cost of new offerings and activities, such as additional majors and graduate degree programs, they raise tuition, their most easily controllable source of revenue. In setting tuition levels, the primary question is not what students are willing and able to pay. Thanks to government grants and loans, the students are less price sensitive in their higher education choices than in other purchase decisions. Because third-party financing reduces student price sensitivity and most schools offer similar curricula, higher education prices can be set on the basis of institutional peer comparison. The most elite institutions charge nearly identical rates and stay in step with similar annual rate increases. The other schools maintain a set discount to the tuition of the elite ones, raising their rates confidently under this steadily rising price umbrella.

THE INNOVATOR'S DILEMMA GETS A BOOST FROM INSIDE INTEL

In 1999 one of the world's most respected executives, Andy Grove of Intel, appeared on the cover of *Forbes* with a relatively unknown Harvard Business School professor named Clayton Christensen. The photo of 6-foot-8 Christensen towering over the highly recognizable Grove drew readers inside to learn about a book, *The Innovator's Dilemma,* that had been in print since 1997. Grove wasn't the first high-profile executive to discover and apply the principles of disruptive innovation, but his compelling articulation of them powered *The Innovator's Dilemma* to notoriety all but unheard of for a book based on a doctoral dissertation. In a 1997 presentation made by Christensen to Intel's senior managers, Grove recognized that the innovation by steel mini-mills that disrupted powerful companies such as U.S. Steel was set to occur in computer chips, and he and his team responded to assure Intel's continued competitiveness. *Forbes* quoted Grove as saying, "What's valuable about Clayton's ideas is that they give you a framework. They allow a business to learn from the experience of others. The specifics are different, but you can move the generality over to your business and then go down into your specifics."[25]

The popularity of *The Innovator's Dilemma* derived both from the broad applicability of its innovation theory to many industries and also from its optimistic premise that the best institutions actually aren't prone to be disrupted because they lose their way or make outrageous mistakes. Christensen told *Forbes*, "I thought, 'These people are at least as smart as I am. There must be a reason why such smart people make bad decisions.'"

Working from this generous assumption allowed Christensen to make the counterintuitive discovery that the sustaining innovation made by established companies on behalf of their best customers can set institutions up for disruption. Kodak Chairman George Fisher described

Christensen's finding this way: ''Even good people get locked into processes that may be totally inappropriate to deal with a new technology attacking from underneath.''

The Risk of Disruption

Much of what universities are doing is standard management practice: improve the product; give customers more of what they want; watch the competition. But it leads even great enterprises to fail, as detailed in *The Innovator's Dilemma.* Inevitably, while the industry leaders focus on better serving their most prized customers and matching their toughest competitors, they overlook what is happening beneath them. Two things are likely to be occurring there. One is growth in the number of would-be consumers who cannot afford the continuously enhanced offerings and thus become nonconsumers. The other is the emergence of technologies that will, in the right hands, allow new competitors to serve this disenfranchised group of nonconsumers, as shown in Figure 1.2.

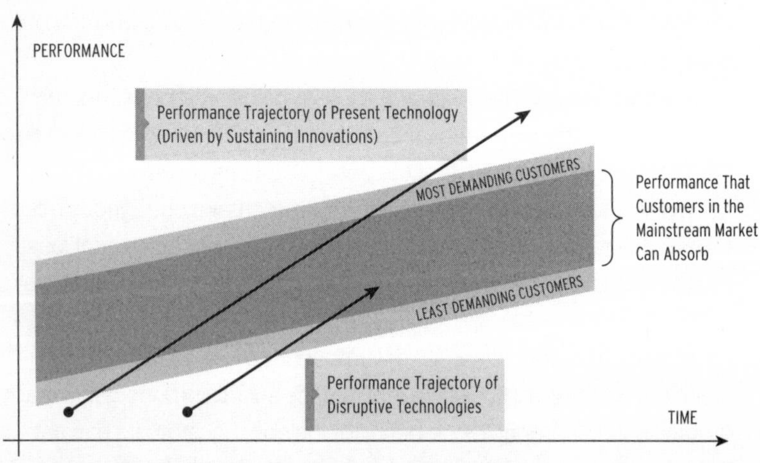

FIGURE 1.2 The Path of Disruptive Innovation.

In most industries, the pattern of sustaining innovation is broken by a disruptive technology. The first Apple computer was such a game-changing technology. Before the Apple, only university professors and graduate students at large universities had access to the bulky mainframe or minicomputers operated by specialists to whom computational requests, such as statistical analyses of data, were submitted. The high cost of these computers meant that they had to be shared by hundreds or even thousands of users. A data request could take days to be filled. If the output data revealed a flaw in the original request or an intriguing outcome calling for follow-up analysis, the user had to repeat the time-consuming process.

The Apple, by contrast, was affordable by high schools and families. Of course, it had only a tiny fraction of the power of traditional computers and was thus useless for universities and large companies. But, through continuous innovation and improvement, its performance improved over the years; so did the performance of its cousin, IBM's PC (personal computer). In time, what had been products acceptable only to nonconsumers of mainframe and minicomputers unseated these incumbents. The minicomputer disappeared entirely, the victim of a disruptive technology.

Historically, higher education has avoided such competitive disruption. There are several reasons for this past immunity. One is the power of prestige in the higher education marketplace, where the quality of the product is hard to measure. In the absence of comparable measures of what universities produce for their students, the well-respected institutions have a natural advantage; because they have been admired in the past, they are presumed to be the best choice for the future.

A related stabilizing force is the barrier to disruptive innovation created by accreditation, a process by which representatives of established universities periodically participate in judging the fitness of established institutions and would-be newcomers. In doing so, they tended to apply the standards of practice in their own institutions. Thus, conformance to tradition became the price of continued accreditation and of entry to the industry.

Another reason for the lack of disruption in higher education has been the absence of a disruptive technology. Since the time that universities first gathered students into classrooms, the learning technologies—lectures, textbooks, oral and written examinations—have remained largely the same. Even when computers were introduced into the classroom, they were used to enhance the existing instructional approaches rather than to supplant them. Lectures, for example, were augmented with computer graphics, but the lecture itself persisted in its fundamental form.

Until the relatively recent emergence of the Internet and online learning, the higher education industry enjoyed an anomalously long run of disruption-free growth. In times of economic downturn, there were cries of alarm and calls for reform. But for the elite, well-endowed private schools, a bit of budget tightening sufficed until the financial markets recovered. The demand for the prestige the elite schools confer far exceeds the supply, allowing them to cover rising costs with tuition increases and fundraising campaigns. Even many less prestigious universities benefit from accreditation, which has elevated them over nonaccredited institutions. Public universities also enjoy the long-term commitment of taxpayers. In the absence of a disruptive new technology, the combination of prestige and loyal support from alumni and legislators has allowed traditional universities to weather occasional storms. Fundamental change has been unnecessary.

That is no longer true, though, for any but a relative handful of institutions. Costs have risen to unprecedented heights, and new competitors are emerging. A disruptive technology, online learning, is at work in higher education, allowing both for-profit and traditional not-for-profit institutions to rethink the entire traditional higher education model. Private universities without national recognition and large endowments are at great financial risk. So are public universities, even prestigious ones such as the University of California at Berkeley.

Price-sensitive students and fiscally beleaguered legislatures have begun to resist costs that consistently rise faster than those of other goods and services. With the advent of high-quality online learning, there are new, less expensive institutional alternatives to traditional universities, their standing enhanced by changes in accreditation standards that play to their strengths in demonstrating student learning outcomes. These institutions are poised to respond cost-effectively to the national need for increased college participation and completion.

A disruptive technology, online learning, is at work in higher education, allowing both for-profit and traditional not-for-profit institutions to rethink the entire traditional higher education model.

For the vast majority of universities change is inevitable. The main questions are when it will occur and what forces will bring it about. It would be unfortunate if internal delay caused change to come through external regulation or pressure from newer, nimbler competitors. Until now, American higher education has largely regulated itself, to great effect. U.S. universities are among the most lightly regulated by government. They are free to choose what discoveries to pursue and what subjects to teach, without concern for economic or political agendas. Responsibly exercised, this freedom is a great intellectual and competitive advantage.

Traditional universities benefit society not just by producing intelligent graduates and valuable discoveries but also by fostering unmarketable yet invaluable intangibles such as social tolerance, personal responsibility, and respect for the rule of law. Each is a unique community of scholars in which lives as well as minds are molded. Pure profit-based competition would produce fewer of these social goods, just as increased government regulation would dampen the great universities' genius for discovery.

The DNA of the University

Ideally, the faculty members, administrators, and alumni who best appreciate the totality of the university's contributions to society will, in the spirit of self-regulation, play a leading role in revitalizing their beloved institutions.[26] They have the capacity to determine their own fate and in so doing take the indispensable university to new heights. In performing that critical task, they must understand not only current realities, especially the threat of competitive disruption, but also how universities have evolved over the past several hundred years. Even more than most organizations, traditional universities are products of their history. That history is shared, because most universities have emulated a handful of elite American schools that began to assume their modern form a century and a half ago. Prominent among them were Harvard, Yale, Johns Hopkins, Cornell, and MIT. Together, they have evolved to share common institutional traits, a sort of university DNA.[27]

Much as the identity of a living organism is reflected in its every cell, the identity of a university can be found in the structure of departments and in the relationships among faculty and administrators. It is written into course catalogs, into standards for admitting students and promoting professors, and into strategies for raising funds and recruiting athletes. It can be seen in the campus buildings and grounds. These institutional characteristics remain the same even as individual people come and go.

Pioneering institutions such as Harvard and Yale first began granting Ph.D.s in the mid-nineteenth century. As graduates of their doctoral programs joined the faculties of other universities, they took their experiences and expectations with them. With the support of ambitious university presidents, they strove to make their new academic environments like those from which they had come. This internal drive was reinforced by external systems for accrediting, classifying, and ranking universities. It also became embedded in a common academic culture. As a result, even the smallest and most obscure universities bear many of the essential traits of the greatest ones.

University DNA is not only similar across institutions, it is also highly stable, having evolved over hundreds of years. Replication of the DNA occurs continuously, as each retiring employee or graduating student is replaced by someone screened against the same criteria applied to his or her predecessor. The way things are done is determined not by individual preference alone but by institutional procedure written into the genetic code.[28]

There is evolution in the university, though its mechanism typically is not natural selection of random mutations. As a general rule, the university alters itself only in thoughtful response to significant needs and opportunities. Entrepreneurism occurs within fixed bounds; there is rarely revolution of the type so often heralded in business or politics. This steadiness is a major source of universities' value to a fickle, fad-prone society.

Yet the university's steadiness is also why one cannot make it more responsive to modern economic and social realities merely by regulating its behavior. The genetic tendencies are too strong. The institutional genes expressed in course catalogs and in standards for admitting students and promoting faculty are selfish, replicating themselves faithfully even at the expense of the institution's welfare. A university cannot be made more efficient by simply cutting its operating budget, any more than a carnivore can be converted to an herbivore by constraining its intake of meat. Nor can universities be made by legislative fiat to perform functions for which they are not expressly designed. For example, requiring universities to admit underprepared students is unlikely to produce a proportional number of new college graduates. It is not in the typical university's genetic makeup to remediate such students, and neither regulation nor economic pressure will be enough, alone, to change that.

A university cannot be made more efficient by simply cutting its operating budget, any more than a carnivore can be converted to an herbivore by constraining its intake of meat.

Bigger and Better

In at least one critical respect, organizations are like living organisms: they seek not only to survive, but to grow. Once the typical organization has more than a few employees and has experienced a degree of success, predictable genetic tendencies switch on. These tendencies start to dominate planning and investment processes, driving the organization to make things bigger, better—or both. To diminish in size or quality is to violate the genetic code, to introduce a mutation unlikely to survive the natural institutional response. Becoming bigger and better is "in the genes."

In at least one critical respect, organizations are like living organisms: they seek not only to survive, but to grow.

Members of the university community readily recognize this tendency. With rare institutional exceptions, quantity and quality in the academy continually grow. Courses become more numerous and more specialized. New degree programs are created. More qualified faculty are sought, as is entry into more prestigious athletic conferences. New buildings are added and older ones upgraded.

Proposals for focusing effort or economizing, by contrast, are rare, particularly when there are valid concerns for quality. The aversion to shrinking or simplifying is more than just a matter of personal preference; it is driven by institutional decision-making systems, individual rewards, and culture. For example, no risk-averse department chair can think seriously about cutting courses or degree programs; even if such a proposal could be pushed through the curriculum committee, the only reward to the chair would be ostracism by his or her colleagues. For similar reasons, no athletic director can view dropping a popular sport or moving into a less expensive conference as a good career move, nor can a university president take lightly the risk of offending a major donor who has a building dream. Through mutually reinforcing formal and informal systems, the university continually demands bigger and better.

Though the Carnegie classification system supercharges this tendency, it is by no means unique to higher education. Most established organizations, including for-profit companies, readily adopt new technologies that show potential for enhancing their size and standing. However, they are much less likely to see the value of innovations that would reduce the price a customer pays, especially when quality might be adversely affected. As an illustration, the established makers of X-ray equipment, General Electric, Siemens, and Phillips, quickly adopted CT, MRI, and PET imaging technologies as they were developed.[29] Each of these new technologies allowed them to make enhanced, more expensive equipment that vaulted them ahead of the competition and generated better profit margins. However, for thirty years they persistently overlooked the potential of ultrasound technology, which was simpler and more affordable for customers. The bigger-and-better tendencies built into their institutional DNA—through systems such as profitability-based compensation for executives and salespeople—made ultrasound seem unattractive, particularly in its infancy, when the image quality was relatively low.

Because new entrants to an industry typically begin at the bottom of a market, selling simple, affordable products to easily satisfied consumers, the bigger-and-better tendencies in established institutions can blind them to disruptive technologies such as ultrasound. This tendency on the part of incumbents gives innovative entrants time to operate out of harm's way; they can perfect the new technology without interference from resource-rich competitors. Thanks to this competitive grace period, products that initially could be sold only to low-end customers of no interest to the incumbents steadily improve in quality.

A familiar example of the bigger-and-better cycle can be seen in automobiles. When Toyota entered the lowest tier of the car market with its subcompact Corona, it was secure from General Motors (GM), because GM's institutional DNA was driving it upward, to make bigger and better vehicles such as SUVs and trucks. Toyota had decades to improve its subcompacts to the point that they were recognized as something better than just the cheapest car on the market. Beginning in the 1980s, GM finally took notice of Toyota. GM tried to respond with smaller cars of its own, but by then Toyota had the edge. GM watched Toyota grow to become the world's most profitable car company.

Toyota upended the global auto market by embarking on an upward march of its own. The Corona was followed by the Tercel, the Corolla, the Camry, the Avalon, the 4-Runner, and ultimately the Lexus. The bigger-and-better tendency found expression in Toyota's institutional DNA and began to drive Toyota's decisions just as it had GM's. Toyota's attention to the Lexus, for example, made it more difficult for the company to see and respond to what is happening in the world below it. New competitors such as Hyundai have been the beneficiaries, though the bigger-and-better tendency now drives them as well. This genetic tendency is similarly embedded in retail companies, telecommunication equipment manufacturers, steel companies, hospitals, computer producers, and companies in scores of other industries—with the same results we see in automobiles. They are obsessed with bigger and better, and all but paralyzed from moving toward simpler and more affordable.

Two Schools of Thought

As we'll see in the stories of Harvard and BYU-Idaho, the bigger-and-better tendency is powerful in higher education. Still, it can be overcome. The first step is to understand Harvard better.

The bigger-and-better tendency is powerful in higher education. Still, it can be overcome.

Though a prodigious innovator and an unrivaled trend-setter, Harvard was not first with every key university feature. Well into the twentieth century, it adopted practices and policies both from the great European universities and from elite American ones.[30] Nor can all of the most prominent and costly features be traced back to it. For example, Harvard has few of the financial and behavioral problems associated with intercollegiate athletics at other universities. Likewise, its undergraduates uniformly complete their bachelor's degrees in four years, in contrast to the majority of students elsewhere, who take longer or fail to graduate altogether. In fact, the costs that many universities bear in emulating Harvard are greater because they have adopted the Harvard DNA imperfectly; as in the biological world, university clones inevitably suffer from defects not present in their donor. A case study of Harvard's evolution to greatness is a good way not only to explore typical university DNA but also to discover what has been lost in the process of institutional imitation.

Another helpful step in changing the university's DNA is to study institutions that are in the process of making such changes. The tendency to emulate Harvard is widespread, but it is not universal. To varying degrees, many institutions are taking different paths.

TWO UNIVERSITIES WITHOUT HARVARD ASPIRATIONS

Two of the country's biggest universities, Arizona State and Ohio State, which enroll 70,000 and 64,000 students,[31] respectively, are led by presidents who explicitly reject Harvard imitation. Arizona State's Michael Crow and Ohio State's Gordon Gee were identified by *Time* in 2009 as among the country's ten best college presidents; Gee, in fact, topped the list.[32] Both are leading efforts to make their giant, well-respected institutions different from Harvard.

Michael Crow describes Arizona State's intent to become a "New American University," one more accountable for educational attainment, math and science educational outcomes, and national competitiveness. He points to a lack of institutional differentiation as a liability in American higher education: "[I] don't know if it's necessarily good for every private university in the United States to think that its mission is to emulate and ultimately topple Harvard as the number one university." Arizona State's goal, by contrast, is to augment rather than copy the nation's top universities, by striving for academic excellence while still being widely accessible to students and engaged in its local community.[33]

Gordon Gee, whose Ohio State is one of the sixty-three members of the elite, research-oriented American Association of Universities, nonetheless celebrates its commitment to the values and purposes of the "land-grant" colleges created by the federal government in the darkest days of the Civil War. The congressionally stated function of these colleges is to teach not only "scientific and classical studies," but also "agriculture and the mechanic arts . . . to promote the liberal and practical education of the industrial classes."[34]

Gee takes pride in Ohio State's land-grant heritage:

> We embrace it, and we treasure the enormous contributions made in agriculture, engineering, medicine, law, veterinary sciences, and so many other fields of study . . . . And we make no apologies for also working to ensure that our graduates have the skills needed to thrive. Truly, the great universities of today and tomorrow will honor their histories while also changing for the future.[35]

In addition to touching lightly on the stories of more than a dozen institutions that are changing for the future, we'll study one at the same level of detail as Harvard. That school, BYU-Idaho, began as a frontier academy with an eye on Harvard, and soon had adopted many of its bigger-and-better tendencies, including the tendency to abandon the less educated students it was originally created to serve. However, the university's leaders, including a number with firsthand understanding of the Harvard model, altered the university's course. The faculty, administrators, and students of BYU-Idaho, like their counterparts at other universities and colleges, know that organizations must drive to improve, or else lose their vitality. But BYU-Idaho has adopted a unique definition of bigger and better.

The headline-grabbing genetic changes at BYU-Idaho, made in 2000, included the elimination of a successful intercollegiate athletic program and the creation of a year-round academic calendar designed to serve as many students in the summer as in the fall and winter. These outwardly visible modifications paled, though, in comparison to the effects of other alterations of the traditional university DNA. BYU-Idaho's creators made unusual decisions about the three choices that determine the productive capacity of a university community: which *students* it serves, what *subject matter* it emphasizes, and what types of *scholarship* it pursues.

Specifically, BYU-Idaho determined to serve only undergraduates, with the goal of providing even ordinary students a first-class education via a focused set of academic offerings. Scholarly activities were focused on the scholarship of teaching and learning rather than traditional discovery research. These choices stand in stark contrast to the most prevalent definition of bigger and better in higher education, which favors graduate students over undergraduates, expansive course catalogs over selective ones, and specialized discovery scholarship over more integrative or applied forms.

The administrators and faculty members of BYU-Idaho also chose unique *success measures* to align their activities and incentives with these strategic choices. For example, among BYU-Idaho's most watched statistics is the percentage of students admitted, rather than the percentage denied. Likewise, the institution's goal is to decrease tuition relative to inflation, rather than increase it. The university is designed, at the cellular level, to achieve these goals. Serving more undergraduate students at higher quality and lower cost is an objective built into the university's organizational design, into its standards for admitting students and promoting faculty, and into its year-round academic calendar, course catalogs, and pedagogical approaches. It is also the driving reason behind the university's emphasis on online learning.

Rather than incorporating wholesale the genetic code of the great research institutions, BYU-Idaho is a product of genetic reengineering. It benefits from many of the educational innovations of Harvard, including some commonly ignored ones. But instead of imitating the most prestigious universities, it is designed to play a complementary role, serving students who seek a different kind of educational experience. Much of BYU-Idaho's genetic design was put in place before Spellings, Bok, and Lewis raised their concerns about the quality, cost, and accessibility of undergraduate education, though it was precisely those challenges that BYU-Idaho's founders sought to address. It is not only students who have benefited. The university's operational efficiency allows it to pay its faculty members more; by McKinsey's analysis, they make roughly 15 percent more in total compensation than their peers at comparable institutions.

The Power of Uniqueness

BYU-Idaho is of course a unique case, and some might doubt its usefulness as a model for other institutions. For example, short of *force majeure,* few university communities would accept the wholesale elimination of intercollegiate athletics or the implementation of a year-round academic calendar. Likewise, few tenured university professors would willingly bear teaching loads equivalent to those of community colleges, as BYU-Idaho faculty members do.

Yet, owing to a potent combination of financial downturn and looming competitive disruption, *force majeure* is a growing reality for many institutions. Moreover, much of what BYU-Idaho has done, especially its innovative use of online learning technology, was being done by other universities even before the downturn. Innovation at forward-looking institutions is now accelerating; many are considering heretofore unimaginable changes.

As we'll see, the key to successful innovation is not to imitate what BYU-Idaho—or any other university—has done. To the contrary, success in an increasingly competitive higher education environment requires each institution to identify and pursue those things it can do uniquely well. A strong sense of uniqueness has long been a driving force behind Harvard's success. Even when Harvard borrowed traits from other institutions, as it did from the great European universities in the 1870s, it did so with innovative twists that accounted for its unique strengths and needs. Harvard succeeded in becoming Harvard in large part because it never tried to become anything else.

Due to their uniqueness, Harvard and BYU-Idaho provide useful case studies for the many universities seeking a sustainable future in an increasingly competitive environment. So do the other innovative schools we'll encounter. Little-known features of these unique institutions offer hope for others as they seek to find their niches.

A NONCONFORMIST'S UNIVERSITY

In *Winning by Degrees,* McKinsey urged policymakers to foster uniqueness even as they seek increased higher education productivity. "Grant policies," the authors said,

> should foster productivity innovatively, for example, through sharing best practices, or introducing competitive grants and results-based funding. But they should not dictate how better productivity is achieved. This report shows that creative institutions can improve productivity in different ways, as long as they stay focused on the goal of educating more students for the same cost while maintaining or raising quality and access.[36]

All of the eight schools profiled in *Winning by Degrees* achieve their superior productivity in different ways, but one in particular, private, nonprofit Southern New Hampshire University (SNHU) has, like

BYU-Idaho, created a unique blend of the traditional and emerging models of higher education. SNHU's eclectic blend of old and new reflects the background of its nonconformist leader, Paul LeBlanc, who once led an effort to unseat the president of the college where he taught and departed academe for a time to do a stint as vice president of new technology at book publisher Houghton Mifflin.

In addition to its 300-acre residential campus in Manchester, SNHU operates five extension centers, a large online program, and a variety of low-residency programs. Almost all of its courses and programs are available online, allowing students to choose not only their preferred place of study but also the learning medium. Nearly half of its roughly 7,300 students work through SNHU's extension centers and online learning channels. (SNHU distinguishes its learning sites as "On Campus," "On Location," and "Online.")

SNHU's curriculum is both liberal in the traditional sense and also employment focused. The curricular focus on what comes after graduation, combined with a well-supported internship program, helps SNHU place more than 95 percent of its students by the time they graduate.[37] None of these students graduate with more than five years' worth of credits, compared to 20 percent of students at peer institutions.[38]

To see both the dangers of imitation and the potential to innovate and thrive in the new higher education environment, we'll move back and forth between urbane Cambridge, Massachusetts, and rural Rexburg, Idaho. Like the other innovative institutions we'll see, BYU-Idaho is not a finished product. Nor is it entirely immune to the expensive inclinations of traditional universities. But, having abandoned its early strategy of Harvard imitation, it is now focused in its choices of students, subjects, and scholarship and designed to produce effective learning at low cost. By selectively borrowing the best practices of others while pursuing its own unique mission, BYU-Idaho has established a sustainable competitive position and secured a bright future. Other institutions, from the largest research universities to the smallest colleges and institutes, can do the same. Many already are.

PART TWO

The Great American University

All the insights, noble thoughts, and works of art that the human race has produced in its creative eras, all that subsequent periods of scholarly study have reduced to concepts and converted into intellectual property—on all this immense body of intellectual values the Glass Bead Game player plays like the organist on the organ. And this organ has attained an almost unimaginable perfection; its manuals and pedals range over the entire intellectual cosmos; its stops are almost beyond number. Theoretically this instrument is capable of reproducing in the Game the entire intellectual content of the universe.[1]

From "A General Introduction"
The Glass Bead Game, by Hermann Hesse

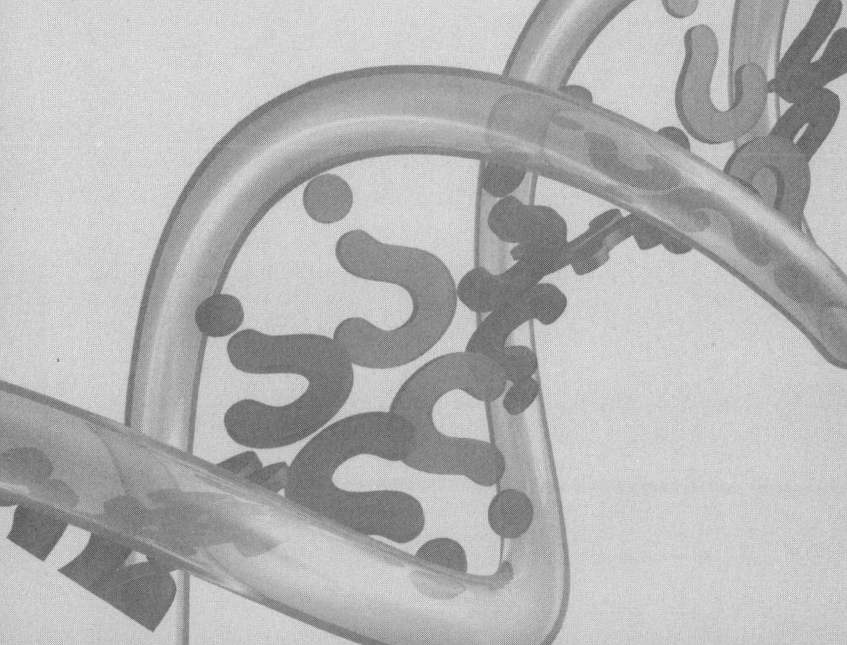

Chapter 2

Puritan College

The earliest settlers of the Massachusetts Bay Colony, who arrived from England in 1630, spent six years putting roofs over their heads, planting crops, building churches, and establishing a civil government before they could address the cause of higher education. But in the spirit of creating the "city on a hill" described by their leader, John Winthrop, as they crossed the Atlantic on the *Arbella,* in 1636 the Massachusetts General Court passed an act providing for a "schoale or colledge." Governor Winthrop and eleven other appointed overseers identified a spot up the Charles River from Boston, in Newetowne, at Cow-yard.[1]

Newetowne was renamed Cambridge, and it was to England's University of Cambridge that the new college looked for its institutional DNA. The initial masters and benefactors of the school were Cambridge graduates. They included John Harvard, for whom the college was named after he died in 1638 and left it half of his estate of about £800 and his library of 329 books.

The vision of Harvard's founder's was grand: "the advancement of all good literature, arts, and sciences."[2] In the English tradition, Harvard was an all-male school (that would remain the case for more than three hundred years). Most of the students were young, the youngest in their middle teens. They studied classical subjects such as logic and rhetoric, via learning methods experienced by their Cambridge-trained instructors: readings, recitations, and, as the final hurdle to graduation, oral examinations.

Though Harvard modeled its curriculum and instruction on that of Cambridge and its sister institution Oxford, there were fundamental differences. The most significant was an overt sacred purpose and focus. The school was, to its core, a religious enterprise, intended to train future ministers. The *Veritas* motto now enshrined on its official seal replaced an earlier one, *Christo et Ecclesiae:* "For Christ and the Church."[3] In addition to other classical subjects, Harvard students studied the Greek and Hebrew necessary to read the early versions of the Bible, regardless of whether they intended to join the clergy.[4] In the Puritan tradition, the instruction was dogmatic.

Harvard instilled moral character not only through classroom recitation of scriptural texts but also through devotionals such as morning and evening prayer as well as daily attendance at chapel, where the college president expounded on a chapter of scripture.[5] Sunday, of course, was given over wholly to worship.

Harvard also differed from Cambridge and Oxford in its lack of what is generally considered scholarship, the discovery of new knowledge. Though it soon won recognition of its degrees by the established English universities—an early manifestation of the bigger-and-better tendency—Harvard operated at a much more modest level. For many years, it accepted tuition in the form of farm produce, including livestock.[6] The faculty was small, a president plus two or three tutors, usually recent graduates awaiting ministerial appointments.[7] No faculty member was qualified to give the kind of lectures offered at Cambridge and Oxford. The college did not grant Ph.D. degrees, and its master's degrees required little effort and were widely considered to be of low quality.[8]

To its credit, Harvard College was entirely student focused. Each tutor lived with his students; the instruction, formal and informal, ran from dawn to dusk. But no tutor was a subject matter expert. In fact, the tutors had studied no subject in more detail than their students would. Their value as instructors was that they had walked the same

TABLE 2.1 Harvard's Initial DNA, 1636–1707	
Initial Traits	**Implications**
Small, face-to-face classes	High faculty-student intimacy Low instructional efficiency
Classical, religious instruction	High moral content in the curriculum Narrow curriculum with low practicality for non-pastors
Nonspecialized faculty	Dogmatic instruction High faculty empathy for learners Low faculty expertise

path already and were willing to tread it again, stride for stride with their charges. None could be called scholars in the modern sense of the term.[9] Moreover, the instruction was inherently expensive, given that all learning occurred under direct supervision. The cost was affordable only because instructors were paid so little.

Though Harvard was destined to be one of the biggest and best universities in the world, in its earliest years its educational offering was modest. In the late seventeenth century, its key genetic traits could be characterized as shown in Table 2.1.

The Advent of Secularization and Specialization

In 1708 John Leverett became the first non-clergyman to preside over Harvard. Leverett knew the school well, having earned both B.A. and M.A. degrees and taught there for a dozen years. But he was a man of the world in the best sense, an accomplished jurist, politician, and military commander.

Leverett's appointment ended decades of weak and even absentee leadership at Harvard. His immediate predecessor had resigned due to illness, and the preceding president, Increase Mather, had spent little time in Cambridge during his nine years at the helm. Leverett brought welcome attention and energy to the job. In addition to promoting financial stability and student enrollment growth, he gently steered Harvard in a more secular and liberal direction than his sectarian predecessors would have countenanced.[10] While striving to preserve the moral character of the school, Leverett established the first student club and the first student publication, *The Telltale*. He began a tradition of endowed faculty chairs, several of which were soon occupied by scholars who had been trained in England.

Leverett's decision to take Harvard down a more secular path was understandable. In addition to being all-too-often absent from his post, Increase Mather had played an indirect role in the Salem witch trials, in which his son Cotton was a central figure. Leverett recognized that a less Puritan Harvard would have broader appeal, particularly to students with no intention of becoming clergy, and that graduates educated in a more secular tradition might make greater contributions to civic leadership.

The move away from Puritan orthodoxy and dogma, and from the focus on clergy education, was a modification of Harvard's original DNA that brought both benefits and costs; the same was true of the introduction of endowed chairs, clearly a bigger-and-better move. That can be seen in the person of Isaac Greenwood, the first professor to occupy Harvard's chair of mathematics and natural philosophy. Greenwood had graduated from Harvard and gone

The move away from Puritan orthodoxy and dogma, and from the focus on clergy education, was a modification of Harvard's original DNA that brought both benefits and costs; the same was true of introduction of endowed chairs, clearly a bigger-and-better move.

on to study science in London before returning to Harvard. Fresh with knowledge of the latest scientific discoveries, Greenwood lectured of things not yet in print.[11] His stories of Isaac Newton's experiments and observations represented a substantial improvement over the reading of Aristotelian texts. Greenwood's approach was the beginning in the United States of the college lecture, with students taking notes at the feet of an expert professor. Pedagogically, it represented a great advance over reading and rote recitation. Better still, Greenwood brought laboratory equipment into the classroom, for the first time in the history of American higher education demonstrating the principles he taught.[12] He was Harvard's first modern scholar.

Greenwood's innovative approach was also the beginning, though, of divided faculty attention, with professors splitting their time between teaching students and exploring new discoveries in their specialized fields of knowledge. In some respects, the greater scholarly expertise was better for students, allowing them greater depth and practicality in their studies. However, it came at the expense of breadth of knowledge and student–teacher intimacy. Specialists such as Greenwood brought more relevant ideas to the classroom, but as mentors they were both narrower in their interests and more distant from the daily student experience. We can see that change to Harvard's DNA on many university campuses today.

The more immediate problem, in Greenwood's case, was his private life. After just ten years on the job, during which he published the country's first modern science textbook, he was fired for "various acts of gross intemperance, by excessive drinking."[13] Greenwood's moral weakness was unique among the faculty but indicative of a broader trend among students. The records of that time are, according to noted Harvard historian Samuel Eliot Morison, "full of 'drinking frolicks,' poultry-stealing, profane cursing and swearing, card-playing, live snakes in tutors' chambers, bringing 'Rhum' into college rooms, and 'shamefull and scandalous Routs and Noises for sundry nights in the College Yard.'"[14]

Harvard's classrooms continued to secularize under scholars such as Greenwood's successor, John Winthrop. Winthrop, second great-grandson and namesake of the founding governor of the Massachusetts Bay Colony, was a first-rate scientist even by European standards. He was also unbound by religious orthodoxy, daring to speculate that disasters such as the great Lisbon earthquake on All Saints Day 1755 had natural rather than divine origins.[15] For this he is recognized today as an early contributor to the science of seismology. At the time, "he attracted the opprobrium of the clergy, the admiration of Harvard students, and the curiosity of the laity."[16]

The pursuit of discovery, which required a more secular view of the world, also required more academic specialization. That trend was evident among not only Harvard's professors but also its tutors. Beginning in 1767, tutors specialized by subject rather than spanning the entire curriculum.[17] From the standpoint of subject matter expertise, the change represented a clear improvement. But the tendency toward curricular narrowing and pedagogical distancing, begun forty years earlier with Isaac Greenwood, was becoming genetically entrenched.

Transition Years

On the eve of the American Revolution, Harvard entered a nearly hundred-year period of relative drift and discontent. The first two presidents of this period were forced to resign, one for personal impropriety and the other for unpopularity with students.[18] Their eleven successors did little better, presiding over terms marked by brevity, student dissatisfaction, and occasional tumult.

The end of Puritan domination of Harvard was signaled just after the turn of the nineteenth century, when Unitarians captured both the presidency and the school's divinity professorship. Though this pivotal event in the shift away from Calvinist orthodoxy embittered some supporters, it did not necessarily mean the end of religious reverence at Harvard, as pointed out by Morison:

The end of Puritan domination of Harvard was signaled just after the turn of the nineteenth century, when Unitarians captured both the presidency and the school's divinity professorship.

Unitarianism of the Boston stamp was not a fixed dogma but a point of view that was receptive, searching, inquiring, and yet devout; a halfway house to the rationalistic and scientific point of view, yet a house built so reverently that the academic wayfarer could seldom forget that he had sojourned in a House of God.[19]

The rationalism of Unitarianism made for a more open, inquiring learning environment for both scholars and students, a cherished trait of today's universities. However, the classroom experience changed little. In the early 1800s, the college remained inbred, with nearly all of its instructors schooled exclusively at Harvard.[20] The subjects of study and teaching methods stayed largely the same, as these former students replicated their classroom experiences for current ones.

There were exceptions to this rule, mainly in the form of a few brilliant instructors trained in Germany, then the scholarship capital of the world. There was, for example, Edward Everett, a professor of Greek who had studied at the University of Göttingen. One of his students, Ralph Waldo Emerson, lauded Everett's "great talent for collecting facts, and for bringing those he had to bear with ingenious felicity on the topic of the moment."[21] That "ingenious felicity," though, apparently didn't embrace the gift of getting quickly to the point, nor of audience sensitivity. This was the same Everett who, having spoken for two hours before Lincoln's Gettysburg address, later confessed to President Lincoln, "I should be glad if I could flatter myself that I came as near to the central idea of the occasion, in two hours, as you did in two minutes."[22]

With the curriculum and pedagogy in relative limbo, Harvard failed to challenge or satisfy its best students. Charles Sumner, a Massachusetts senator and famed abolitionist, declared of his experience,

"I am not aware that *any one single* thing is well taught to the Undergraduates of Harvard College."[23] Another alumnus, Andrew Peabody, who went on to become a Harvard professor and acting president, recalled, "A youth who was regular in his habits, and who made some sort of an answer, however wide of the mark, at half of his recitations, commonly obtained his degree."[24]

In 1823 the discontent spilled over. That was the year of a "Great Rebellion" that resulted in the expulsion of thirty-seven students (more than half of the unruly graduating class) as they were on the verge of receiving their diplomas.[25] The immediate cause of the rebellion, factional brawling over the chosen commencement speaker, was only the tip of an iceberg of dissatisfaction that had manifested itself for years in large-scale food fights and destructive pranks.

In 1825 Harvard president John Kirkland, a gentle pastor beloved by the students notwithstanding their dissatisfaction with the institution, responded to the discontent with seminal changes to the undergraduate curriculum. For the first time in nearly two hundred years, students were allowed to choose a subject; in place of part of the Latin and Greek requirements, they could opt for French, Italian, German, or Spanish.[26] At the same time, control of the curriculum, which had resided with collegewide boards, was given over to newly created faculty departments. Putting responsibility for curriculum development with the specialists who knew the subject matter best, it was thought, would result in greater curricular innovation and thus better student learning experiences.

Departmentalization of the curriculum did in fact make for better individual courses. It also facilitated better scholarship, as academic specialists gathered into departments could more easily share ideas. But the introduction of departments also modified Harvard's DNA and was a de facto driver of the school's choices about its subject matter and scholarship. In the decades to come, the departmental structure would lead not only to broader study options and better scholarly research, but also to course offerings that both narrowed and proliferated. In addition, it would distance the academic disciplines from one another.

Over time, the net effect would be to increase the cost and complexity of providing undergraduate education, particularly cross-disciplinary elements of the curriculum such as general or liberal education.[27]

The educational reforms of this era also included the introduction of grades, a tool for challenging indolent students and rewarding conscientious ones.[28] In a related attempt to improve student behavior, a long summer vacation was introduced. Ironically, the traditional academic calendar was instituted at Harvard not for pedagogical reasons or even out of agricultural necessity but to accommodate student preferences.[29] The theory was that disruptions such as the Great Rebellion occurred most often in hot weather; without modern air conditioning systems, it seemed safer to send students home during the summer months.[30] In those days, when faculty salaries and building costs were relatively low, the cost of a long summer break was modest. Before long, though, the truncated academic calendar would become much more expensive.

Notwithstanding these significant innovations, the Harvard curriculum remained relatively rigid and stale. In many cases, faculty preference for the established order thwarted proposed curriculum changes. Professors at Harvard found support in an influential report issued in 1828 by Yale University that reasserted the primacy of the classical curricular model that allowed students little or no choice of subject matter.[31] In New Haven, Connecticut, as well as Cambridge, Massachusetts, recitation, the rote restatement of reading and lecture material, continued as the dominant pedagogy. Greek remained the language of distinction, a requirement not only for graduation but also for admission.[32]

Though the Industrial Revolution transformed the greater Boston area to a degree seen in few other places, Harvard College changed little more in the nineteenth century than it had in the eighteenth. One reason for Harvard's reluctance to innovate may have been the relative failure of experiments by Benjamin Franklin at what would become the University of Pennsylvania and by Thomas Jefferson at the University of Virginia. Both men were ahead of their time with innovations such as an elective, science-heavy curriculum and division of the university into separate colleges. These innovations were prescient, as we'll see, but premature for the faculty of these institutions.

Harvard's commitment to its traditional model of higher education was also a reaction to developments in the world beyond the academy. The more things changed around them, the more academic scholars found a sense of stability and safety in the classical tradition. The supposed virtue of the ancients was seen as an antidote to the venality of the new commerce. Thus, the most respected institutions were the slowest to innovate. Higher education advanced during this period, but not at Harvard or its sister schools. For example, the forerunner of the American Association for the Advancement of Science, the world's largest scientific society and the publisher of the prestigious journal *Science*, was founded not by scholars at Harvard or Yale but at the fledgling U.S. Military Academy at West Point by two dozen cadets.[33]

The more things changed around them, the more academic scholars found a sense of stability and safety in the classical tradition.

Even during this period of relative drift, Harvard made notable changes that helped lay the foundation for the university to come. Professional schools were established in medicine (1782), divinity (1816), law (1817), science (1847), and dentistry (1867). National searches led to the hiring of more-qualified faculty not only for these professional schools but for the college as well. Both professional schools outside of the college and recruitment of the best professors became important elements of Harvard's DNA, though their full effects weren't immediately apparent. For example, the specialized professional schools, which did not then require completion of a college degree, became competitive alternatives to a liberal college education, increasing pressure on the college to introduce more specialized curriculum. Similarly, national searches for faculty heightened the emphasis on scholarship as a selection criterion, in part because research publication and scholarly distinction were more easily measured than teaching effectiveness.

Harvard also established itself during this time as a premier fund-raising organization. The robust New England economy produced new fortunes, and Harvard received large donations not only from its alumni but also from more-distant admirers. From the beginning, the school's presidents established the expectation that they would retain discretion in the use of these donations, though that would prove more and more difficult over time.[34] By the turn of the twentieth century, Harvard's endowment comprised thousands of separate gift funds, many controlled by its deans rather than the president. Some donors with preferred personal causes placed narrow, legally binding restrictions on their gifts. Among present-day Harvard's restricted endowments is one limited to the acquisition of meteorite specimens. Another rewards the best essay on "the true spirit of book collecting."[35] Such narrowly restricted gifts, common in higher education today, are not only inaccessible for general university purposes but may require expenditures not provided for by the donor. Meteorites, for example, must be housed and cared for by curators.

Notwithstanding these seeds of future difficulty, Harvard's relatively unrestricted philanthropic support proved a boon when, in 1865, it severed financial ties with the government of Massachusetts, which had been agitating for curriculum and financial reform (some of which it achieved in the newly established Massachusetts Institute of Technology). The preference for donor rather than state-appropriated funds would become a dominant trait not only of Harvard but of other universities. As shown in Table 2.2, it was one of seven major genetic alterations during Harvard's first two hundred years that together made the institution more secular and specialized. In many respects, these alterations raised the quality of its academic activities, including the education of students. Harvard was getting bigger and better. However, it was also gradually becoming less focused on student instruction and more organizationally complex and resource hungry.

TABLE 2.2 Harvard's Evolving DNA, 1708-1868	
New Trait	**Implications**
Secularization	Freedom from dogma in academic inquiry Increased practicality in the curriculum Tendency toward skepticism
Subject matter specialization	Greater subject matter expertise and depth Better scholarship Enhanced faculty credentials Diminished faculty focus on students Increased emphasis on curricular content and lecturing Increased instructional cost
Departmentalization	Broader study options Enhanced disciplinary collaboration Increased narrowing of scholarship and fragmentation of the curriculum Increased fragmentation of the faculty
Long summer recess	Greater faculty research opportunities Lower utilization of physical facilities
Professional schools	Increased contribution to economic and social welfare Specialized alternatives to liberal education
Private fundraising	Greater discretion in spending Diminished dependence on student tuition and state support Donor limitations and incidental expenses

Harvard weathered the Civil War better than many of its peers. The war's economic impact on New England was relatively positive. The school prospered under a modest but capable minister, Thomas Hill, who raised admission standards and expanded elective offerings, particularly in the sciences.[36] But during Harvard's years of drift, competing institutions had sprung up by the dozens. Some, notably Yale, temporarily eclipsed it in prestige and number of graduates.[37] Innovative newcomers seemed ready to do the same in terms of curriculum and scholarship. By comparison, Harvard seemed adrift. Samuel Eliot Morison summarized the woeful contrast this way:

> Yet Harvard College was hidebound, the Harvard Law School senescent, the Medical School ineffective, and the Lawrence Scientific "the resort of shirks and stragglers." . . . It was a saying that all a Harvard man had to do for his Master's degree was to pay five dollars and stay out of jail.[38]

Fortunately, by the end of the 1860s Harvard was poised for a remarkable renaissance.

Chapter 3

Charles Eliot, Father of American Higher Education

Onto a Harvard stage set for change walked the leading actor in the institution's history, Charles Eliot. Eliot was a Boston Brahmin, born into a family of wealth, political power, and strong Harvard ties. He inherited the family intellect but not its wealth; his father lost everything in the financial panic of 1857, when Eliot was twenty-three. By then, he was a graduate of Harvard working at his alma mater as a tutor. The loss of the family fortune and the resulting responsibility to provide for his parents and three unmarried sisters made an already serious Eliot the more so. At the age of twenty-four, he married and won a professorial appointment in mathematics and chemistry.

Eliot's experience as a Harvard College student had been transformational, and it inspired him as a teacher. As a freshman, he had been particularly blessed by what would become a lifelong association with one of his professors, Josiah P. Cooke, an instructor in chemistry and mineralogy. Cooke had visited Europe, where he observed the laboratory learning environment in which the Germans especially excelled. Harvard lacked anything like that, but upon returning Cooke built a makeshift lab in a basement corner. Young Eliot was among the privileged few students given access to this "poor scholar's lab," where he confirmed his zeal for chemistry. Cooke's mentorship led to coteaching opportunities and a Ph.D. for Eliot.[1]

As a professor, Eliot sought to engage his students in the way that Cooke had entranced him. He was an imaginative, reforming teacher who substituted oral examinations with written ones and created Harvard's first laboratory-based course, an exciting departure from traditional classroom study.[2] He applied hands-on approaches even to mathematics, later recalling:

> I tried to make the teaching as concrete as possible and to illustrate its principles with practical applications. For example, while the class were studying trigonometry I taught simple surveying to a group of volunteers, and with their help made a survey of the streets and open spaces of that part of Cambridge which lies within a mile and a half of University Hall. These volunteers made under my direction a careful map of what was then the College Yard, with every building, path, and tree delineated thereon.[3]

Though Eliot taught well, his truly great gift was for administration. Three Harvard presidents relied on him as a de facto operating executive. Eliot's activities eventually encompassed most of the college's nonacademic functions, from buildings to budgets to student affairs. He also proved to be a skillful fundraiser, with a talent for convincing Boston's wealthy merchants and manufacturers to support scholarly inquiry.[4] During the early Civil War years, his responsibilities grew still greater: he became acting dean of Harvard's Lawrence Scientific School. His innovations there included new general education courses in science.

These administrative activities, as well as teaching classes that he could have avoided, came at the expense of Eliot's scholarly research. That probably cost him the appointment he really wanted: Harvard's prestigious Rumford professorship. He lost that prize to a scholar with German training and a superior publication record.[5] Crushed at being passed over, he left Harvard in 1863, after nine years as one of its most powerful forces.

Declining an offer to lead a cavalry regiment in the Civil War because of his responsibility for his extended family, Eliot followed the counsel of friends and went to Europe. During two years spent primarily in France and Germany, he applied his prodigious intellect and dogged learning approach not only to education but to all aspects of society. He took equal interest in scholars and shopkeepers.

Eliot made three important discoveries. One was the broad range and high degree of specialization of European scholarship. The great French and German universities seemed to excel in a dizzying array of disciplines. The second discovery was the apparent connection between scholarship and national economic productivity. Eliot surmised that the increase in imported European goods he had seen at home was the result of scientific discoveries being translated into commercial practice.[6] Though he felt discouraged to see many scholars working in relative isolation, the ultimate linkage between the discoveries being made in European universities and technical schools and the innovation occurring in European factories seemed clear. Scholarship, he concluded, could be an engine of national productivity and prosperity.

Third, Eliot saw that notwithstanding French and German superiority in scholarship and industry, individual citizens suffered at the hands of undemocratic governments, rigid class structures, and exclusionary school systems.[7] He gained increased appreciation for the value of democratic liberty. He recognized that the rise of his own family to the heights of political, financial, and scholarly success would have been impossible in Europe.

Eliot returned to America in 1865 convinced that great universities could and should do three things: (1) excel in all academic disciplines, with an emphasis on advanced study and the discovery of new knowledge, (2) contribute to social and economic welfare, and (3) provide curricular freedom of choice. He could already see how the third aim—freedom of scholars and students to choose their subjects of study—would create a kind of intellectual free market, one stimulating of excellence in all disciplines, including those with the potential to directly promote societal welfare.

Thanks to work that Eliot would soon undertake at Harvard, the interplay and mutual reinforcement of these ambitions permanently altered the genetic structure of the American university. The types of students served grew to include—and even favor—graduate students in the arts and sciences, who would be of greatest help to the faculty in their research. The range of the university's subject matter interests would broaden. And the university's scholarship would emphasize knowledge discovery and dissemination over instruction.

Lessons from Europe

The America to which Eliot returned was ripe for the changes he hoped to make. With the conclusion of the Civil War, the country stood ready for dramatic expansion of its territory, population, and commerce. Northern businesses that had boomed in wartime retooled to meet civilian needs. Railroads created a vast common market. New industries would soon grow up around inventions such as the electric light, the telephone, and the automobile, and businesses both old and new would benefit from the practices of mass production and scientific management. Significantly for Eliot and his academic colleagues, the number of Americans needing higher education to work in these industries and consume their products would grow substantially.

In 1865 change was brewing even in the historically conservative world of higher education. That year the Massachusetts Institute of Technology (MIT) opened its doors, and philanthropist Ezra Cornell, Western Union's largest stockholder, endowed the university that bears his name. Each of these schools was significant for espousing at least two of the three principles reinforced in Eliot's mind during his travels.

MIT was dedicated to the discovery and application of scientific technology, the forte of the European polytechnical schools and Eliot's second imperative for a great university. So was Cornell; as a land-grant institution supported by the State of New York, it was accountable to provide practical education in fields such as engineering and agriculture.

Both new schools intended to provide far more freedom in subject selection, Eliot's third imperative, than Harvard had ever done.

Cornell also aspired to excel in all fields of scholarship, Eliot's leading imperative for great university status. Its commitment to breadth of study was reflected in the statement of its founder that became the university motto: "I would found an Institution where any person could find instruction in any study."[8]

Ironically—but perhaps providentially—it was MIT rather than Harvard that brought Eliot back home from Europe, offering him a professorship in chemistry; he became one of the school's first ten faculty members. He served the fledgling technical institute faithfully, and his MIT experience gave him not only time to refine his ideas about the connection between research discoveries and economic productivity but also an innovative forum in which to apply some of them.

However, Eliot's ambition to return to and lead Harvard only grew. So did his stature in the eyes of Harvard's Board of Overseers, to which Eliot won election in 1868. He used that institutional platform to publicize his strategy for reinvigorating American higher education, particularly in an influential two-part magazine article published in *The Atlantic Monthly.*[9] When, in late 1868, the presidency of Harvard opened for the fourth time in two decades, Eliot was selected as the man to impart both leadership stability and a new institutional vision.

HARVARD'S GOVERNING BODIES CHOOSE A PRESIDENT

Eliot's selection as president was bold stroke that paid off handsomely but involved real risk. He was young (thirty-five), outspoken, and lacking in scholarly credentials. He had publicly politicked for the job, and he was already on record with a reform agenda. Had the choice been left to Harvard's faculty, his appointment as Harvard's president seems unlikely.[10] However, the real power lay not with the faculty or even with the overseers, elected representatives of the alumni, but with the Harvard Corporation (formally, The President and Fellows of Harvard College), created by Massachusetts charter in 1650. By that charter, the seven-member corporation comprised the institution's president and treasurer, along with five other members chosen by the corporation itself, subject to the counsel and consent of the overseers.[11]

Eliot wasn't the first choice of the corporation: Charles Francis Adams, son of John Quincy Adams and U.S. minister to Britain, declined their offer.[12] Unable to woo a seasoned diplomat, the corporation turned to the young, untested former Harvard professor with visionary ideas. Its members, whose professional positions gave them broad purview not only of the worlds of commerce, law, and politics, but of the universities poised to eclipse Harvard, placed a bet on innovation and the prospect of presidential longevity. They patiently discussed the matter for months with the overseers, who ultimately consented, and Harvard had its man.

The Elective System: Having It All

As Harvard's new president, Eliot lost no time in announcing his plans. In his inaugural address, he declared, "This University recognizes no real antagonism between literature and science, and consents to no such narrow alternatives as mathematics or classics, science or metaphysics. *We would have them all, and at their best.*"[13] That concept of everything at its best, much more easily stated than realized in practice, would become not only Eliot's agenda for the ensuing forty years but also, in time, the burden of universities in America and around the world.

The lynchpin of the young president's strategy for turning Harvard into a great university came to be known as the "elective system." The idea was simple: rather than the college's mandating a standard, classical curriculum for undergraduates, professors would be allowed to choose what to teach. Likewise, students would be able to choose what to study. It is an idea taken for granted today, an essential feature of university DNA, but in Eliot's day it ran counter to the long-established grain.

While election was controversial at the time for its novelty, the reasoning behind it resonated with both faculty and students. Instructors, Eliot successfully argued, teach best the subjects to which they are naturally drawn. The same is true of students, who learn best subjects of inherent interest to them. Eliot felt that mature students who know where they are going in life should be allowed to focus their studies in that direction rather than being required to run a standard curricular gantlet; in addition, they should be allowed to move at their own pace, taking advanced subjects as soon as they are ready rather than working through a lockstep sequence. Eliot also anticipated that the elective system would lead to specialization, affording scholars greater opportunities to bring their discoveries into the classroom. That would both energize faculty members and allow their students to get a jump on graduate education.[14]

In addition to these benefits to scholars and students, Eliot recognized the potential of the elective system to help transform Harvard from a classical college with a handful of mediocre professional schools into a university with a broad, cutting-edge curriculum. By allowing student choice, the college could be freed from Greek and Latin requirements without the outright elimination of those subjects.[15] Through the elective system, Eliot could effectively modernize the curriculum while not specifying what it would be; his curricular innovation thus avoided the political tension that inevitably attends administrative choices of what will and will not be taught.

Eliot also anticipated that freedom of choice would create competitive pressures on faculty to ensure student satisfaction. To this end, he created the academic course as it is known today, with a name, number, and professor identified to teach it.[16] Whereas past students had no advance knowledge of who would be teaching a given subject and no choice about the year in which to take it, now they could pick and choose according to preferred times and professors. In this way, the new elective system elevated teaching standards by market forces rather than by administrative fiat.[17] Eliot the fundraiser also saw one more potential benefit: he expected many students and scholars to pursue applied sciences, thus creating opportunities for him to raise money from Boston's wealthy industrialists.[18]

Eliot wasn't blind to the potential costs of the elective system. His critics cited three risks in particular: the possible loss of (1) coherence, or connectedness among the courses taken by a student, (2) educational breadth, and (3) subject matter depth.[19] The elective system offered no guarantee, in other words, that a student would graduate with an integrated understanding of the fundamental academic subjects and also in-depth knowledge of at least one specialty.

Eliot attempted to dismiss these concerns with the argument that a motivated student would naturally choose a specialty and that the sequential requirements established for progress from one course to the next would create subject matter coherence. As for breadth, he reminded his critics that disagreement over the meaning of "broad" education was precisely the reason for abandoning the old classical curriculum.[20]

He also anticipated another concern: the financial cost of allowing so much curricular freedom.[21] He knew that the elective system would produce a plethora of courses, many of which would have small enrollments and thus be relatively expensive to offer. But Harvard could afford the investment, thanks to a tuition increase and a growing endowment.

THE UNEXPECTED COSTS OF ELECTIVE COURSES

Product proliferation is a genetic tendency of even for-profit organizations, but it is particularly strong in higher education. In the for-profit environment, investors and executives expect to see financial projections of the costs and potential benefits of a new product. They are also likely to evaluate the product's performance against those projections and, when necessary, cull an unprofitable offering.

By contrast, the creation of a new course occurs in an environment that is simultaneously less data driven and less demand focused. Even if enrollments could be accurately forecasted, there is a valid question as to whether student demand should drive decisions about the curriculum; the overriding concern is to provide what faculty members feel is essential to a sufficiently broad and deep education. Thus, a business-style assessment of course creation can be seen as both impractical and undesirable in higher education.

Still, the faculty enthusiasm that Eliot tapped with the elective system comes with a risk of self-interest or at least partiality, as a scholar who has spent years mastering one aspect of a discipline is likely to consider it essential. Moreover, academic collegiality may mean giving the benefit of the doubt to a colleague's new course proposal. The result is a tendency for course catalogs to swell more rapidly than typical business catalogs.

The real difference between the for-profit and academic realms, though, is in the treatment of existing offerings. Once created, a course tends to live as long as a faculty member wants to teach it. The financial data and the executive reviews used to cull an unprofitable product in the business world have, at best, only weak counterparts in traditional universities and colleges. The result is that courses with low enrollments (and thus high delivery cost) may persist alongside those with higher enrollments. A similar disparity in quality is possible. Eliot expected the latter risk to be mitigated by the competition inherent in the elective system. But another of his innovations, a system of tenure for Harvard's professors, would weaken that competitive check on subpar instruction. In time, Eliot's elective system grew more expensive than he anticipated.

A Harvard-Style Innovation

In addition to being expensive, Eliot's elective system was typical of later Harvard innovations in other ways. For one, it built on a sound foundation of preparation. Eliot didn't invent the elective system at Harvard; at the time of his inauguration, students were already choosing nearly 40 percent of their courses.[22] Eliot simply increased both that percentage and the number of electives offered. In the ensuing decades, a liberated faculty introduced courses on subjects of their choosing, often drawing from their personal research activities. In time, students found it possible pursue a single field of study to great depth or, conversely, play the field of knowledge with almost unlimited breadth, a major innovation.

Yet Eliot's elective system was an opportunistic move that wasn't rushed or pressed too hard on the faculty, another hallmark of innovations that he and his successors made. He sensed that the forces of change were on his side. Though a few classicists among the faculty and alumni clung to the old prescribed curriculum, the majority of professors and virtually all students liked the idea of greater choice. It resonated not only with the economic ethos of the day, but with the post-Civil War spirit of liberty augured by Abraham Lincoln's plea for "a new birth of freedom."[23]

In the implementation of the elective system, as in his other innovations, Eliot was confidently patient. The last required course at Harvard didn't disappear until 1899, thirty years after he assumed office.[24] He took courage along the way from the experience of his son, an 1882 graduate who loathed the prescribed classical curriculum for freshmen but reveled in his elective courses, which prepared him well for a distinguished career in landscape architecture.[25] Eliot's patience produced benefits beyond bringing the faculty along at an emotionally comfortable pace; it allowed time for ensuring the quality and continuous improvement of the new courses.

Eliot also let Harvard's elective system be uniquely Harvard's. He was aware of the system of Cornell's founding president, Andrew White, who had the advantage of working from whole cloth. But he didn't copy the elective system of Cornell or that of any other institution. The imitation was left to others. As late as 1890, when Harvard's elective system came into full flower, the typical college specified 80 percent of a student's courses. Little more than decade later, at many schools that figure was down to 30 percent.[26]

Everything at Its Best: Harvard Graduate Schools

An elective system for undergraduates was an important first step toward Eliot's ideal university, as it allowed faculty to specialize as never before. There was still the challenge, though, of taking knowledge discovery and application to the heights he had seen at the great European universities. Achieving that would require more than just a college with freedom of study. Therefore, even as he began to implement the principle of liberty in the curriculum of Harvard College, Eliot undertook the creation of new graduate schools, through which Harvard University would recognize his goals of world-class scholarship and contribution to economic prosperity and social welfare.

As with the elective system, Eliot's innovative approach to graduate education built on what Harvard already did well and, though it found inspiration in the example of other institutions, was uniquely Harvard's. The European universities inspired Eliot, but he had no intention of simply copying them, as he declared in his *Atlantic Monthly* article, "A university, in any worthy sense of the term, must grow from seed. It cannot be transplanted from England or Germany in full leaf and bearing . . . . The American college is an institution without a parallel; the American university will be equally original."[27]

It was partly with Harvard College in mind that Eliot took the first step in creating his university. In 1872 he established what would become the Graduate School of Arts and Sciences, which began to offer advanced degrees, including the Ph.D.[28] By creating Ph.D. programs in fields such as language, history, economics, and chemistry, Eliot provided his faculty with a supply of the graduate students essential to first-rate scholarship. These advanced students would perform the more menial tasks associated with research, such as the collection of experimental data, and would teach undergraduate classes, allowing their professors to focus on the process of making and publishing discoveries. Home-grown Ph.D. graduates would also swell the ranks of qualified prospective faculty and reduce competition for the few Europe-trained scholars in the United States.

Significantly, Eliot gave the Faculty of Arts and Sciences (FAS) responsibility for all college-level instruction. That decision had far-reaching impact on the undergraduate curriculum. On the positive side, it gave Harvard College students direct access to arts and sciences faculty with deep expertise. It also paved the way for college students to pursue advanced studies. One of Eliot's curricular innovations was the opening of courses to students regardless of their year in school, so long as they could meet the prerequisite qualifications. That was true of both undergraduate- and graduate-level courses. Even today, courses offered by the Faculty of Arts and Sciences are identified as "Primarily for Undergraduates," "Primarily for Graduates," or "For Undergraduates and Graduates." Eliot succeeded in opening an impressive array of advanced courses to qualified students of the college. In this sense, he was justified in bragging, "There is no telling where the College ends and the Graduate School begins; they are interfused or commingled."[29]

The downside of giving the Faculty of Arts and Sciences responsibility for the college was that professional disciplines—law and medicine, for example—would not be taught as such to undergraduate students. Those who intended to pursue one of these careers might study complementary subjects, such as history and philosophy for law and biology and psychology for medicine. But college students would graduate with no direct knowledge of the professions. Another consequence of putting the FAS in charge of the college was to set the undergraduate curriculum on the same path of academic specialization and narrowing that the faculty had chosen.

Eliot also created new professional schools in agriculture and horticulture, veterinary medicine, mining and geology, and business. Only the last of these, the Harvard Business School, survived as a stand-alone entity. However, Eliot succeeded in upgrading the already established medical and law schools, which prior to his presidency had required neither bachelor's degrees of entering students nor rigorous examinations of graduating ones.[30] He also raised standards for the faculty of the medical school, preferring scholars over practitioners.

Under his leadership the law school adopted the "case method" of study, now the standard pedagogy for U.S. legal training.[31]

World-class professional schools of medicine, law, and business not only burnished Harvard's reputation for having all subjects at their best, they also reinforced Eliot's vision for the college. With practice-oriented, bachelor's degree-requiring professional schools under the university umbrella, Eliot had an answer to those who challenged the undergraduate curriculum as either too impractical or too diffuse. Liberally educated college graduates could proceed for professional graduate training. The professional schools would require little, if any, specialized preparation in the field, so an undergraduate who had sampled a bit of everything would be at no significant disadvantage.

Having created such a wide array of graduate study opportunities within the university, Eliot saw no reason why students of the college, whom he expected to continue on for graduate education, shouldn't be able to earn a bachelor's degree in three years rather than the traditional four.[32] He appreciated the unique role of the college in providing a liberal education. But he worried about the individual and societal costs of keeping graduate students in school until age twenty-six or twenty-seven when they might otherwise be productively employed.

In the 1890s, Eliot succeeded in reducing the number of credits required for a bachelor's degree. However, his plan to make the three-year degree standard met a full decade of stiff resistance from the faculty. The death knell came in the early 1900s, with a financial crisis caused by falling enrollments and spiraling costs. With such budgetary pressure, Harvard couldn't afford to lose the 25 percent of its undergraduate tuition revenue generated by the fourth year of the bachelor's degree program. The three-year bachelor's degree, which like other Harvard innovations would likely have been taken up into the DNA of other universities, died a victim of fiscal exigency that persisted through the end of Eliot's presidency.

Faculty Prerogatives and Influence

That the faculty could thwart Eliot in a major initiative in his fourth decade as president shows how their power had grown under his leadership. He presided over a fourfold growth in the number of both students and professors at Harvard.[33] But that statistic understates the real increase in the size of the faculty. By the end of his presidency there were nearly two hundred professors and more than four hundred teachers and researchers who were not professors, or two full-time employees to support each professor in teaching and research activities.[34] The faculty, broadly defined to include these teachers and researchers, grew by twelve times during his tenure.

Eliot made this investment in faculty growth because his world-class university required simultaneous specialization and breadth. Discovery research of the kind he had seen in Germany necessitates focus: discovering something new in an already well-studied field is most likely when the range of inquiry is narrowed. For this reason, scholars tend to specialize. Covering the full range of academic subjects requires hiring a host of such scholarly specialists.

At the same time, the work of educating students, including undergraduates, must go on. Yet the research of university scholars not only limits their time in undergraduate classrooms, it also distances them intellectually from the relatively rudimentary subjects taught there. Eliot believed in the compatibility of teaching and research, but he knew from firsthand experience that scholarship requires focused effort and discretionary time. Prizing both research and high-quality teaching, he supported the hiring of apprentice teachers, often graduate students, to lead discussions among students in small "sections." These supplemental instructors helped preserve a degree of teacher–student intimacy even as professors devoted more time to research and as enrollments in the largest courses they taught grew into the hundreds.[35] This arrangement would become a permanent feature of many large research universities.

Eliot supported the faculty in other ways. He championed freedom of academic inquiry and speech, and he implemented a system of tenure, ensuring lifetime employment until the age of retirement.[36] During his term as Harvard's president he also created a pension system and implemented three across-the-board increases in faculty salaries.[37] In another effort to attract first-rate scholars and support them in their work, he invented the academic sabbatical, by which each seventh year can be taken for full-time research.[38]

Eliot also established a tradition of involving the faculty in the administrative decisions of the university. He consulted with department members in faculty hiring decisions and granted them control over honors degrees and graduate programs.[39] He also respected a tradition that predated him of significant faculty self-determination in financial matters. In fact, Eliot's demonstrated regard for the faculty exceeded that of his Harvard predecessors and his contemporaries at other institutions. It won him broad admiration. One professor observed, "I have seen a great president content year after year to lay his most cherished projects before a large faculty and labor year after year to bring this faculty to his own way of thinking, convinced that in this assembly he had, on the whole, the most intelligent and fair-minded body of men in the world, for his purposes."[40]

Student Freedom

Eliot believed that the principle of academic freedom applied not just to scholars but to students. In addition to granting unrestricted course selection, he gave up the college tradition of *in loco parentis*, or exercising parental authority over student behavior outside of the classroom. In fact, even class attendance was optional for a time, until a father's discovery that his son, presumed to be studying in Cambridge, was in reality vacationing in Cuba; after that, professors were expected to take roll.[41]

Eliot reduced restrictions on students in other ways. Chapel became optional, and most forms of student misbehavior were ignored, the rigid discipline of the past being associated with Puritanism and the old classical curriculum.[42] Perhaps because as a student he preferred faculty mentoring to fraternizing with his fellows, Eliot generally neglected student social life.[43] He also ignored calls for more on-campus housing for the growing student body, reasoning that private investors would meet the need and that university resources ought to be focused on more strategic purposes.[44]

Not surprisingly, student behavior degenerated. With academic standards so low (a bachelor's degree could be won with D's in half of all courses taken), students made little effort in the classroom, often relying on private tutors to cram for final exams. [45] Harvard gained the reputation of being "the hardest college to get into and the easiest to stay in."[46] Students elevated extracurricular life to an art form. Social and athletic clubs flourished, and a pronounced class system developed, with the wealthier students abandoning on-campus housing in favor of elegant private dormitories that came to be known as the "Gold Coast."[47]

At the same time, athletic rivalries transfixed the Harvard community. The university was, to Eliot's chagrin, a football pioneer, playing its first intercollegiate game in 1874. He characterized football as "a brutal, cheating, demoralizing game" and saw no future for it. "It is very improbable that a game which involves violent personal collision between opposing players can ever be made a good intercollegiate game," he opined.[48]

Events soon proved him very wrong. Shortly after the turn of the century, Harvard's team, a perennial national powerhouse, was drawing crowds of up to 40,000, the largest in the country.[49] Students and alumni rejoiced in the new outlet for their emotional energies. But the cost was substantial. Harvard's football stadium, built in 1903, carried a $310,000 price tag. Fortunately, the alumni made a gift of the stadium. Had that amount been deducted from student-related revenues that year, it would have consumed more than half of the total.[50]

Eliot's Influence on Secondary Education

By the turn of the twentieth century, Eliot's attention and sphere of influence had broadened to include America's entire educational system. His prestige and impact were particularly pronounced in secondary education. It is hard today to imagine a university president making high school reform a personal priority. But for Eliot the cause was one not only of public good but of practical necessity for his fledgling university.

When Eliot assumed office in 1869, Harvard needed fewer than two hundred qualified applicants to fill its freshman class. The level of qualification required was modest, given the loose standards and low expectations inherent in the college curricula of the day; Harvard and its peers were, at the time, still providing the equivalent of the final years of a high school education. And, because Harvard drew most of its students from the relatively elite private preparatory schools of New England, their preparation, though rudimentary, was at least fairly even.

That changed, though, as Eliot sought to increase both the size and the intellectual rigor of the university. The problem of attracting qualified students was exacerbated by competition from an army of new institutions, including MIT, Cornell, Stanford, Johns Hopkins, the University of Chicago, and dozens of land-grant colleges from Massachusetts to California. In the face of such pervasive competition, and given the imperative to grow in both size and quality, the traditional feeder system of private college prep schools proved inadequate. For the first time, a Harvard president had to be concerned about public high schools.

Early on, Eliot opposed public support for high schools, viewing them as all but incapable of producing college-ready graduates.[51] He argued for bifurcation of secondary education, along German lines, with high schools providing only trade preparation and leaving college preparation to private schools.[52] This was consistent with his view of Harvard as equal to a German university, supported by preparatory schools similar in quality and content to the German gymnasia that emphasized liberal education.

By the late 1870s, though, he could see that private academies would produce too few students to supply large universities. It was a problem common in the rise of other great enterprises of the day. Henry Ford, for example, faced a similar challenge as demand grew for his competitively disruptive Model T cars, which were affordable to the working class. The independent steel manufacturers of the day couldn't supply steel at the consistently high quality and low cost his operation required. Thus, Ford established his own mill at River Rouge, next to his Dearborn, Michigan, assembly plant. This kind of "vertical integration" would become a hallmark of efficient manufacturing in the twentieth century.

Eliot, though, was ahead of his time in seeing a way to avoid the high costs of vertical integration. He recognized that what Harvard needed was not its own captive feeder schools but a set of educational standards to which all of the nation's leading secondary schools would adhere. He rightly surmised that Harvard had the clout to set such standards and to effectively offload college preparation to secondary schools.

> *[Eliot] recognized that what Harvard needed was not its own captive feeder schools but a set of educational standards to which all of the nation's leading secondary schools would adhere.*

In the beginning, Eliot tried out his ideas locally. He began to attend meetings of the Massachusetts high school teachers association and went so far as to convene a gathering of secondary school teachers with his faculty.[53] He even proposed complete curricula to two local high schools as they underwent reform.

In time, he took his case for better college preparation to the national level. In 1892 he chaired the National Education Association's "Committee of Ten," leading educators who adopted his fourfold classification of elementary knowledge—language, history, mathematics, and natural science.[54] He also contributed to founding of the College Entrance Examination Board, which would later administer the Scholastic Aptitude Test (SAT).

Eliot's overarching aim was to make all public high schools capable of producing college-ready graduates. In particular, he hoped that high schools could perform the liberal education function that had previously belonged to the colleges; it was in high school, he felt, that students should gain broad exposure to language, history, mathematics, and natural science. That would allow college to become a place of more specialized study or, if necessary, provide for undecided students the opportunity to discover their particular passion.[55] It would also allow the great universities to move "up-market," in today's terms, focusing on more sophisticated, better-heeled consumers. In other words, part of Eliot's objective was to enlist the support of secondary schools in Harvard's drive to be bigger and better.

Recognizing that not all high school students would pursue university education, Eliot nonetheless advocated a comprehensive approach in which students bound both for universities and for technical training would not be separated, as they were at a young age in Germany. This system, which can be seen in the DNA of American high schools even today, would favor the late bloomer and preserve a student's choice of an educational path until the eighteenth year. The downside was that the liberal curriculum he advocated, with its emphasis on what he called "mental training" rather than vocational preparation, would leave non-university-bound students poorly prepared for the workplace. Initially, he saw this problem as a minor one, given his belief that high school enrollments would be limited to a higher class of student, as the private preparatory schools were.[56]

The weaknesses of Eliot's liberal curriculum for American high schools became apparent as they broadened their reach to encompass all students, including a majority who would not attend a university or four-year college. Eliot responded by advocating proficiency-based grouping, suggesting that the less academically gifted students should proceed at a slower pace.[57] This tracking of students helped teachers to focus their efforts but made it less likely that a late bloomer would break through to the ranks of the college bound. Eliot's design also placed on the high schools the burden of being truly comprehensive, of trying to address both his liberal curriculum and workplace preparation.

Being tasked with two such different functions, as they still are today, means that many public high schools struggle to perform either well.[58] The consequences can be seen in the declining earning power of a high school degree and the decreasing percentage of high school students who enter and complete college.[59] The gap created by the university move "up-market" is also manifested in the call for community colleges to play a larger role in higher education and in the growing success of for-profit educators in serving students lacking the necessary preparation and credentials to access traditional universities and colleges. Nonetheless, in simultaneously raising the performance bar and standardizing the curricular approach of high schools across the country, Eliot laid the foundation for the remarkable growth of higher education in the twentieth century, and for the unprecedented economic prosperity that accompanied it.

MOVING GOALPOSTS

In 2008 Clayton Christensen and colleagues Michael Horn and Curtis Johnson published *Disrupting Class: How Disruptive Innovation Will Change the Way the World Learns.* They made the provocative argument that U.S. public education has improved over time notwithstanding the fact that "society just keeps moving the goalposts on schools by changing the definition of quality and asking schools to take on new jobs."[60]

In support of this "moving-the-goalposts" argument, Christensen and his colleagues pointed to the job of educating everyone for either university study or immediate employment that devolved to public high schools in Eliot's day.[61] This new job came on top of the Jeffersonian responsibility to inculcate democratic values and prepare a relative few for civic leadership. The public schools' response was admirably effective, as chronicled in *Disrupting Class*:

> In 1905, only a third of children who enrolled in grade 1 made it to high school, roughly a third of those graduated from high school, and even fewer went to college. By 1930, by contrast, over 75 percent of students were entering high school, and almost 45 percent graduated.[62]

But the goalposts continued to move, as high schools were required to respond to racial and cultural integration, *Sputnik*-motivated increases in demand for science and math education, and the rising expectations of affluent Americans, who wanted their children to have broad extracurricular opportunities and a head start on college via Advanced Placement courses. In addition, population growth meant that high schools originally designed to serve a hundred students enrolled, on average, nearly a thousand.[63]

The design for public high schools created by Eliot and others proved remarkably robust over the next hundred-plus years. However, the jobs required of these institutions would become increasingly difficult to perform as the nation's colleges and universities climbed the ladder in pursuit of Eliot's definition of the best education.

Eliot's Innovative Influence

Eliot's effect on higher education is hard to overestimate. By placing graduate schools atop the college and introducing the elective system, he gave students a vastly expanded choice of courses and allowed them to better prepare for graduate study and work. Professors enjoyed more time for scholarship, as many teaching duties could be delegated to graduate students, whose services cost the university relatively little. The university benefited in other ways. It found an increased ability to attract scholarly specialists and funding from industry-minded donors. The added funding and the lower cost of instruction also allowed it to grow student enrollments.

The new approach required tradeoffs on certain dimensions of performance. For example, some graduate students taught less effectively than the professors they replaced in the classroom. There was also less cohesiveness in the undergraduate curriculum. As we'll see, though, Eliot's immediate successor introduced sustaining innovations to ameliorate these problems so that, over time, Harvard's quality grew steadily on all dimensions.

The power of Eliot's innovative university model resulted in other institutions either following Harvard's lead or seeing a steady erosion of their influence. Most copied Eliot's elective system, as well as his superimposition of a German-style university for graduate students on an English-style college for undergraduates. Institutions that didn't adopt these innovations, including the great universities of Europe as well as American liberal arts colleges that continued to serve only undergraduate students and hewed to a classical curriculum, began to decline in relative influence. Many of these colleges survived, but they did not participate proportionally in the higher education growth that soon began to sweep the U.S.[64]

AN INNOVATIVE LIBERAL ARTS COLLEGE

Some liberal arts colleges have not only survived but are thriving, thanks to DNA-enhancing innovations that are important for universities as well. Westminster College was founded in 1875 as a mission school by the First Presbyterian Church of Salt Lake City and received regional accreditation in 1949 as a liberal arts college.[65]

Even as the college grew in the 1960s and 1970s, it struggled to compete with bigger public institutions that enjoyed the benefits of low tuition and high profile. In the 1980s, the school changed tack, deciding to compete on the basis of quality rather than low price. With the 1995 appointment of President Peggy Stock, Westminster assumed the features of an elite liberal arts college, raising faculty salaries, adding new buildings that included three residence halls, and pursuing a student-centered "vision of excellence."[66]

In 2002, under Stock's successor, Michael Bassis, Westminster undertook innovations to increase its visibility, vitality, and fiscal health. Most fundamentally, it shifted its paradigm from teaching to learning.[67] To this end, Westminster refocused its programs on measurable collegewide learning goals, which emphasize skills and attributes critical to long-term success. It reduced the emphasis on lectures, textbooks, and seat time in favor of active, collaborative, and experiential learning. E-portfolios were introduced to enable students to draw on the full range of their experiences in demonstrating achievement of these learning goals. Bassis and his colleagues are now building programs that blend online and face-to-face learning that they call "high-tech, high-touch."[68] Noting the innovation imperative facing not only liberal arts colleges but also traditional universities, Bassis has said:

> In some fields, and for some students, high-tech/high-touch may not be the most effective instructional design. But it is a model that may help many brick-and-mortar institutions increase both their quality and affordability. If they don't integrate online or other alternative forms of learning into their programs, more than a few are likely to fail.[69]

Though Eliot put Harvard on a path to excellence, his design also bore traits that became steadily more costly, both financially and in terms of the undergraduate student learning experience. His strengthening of the academic departments produced tremendous growth in the number of courses taught; that led to increased financial costs. Harvard's definition of scholarship, which emphasized German-style knowledge discovery, put instruction at risk. Other elements of Eliot's design, such as faculty and student autonomy, similarly proved to be more costly than he foresaw. So did his system of tenure and student selectivity. Intercollegiate athletics, an Eliot-era addition to Harvard's DNA that he resisted unsuccessfully, was another liability in the making. Harvard's genetic evolution under Eliot, with its positive and potentially negative implications, is summarized in Table 3.1.

TABLE 3.1 Harvard's Evolution in the Charles Eliot Era, 1869-1909

New Trait	Implications
Comprehensive, elective curriculum	Broader study options
	Opportunity for greater depth of study and self-pacing
	Opportunity to bring more advanced scholarship into the classroom
	Competitive incentive for teachers
	Potential loss of curricular breadth and subject matter depth
	Tendency toward fragmentation of the curriculum
	Proliferation of courses and a decrease in students-per-class in advanced courses
Graduate schools atop the college	Low-cost supply of graduate instructors and research assistants
	Elimination of pressure on the college to provide professional preparation; greater freedom to emphasize liberal education
	Further narrowing of the college curriculum

continued overleaf

TABLE 3.1 *(Continued)*

New Trait	Implications
Increased organizational complexity and cost	
Faculty self-governance	Greater curricular depth and rigor Increased excellence in scholarship Potentially decreased faculty attention to undergraduate instruction and increased instructional cost
Tenure and other faculty benefits	Increased faculty stability Increased institutional cost
Student freedoms	Increased social activity Decreased academic and social discipline More off-campus living Social cliques
Intercollegiate athletics	Alumni engagement Student distraction Increased institutional cost
College entrance standards	Tighter high school performance standards Greater awareness among high school students of college opportunities Reduced need for new student remediation Dual burden of college prep and career prep on high schools

Eliot effected these lasting changes in Harvard's DNA with an admirable combination of foresight and patience. It was thirty years, for instance, between the time he first proposed standardized college entrance exams and Harvard's institutional decision to participate in the system, which by then had become commonly accepted.[70] By the end of his four decades at the helm, he was almost as well known and respected as the university itself. The names Harvard and Eliot inspired veneration and emulation. That was true not only in the academic citadels of the East, but also in the smallest schools of the West, including a modest institution founded to serve the children of a hardy group of pioneers.

Chapter 4

Pioneer Academy

In 1888, at roughly the midpoint of Charles Eliot's presidency at Harvard, an academy for primary and secondary school-aged children was founded in rural Rexburg, Idaho, a farming community with a population of just three thousand. Boston, by contrast, was approaching half a million.[1] Founded by Mormon pioneers who were building communities throughout the west, the school in Rexburg embodied many of the Puritan virtues of early Harvard College: religious conviction, frugality, hard work, self-sacrifice. It also shared many of Harvard's ambitions.

A High Regard for Education

Joseph Smith, founder of the Church of Jesus Christ of Latter-day Saints (commonly know as the Mormon Church) wrote in 1832 of the importance of learning. His ideal curriculum included "things both in heaven and in the earth, and under the earth; things which have been, things which are, things which must shortly come to pass; things which are at home, things which are abroad; the wars and perplexities of the nations, and the judgments which are on the land; and a knowledge also of countries and of kingdoms."[2] It was bold doctrine for a twenty-seven-year-old frontiersman speaking more than three decades before Eliot declared that Harvard would have all academic disciplines at their best. The poverty of Joseph Smith's New England family prevented him from attending organized school past the second grade. However, with the help of tutors, he spent his life studying a broad range of subjects, including astronomy, history, languages, and law.

Joseph Smith was also a builder of schools. In the frontier settlements of Kirtland, Ohio, and Nauvoo, Illinois, he directed the early Mormon pioneers to create schools at the same time they were constructing homes. School-building became a pattern for these pioneers when they went west, beginning in 1847, under the direction of Brigham Young. Soon after the religious refugees from the then–United States founded Salt Lake City, Young sent groups to colonize the intermountain region. As they established new settlements on frontiers ranging from southern Alberta to northern Mexico, they built schools for their children, both boys and girls.

One such school, or academy, was established in 1888 by Thomas E. Ricks. Ricks led a congregation of Mormon pioneers who were sent to settle in eastern Idaho's Upper Snake River Valley, 60 miles west of Jackson, Wyoming, and an equal distance to the southwest of what would become Yellowstone Park. Ricks was directed by the church's board of education in Salt Lake to create a school similar to Brigham Young Academy, established thirteen years earlier in Provo, Utah. Rexburg's new Bannock Academy took its name from an indigenous Indian tribe and began operation in a converted log church house.

The relationship between the church board in Salt Lake and the academy's local board of education was complex and imprecisely defined. The church board had ultimate say on matters of policy, such as degree programs to be offered. The board also provided what financial support it could. However, the tenuous finances of the church, which had been disincorporated in 1887 by the anti-polygamy Edmunds-Tucker Act, made local contributions necessary. At the founding of the academy the board pledged to pay the principal's salary, but local supporters were required to outfit the building. For the purchase of desks Thomas Ricks raised $186.10 in cash, forty bushels of wheat, and two steers.[3]

The Early Years in Rexburg

The academy's first principal was Jacob Spori, a Swiss immigrant who had presided in his homeland over a school similar to the German gymnasia that Eliot admired. Spori brought impeccable credentials to the job, including degrees in mathematics and arts and music. He spoke nine languages, several of which he learned as a missionary to the Ottoman Empire and Palestine. In fact, he proved overqualified for the realities of the classroom. For all of his linguistic gifts, his English was difficult to understand, particularly for the elementary school-aged children who comprised the majority of his students.[4]

The academy's local founders held lofty expectations of its role and influence. At the dedication ceremony Ricks specified that it should "give spirituality precedence over worldliness." Spori boldly predicted, "The seeds we are planting today will grow and become mighty oaks, and their branches will run all over the earth."[5] The reality of that first year was more modest. Eighty-five students enrolled, paying between $2 and $4, depending on grade. They studied the subjects typical of today's elementary schools, plus Mormon religion.[6]

From the beginning the academy struggled financially, as some families sought to cover tuition with labor or produce and others failed to pay altogether. In response to a $177 end-of-year deficit, Spori offered to forego his salary the second year. While living with his family in an empty granary, he farmed and worked on the railroad, sharing his earnings with two assistant teachers.[7] By the end of that year, he felt compelled to resign so as to put his own financial house in order.[8] Faculty sacrifice and institutional struggle proved to be hallmarks of the fledgling academy. Enrollments fell as the academy shifted its focus to high school in the late 1890s; the earlier

The academy's local founders held lofty expectations of its role and influence. At the dedication ceremony Ricks specified that it should "give spirituality precedence over worldliness."

grades were dropped with the advent of public elementary schools. One short-term principal followed another, the first four of them coming and going in what amounted to one-third of Eliot's forty-year term.

The academy survived, thanks largely to an assessment on local Mormon congregations and additional support from Salt Lake City. At the turn of the century, the board approved the construction of a three-story, $40,000 stone classroom building; board members also gave the school a new name, Ricks Academy, to honor its founder. Teacher training was added to the curriculum, making the academy both a high school and a "normal" school. In 1902 a relatively encouraging 65 of 165 students who started in the fall stayed through May. By 1905, the academy had thirteen faculty members and rivaled the state university in Moscow, Idaho, in size. At the dedication of the new classroom building, which came in over budget at a total cost of more than $60,000, a senior student predicted of the academy that "other departments will be added until it shall embrace all branches of learning."[9] By the end of Eliot's tenure at Harvard, his test of a first-rate university embracing all subjects was shared even by teenagers on the western frontier.

Notwithstanding its religious affiliation, the academy wasn't without behavior problems. Ezra Dalby, who became principal in 1901 and remained at his post for an unprecedented thirteen years, bemoaned the "evil habits" (drinking, in particular) that a few students brought with them to campus. Like early Harvard College, Ricks Academy's religious mission pervaded its curriculum, in the form not only of religion classes but also required daily chapel services and special degree programs for future missionaries and Sunday school teachers. The majority of students were immature but earnest, both irking neighboring homeowners with their hi-jinks and disappointing downtown saloonkeepers with their temperance. Girls were welcome from the outset, though in the early years boys outnumbered them almost 3 to 1. However, in some things they were favored: boys were charged 25 cents for admission to school dances, while girls paid only 20 cents.[10]

Adopting Traits from the Great Universities

As the academy's student body grew, so did its curricular offerings. By 1907, Ricks offered four-year high school and normal programs, three-year commercial and domestic science programs, two-year tracks for junior high school-aged students, and shorter courses of study in fields such as music, art, elocution, cooking, and sewing. Programs in agriculture and "mechanic arts" were added, the latter housed in its own two-story building.[11]

Education at Ricks was far different from the kind offered at Harvard College under Charles Eliot. Nor could Ezra Dalby, holder only of a bachelor's degree from the University of Utah and a journeyman high school principal, match Eliot's rich academic background. Yet Eliot might have applauded Dalby's view of the high purpose of education:

> There is only one school period in life. The few years that have been set apart for this purpose in the life of a child are very sacred. Fearful will be the responsibility of the parent who crushes the ambitions and hopes of a child whose whole soul is on fire to learn and know. Many boys and girls in our community will never realize their highest possibilities, because of beets and grain and factory. We pay an awful price sometimes for material prosperity. Our bank account is often purchased at the expense of our children's future generations.[12]

Academy classes ran six days per week, from late October to early May, to compensate for a shortened academic year that accommodated early October potato harvest and spring planting. The faculty welcomed the long work week, which made for more serious students. As Dalby reported, "We have found the practice of having six days of school a week and a shorter term to be beneficial to the students, not only in the matter of having more time to work on farms, but also in the matter of discipline."[13]

The academy adopted a sixteen-credit system for its high school degree, with four credits or eight half-credits taken each year. Most college students wouldn't recognize such an odd curricular configuration, but Harvard College students both then and now would—it was similar to their system, still used today.[14] Each Ricks Academy course received an independent number rather than being part of a set program, and all courses were elective, except for English and religion. Just a few years after Eliot concluded his term as president, evidence of Harvard's DNA and ambitions could be seen in the curriculum of a rural Idaho school.

The academy also sought to emulate Harvard athletically. In 1909 a local power company worker purchased a football from a mail order catalog. A team soon formed, with an academy student as coach. Basketball was under way already, accompanied by complaints about the lack of a campus gymnasium. Players and fans cited having to play at the local armory as the reason for a losing record. Dalby himself worried that "many of our students will become dissatisfied, and perhaps go to some other school where the accommodations are better." The academy board tried to appease students with a new maple floor and basketball hoops in the third-floor auditorium of the classroom building, as well as the announcement of plans to install dressing rooms and showers.[15]

The academy adopted the academic tradition of fundraising, with its attendant benefits and costs. Two wealthy community members gave $500 to establish a library collection. Five weeks after the gift had been accepted, one of the donors appeared before the academy's executive committee to complain that the institution was losing strength, as evidence by declining enrollments. The donor made no mention of Dalby, but the implication was clear. While the principal was popular with students and a vocal critic of Rexburg's saloon owners, he was nonetheless too intellectually progressive for many in the religious community.[16] Though the academy offered a limited slate of summer classes, Dalby had encouraged faculty members to spend that time studying at leading universities. They brought back secular philosophies that included the theory of evolution and literary "higher criticism" of religious texts. Some were openly critical of the academy's conservatism.

One faculty member, Dalby's brother Oliver, authored and shared with his faculty colleagues a paper entitled "The Defects of Our Church School Theology."[17]

In teaching the theory of evolution and engaging in higher criticism, Ricks Academy faculty members were following the developing trend not only at secular schools but also at Brigham Young Academy (by then Brigham Young University).[18] In later decades, the board would guide its educators in harmonizing secular and sacred viewpoints. But in 1914, Dalby was ahead of his time in Rexburg, and the local academy board, composed entirely of church members, voted to replace him and all but three other members of the faculty. It was a challenge to academic freedom at Ricks the likes of which would never be seen again.

The DNA of Ricks Academy

At the time of Ezra Dalby's departure, the academy had, in a mere twenty-six years, copied many elements of the Harvard DNA. Though it offered courses in far fewer academic disciplines than Harvard did, it aspired to adding as many as possible. Its faculty were organized into departments, albeit small ones. The curriculum was structured along Harvard lines, and competitive athletics and fundraising, though modest in absolute terms, had already become major campus forces. From Harvard, Ricks Academy copied:

- Small, face-to-face classes
- Subject matter specialization, with aspirations of comprehensiveness
- Departmentalization
- Private fundraising
- Intercollegiate athletics

There were, however, significant differences in the Ricks Academy DNA (see Table 4.1). For the time being, it was different in undergraduate student focus, cost effectiveness, and accessibility. It also provided

TABLE 4.1 The Unique Traits of Ricks Academy, 1888–1914	
Unique Traits	**Implications**
Religious orientation, strict moral code	Value-laden curriculum High social cohesion Limited discipline problems Restricted conduct
Partial summer operation	More students served Lower cost per student
No graduate programs	Young-student focus Lower institutional cost Limited institutional prestige and research support
No tenure or rank, limited self-governance	Teaching-oriented faculty Lower instructional cost Limited scholarly notoriety
Open admission	High accessibility Need for new student remediation

a unique social and moral environment. Of course, it lacked any semblance of research scholarship or opportunity for advanced study, though there would be stirrings in those directions in the not-too-distant future. The bigger-and-better tendency had only begun to work in Rexburg.

Ricks Academy had come far under Dalby, just as Harvard had under Eliot. But at both institutions, change was in the wind—and in the DNA. Harvard was set to change first.

Chapter 5

Revitalizing Harvard College

Charles Eliot's legacy, though prodigious, was not without its critics at Harvard. Among them was Abbott Lawrence Lowell, Eliot's successor. Lowell, like Eliot, was born into a family of privilege and prominence with deep Harvard ties.[1] A. Lawrence Lowell was a sixth-generation Harvard alumnus, having graduated with highest honors in mathematics from Harvard College and then from the law school.

Also like Eliot, Lowell was the beneficiary of special mentoring as a college student. His gift for math drew the attention of Benjamin Peirce, America's foremost mathematician. Lowell excelled under Peirce's tutelage, so much so that Peirce arranged to have Lowell's college honors thesis published by the American Academy of Arts and Sciences.[2]

Entirely unlike Eliot, Lowell never knew even the slightest financial hardship. Embarking in 1880 on the practice of law, he found the work tedious.[3] Family wealth allowed him to redirect much of his time to writing. An astute observer of the role of political parties on government, he published two studies that won him scholarly recognition and an appointment as a lecturer at Harvard. A professorship of government soon followed, though he arranged to teach only half-time so as to continue writing (thus avoiding Eliot's problem of letting other duties impinge on his scholarship). The balance worked well, as Lowell was able to publish several acclaimed books and also win distinction as a teacher. His Government 10 course was one of the college's most popular, with more than four hundred students enrolled.[4]

Serving on the faculty during the last of Eliot's four decades as Harvard's president, Lowell saw and studied both the good and the less desirable aspects of the great university Eliot had forged. He was particularly troubled by the loss of what he called "the collegiate way of living." As a Harvard College student, Lowell had excelled not only in the classroom but also on the field of athletic competition, where he set school records in the 880-yard and mile footraces.[5] He had likewise enjoyed his residential living experience, through which he made lasting friendships with both fellow students and faculty mentors.

When he returned to Harvard twenty years later, in 1897, there was obvious evidence of the breakdown in this collegiate way of life. Even the casual observer could see it, for instance, in the Gold Coast of private dormitories lining Cambridge's Mount Auburn Street, to which wealthy students had increasingly resorted since the beginning of Eliot's presidency. The Gold Coast was only the most visible evidence of two disturbing trends: growing class distinctions among students and the elevation of leisure pursuits over studies.

Lowell discovered more evidence of these trends in formal studies he made of undergraduate education while serving on ad hoc faculty committees.[6] He found that students were studying far less than the faculty and administration thought.[7] As a kind of battle cry to abandoning the study hall in favor of the playing field or pub, many students invoked the Mark Twain witticism, "Don't let your studies interfere with your education."[8] They further eased their consciences with the slogan, "C is the gentleman's grade."[9] Even relatively serious students spent little time studying. One freshman, upon learning of the Harvard College expectation that he study at least seven hours each school day, including class time, replied, "Nobody I know works seven hours a day!"[10] Many students employed paid tutors, or "crammers," to help them win passing marks, their "gentleman's grades."[11]

Lowell observed the students' disconnectedness not only from one another and from their studies, but also from the faculty. The college's largest courses were enormous, some with enrollments in excess of five hundred.[12] Professors typically lectured to these vast groups of students once each week. Much of the real teaching, conducted in smaller and more frequently convened sections, was delegated to assistants.

Equally disturbing to Lowell was the tendency of undergraduate students to abuse the elective system. They clustered at the extreme ends of the curricular spectrum. The majority took courses for idiosyncratic reasons: a subject of interest, a popular professor, friends in the class. These students graduated having studied nothing in any real depth. Nor, because of the randomness of their choices, were they likely to have obtained a broad educational foundation.[13]

At the other end of the spectrum, some students pursued one discipline in great depth to the exclusion of others. Not only did the absence of required courses make this possible, the structure of the university and the content of its course catalog tended to encourage specialization by ambitious students. Shortly after Lowell assumed the presidency, only 12 percent of Harvard's courses were designated "For Undergraduates Only."[14] Nearly three times as many carried the label "For Both Undergraduates and Graduates." Given the relative abundance of specialized courses, an enterprising student with a clear view of his future was naturally inclined to treat college as focused professional training.

What Lowell saw, in the aggregate, was the loss of much of what he cherished in his Harvard College education: strong social ties; the competitive spur to excellence; a broad foundation for success in fields as diverse as mathematics, law, and political science—the ones he had pursued. In general, he felt the need to take Harvard back to its roots, by refocusing on undergraduate students and their learning experience, broadly defined. Years before the end of Eliot's term, he began agitating for reform. It is much to Eliot's credit that he not only countenanced this potentially subversive activity but also made no effort to prevent Lowell's ascension to the presidency. Not so creditable were the retiring Eliot's warnings to Harvard's governing boards about Lowell: Eliot urged "incessant watch against [his successor's] defects of judgment and good feeling."[15] Still, Eliot accepted the inevitability of innovation and change, given that he had made both a new Harvard tradition.

Lowell's Strategy

Lowell, a scholar of government and politics, was a gifted strategist with the university's best interests at heart. Like Eliot, he had spent many years preparing to assume Harvard's presidency. During that time he had seen the weaknesses inherent in Eliot's model, borrowed mainly from the great German universities, which emphasized graduate education, diverse fields of inquiry, and discovery scholarship. When he became president, Lowell brought a clear conception of the changes he hoped to make, many of them drawn from the great English universities, particularly Oxford and Cambridge, upon which Harvard College had been originally modeled. He already had both the need for those changes and the innovations that would facilitate them well articulated, as became apparent in his inaugural address.

He began his speech, on that October day in 1909, with a description of the social and intellectual benefits of "the college of the old type," in which students were "constantly thrown together" and provided a "universal foundation of liberal education."[16] Tipping his hat only slightly to the "unanswerable force" with which Eliot had shown the need for curricular choice, he proceeded to describe how the elective system, along with the growth in the number of students and their tendency to live off-campus, had "broke[n] down the old solidarity" of the college and led to a loss of public esteem for college education.

Lowell raised and summarily dismissed the possibility of Harvard's adopting a German model of education for the college, one focused on career preparation, as the university's professional schools were. American high schools he pointed out, were incapable of educating students at the level of the German gymnasia; in his mind, Eliot's attempt to make the high schools responsible for what had been the early years of a college education had failed. Moreover, Lowell felt that the American republic needed "a freedom of thought, a breadth of outlook, a training for citizenship" that only the college could offer. Rather than reducing Harvard's emphasis on undergraduate education, he wanted to increase it. Responding to Eliot's argument that the college experience be limited to three years instead of four, he asked rhetorically, "May we not feel that the most vital measure for saving the college is not to shorten its duration, but to ensure that it shall be worth saving?"

Lowell alluded to the types of innovations that would make the college worth saving. Two reflected his admiration of the great English universities, with which he had become familiar as a scholar of that nation's government. One was to recreate, through college dormitories of the English type, the collegiality of the old Harvard, with students spending time together not only in the classroom but in informal settings where they could freely discuss both their studies and their professional aspirations. As in the colleges of the English universities, they would be presided over by scholars resident in their living quarters.

Another idea drawn from Oxford and Cambridge was a system of honors designations, intended to simulate healthy competition in academic achievement. The third notion was uniquely American and the innovation for which Lowell would become best known. It was a college curriculum that would provide both professional preparation of the German type and also English-style liberal education.

An Unsustainable Financial Reality

Lowell's high aspirations for social and curricular reform had to be undertaken in the face of pressing financial realities. In spite of generous philanthropic support, the university's operating budget trends were unsustainable.[17] Eliot had spent forty years establishing new graduate schools and physical facilities. His elective system had produced an explosion of new courses to be taught, and his drive for excellence in all fields of scholarship meant that new hires were needed both for the classroom and for the research laboratories and libraries.

All the while, tuition had remained constant, at $150.[18] Eliot had recognized and defended the costs of his innovations, particularly the elective system and its proliferation of specialized courses. "Like most things worth having," he said, "it is expensive."[19] He was reluctant, though, to increase the financial burden on students (or to break ranks with Yale and Princeton universities, whose tuition rates were similar).[20] Optimistic that philanthropy would continue to grow, he stayed the course with tuition.

However, enrollments were falling, due in part to competition from rivals both old and new, many of which had recognized the deficiencies of a pure elective system and were reinstituting some required courses. At the same time, frugality measures taken at Harvard had included the cutting of graduate courses and the refusal to match external job offers, which in turn led to the loss of high-profile faculty.[21] The institution faced a potential downward spiral, with quality-defeating cost cuts leading to even greater declines in revenues.

Remarkably, Lowell kept tuition at its $150 level (about $3,700 in 2011 dollars) for the first seven years of his presidency. Rather than raise Harvard's price, he found ways to manage its costs and to stimulate nontuition sources of revenue. His strategy, which amounted to a significant modification of Harvard's DNA, had three components: rebuilding a sense of community, assuring educational breadth and depth, and promoting academic excellence. Lowell saw these initiatives as interdependent and potentially reinforcing. He began work on all three in his first year as president.

Fostering Community at Harvard

One of the earliest of Lowell's community-building innovations, the creation of the Harvard Extension School, wasn't among the most strategic such actions he hoped to take. It was, however, the most immediately feasible, and it took the university in a symbolically important direction. The precedent for offering evening courses to community members had already been established by the University of Chicago, and doing so required neither additional fixed investment in facilities and faculty nor alteration of any daytime activities. It also comported with Lowell's belief that education should be available to all who desired it and with his vision of a Harvard less aloof from its surrounding community. Today such extension programs, which generate both goodwill and incremental income, are standard features of many universities. Increasingly, they offer courses online, thus providing a foundation for responding to emerging competitive threats, as we'll see. However, in Lowell's day extension programs offering full degrees rather than just courses were relatively rare; even today many universities refer to this kind of study as "continuing education" and are more likely to offer certificates than degrees. This was one of several Lowell innovations that wasn't broadly adopted.

Another of Lowell's strategically important but not widely reproduced innovations refocused Harvard on its student housing. He required freshmen to live in the school's dormitories, as most students had done in the early days. He reasoned that housing all freshmen together, under close supervision, would not only allow Harvard to admit students at a younger age but also set a tone for their subsequent years of study. "A boy's career in college is largely determined," he believed, "by the conditions of his freshman year, and it ought to be possible to organize that year so as to improve the whole state of the college intellectually and socially."[22]

Although this new policy meant that four new dormitories had to be built, Harvard reaped a good return on its investment. The sum total of room and board, at $200 and $140 respectively,[23] amounted to more than twice the price of tuition but was still below the Gold Coast market, where Harvard undergraduate Franklin D. Roosevelt had paid $400 in rent alone for his corner suite in a building with an indoor swimming pool.[24] Most important to Lowell, the investment in dorms replaced a fragmented, class-based system of freshman housing with one conducive to his ideal collegiate life.

Nearly two decades later, a philanthropic windfall allowed Lowell to make this housing opportunity available to all Harvard College students. In 1928 a $10 million gift from Standard Oil heir and Yale alumnus Edward S. Harkness funded a house system similar to those of the great English universities.[25] Harvard built seven new dormitories, in which sophomores, juniors, and seniors not only lived but also studied, under the tutelage of a master, resident dean, faculty members, nonfaculty advisors, and graduate students.

The house system allowed Lowell to recognize two educational ambitions. One was to have students of differing backgrounds and professional objectives rubbing shoulders, sharing important ideas not only in the classroom but also over meals and in social activities.[26] The other goal was to bring the faculty back into the extracurricular lives of the students.[27] House masters taught in the formal sense, but they also served as role models. Along with their spouses, many became surrogate parents to the students, often living in the same house for decades. Younger faculty tutors likewise performed both formal and informal services; they not only explained the content of specific courses but also offered tips for "navigating the system," teaching students how to choose the right professors and the sequence of courses to ensure good learning and high marks.

Through the freshman dorms and the houses, which serve nearly all Harvard undergraduates today, Lowell reintroduced to the university's DNA one of the most educationally and socially powerful traits of early Harvard College. The system of comingled living and learning was copied only by a few other institutions, mostly elite private colleges like Harvard that could afford the high financial cost, though on-campus dormitories serving at least a fraction of undergraduate students became a standard feature of traditional universities. By his retirement, in 1933, Lowell could claim not only to have revitalized Harvard College's sense of community but to have taken it to new, exemplary heights.

Breadth and Depth in the Curriculum

Lowell worked an even more influential change in the college's curriculum. He was not the first university president to introduce a distribution requirement, elsewhere more commonly called general education (GE) or liberal education. However, he was the first to create a combination of distribution and concentration requirements (the latter known at most schools as a major). For this innovative but soon-to-be-ubiquitous system of general education-plus-major he coined a memorable tag line: "The best type of liberal education in our complex modern world aims at producing men who know a little of everything and something well."[28]

The purpose of simultaneous distribution and concentration requirements was to promote a degree of classical well-roundedness and also impart the specialized knowledge needed for a trade or for pursuit of advanced studies. In theory, it was an Aristotelian golden mean, the ideal combination of two desirable but competing extremes.[29] In practice, it proved difficult to achieve, as Lowell himself conceded.

Ready-made components for concentrations already existed, thanks to Eliot's success in creating graduate curriculum. The foundational courses for Ph.D. programs served equally well as building blocks for concentrations.[30] They were already there in the catalog, many bearing the name "For Both Undergraduate and Graduate Students."

It was more difficult to find courses well suited to the distribution requirement, which was meant to assure a degree of breadth in an undergraduate student's education. Lowell recognized two main challenges.[31] One is the inherent difficulty of creating a course for uninitiated students that provides a true synthesis of a subject rather than merely laying the foundation for further study. The typical introductory course, which must treat in detail the fundamentals of a discipline, such as chemistry, offers little insight into its connection to other disciplines, let alone the role of that science in the broader world. Faculty members trying to summarize their discipline for students in a single dose face a curricular

Catch-22. Broad perspective is hard to achieve absent a modicum of basic understanding, and in most disciplines the latter requires at least one course unto itself. As Lowell admitted, "Instruction that imparts a little knowledge of everything is more difficult to provide well than any other."[32] His proposed solution was to have these difficult-to-teach courses delivered by "the leading men of the department," those with "mature minds, who can see the forest over the tops of the trees" and possessed of "unusual clearness of thought, force of statement, and enthusiasm of expression."[33]

Lowell also recognized, though, the "serious obstacle . . . that many professors, who have reaped fame, prefer to teach advanced courses, and recoil from elementary instruction, an aversion inherited from the time when scholars of international reputation were called upon to waste their powers on the drudgery of drilling beginners."[34]

In fact, it wasn't just already-tenured professors who faced this disincentive to teaching courses for nonspecialists. The university Eliot created still aspired to offering its students a broad education, but it rewarded its faculty for specialization. A Ph.D. had become de rigueur for entrance to the professoriate, and the plaudits, promotions, and pay raises went to those faculty members who were recognized by fellow scholars for their published work.

Lowell's Curricular Compromise

Lowell saw the organizational disincentives to teaching general courses, just as he did the intellectual challenge of designing them. Because the system of faculty scholarship had been firmly established before his time, he made the best of things by aligning the distribution requirements with the graduate departments created to grant Ph.D.s.[35] In other words, his distribution system did not necessitate the creation of cross-disciplinary courses; a student could satisfy the distribution requirements by taking discipline-specific offerings already in the catalog as long as they were unrelated to the student's concentration, or major. Also, as the price of exposing young undergraduate students to senior professors, Lowell condoned the practice of offering small sections in which junior faculty led discussions and gave exams. "Such a policy," he said, "brings the student, at the gateway of a subject, into contact with strong and ripe minds, while it saves the professor from needless drudgery."[36]

A Scholarly Solution Shop and an Instructional Value-Added Process

Lowell's system of distribution and concentration requirements conceded the new university reality of academic specialization, while still providing a way for an increasingly balkanized institution to produce graduates "who know a little of everything and something well." It was an uneasy compromise that universities still struggle to strike today. Much of the challenge is that they are operating two fundamentally different enterprises under a single institutional roof. The one enterprise, knowledge discovery, can be characterized as "solution shop."[37] In this part of the university, scholars draw upon their subject matter expertise and intuition as they seek to diagnose and recommend solutions to unstructured problems, such as splitting the atom or managing national economies. The consumers of these discoveries are not the university's students so much as fellow scholars and nonacademic experts in the field.

The other main enterprise in the university, the instruction of students, is a "value-adding process."[38] The value added is to students, who know more when they leave the university than when they entered. This process is less dependent on creative instinct and original insight than the work of knowledge discovery. Though teaching requires expertise and judgment, it is repetitive, so it can be embedded in standardized curriculum and delivered at reasonably high quality by teachers with less subject matter expertise and scholarly intuition.

That is why the best Lowell could hope for was a modicum of participation by senior scholars in his proposed distribution courses. Harvard's tenured professors justifiably concluded that their highest and best contributions to the university were to be made through original research rather than teaching undergraduate students. Most of that work was delegated to graduate students and tutors, whose more limited training and capability meant that their opportunity cost of teaching was lower.

The problem, though, was—and is—that students pay not only for this less expensive instruction but also for whatever portion of a university's scholarship is not covered by research grants or donors' gifts. Put differently, undergraduate tuition often subsidizes scholarship. In addition, students bear other less quantifiable but nonetheless significant costs. Academic departments are better organized to facilitate specialized scholarship and curriculum development than to create cross-disciplinary general education courses and majors. Undergraduate students who do not choose to specialize in one discipline, as though they are headed for graduate studies in the same field, must browse back and forth across departments, attempting to create an integrated learning experience for themselves. Though Lowell couldn't see it at the time, the costs to students of the university's conflation of scholarly and instructional activities, with the former being dominant in the departments, would steadily grow.

Lowell implemented the system of distribution and concentration in his first year as president. Of the sixteen full-year courses required to graduate from Harvard, a student had to take at least six in his area of concentration and at least four in other subjects.[39] As noted by Harry Lewis, "Lowell's dream of general courses that were not introductory did not materialize during his presidency. Nor did he ever resolve the problem that the 'clearness of thought, force of statement and enthusiasm of expression' so valuable in college teachers were qualities largely unrelated to scholarly excellence."[40]

Nevertheless, as the most effective compromise among the competing interests of scholars and students, Lowell's system of distribution and concentration soon became the curricular model of choice in American-style universities.

Lowell's system of distribution and concentration soon became the curricular model of choice in American-style universities.

Promoting Student Excellence

Having struck an imperfect but workable balance between the liberal and practical aspects of a college education, Lowell turned his attention to the problem of undergraduate dilettantism. He conceded only grudgingly the necessity of granting all graduates a standard degree.[41] It piqued him that a half-dedicated student received the same college credential as a diligent one. Over time, he perceived, this lack of academic distinctions had eroded both students' ambitions and the value of the college degree.

Ironically, Lowell's inspiration for solving this problem came partly from athletic competition, one of the causes of Harvard's student dilettantism. Recalling his own experiences as an athlete and observing the intensity of college athletic rivalries, Lowell saw a model for bringing greater competition to the classroom. He observed the zeal with which students sought athletic glory even though they had no intention of making a career of athletics.[42] How much easier it should be, he reasoned, to bring a competitive spirit to the classroom, where students prepare for their life's work. The key was merit-based prizes such as those awarded to athletes. He was willing to risk the potential downsides, including a decrease in collegiality and intrinsic motivation to learn, for the sake of greater academic excellence.

Lowell knew that no single measure would be enough; as he liked to say, "A blanket cannot be lifted by one corner."[43] Among the first of his competition-stimulating innovations was the creation of the grading curve. During the Eliot years, he had seen how students flocked to courses taught by lenient graders, doing themselves a double dose of educational damage: they not only studied less diligently in these massive courses, but also enjoyed less student-teacher interaction. Focusing especially on high-enrollment courses, he used his normal grading curve, with C's predominating, to stimulate competition for A's.[44]

Borrowing a tradition from England's universities, Lowell also pushed through a measure to have Latin honors—*cum laude, magna cum laude,* and *summa cum laude*—noted in the commencement program and alumni catalogue. These, he foresaw, would become the academic equivalents of newspaper box scores and athletic record books.[45] He also created a new form of academic recognition: "honors," "high honors," and "highest honors" designations; these were tied to a student's concentration and required a thesis, in addition to the standard coursework. To help students win the high grades and write the theses that would earn them graduation honors, Lowell introduced a system of tutorials through which individuals and small groups received focused instruction. Specialized tutors, working at the direction of the academic departments, supplemented the efforts of those in the houses.

The reinforcing system of incentives and supports for academic excellence took hold with generally gratifying results. The balance of student interest and effort shifted markedly during Lowell's presidency. The A replaced the C as the "gentleman's grade," and many of the hours spent in the Eliot era on socializing and athletics were redirected to study, which Harvard's athletic director called the school's principal sport. "This," wrote Samuel Eliot Morison, "was Mr. Lowell's greatest achievement; he 'sold' education to Harvard College."[46]

Lowell's achievement was not without its costs. In *Excellence Without a Soul*, former Harvard College Dean Harry Lewis wrote, "Nothing I saw during my eight years as dean brought Harvard as much scorn as the grades and honors it awards."[47] The problem for Lewis and his fellow professors was the *Boston Globe*'s 2001 discovery that more than half of Harvard College grades were A's and A-minuses, and that more than 90 percent of graduates earned honors. A *New York Times* article declared, "Harvard, long a center of excellence in so many forms, is becoming known as a pioneer in grade inflation, too."[48]

In *Excellence Without a Soul*, Lewis explored the myriad potential causes of grade inflation, from the pernicious—such as untenured faculty members' fears of low student evaluations—to the laudable, ever-better-performing teachers and students. Lewis also enumerated the downsides of promoting academic excellence through grades: course selection becoming a game of identifying lenient graders; demotivation and alienation of students who cannot excel relative to their peers; excellence calculations being "inaccurate to the point of fraud."[49] Given the prevailing attitudes toward academic achievement he inherited, Lowell's introduction of grading curves and honors represented an improvement over the status quo. Even today, the difficulty of measuring in absolute terms what a student has learned makes relative ranking and the awarding of academic honors an attractive, practical alternative. But the system was and is an imperfect one.

Lowell and the Cause of Academic Freedom

University professors in particular are indebted to Lowell for another achievement in the realm of academics. From his bully pulpit at the nation's greatest university, he powerfully articulated a broad definition of academic freedom. Though Eliot had supported freedom of inquiry and speech for the faculty in principle, no case of great consequence had come before him.[50] World War I forced upon Lowell a host of such cases, as Harvard faculty members spoke out on both sides of the issue of American involvement. In a particularly difficult instance, he withstood strong pressure to dismiss psychology professor Hugo Munsterberg, a German American, who spoke publicly in defense of the German cause. In Lowell's annual report for 1916–1917, at the height of the war, he explained his reasoning not only in the Munsterberg case, but in terms of broad principle.

From his bully pulpit at the nation's greatest university, [Lowell] powerfully articulated a broad definition of academic freedom.

Lowell explored the freedom of professors to speak according to conscience in two realms: the classroom and the world beyond it. In each of those realms, he distinguished between those statements related to the professor's expertise and those not. In the classroom, he asserted, "The teaching by the professor on the subjects within the scope of his chair ought to be absolutely free."[51] At the same time, though, he spoke of the students' right "not to be compelled to listen to remarks offensive or injurious to them on subjects of which the instructor is not a master." Thus, academic freedom in the classroom is complete but conditioned on expertise. Of course, Lowell likewise asserted the right of professors to share, unfettered, their expertise outside of the classroom, as the publication of research and the dissemination of knowledge requires this.

It was in the matter of public speech unrelated to the academic discipline that Lowell's logic took an asymmetrical twist. Lowell posed the hypothetical case of a professor of Greek who publishes an article on "the futility and harmfulness of vaccination" and cites his university affiliation, but does not identify his discipline as unrelated to medicine. In this case, Lowell granted, the professor "is misleading the public and misrepresenting his university."[52]

Yet, he argued, even in such circumstances the university must not impose any expectation other than "sincer[ity]." The reasons for allowing such a risk of injury to the institution and to the public, he felt, were two. First, academicians should not, by virtue of their profession, be subject to greater constraints on public speech than lawyers, physicians, engineers, and others. Such constraints would "tend seriously to discourage some of the best men from taking up the scholar's life." Second, Lowell argued, if universities did restrain faculty members' communications in select instances, they would by implication be endorsing their statements in all others. "If the university is right in restraining its professors, it has a duty to do so, and it is responsible for whatever it permits. There is no middle ground."[53]

It was reasoning atypical of Lowell; he was a master of finding the golden mean, or middle ground. Moreover, having run his own legal practice, he would have appreciated that an attorney could expect to be dismissed from a firm for behavior not worthy of disbarment from the profession, yet inimical to the partnership. In fact, the 1940 academic freedom statement of the American Association of University Professors (AAUP) took a more temperate position, noting that a college and university teachers' "special position in the community imposes obligations," including being accurate, restrained, respectful, and "making every effort to indicate that they are not speaking for the institution."[54] The AAUP statement also makes allowances for limits to individual freedom based on an institution's religious or other special mission. In this case, the impassioned proposal of a Harvard president did not take hold in the traditional university's DNA. However, Lowell's championing of the cause of academic freedom strengthened it as a guiding principle of American higher education and thus reinforced the autonomy of the professoriate.

When Lowell retired, after twenty-four years at the helm and at age seventy-six, he had not only revitalized Harvard College but taken it to

TABLE 5.1 Harvard in the Lowell Era, 1909–1933

New Trait	Implications
Residential house system	More unified collegiate community Social and academic support for students Significant expense Limitation of student social freedoms
Curricular distribution (GE) and concentration (majors)	Balance of subject matter depth and breadth Increased demand for less popular subjects Tendency toward delegation of instruction in distribution courses
Grading curve and academic honors	Increased incentive to excel academically Potentially decreased intrinsic motivation to learn Student pressure on faculty for generous grading

an unprecedented level of quality. By innovatively combining elements of the old Puritan college with Eliot's curricular free market, he had also finalized much of the essential DNA of undergraduate education. (See Table 5.1.) Grading curves, honors designations, general education, and majors would soon become known to most university undergraduates. That was true even at Ricks Academy, which before the end of Lowell's presidency at Harvard would become Ricks College.

Chapter 6

Struggling College

The principal who replaced Ezra Dalby in 1914 at Ricks Academy, A. B. Christensen,[1] was an accomplished scholar, an academic who had experienced firsthand some of the biggest and best institutions. Holder of a bachelor's degree in literature from the University of Michigan, he had subsequently studied at Oxford University and the University of Berlin.[2] When approached by the board about leading Ricks, he was happy teaching literature and biblical history at Brigham Young University (BYU), Ricks's sister institution in Utah. The academy was both little known and small, having graduated only thirty-one students the year before. Christensen was willing to accept the job in remote, inclement Rexburg for only two years.[3] In that time he planned to achieve two clear goals: creating a two-year college program to complement the high school curriculum and building a gym.

The college program would be added without incident or notable cost, one year at a time, beginning in 1916. The gym, though, proved a more expensive prize, at least in the near term. The initial cost was estimated at $30,000 to $40,000 but was revised upward to $55,000 to $60,000. Each church congregation in the region accepted a higher assessment to cover the increased cost. Construction finally began in mid-1917, thought it was not completed until 1918 due to labor shortages attendant to World War I. The building contractor also experienced difficulty excavating the lava rock underlying the site. The final cost was $82,000.[4]

In the meantime, Christensen pushed his agenda ahead. He expected that the new gym would free up the classroom building's third-floor auditorium, with its improvised basketball court; in that space he planned to create an expanded school library, one befitting a two-year college. To hurry the process, he took several library chairs to the auditorium and, under cover of darkness, screwed them to the floor. That act of presidential *force majeure* drove not only basketball games but also dances off campus until completion of the gym—three years later and one year after Christensen's return to BYU. When that day finally came, a coach was hired and a fine basketball tradition began.[5]

New principal George S. Romney,[6] a product of the Mormon pioneer colonies in Mexico's northern state of Chihuahua, couldn't match Christensen's elite academic credentials. He had married and gone to work with only an eighth grade education. He was thirty-one when he graduated with a high school degree from Ricks Academy's sister institution, the Juarez Academy. Notwithstanding the disadvantages of this slow start, Romney was as determined as any of his predecessors to get higher education, and at the best possible universities. After his family was driven from Mexico by revolution, he graduated with a bachelor's degree from the University of Utah while working full time as a custodian and providing for a family of that would grow to include eleven children. Later, while presiding at Ricks, he spent summers at Stanford University, where he earned a master's degree. Upon leaving Rexburg, at age fifty-seven, he pursued additional graduate studies at the University of Chicago.[7]

In Romney's first year, he saw the realization of both of his predecessors' dreams: the gym building opened, and Ricks Academy became Ricks Normal College. Consistent with the bigger-and-better tendencies of higher education, the new college dropped the first two years of high school; it also sought and won state accreditation as a two-year college. The student body, drawn almost entirely from southeastern Idaho, surpassed five hundred students, with some of the increase attributed to the announcement of a football program. Many students stayed for summer school, which boasted an enrollment of more than three hundred and offered training for local teachers as well as faculty-supervised internship credit for students working their family farms. The latter program proved both popular and highly economical, with the internship credit being granted at one-tenth the full-time student price. Night school was similarly well subscribed.[8]

In Romney's first year, he saw the realization of both of his predecessors' dreams: the gym building opened, and Ricks Academy became Ricks Normal College.

High Standards and Aspirations

The new two-year college could claim high educational quality. Though it was not selective, it required a high school diploma and conferred academic honors. In good years, 100 percent of its teacher education graduates passed the state certification examination and found jobs. Ricks Normal also hewed to the moral standards of the old academy. Its code of honor held that "the standard of Ricks is clean living; that neither boys nor girls should use tea, coffee, tobacco or alcohol; that pure language only be used; that chastity and virtue are more precious than life."[9]

THE ACADEMIC TRADITION OF HONOR

The Ricks honor code of the early 1900s persists in its fundamental form at BYU-Idaho.[10] Its rules of moral conduct apply equally to students and university employees. Honor codes of such broad subject matter and applicability are rare. However, the concept of academic honor predates the founding of Ricks College and undergirds much of the traditional higher education system.

Thomas Jefferson urged the creation of student-governed honor systems at both the College of William and Mary and the University of Virginia. Today incoming William and Mary students take the following pledge: "As a member of the William and Mary community, I pledge on my honor not to lie, cheat, or steal, either in my academic or personal life. I understand that such acts violate the Honor Code and undermine the community of trust, of which we are all stewards."[11] At both institutions, power is vested in student councils to judge their peers' conformance to the honor code and, based on sufficient evidence, dismiss them from school. The University of Virginia cautions prospective students: "U.Va. students benefit from the freedom and security provided by the Honor System; every student must agree to live by and support the spirit of honor. Applicants who are not prepared to embrace this freedom and accept this responsibility should not apply for admission."[12]

In the 1970s, students at Pennsylvania's Haverford College created an honor system encompassing not only academic behavior but all social interactions. Rather than rules of behavior, the foundation of the code is the aspiration to "live together, interact, and learn from one another in ways that protect both personal freedom and community standards." Though the code, which is reratified annually, provides for honor councils, the goal is for individual students to resolve disputes one on one, without resorting to the involvement of others. Haverford students commit to engaging in constructive "confrontation," defined as "initiating a dialogue with another community member, with the goal of reaching some common understanding by means of respectful communication."[13] Benefits of this rarified system of honor include unproctored exams, dormitories without resident assistants, and the ability to enroll without making a financial deposit.[14]

Just four years after Ricks achieved junior college status, the local board began planning the jump to senior college. The first step was the 1923 elimination of all high school classes, a decision that caused revenue to fall, though it did not leave these students unserved, as the public high schools in and around Rexburg were growing in size and quality. The church board of education determined that the financial strain attendant to this move up the educational ladder would have to be dealt with at the local level, where the decision had been made. In addition to making up the budget deficit caused by eliminating high school offerings, local church congregations were tasked with recruiting college-aged students and augmenting the school's meager library.[15]

Meanwhile, expansion of competitive sports programs continued apace. The school's athletic director went to the University of Chicago for a full academic year in 1927, to study Alonzo Stagg's renowned football system. Upon his return, he hired a young football coach trained by the University of Notre Dame's Knute Rockne. With fewer than twenty full-time instructors, Ricks could claim to have, on a percentage basis, an unusually football-literate faculty. Expectations in the community ran high; at a public meeting presided over by the president of the Rexburg Chamber of Commerce, eager boosters launched a drive to fund a new football field.[16]

Hard Economic Times

But football glory, along with the leap to four-year college status, was put on hold by the Great Depression. The task of seeing the college through a difficult decade fell to Hyrum Manwaring, a longtime faculty member with an enduring vision of the college's potential. Another academic late bloomer, Manwaring completed high school at Brigham Young Academy at age twenty-nine.[17] He continued for bachelor's and master's degrees at BYU, and later earned a doctorate from the University of California, while serving on the Ricks faculty. He was studying at George Washington University when asked by the board to come back to replace Romney. Years later, he would recall, "This was a hard decision to make, as none of the family cared to return to Rexburg and I felt that under the new policy of the Church there was little chance for Ricks College to live, much less grow and develop."[18]

The policy of the church to which Manwaring referred was a decision to either close its schools or turn them over to state governments. From their beginnings as academies sponsored primarily by local church congregations, these schools had lived hand to mouth financially. The church board of education had tasked the local education boards with self-sufficiency in operating expenses but typically ended up supplying the bulk of new building funds.

Even before the Crash of 1929, the financial burden on the central church had become unsustainable. The problem was growing costs, driven not just by expanding enrollments but also by the climb from academy to college status. Higher education, particularly as practiced by ladder-conscious academicians and college boosters, had become unexpectedly expensive, with no apparent end to the upward cost creep. At the same time, public higher education opportunities were expanding, reducing the need for a church-sponsored system.

In the 1920s, the board had closed other Idaho schools but maintained its commitment to Ricks, the largest and strongest of the group. The Depression, though, put Ricks on the same auction block. Rumors of closure produced embassies of community leaders to church headquarters, letter-writing campaigns, and local student-recruiting drives. Rather than close the school outright, the board determined to give it to the State of Idaho. Preferring this outcome to closure, Ricks's local supporters went to work dressing it up for sale. They advertised the value of the physical plant as being $250,000 and operating needs as $50,000, with 250 students expected to enroll.[19] They also eliminated church religion courses from the curriculum, so as to make Ricks a more attractive candidate for state acquisition.

It was a difficult time to be selling even an institution as academically successful and locally well supported as Ricks. With the state's budget under unprecedented strain, political opponents found it easy to argue for deferral of the issue, at least until the economy improved. Opposition from the University of Idaho in Moscow and its branch campus in Pocatello was particularly strong, contributing to a 23–20 legislative vote against the acquisition in the 1931 session.[20]

Expecting success in the next session, two years later, Manwaring and his colleagues soldiered on with the support of the church board of education. In 1,500 packets sent to potential students, Manwaring argued that the downturn was in fact the best time to be in school: "When times are normal again, there will be a great call for young men and young women who are prepared for responsible places. [C]ome and rent an inexpensive room, bring most of what [you] need to eat from home, and get along with a very little money."[21] In an attempt reminiscent of Eliot's efforts to manage his supply of students, Manwaring joined other faculty members in making recruiting visits to Idaho high schools, paying his own out-of-pocket expenses, as they did. When a new student paid his tuition in-kind, with a cow, it was turned over to one particularly zealous faculty member as compensation for his recruiting efforts.[22]

Hoping to present the college as a going, viable concern in the coming legislative session, Manwaring led other extraordinary efforts to boost enrollment. A bus line to Idaho Falls, a larger community 30 miles to the south of Rexburg, was instituted. Football was also promoted as never before. Some of the land for the new field had been acquired, but Manwaring and Rexburg mayor Arthur Porter, a former Ricks faculty member, urged supporters to contribute the funds necessary to secure the remaining property. The two of them set the example with donations of their own.[23]

The lynchpin of the football promotion strategy was a two-game series with a Hawaiian high school, McKinley. Ricks guaranteed $3,500 in travel expenses for the McKinley squad's visit to Rexburg, an amount equal to roughly 5 percent of the school's annual operating cost. Union Pacific did its part, offering a special rail fare of one penny per mile for fans from surrounding states. The game was played at the county fairgrounds, with 5,500 in attendance. Ricks lost by a touchdown but scored a financial victory—enrollments during this period reached record heights, more than two hundred, with the fall term (football season) being extraordinarily high.[24]

"The State Would Not Have It"

In 1932 Manwaring invited the University of Idaho's president to deliver the spring commencement address, in an undisguised attempt to woo him as a potential acquirer of the school. But with public officials' salaries being cut, a bill authorizing the acquisition of Ricks was withdrawn by its supporters from the 1933 session, in the hope of better economic times and a more favorable political climate in 1935. Struggling to meet its members' basic welfare needs, the church reduced its financial appropriation to the college. The balance was to be made up by local congregations, effectively making the church a minority partner in the enterprise.[25]

Rather than better times, 1935 brought another political defeat. Manwaring was dejected but determined to persevere:

> The school did not seem to belong to anyone, or to have a place in educational circles. The Church did not want it, the state would not have it, and the [local] board did not know what to do with it. The president and faculty just went ahead and ran it the best they could with their very limited budget and the trying conditions of the financial depression.[26]

Even in these dark years, the college advanced in status. In 1936 it won regional accreditation, the ultimate form of general acceptance for U.S. colleges and universities. That was a source not only of individual satisfaction for its faculty but also another selling point for the institution. Nevertheless, in 1937 the attempt to become a state school went down to defeat yet again. In addition to the expected opposition from legislators allied with state colleges and universities, the debate elicited criticisms from some legislators who argued that higher education was a "racket," with colleges mainly interested in athletics at the taxpayers' expense.[27]

Fortunately, the church board of education now felt that the improved economic situation would allow the church to keep Ricks

College. It appropriated $25,000 annually, enough to make up the gap left after tuition payments ($75 per student) and local community support.[28] The newest member of the church's three-man First Presidency, David McKay, may have encouraged the board's policy reversal. McKay had served as principal of Ricks's sister institution, Weber Academy in Ogden, Utah, at the turn of the century. In 1933 then Weber College had been given to the State of Utah. McKay, elevated to the First Presidency in 1934, would become a fast friend to embattled Ricks College for the next three decades.

A Return to Religious Values and Growth Aspirations

Reaffirmation of church support brought the return of religion courses, which had been replaced in the curriculum by ethics offerings in anticipation of Ricks's becoming a state college. In fact, after 1937 religion study was made mandatory from enrollment through graduation.[29] In this respect, Ricks eschewed an element of traditional university DNA, the tendency to secularism, which first took hold at Harvard in the 1700s. The board reasserted the importance of religious education and clarified its relation to secular studies. David McKay's colleague in the First Presidency, J. Reuben Clark Jr., spoke definitively on the matter in 1938. Clark, a former U.S. State Department lawyer and ambassador to Mexico, challenged the church's teachers to have courage in their instruction:

Reaffirmation of church support brought the return of religion courses, which had been replaced in the curriculum by ethics offerings in anticipation of Ricks becoming a state college.

> I mean intellectual courage—the courage to affirm principles, beliefs, and faith that may not always be considered as harmonizing with such knowledge, scientific or otherwise, as the teacher or his educational colleagues may believe they possess. [Ultimate truths] are not changed by the discovery of a new element or a

new ethereal wave, nor by clipping off a few seconds, minutes, or hours off a speed record.[30]

Clark's argument for courage of spiritual conviction in the pursuit of knowledge was buttressed by the church's leading scientist, Dr. Henry Eyring, a theoretical chemist whose work won him the Priestley Medal, given to one American chemist annually. To the encouragement of teachers at Ricks and other church schools, Eyring reasoned that

> the scientific method which has served so brilliantly in unraveling the mysteries of this world must be supplemented by something else if we are to enjoy to the fullest the blessings that have come of the knowledge gained. It is the great mission and opportunity of religion to teach men "the way, the truth, the life," that they might utilize the discoveries of the laboratory to their blessing and not to their destruction. There is a need for added spirituality, of the kind that leads to brotherhood, to go hand in hand with the scientific progress of our time. [F]or me there has been no serious difficulty in reconciling the principles of true science with the principles of true religion, for both are concerned with the eternal verities of the universe.[31]

A FAMILY OF GRATEFUL STUDENTS

In 1850 a fifteen-year-old German gymnasium student named Henry Eyring was orphaned by the loss to cholera of his father, an apothecary weakened by the untimely passing of the boy's mother and the bankruptcy of the family business. The principal of the gymnasium, Dr. Edward Jacobi, agreed with his wife, a distant relative of the boy, that they would keep him in school by paying his tuition out of their modest salary. The grateful graduate, who immigrated to America, would later write of Dr. Jacobi, "I wish his name handed down to my posterity as my true benefactor."[32]

The blessing of higher education granted by Dr. Jacobi passed from this Henry Eyring to a namesake, a grandson who took a Ph.D. in chemistry at Berkeley, taught at Princeton and the University of Utah, and won the Priestley Medal in 1975. The tradition of higher education—and of naming sons Henry—continued in the succeeding generations. Henry Bennion Eyring, son of the chemist, would study at Harvard, teach at Stanford, and, in 1971, become a president of Ricks College. His first son, Henry Johnson Eyring, coauthored this book as a BYU-Idaho administrator.

Threat of closure or transference to the state had no sooner passed than the aspiration to grow the college reasserted itself. The 1937 homecoming committee chose the theme "A Bigger and Better Ricks College." The church board of education, though, signaled its intent to closely manage growth by disbanding the local education board. World War II also put a brake on expansion. After record enrollments in 1940, the college spent the next four years augmenting the draft-depleted student body with early-admitted high school seniors and with military recruits who earned their associate's degrees at government expense before deployment.[33] As would be the case at Harvard, downward enrollment pressure was tempered by these armed services programs and by growth in the female student population.

In 1944 sixty-seven-year-old Hyrum Manwaring stood down, after thirteen years of dedicated, courageous service. The school had evolved significantly during his presidency and those of his two predecessors, Christensen and Romney, as show in Table 6.1. The previously adopted traits of subject matter comprehensiveness, academic specialization, and athletic competition became more pronounced as the academy made the leap to college status. Those inevitably created new costs. The quality of a Ricks education had increased, not only because students could pursue their studies to a higher level but also because of

TABLE 6.1 Ricks College Evolution, 1914-1944	
New Trait	**Implications**
Two-year status	Advanced study opportunities and a college credential for students End of the high school program Growth of subjects and specialization
Admissions standards and honors	Basic student preparedness Mixed blessing of academic competition
Recommitment to values	Increased moral content in the curriculum Potential for dogmatism

the introduction of admissions standards and academic honors. There was also an institutional recommitment to teaching the values central to its students' religious faith. The school had also expanded its summer school and won increased support from its sponsoring institution; both of those achievements would prove valuable in the future.

Hyrum Manwaring's greatest achievement was in seeing the college through economic depression, war, and a lonely fight for survival. The way had been painfully difficult, and there was little reason to hope for better things in the immediate future. That was true, at the time, even at Harvard, though much more had changed there during the long years of depression and war.

Chapter 7

The Drive for Excellence

The DNA of Harvard University was not entirely set by the time A. Lawrence Lowell gave up its helm in the early 1930s. Charles Eliot had established the institutional structure, which mingled graduate students with undergraduates. He had also broadened the curriculum to include all academic subjects. By reordering the college, Lowell brought much needed rationality to the university's broad choice of students and subjects. There was, though, still the matter of scholarly excellence, to which neither Eliot nor Lowell had given much attention. It was left to Lowell's successor to do that.

Appointed in 1933, James Bryant Conant was the first world-renowned scholar to lead Harvard. Already decorated for his research in organic chemistry, he was recognized during his presidency with the Priestley Medal. Had he not left the laboratory to lead Harvard, he might have contended for a Nobel Prize.[1]

Even more than Eliot and Lowell, Conant owed his success to generous academic mentors. His scientific career began with a gifted and dedicated high school teacher, at Roxbury Latin School, who recommended him to the Harvard chemistry department. Among the most significant of Conant's mentors there was Charles Loring Jackson, America's first and most prominent organic chemist. Like so many other leading-edge chemists, Jackson had studied and conducted research in Germany. He shared the benefits of that training with Conant, along with connections that allowed him to take a German tour of his own. That experience led to a tremendously productive period of laboratory research and the opportunity to serve as chair of the chemistry department, his only administrative experience before being tapped to lead Harvard.

Unlike his distinguished predecessors Eliot and Lowell, Conant was a first-generation Harvard man. His ancestors on both sides were early New Englanders, but his family lacked ties to the Boston aristocracy.[2] His father was an engraver whose work in copper etching provided his first contact with chemistry.[3] The contrast between self-made Conant and his privileged predecessor Lowell came starkly into focus as the two discussed the transfer of office. When Conant asked what salary he would draw as president, Lowell replied that he did not know, as he had always donated his compensation back to the university.[4] Conant, to his chagrin, felt compelled to haggle for more than the $20,000 initially offered.[5]

His up-by-the-bootstraps, outsider's perspective may have helped Conant see that while Lowell had been revitalizing Harvard College, the university had lost some of its academic luster.[6] Lowell's emphasis on the college, though invaluable, had not been equaled by his investment in scholarship, the established coin of the realm in higher education. Thus, while Harvard had reasserted its educational leadership and grown tremendously in physical and financial resources, it was no longer preeminent in many fields of scholarship. As Samuel Eliot Morison observed, "In certain departments of knowledge, a chair in Harvard University was no longer recognized as an academic first prize."[7]

Conant worried that the university was contributing less than it should to the welfare of the country and the world, in a time of desperate economic and political need. During the Roaring Twenties, it had been natural

Conant worried that the university was contributing less than it should to the welfare of the country and the world, in a time of desperate economic and political need.

to focus on campus investments such as the house system and other building projects. But the times had changed dramatically, and the university's capacity to serve practical societal ends lagged that of some of its peer institutions. Conant thought Harvard could do more, particularly in the physical and social sciences.

Fortunately, the university's finances were relatively well ordered. Thanks to generous donors and wise budget officers, it had survived the worst of the Depression without cuts in salaries, staff, or services.[8] Costs had risen substantially during Lowell's tenure; he had not only doubled the university's physical footprint but also allowed the salary of the university's highest paid professors to more than double, from $5,500 in 1918 to $12,000 in 1930.[9] But Lowell's Harvard had also set records in philanthropic giving. In addition to the Harkness gift for the house system, which in the end totaled more than $13 million, a postwar fundraising campaign had netted a similar amount. In spite of the stock market crash, during Lowell's term the university's endowment grew from $20 million to $126 million.[10] Tuition revenues also rose: beginning in 1913, the price of a year at Harvard climbed in stages from $150 to $400.[11] The net effect was a balanced budget, even in the worst of economic downturns. Few other universities were so financially fortunate. Though the times dictated prudence, it was not unreasonable for Conant to hope to raise Harvard's scholarly standards and increase its social impact.

Conant's Meritocracy

He did so by the application of principles and procedures that collectively came to be called "meritocracy." The Harvard of Eliot and Lowell was, for all its strengths, clubby and inbred. New students and faculty tended to be drawn from the same narrow pools. In the case of the students, those pools were the elite private and public high schools of New England.[12] Faculty were too often from Harvard's own graduate programs. These sources produced more than their share of capable candidates. But students from the elite New England secondary schools were as likely to have been admitted for reasons of family wealth and social standing as for intellectual capability. Likewise, personal connections gave Harvard graduate students the inside track to new faculty appointments. Conant saw the undesirable consequences of these non-merit-based structural preferences more clearly than had his immediate predecessors, both of whom were so supremely well connected that they may have been oblivious to them.

Selecting new students and faculty on the basis of demonstrated merit would not only raise the standard of performance at Harvard, Conant reasoned, it would also spread limited opportunities for educational advancement more broadly. He worried that, in a world of low growth and limited social mobility that seemed to be the new normal in those years of economic depression and political isolationism, it was incumbent on Harvard and the nation to improve "the selective machinery in our school system which should sort out those who can profit most by four years of college and a subsequent professional education."[13] Bringing the best students to Cambridge, Conant believed, would serve not only Harvard but also the country.

He wasn't without enticements for recruiting new professors. Under Lowell the faculty had received additional research funds, reduced teaching loads, and an occasional semester entirely free of teaching responsibility.[14] The introduction to the academic calendar of six weeks' worth of reading periods gave them additional time for scholarship. Conant added other perquisites, including the new position of University Professor, which entitled the scholar so designated to work across traditional departmental boundaries.

In attracting faculty Conant also had the benefit of Harvard's financial stability, a rare asset in the mid-1930s. Within a few years, he had hired a clutch of distinguished professors from around the world, especially out of economically and politically unstable Europe.[15] But the austerity of the time prevented the full realization of his dream to recruit the world's best scholars to Harvard. That would have to wait until the exigencies of the Great Depression and the war were past.

Up-or-Out Tenure

Conant was more immediately successful in raising the scholarship bar for Harvard's young faculty members. He did so via a system of up-or-out tenure. Rather than being able to stay indefinitely as untenured faculty members, newly hired assistant professors would have eight years to demonstrate their worthiness for tenure.[16] That demonstration would be made not just to committees internal to the university, but also to external reviewers, peers from a candidate's academic discipline.[17] This system of peer review fostered merit-based competition in tenure, undercutting the tendency toward faculty cronyism and inbreeding, thus benefiting the university. It also benefited the candidates. Thanks to unbiased peer review, the worthy prevailed. The eight-year time limit for a tenure decision prevented the university from stringing the others along.[18]

Conant's implementation of up-or-out tenure also solved a practical problem left by Lowell. With the creation of the house system, Lowell had significantly expanded the faculty through the hiring of tutors for the houses. By the mid-1930s many of these tutors had been around long enough to hold expectations of tenure. However, they lacked the scholarly star power that Conant wanted to maximize through the tenure system. They also represented a growing financial cost. As with innovations such as Eliot's elective system and Lowell's system distribution and concentration, Conant's up-or-out tenure had both long-term strategic and immediate tactical benefits.

There were, though, unintended casualties of the new tenure system. One partial casualty was faculty collegiality and commitment to the institution. An untenured faculty member was now more inclined to view his departmental peers as competitors and the needs of the community—including students—as secondary to the tenure goal. Over time, undergraduate students have been particularly affected by this change in university DNA. Conant made it clear that good teaching, a point of pride for Lowell, would not compensate for mediocre scholarship, by this time clearly defined as research and publication.[19] However, his tenure system tended to skew the efforts of tenure-track faculty toward scholarship and away from teaching. With so much of the undergraduate teaching load carried by junior professors and graduate assistants with tenure aspirations, the research emphasis of the process inevitably drew attention away from the classrooms and study halls.[20] Lowell's beloved tutorials in particular suffered. By 1950, three out of four tutorials were staffed by graduate students; some departments had voted to eliminate them altogether.[21]

The new tenure system also widened the gulf between the haves and have-nots on the faculty. Many Harvard departments began to focus their searches for tenure candidates outside the university. The test of worthiness for a tenured position was recognition as being "the best" in one's field. In later years, Dean Henry Rosovsky of the Faculty of Arts and Sciences would describe the search process Conant instituted this way: "At Harvard we ask a traditional question: who is the most qualified person in the world to fill a particular vacancy, and then we try to convince that scholar to join our ranks."[22]

Successful scholars thus became sought-after free agents. This had been happening ever since the German model of scholarship was adopted in the late 1800s. The new universities created by wealthy philanthropists used their capital to attract the world's best scholars, often poaching from one another. Cornell, one of the first to play this game, gained early prominence only to find itself outbid for its own faculty by new universities founded by John D. Rockefeller in Chicago and Leland Stanford in Palo Alto, California.

Conant's drive for excellence required Harvard to enter this free agent market for scholarly talent, a financial competition he preferred to avoid. His goal was to set newly tenured faculty members' salaries at a consistent level across the university.[23] But that goal conflicted with his drive to recruit "the best." For example, in the early 1950s the nation's most promising young geneticist, a twenty-six-year-old from Wisconsin, demanded a full professorship, a paid position for his wife, the promise of additional faculty appointments in his field, lab space and research funding, and no teaching except of graduate students. On top of that, he refused to wear a necktie to work.[24] University officials declined this tall order and watched their lost quarry win a Nobel Prize just seven years later. In time, Harvard would find a balance, eschewing bidding wars but deviating as necessary from Conant's goal of parity in faculty salaries, so as to be competitive in recruiting "the best," and to recognize the higher salaries available outside of the academy in fields such as science and business. Meanwhile, Harvard graduate students and junior faculty, the workhorses of undergraduate instruction, labored under the apprehension that, when tenure time came, they would need to find other employment, as they were unlikely to be deemed the world's best candidate in their field.

Conant's tenure system, with its emphasis on finding the world's premier scholars, also made Harvard's curriculum more specialized and graduate-student focused. Many of the most noted scholars in a field had found some subspecialty in which to make discoveries. Their teaching preferences reflected this narrowness. Specialty offerings proliferated; in the latter part of Conant's presidency, most departments offered two to three times as many courses as in Eliot's day.[25] With the student body growing less rapidly than the course catalog, this meant that many offerings operated at less-than-economical levels. A Conant-commissioned report revealed that 169 courses had fewer than five students. Handwritten notes on the margin of this report reflect his surprise and dismay: "This is ridiculous"; "My God!" [26] Ridiculous or not, academic specialization, with its attendant costs, was by then firmly embedded in the university's DNA. Fortunately, Harvard could afford those costs.

Merit-Based Admissions

Conant also introduced meritocratic measures for the recruitment and evaluation of the best students. The need to access a bigger, broader pool was clear. Harvard College was admitting more than two-thirds of all applicants, and it had the highest percentage of students from its home state of any major school.[27] To draw more candidates outside of the New England region, Conant created national scholarships that included target regions such as the Midwest.[28] Anticipating that students in these distant regions would need greater financial support, he included need-based aid up to several times the cost of tuition.[29] Though the combination of merit and need-based student support was rare at the time,[30] packages of scholarships and financial aid would soon become standard features of the traditional university. The cost at Harvard grew large: by 2010, 60 percent of Harvard College students received some portion of $158 million in financial aid from the school, with the average grant estimated to be $40,000.[31]

The immediate challenge became judging the merit of the new candidates that Conant hoped to admit. Few of them had experienced the kind of classical curriculum found in New England's private preparatory schools and elite public high schools. It wasn't fair to judge them on what they knew of Homer or Milton or classical languages, which is what the entrance examinations pioneered by Eliot and the College Board at the turn of the twentieth century did. Those tests required essays, rather than multiple choice responses, and included sections testing not only English but also French, German, Latin, and Greek.[32]

To implement a standardized, widely administered test of merit that wouldn't penalize students from ordinary high schools, Conant and his Harvard colleagues turned again to the College Board. The new screening mechanism he advocated for wide adoption was the SAT, an evaluation instrument developed in the 1920s by Princeton psychologist Carl Brigham.[33] Unlike the early entrance exams, the SAT was a form of IQ test that attempted to measure academic potential separate from the knowledge of specific subjects, other than English and math. The test wasn't perfect. It assessed primarily word familiarity, which of course depended to a large degree on formal education.

Brigham himself soon disavowed the SAT as a true measure of native intelligence.[34] That others share his view is evidenced by the time and money today's college applicants spend in test preparation.

However, the SAT yielded better results than the old college boards that Eliot helped create. It could be administered and scored much more reliably, and it predicted college success better.[35] While it still favored students with more education, it leveled the playing field for those who hadn't attended New England's college prep schools. The SAT proved tremendously popular and influential, thanks largely to the efforts of Henry Chauncey, the Harvard assistant dean and scholarship committee chairman who first brought the test to Conant's attention. He left Harvard and founded Educational Testing Services (ETS), which marketed and administered the SAT nationwide.[36]

By making the SAT the national standard for college admissions, Conant and Chauncey gave Harvard and other elite colleges access to the country's brightest students. They also paved the way for remarkable growth in American higher education. Administration of the SAT was a much less expensive way of ensuring high-quality student "inputs" than Henry Ford–style vertical integration. Its adoption as a national standard allowed colleges and universities to deliver standardized curriculum to the masses at very low cost, putting a college education within reach of all high school graduates, much as Ford's integrated manufacturing process made Model T cars affordable even for his factory workers.

At the same time, though, Conant's use of the SAT ultimately produced a further narrowing of the types of students Harvard served; only the brightest and best prepared could win admission. With Eliot's emphasis on graduate and professional schools, the proportion of the university's students who were undergraduates had fallen. With Conant's added emphasis on the SAT, Harvard's accessibility by undergraduate students of ordinary intellect would plummet. That happened when Conant's system of meritocratic admission met a wave of student demand after World War II.

THE UNFORESEEN COSTS OF STANDARDIZED TESTING

Thanks to innovative policies and procedures created by admissions personnel in the 1970s, a near-perfect SAT is not a requirement for admission to Harvard College. Rather than applying a quantitative formula, admissions officers invest extraordinary time and effort in judging intangibles such as "strength of character" and "ability to overcome adversity." Standardized tests factor in, but not decisively. As the college's admissions website says, "We regard test results as helpful indicators of academic ability and achievement when considered thoughtfully among many other factors."[37]

Nonetheless, Harvard's huge pool of qualified applicants means that its students' standardized test scores are among the highest in the country, and no farsighted applicant to it or any other selective school sits for the SAT or ACT unprepared. Test preparation strategies range in cost from few dollars for a used book to a few hundred dollars per hour for private tutoring, with the sum of options in between amounting to a multibillion-dollar industry.[38] Rankings-conscious institutions also pay a price, offering scholarship packages to high-scoring applicants.

In addition to this financial cost, there is the social cost of unequal preparation for the economically disadvantaged, as pointed out by Nicholas Lemann, author of *The Big Test: The Secret History of the American Meritocracy.* Lemann has noted how Conant's attempt to blunt the power of privilege—by substituting a standardized test for personal connections in the admissions process—ironically created a new form of privilege and a fierce drive to secure it, via admission to an elite university. In a PBS interview exploring the strengths and weaknesses of standardized assessment, he observed, "It would horrify [Conant] to see the way in which people regard getting high test scores and getting selected for these universities as a kind of way to get stuff—to get the goodies in America. That is not what the system was built for.''[39]

Harvard During World War II

World War II turned Harvard on its head. The draft caused the population of traditional students to shrink dramatically. Four hundred faculty members, a quarter of the total, also joined the war effort. Filling the classrooms and keeping the university running required drastic measures; the faculty who remained voted unanimously to teach year-round, with no increase in salary.[40] Students were inducted in February and June, in addition to the usual September entry point, and the professional schools admitted candidates without bachelor's degrees.[41] The university's classrooms and dorms were rented out to the Army and Navy for the training of their personnel.

Most of these measures were temporary. But one important change, the inclusion in Harvard's classrooms of women from its sister institution, Radcliffe, proved lasting. It would be twenty years before female students received Harvard diplomas, and almost thirty before they took up normal residence on the campus, but the door to equal educational opportunity had been opened.

The war also provided an unexpected boost to Conant's drive for meritocracy. Peacetime and the G.I. Bill brought a flood of applicants—20,000 in 1946. These prospects hailed from around the country, and from all social and economic strata. Rather than admitting two of every three applicants, Harvard could choose one in fifteen, with an eye to diversity as well as academic excellence. The swollen postwar tide of applicants soon ebbed, but the makeup of the student body would never be the same. Meritocracy in admissions, designed to inhibit social inbreeding at a time of low demand, would create a new kind of elite as more and more students vied for a prized spot at Harvard.[42]

The Rise of Government-Funded Research

The war brought two other major changes to Harvard, one pervasive and permanent, the other less so. The more lasting change was the rise of government-funded research. During World War I university scientists had been enlisted, both in the military sense of the term and also on a project basis, to create weapons and equipment. In fact, Conant was among the most prominent of these serviceman-scientists. He left Harvard to join the Chemical War Service, where he oversaw the development of poison gas and gas masks and became "practically a section of the War Department."[43] By the conflict's end, he had been promoted to major.[44]

Conant's involvement in the Second World War was much more strategic and high profile. He chaired the National Defense Research Committee (NRDC), the federal government's vehicle for mobilizing civilian scientists and engineers, and for funding research in university and company laboratories.[45] He also played a personal role in expediting the development of the atomic bomb; his position at Harvard provided cover for covert recruitment visits to the nation's leading scientists.[46]

Conant's work in Washington gave Harvard an inside track on government-funded research contracts.

Conant's work in Washington gave Harvard an inside track on government-funded research contracts. Its $31 million in NDRC grants put it behind only science and engineering specialists MIT and Cal Tech as a player in the world of sponsored university research.[47] Harvard scientists made valuable contributions to military communications and to the development of radar, napalm, and the atomic bomb.

The war's end brought a decrease in government-funded research, but its role in the university was established. The volume of research contracts and grants would grow with the coming of the Cold War and the creation of agencies such as the National Science Foundation and the Atomic Energy Commission, both of which Conant advised. Government research funds produced not only economic benefits to the university but also scholarly ones. Money attracted discovery-minded scientists. Particularly in the physical sciences, the growth of external research funding coincided with a rise in the number of world-class scholars at Harvard. Four candidates tenured in physics in October 1945 went on to win Nobel Prizes.[48]

The new externally funded research came with costs. Faculty and administrative time was taken up in grant writing and regulatory compliance, and the programmatic nature of some of the research made it more difficult for professors to carve out time for teaching. External funding also widened the haves-and-have-nots divide in the university, creating greater opportunities for scientists than for other members of the faculty. Still, the net effect for Harvard was positive. The war indirectly enhanced the quality not only of its student body, but of its scholarship as well.

The Redbook

The war produced yet another benefit at Harvard, one to the undergraduate curriculum. In addition to being concerned about the merits of the university's scholars and students, Conant was intent on raising the academic rigor and social usefulness of the college curriculum. Lowell's distribution requirements were an improvement over Eliot's elective free-for-all, but they failed to promote either a truly general education or academic excellence. As in Eliot's day, some students sought out the curricular path of least resistance, congregating in easy courses known colloquially as "bow-wows."[49] Distribution requirements produced a general education that was, in Conant's view, spotty, shallow, and bereft of moral authority.

The specter of war, to say nothing of its actual horrors, stimulated a redesign of the core undergraduate curriculum of which even Harvard's Puritan founders might have been proud. The West's narrow escape from totalitarianism temporarily unified academicians separated by their specialties. A committee of twelve well-regarded Harvard scholars sought broad input and published a 267-page volume called *General Education in a Free Society*, or, in reference to its crimson binding, the "Redbook."

The Redbook's authors stated their view that a fundamental purpose of education is to promote freedom. That, they declared, requires a degree of commonality of "traits and outlooks" among the citizenry: "A successful democracy (successful, that is, not merely as a system of government, but as democracy must be, in part as a spiritual ideal) demands that [certain] traits and outlooks be shared so far as possible among all the people."[50]

"Unless the educational process includes . . . some continuing contact with those fields in which value judgments are of prime importance, it must fall far short of the ideal."

—The Redbook

In addition to advocating common traits and outlooks, an educational goal abandoned for practical purposes by both Eliot and Lowell, the authors quoted Conant on the importance of values: "Unless the educational process includes . . . some continuing contact with those fields in which value judgments are of prime importance, it must fall far short of the ideal."[51] The main writer on the project, a young professor of Greek literature named John Finley, went so far as to suggest that "if many courses should set forth our view of life as rooted in a humane tradition, it seems only fair that some should set it forth as rooted in a religious tradition." Conant wouldn't go so far. He doubted "if a secular university today can take the step necessary to put its argument on the plane of absolute values."[52]

As ultimately adopted by the faculty, the new general education (GE) program lacked not only grounding in absolute values but also any single course required of all students. Yet it did, as recommended by the Redbook, require that courses designed specifically for general education comprise more than a third of the undergraduate curriculum.[53] This represented a substantial increase over the 25 percent required in Lowell's day.[54] No courses from a student's concentration could be "double counted" for GE credit, though that curricular compromise would creep into later versions of the system.[55]

The new GE program also specified that students take at least one course in each of three areas: humanities, social sciences, and natural sciences. To the Harvard faculty's credit, many courses met Lowell's ideal that distribution requirements give students a synoptic view of a broad area of learning, rather than a mere introduction to a narrow academic discipline. Well-received offerings such as "Western Thought and Institutions" and "Principles of Physical Science" met the Redbook's standard of "form[ing] a comparatively coherent and unified background for an understanding of some of the principal elements in the heritage of Western civilizations."[56]

The Redbook improved general education for a generation of students not only at Harvard but elsewhere: 40,000 copies were purchased, many by representatives of other universities, some of which introduced general education programs modeled after Harvard's.[57] Yet the effect in Cambridge was not long lasting. Courses consistent with the Redbook's broad vision were popular with students but difficult to teach, both because they spanned traditional disciplines and because of the high student–teacher ratios.[58] Newer offerings tended to be narrower, more rooted in a single academic discipline.[59] Conant saw that coming. He knew that the gravitational pull of the university's departments would inexorably bring cross-disciplinary courses back within the traditional lines of scholarship. However, his hoped-for separate department for general education, which might have resisted this tendency, never materialized.[60]

The prosperity of the 1950s and social turmoil of the 1960s soon brought a shift away from postwar idealism. Confidence in great books and historical Western values, temporarily revived by the Allied triumph over totalitarianism, waned. By the early 1970s, some faculty members were calling the Redbook's view of the world "chauvinistic and dated."[61] The war had temporarily changed patterns of thought and behavior, but the specialization and skepticism written into the university's DNA inevitably reemerged.

The Redbook and High School Education

Paradoxically, the Redbook's most lasting impact may have been not on Harvard or other colleges but on American high schools. In fact, secondary education was arguably its primary focus. In charging the committee's members, Conant advised them that "the general education of the great majority of each generation in high schools [is] vastly more important than that of the comparatively small minority who attend our four-year colleges."[62] Like Eliot before him, Conant appreciated the importance of ensuring a steady supply of well-prepared students for Harvard and other universities. However, he was also genuinely concerned for the welfare of that majority of Americans whom he presumed would not seek college education.

The committee took the challenge to heart, devoting more of the Redbook, by page count, to advice for secondary schools and "community" education than to proposals for Harvard College. Several trends in the realm of high school education concerned them. One was the explosive growth of high school participation and associated changes in the profile of the typical student. Between 1870 and 1940, they noted, laws making secondary education mandatory led to a thirty-fold increase in the percentage of Americans attending high school. Not surprisingly, the fraction of those students going on to college fell, from 3 in 4 to just 1 in 4.[63]

Another trend of concern was diffuseness in the high school curriculum. To meet the varied interests and abilities of their exponentially larger and more diverse student bodies, and in response to the rapid advance of knowledge, high schools introduced more courses.[64] In this respect, they were little different from colleges, where electives had come to rule.

Still, the Redbook's authors lamented the tendency of elective offerings to foster concentration in a particular field of study at the high school level.[65] They worried that societal cohesion required imparting shared values to future scholars and tradesmen before they parted ways to lead separate lives. The authors also aspired to exposing young people to "the good." They worried especially about students in rapidly growing cities, where the social functions of the traditional community had broken down.[66] High school, they reasoned, was the last and best opportunity for doing those things, and general education was the vehicle. Their recommended curriculum bore striking resemblance to the one put forward by Eliot's Committee of Ten, whose focus was college preparation. They reasoned that a general education in the humanities, social studies, and science and math would serve not just future college and technical school students but also the 75 percent of high school graduates going directly into the workplace.

Their logic rested on a presumption that today seems shortsighted and even blithe—that the majority of these students would take one of the 60 to 65 percent of U.S. jobs requiring "no previous training." They derided the value of high school "vocational and trade courses, regarded as inferior, made up of inferior students, and taught by inferior teachers." Better, they reasoned, for those going straight from high school to work to pursue liberal studies. "For these students," declared the Redbook, "their whole high school education is in the truest sense general education."[67]

The Redbook offered detailed opinions about the preferred structure of this general education. English literature ought to be studied through all four years, via "great works." By great the Redbook meant difficult, citing approvingly the dictum that "if it were easy the book ought to be burned, for it cannot be educational." All students, the Redbook's authors felt, should also study a foreign language, ideally Latin or French, for the sake of better understanding English. Those seeking a deeper appreciation of the humanities should recognize Russian and Greek as superior to German and Spanish, the latter being valuable more as "tools." Art—music, painting, drawing, and modeling—should be studied by all students for aesthetic reasons, but not for either career preparation or creative self-expression.[68]

The Redbook was equally prescriptive about the ideal curriculum in the social sciences and in the physical sciences and math. Four years of history: world and European first, then American history, including government, economics, and "contemporary society." At least three years of physical science: biology, chemistry, and physics, in that order. A three-year sequence of math: algebra, geometry, and trigonometry, followed by calculus, for the mathematically gifted. Education in mental and physical health was also recommended.[69]

That the Redbook's authors wanted good education for all high school students is beyond dispute. They can hardly be faulted for failing to imagine, in a country only just emerging from decades of isolationism, a global economy that would soon expose unskilled factory workers to competition from around the world. In fact, the general education they prescribed for all high school students was well-timed for the growing fraction of those students who would attend college with the help of the G.I. bill and other federal aid programs.

Yet their prescriptions, reflected in high school curriculum to this day, did not only presume that students headed directly to work could prepare sufficiently via the mere one-third of the curriculum not consumed by general education. The Redbook also presumed that high school teachers could do what college professors would not: teach required courses "characterized mainly by broad integrative elements," rather than specialized electives.[70] Ironically, a general education curriculum that was too rigid and too difficult to deliver for Harvard students and faculty became the standard for American high schools.[71]

The Redbook's authors may have failed to appreciate the extent to which Harvard's academic rise had distanced it from the kind of students the institution had served in its earliest days, when sixteen-year-old freshman were taught not only Latin and Greek but also the fundamentals of English composition and arithmetic. The authors' suggestions that "easy" books cannot be educational and that vocational training is inherently "inferior" indicate that Harvard's professors had lost sight of a large portion of the potential higher education market, the one below them, in which ordinary high school graduates (and nongraduates) need remedial liberal education and practical career preparation. Today, the universities and colleges that have emulated Harvard may be making a similar misjudgment, as evidenced by the growth of for-profit institutions that increasingly cater to "at-risk" students who might otherwise be nonconsumers of higher education.

The Ivy Agreement

The postwar years saw one change to Harvard's DNA that was not only permanent but had been a long time in coming: the end of big-time football. Harvard's intercollegiate football tradition could hardly have been richer. In the opening decades of the twentieth century, its squad was a perennial national powerhouse. From 1911 to 1915 it won thirty-three consecutive games, producing three perfect seasons. In 1920, it secured its seventh national championship with a Rose Bowl win.[72]

Harvard left its mark not only on the record books but on the game itself. Its early players and coaches were among those who defined the rules of college football and created what would become the National Collegiate Athletic Association (NCAA). Harvard built the first concrete stadium, an architectural wonder seating more than 30,000 people. The stadium stimulated, indirectly, one of the football's most important innovations, the forward pass. Before 1906, the ball could be advanced only on the ground. Because of this limitation, as the game became more serious it grew brutal. Giant ball carriers and blockers drove straight ahead, often with arms locked, into opposing behemoths on the defensive line. Size and strength trumped speed and strategy.

Rule makers considered several options for opening up the game, the most popular of which was widening the field by 40 feet, to reward agility. But Harvard's immovable stands, completed just three years before, ran down to the edges of the field. Other gridirons might be adjusted, but not the nation's premier football facility. Hence, the adoption of one of the alternative proposals: allowing a forward pass.[73]

Harvard also established the tradition of sparing no expense to build a winning program. The alumni who helped pay for the new stadium couldn't bear to sit in it and watch Yale win. They pressed for the hiring of Bill Reid, a former Harvard football hero, as the university's first paid coach. When Reid declined the athletics committee's initial offer of $3,500, the alumni contributed a matching amount. The $7,000 starting salary of the twenty-six-year-old football coach exceeded by 30 percent that of the university's highest-paid professor and was comparable to President Eliot's, who had served in his capacity for thirty-six years.[74]

Eliot's successors were no happier than he had been about the trend toward big-money football. Lowell, who valued athletic competition, preferred that it be intramural, loosely organized competition among fellow scholar-athletes for its own sake. His ideal intercollegiate football schedule would have had just one game per year (with Yale). The most prolific builder in Harvard's history, he nonetheless rebuffed alumni offers to fund a new stadium.[75]

Intercollegiate athletics looked even less attractive to Conant as he grappled with Depression-era budgets. Football gate receipts had paid for all other competitive sports in the Roaring Twenties, but they failed to cover the freight during the lean 1930s.[76] Even in the good times, the game had been difficult to manage. Reid was called twice to the White House by Harvard alumnus Teddy Roosevelt to discuss football violence and casualties, including the deaths of eighteen players from around the country in the 1905 season.[77]

Revisions to the rules and the introduction of protective equipment ameliorated these life-or-death concerns, but big-time football still seemed incompatible with Conant's vision of scholarly excellence and social consciousness. As competition from larger schools increased, there was pressure to reduce admissions standards for athletes.[78] Pending proposals for a "two-platoon system," with players specializing on either offense or defense, would only worsen the problem.

Recognizing the handwriting on the wall, Harvard joined seven sister institutions—Brown, Columbia, Cornell, Dartmouth, Penn, Princeton, and Yale—in an Ivy Group Agreement by which football and all other intercollegiate sports would be bound. The soon-to-be members of the Ivy League agreed to hold all students to common academic standards, to offer no athletic scholarships, and to participate in no postseason games. In addition, professional participation in *any* sport by a student-athlete would preclude collegiate participation in all sports.

Harvard joined seven sister institutions—Brown, Columbia, Cornell, Dartmouth, Penn, Princeton, and Yale—in an Ivy Group Agreement by which football and all other intercollegiate sports would be bound.

Overlaid on the Ivies' relatively small student populations, these strictures effectively meant the end of nationally competitive football. Harvard not only did not win another national championship, it waited nearly twenty years for an outright Ivy League football title. Yet there were compensating benefits. With football expenses under control, there was more money for other sports, in which Harvard and the other Ivies continued to compete well nationally. Also, intramural athletic participation, which had doubled with the creation of the house system, became an even stronger tradition.[79] By 1979, three-fourths of Harvard undergraduates would be participating in intramurals.[80] Lowell, who championed "athletics for all," would have been pleased.[81]

Conant likewise was satisfied with the effects of the Ivy Agreement, though by this time larger matters engulfed him. In 1953 President Dwight D. Eisenhower called him into service as the U.S. high commissioner to Germany. He left Harvard with three weeks' notice to the school.[82] With the subsequent creation of the Federal Republic of Germany, he became U.S. ambassador.

Even before these presidential appointments, Conant had brought Harvard national recognition not seen since Eliot's day. He appeared on three *Time* covers during his presidency. The caption on the last of these, in September 1946, read, "A scholar's activities should have relevance." Certainly Conant made Harvard's scholarship nationally relevant as never before. He also laid the foundation for scholarly excellence not only at Harvard but at other elite universities. His rank and tenure system quickly became ubiquitous, as did SAT screening of college applicants. His alterations to Harvard's DNA had profound implications. (See Table 7.1.)

The Essential Genetic Structure

By the end of Conant's administration the dominant traits of the university were set. Harvard would grow larger and more complex, and it would continue to change, becoming wealthier, worldlier, and more diverse. But, by the early 1950s, Conant and his predecessors had fixed the policies that would ultimately determine the quality and cost of a Harvard education, as well the number and type of students it could serve. As these policies were copied, incompletely, by less prestigious and less resource-rich universities, they had tremendous impact on higher education.

Elements of the genetic design originally set by Eliot and Lowell for Harvard have a particularly powerful effect on college students. The overlay of German-style graduate schools and research objectives on an undergraduate college naturally tends to draw senior faculty away from undergraduate teaching; their focus shifts to scholarship and to working with graduate students, leaving the younger students in the hands of less experienced instructors.

Along with Eliot's elective system, the university's graduate programs and scholarly ambitions foster a narrowing of the curriculum.

TABLE 7.1 Harvard Evolution in the Conant Era, 1933–1953	
New Traits	**Implications**
Up-or-out tenure	Increased scholarly excellence Decreased attention to teaching Decreased collegiality and commitment to the institution
Faculty salary and workload distinctions	Increased incentive to win tenure Flexibility in recruiting scholarly stars and approximating market rates outside of higher education Increased salary costs Envy and division
SAT-based admissions selectivity and merit scholarships	Merit-based fairness in student selection Greater opportunities for poor students Increased cost
Externally funded research	Attraction of world-class researchers New opportunities for social contribution New costs of grant writing and regulatory compliance Distraction from teaching Accentuation of haves/have-not's disciplinary divide
	continued

TABLE 7.1 *(Continued)*

New Traits	Implications
The Redbook/General Education	Enhanced course quality Broader range of required studies Increased emphasis on values Liberal education prescriptions for high school students (good for future college students, but at odds with technical training needs of others)
The Ivy Agreement	Reduced financial expense Elimination of admissions exceptions for athletes Increased zeal for intramurals Decreased affinity and support from some alumni Loss of athletics' contribution to the university's public profile

So do the creation of departments and the deference that university presidents, in the tradition of Eliot and Lowell, pay to them. Given the choice, as they are in the spirit of academic freedom, faculty organized into departments naturally create courses reflective of their high degree of specialization.[83]

When applied with the intent to promote only "the best," Conant's up-or-out tenure system supercharges those tendencies. With one's livelihood at stake, the preference of some faculty members for discipline-focused scholarship over instruction becomes a self-preservation mandate for all. The survivors of the process expect to be paid more while teaching less, as do star recruits from other universities. The greater absence of senior professors from undergraduate classrooms affects not only the quality of instruction but also its cost. The university's hope is that its faculty scholars will secure research grants to cover a portion of their increased salaries and absence from the classroom. That failing, though, professors who spend less time in the classroom become relatively more expensive when they are there, as each teaches fewer students per year. The more established and research-oriented a university becomes, the more its instructional costs tend to grow.

Simultaneously, the academic calendar's long summer break, set in the early 1800s, means that utilization of the physical plant remains low by the standards not only of manufacturing businesses but also of human service providers such as hospitals. The American-style university is by design hungry for expensive brick-and-mortar investment and relatively inefficient in its use. That is particularly true of intercollegiate athletic facilities, which sit mostly idle even when school is in session.

Because of the high cost of its scholarship, instructional activities, and physical facilities, the university is always alert to new sources of revenue. Among those are tuition increases, alumni philanthropy, and, in the case of public universities, new legislative appropriations. Even with increased revenues, though, the inherent unprofitability of the collegiate enterprise necessitates restricted enrollments. Scarce seats are reserved for the most intellectually gifted, as determined primarily by Conant's SAT. Often these applicants come from economically privileged backgrounds. Still, inter-institutional competition requires the less prestigious schools to offer scholarships even to students with the capacity to pay their own way.

> *We crush the enthusiasm out of our young faculty.*[84]
>
> —Gordon Gee, president of Ohio State University

Collectively, Conant, Lowell, and Eliot imbedded in the university's DNA the decision to serve fewer of the country's typical undergraduate students, to make the curriculum expansive in the aggregate but narrower and more arcane at the level of individual courses, and to focus more faculty attention on research scholarship. For students, universities fashioned after this model are expensive and difficult to access; they also provide preparation more appropriate to advanced study in graduate school than to the workplace. For most faculty, particularly the untenured, such universities are pressure cookers that tend to inspire apprehension, envy, and a sense of organizational and intellectual fragmentation.

Some decisions made before Eliot's time have proven fateful in our day. One is the creation of a pedagogy that presumes face-to-face interaction between teacher and student. Another is the gradual abandonment of early Harvard College's blend of rationality and moral values. We'll see later how those decisions make the modern university vulnerable to new forms of competition.

Table 7.2 summarizes the widely adopted elements of the traditional university's DNA, roughly as they developed chronologically at Harvard, as well as traits that didn't transfer.

Harvard's Advantages

Harvard enjoys prestige and resource advantages that blunt many of the negative effects of its genetic tendencies on undergraduate education. Because it attracts the world's leading scholars *and* provides house and tutorial systems, a Harvard undergraduate student can experience the best of both the German research university and the English college. In the words of Henry Rosovsky, who began his Harvard studies near the end of Conant's tenure, "The people who wrote the books stood at the lectern."[85] While world-famous scholars lecture, the house masters and tutors provide personal mentoring akin to that of the early Puritan college.

Likewise, Harvard's ability to draw gifted students and, as necessary, pay for their education, creates tremendous opportunities for learning from one's fellows. They are, to quote Rosovsky, "students from every state and many foreign countries selected by rigorous standards—a

TABLE 7.2 Traditional University DNA
Strategically Significant Traits Copied from Harvard
• Face-to-face instruction • Rational/secular orientation • Comprehensive specialization, departmentalization, and faculty self-governance • Long summer recess • Graduate schools atop the college • Private fundraising • Competitive athletics • Curricular distribution (GE) and concentration (majors) • Academic honors • Externally funded research • Up-or-out tenure, with faculty rank and salary distinctions • Admissions selectivity
Harvard Traits That Didn't Transfer Generally
• Extension school (degree programs for nontraditional students) • Residential house system • Ivy Agreement (limitations on competitive athletics) • Four-year graduation

diverse, contentious, and marvelously stimulating cohort."[86] Thus, even as Conant's Harvard increased its commitment to scholarly excellence across an ever-expanding range of subjects, its undergraduate students continued to enjoy a first-rate educational experience.

Harvard has also made two important decisions that most other schools have not. One is to restrict intercollegiate athletic competition. The other, which is less visible, is actually more valuable to its students. Notwithstanding the growth of curricular offerings attendant to specialization and departmentalization, the standard time-to-graduation for a Harvard College student is still four years. That compares to a national average closer to five.[87] Undoubtedly, part of the difference lies in Harvard's students' superior academic ability, their full-time focus on their studies, and the financial incentive to move quickly inherent in the College's high tuition rate. There is also a strong desire to graduate "with my class."

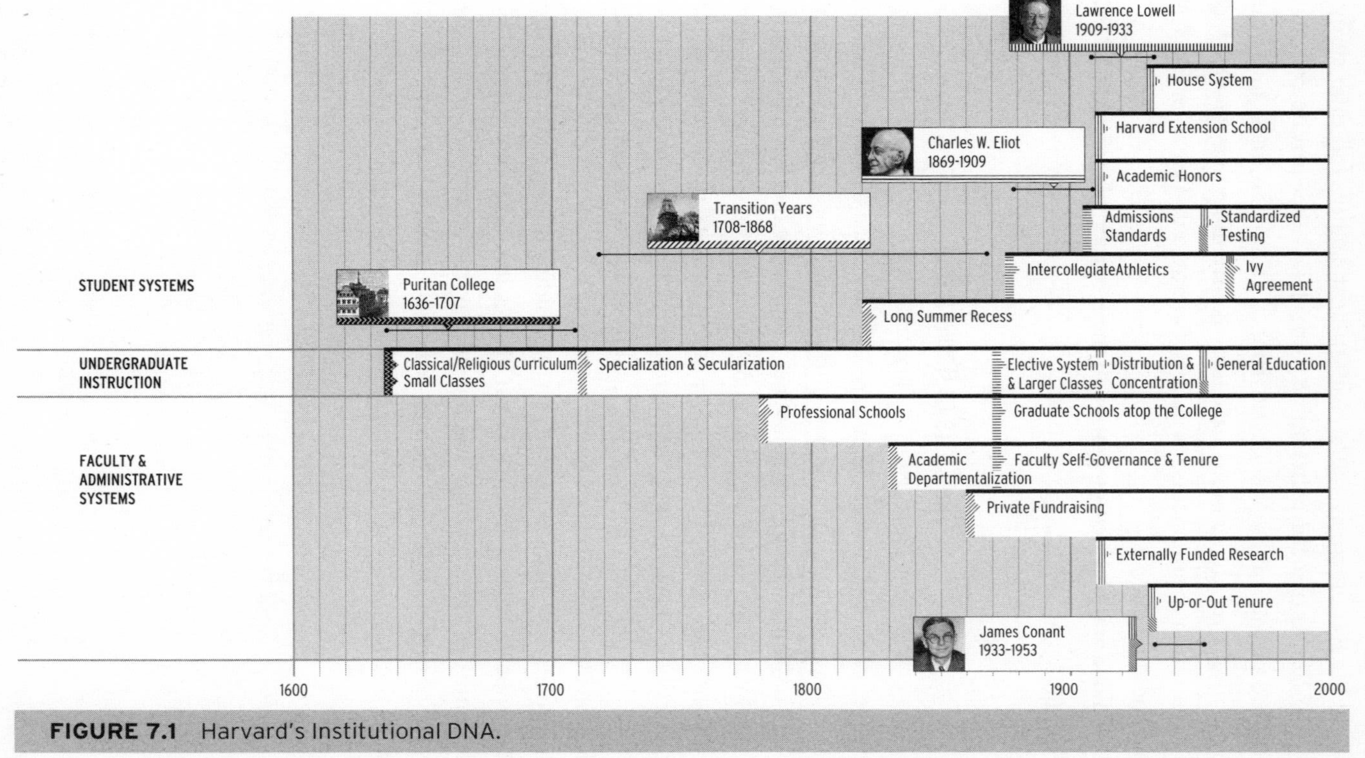

FIGURE 7.1 Harvard's Institutional DNA.

However, there is more than student ability, full-time study, high prices, and social cohesion at work. Like other private colleges, Harvard provides more student advising.[88] It has also made four-year graduation structurally more feasible by constraining the growth of its concentration requirements, or majors. Failure to do that elsewhere has become epidemic.

For a graphical representation of the evolution of Harvard's DNA, see Figure 7.1.

The Costs of Harvard DNA

In spite of its uncommon advantages, the burdens of the institutional DNA have proven increasingly difficult even for Harvard to bear. The presidents who followed Conant found they had limited capacity to influence the university, let alone to innovate as he and his predecessors had done. Two of Conant's successors made funding the university's voracious appetite for resources their primary focus. Two others attempted to increase the quality of undergraduate education; they met with some success but also growing resistance. A fifth successor to Conant, who had the misfortune of presiding during the most severe economic downturn since the Great Depression, came face to face with the limits of the university's ability to pay for everything at its best. None of this was foreseen, though, either at Conant's Harvard or at the many institutions bent on becoming like it, including Ricks College.

Chapter 8

Four-Year Aspirations in Rexburg

Hyrum Manwaring's successor, forty-one-year-old John Clarke, held bachelor's and master's degrees from Brigham Young University (BYU). He came to Rexburg, Idaho, in 1944, having started his teaching career in the public high schools. More recently, he had directed two church "institutes." These institutes were created to offer Mormon religion courses when two former church colleges, one in eastern Arizona and the other in southern Utah, had been given to those respective state governments. The institute buildings bordered the college campuses, allowing students to make religious study a regular part of their higher education as well as to enjoy association with others of their faith, not unlike Jewish Hillel centers.

The end of World War II brought a flood of new students to Ricks, and Clarke wasted no time in preparing to serve them. He undertook a building program that included overdue renovations and the construction of several new facilities, including a large industrial arts (or "shop") building. The college secured Federal Public Housing Authority aid to purchase military surplus buildings, which were converted into a cafeteria and apartments for married students, mostly veterans; it was the beginning of on-campus housing at Ricks. The year 1947 saw record enrollment growth and marked the first time that students had to preregister rather than simply appearing without notice on the first day.[1] The student body continued to be overwhelmingly

Mormon, but an increasing number were coming from outside of Idaho.[2]

Clarke also sought the opportunity to move Ricks up the higher education ladder, to fulfill the dream of "A Bigger and Better Ricks College." Citing new Idaho legislation requiring four years of training for teachers, he secured the church board of education's blessing for four-year college status in 1948, finally realizing former Ricks president George Romney's goal of twenty-five years earlier. With the new status came the requisite organizational structure. On top of the existing departments, Clarke created five "divisions," each analogous to the colleges that comprise a typical university. Within a year, the five divisions had become six.[3] In assuming four-year status, Ricks took on both the organizational structure of a university and the genetic tendency to subdivide.

The early 1950s brought plans for a football stadium, a library, dormitories, and an auditorium to seat eight hundred. Organizers of a $50,000 fundraising drive focused on the stadium, reasoning that enthusiasm for it would stimulate support for the other projects. A Bleacher Athletics Club formed in 1951 to raise money for football scholarships. In 1952, the board appropriated $112,000 for the auditorium, having spent $400,000 on physical plant enhancements during the preceding six years; it also funded property acquisitions that increased the college's holdings to 260 acres. In early 1952, Clarke announced an expansion of the planned auditorium to include additional classroom facilities and seating for one thousand, a number greater than the student enrollment.[4]

Clarke was right to anticipate enrollment growth; the student body doubled between 1948 and 1953. Course offerings grew at a faster pace, though, from 282 to 655. Ricks also grew quickly out of the two-year-degree business. Just five years after the announcement of four-year college status, bachelor's degrees granted outnumbered associate's degrees by more than 10 to 1.[5] The enthusiasm in the community for Ricks's apparent progress toward university status could be seen in a new residential development just east of the campus. Two of its avenues were named Harvard and Cornell. A later development included an avenue called Yale.

Strategic Repositioning

1953 was the year that Ernest Wilkinson, recently installed president of BYU, received the assignment to head the Mormon Church's new unified school system, in which Ricks was the second-largest institution.[6] A successful Washington attorney and holder of a doctorate from Harvard Law School, Wilkinson was already renowned at BYU for his take-charge leadership style.

Wilkinson's reputation preceded him in Rexburg. From the moment of his appointment, doubts began to fly about the future of Ricks College. Those doubts were fueled by speculation over repeated delays in the groundbreaking and construction of the new auditorium. Inquiries to Salt Lake, though, produced assurances from David McKay, then president of the church and chairman of the board, that Ricks's status would not change.[7]

In reality, Wilkinson had dramatic plans for changing the college. Seeing the potentially competitive relationship between BYU and Ricks, both now four-year schools, he felt a concern that would be voiced several years later by James Bryant Conant, Harvard president emeritus. Conant, after touring the nation to study secondary and higher education in the United States in the late 1950s, described his "sense of horror at the disarray [he] found in a number of large and important states."[8] Among other problems, he saw the effects of Carnegie climbing by small colleges in state higher education systems that already had well-established universities.[9] This ambition by would-be up-and-comers sub-optimized a state's overall system, pitting schools against one another in a competition for finite public funds and leaving seekers of associate's degrees and technical certificates underserved.

Wilkinson recognized these problems before Conant, then still at Harvard, began his formal study of them. He admired the centrally controlled State of Utah system, which had kept Weber State College and the other church academies it acquired in the early 1930s at two-year status, preventing competition with the University of Utah, the state's premier research institution, and with Utah State, its agriculture and applied science university. As the new head of a churchwide coordinating system for higher education, Wilkinson quickly sought to place similar bounds on Ricks College.

His strategy for repositioning Ricks had two prongs. One was returning it to two-year status, a move he pushed through in 1955. President Clarke learned of the change by letter. In response to his reply, which expressed "shock" and "anguish," he and his colleagues received the following written explanation: "After long and careful consideration we have come to the conclusion that Ricks College will be of more service to the Church, and have a greater destiny as an integral and permanent part of the Church school system, by being a first-class junior college than by continuing as a relatively small four-year college." The change was to become effective in 1956–1957 school year, with current upperclassmen encouraged to transfer to BYU. "Brigham Young University," the explanatory letter continued, "is to be the senior university of the Church with Ricks College a strong junior college." The commitment to strengthening Ricks in its new, supportive role in the broader system was manifested in a pledge to complete not only the auditorium but also the other planned facilities.[10]

Some Ricks faculty members resigned rather than be limited to teaching a two-year curriculum, but most stayed. The board granted a 5 percent salary increase to show its commitment to creating a first-rate junior college. Overall enrollment fell only slightly with the elimination of upperclassmen, as postwar demand for college education swelled the ranks of freshmen and sophomores. The change was hard, though, on the athletic teams, which had losing seasons after unusually successful 1955–1956 campaigns. Football wouldn't have another winning season for eight years.[11]

Though disappointing to the college's supporters in Rexburg, the new strategy made good sense for the larger church higher education system. By reverting to two-year status, Ricks would be able to serve twice as many students. Associate's degree graduates could transfer to BYU, where the expense of creating upper-division programs, requiring specialized and Ph.D.-credentialed faculty, would be concentrated and contained. In response to complaints from the local newspaper publisher, a letter from church headquarters that was probably drafted by Wilkinson did more than imply that the Ricks team had underestimated this expense: "The provision for a four-year course to meet the requirements of teachers was never developed to a point that insured stability because it was never fully realized how expanded it must become to meet the requirements for the issuance of bachelor's degrees." The letter also revealed a vision of other junior colleges yet to be created. "Now, with a unified Church School System, more perfectly organized to meet the anticipated needs of the future, Ricks may take its place with an assurance that it will be one of what we hope to be many Junior Colleges serving a great purpose in the educational system."[12]

A SYSTEM-BASED APPROACH TO HIGHER EDUCATION

Though Ernest Wilkinson had the weight of church authority behind him in literally putting Ricks College in its place in the new system of higher education, the model was neither original nor unique to ecclesiastically sponsored universities and colleges. Wilkinson was among many system administrators who recognized the need to rationalize the growing investments in American higher education. In 1940 fewer than a third of states had a central mechanism for regulating or at least coordinating their systems; by 1970, nearly all did.

Some states, including New York, North Carolina, Texas, and Utah, created central boards for all public institutions. Others, such as California, had boards that were merely advisory, with greater autonomy retained by individual institutions or subsystems, such as the

University of California campuses.[13] The latter approach was favored by faculty and other employees as preserving self-determination, a guiding principle in American higher education and a key reason for Harvard's seeking corporate independence from the Commonwealth of Massachusetts in 1865. However, the bigger-and-better tendency, particularly as supercharged by the Carnegie ladder, has reinforced the wisdom of state coordination, as we'll see.

A Bridge Too Far

Wilkinson was premature in predicting the recreation of the church junior college system that had been, with the exception of Ricks, given away during the Great Depression. He also overplayed his hand on the second part of his strategy for Ricks, moving the college from Rexburg to nearby Idaho Falls. On paper, this was another logical repositioning. Idaho Falls was larger and offered greater current and future economic prospects. In addition, it was likely to get its own state junior college at some point, creating competition for Ricks unless a preemptive move was made.

The Rexburg campus also carried liabilities Wilkinson hoped to eliminate. One was an aging infrastructure badly in need of renovation. The newer of the college's two main buildings was thirty-five years old, and both were poorly engineered by modern standards; fire had nearly destroyed each on more than one occasion. On top of past-due plant maintenance, there was the political liability of local influence on the college. The community tradition of unstinting support for Ricks was a two-edged sword. Many who had given money to keep the college alive seemed to view themselves as shareholders, with associated control rights. Now that the board planned to centrally finance the college's operations and substantially expand the physical plant, it seemed prudent to make that investment in a new location.

Wilkinson announced the move to Idaho Falls, which had been rumored since his appointment to oversee Ricks, in 1958. Local church, city, and business interests quickly aligned in opposition. It was one thing to lose four-year status for Ricks, but another to lose the college altogether. There was also a sense of betrayal, as three years had passed since the promise of new buildings, one of which, the auditorium, was finished.[14]

The ensuing three years saw a campaign of unrelenting resistance conducted via mail, newspaper, and public gathering. Rexburg's citizens argued the lifestyle and moral advantages of their bucolic community, while boosters in Idaho Falls made counterclaims, citing the greater economic potential and intellectual vitality of their city. President David McKay took an active personal interest, visiting the campus several times during this period. He ultimately determined that Ricks would stay in Rexburg, ending the dispute with the announcement of three new buildings. Wilkinson, to his credit, moved the building program forward posthaste.[15] Rexburg's relieved citizens later joked that the college wasn't moved to Idaho Falls because the buildings got stuck at the Snake River railroad bridge.

Expanding in the 1960s

In spite of the uncertainty of the college's future during the late 1950s, growth continued apace. In 1961, Ricks employed sixty-eight full-time faculty members, a 50 percent increase in just four years. Tuition of $210 per year (less than one-seventh Harvard's rate at the time) kept students coming in record numbers. The board approved $2.7 million to start the construction of science, library, heating plant, and dorm buildings. Within two years, nine new structures were complete, with others in planning stages. The decade of the 1960s, in which the baby boomers came of college age, brought the same growth to Ricks that it did to other campuses. By 1970, the college had more than 5,000 students and 200 faculty members. It was also beginning to grow well beyond its eastern Idaho region; among the 5,000 students were representatives of all fifty states and eighteen foreign countries.[16] Many of these students came to Rexburg with the intent of beginning college in a small, friendly environment but then going elsewhere to get a bachelor's degree. Ricks made the most of this trend by declaring itself "a great place to start."

Growth in size and in the number of students transferring to four-year schools naturally rekindled desires for advancement in academic standing. In 1966 the alumni association published a 22-page document arguing for the return to four-year college status. In fact, informal efforts to reintroduce bachelor's degrees had resumed just one year after the resolution of the Idaho Falls relocation issue. In 1962, local public high school superintendents had sent a letter to church headquarters urging four-year credentialing of teachers. An Idaho Falls newspaper editorial asserted the need for a bachelor's degree-granting college to fill a pressing need in the area. Ricks president John Clarke privately longed for the return to four-year status, though he publicly supported the board's more modest vision for the college until his retirement in 1971.[17] The college grew in size and complexity during his twenty-seven years of service but genetically remained little changed (see Table 8.1).

TABLE 8.1 Ricks College in the John Clarke Era, 1944-1971

New Traits	Implications
Campus housing	Enhanced campus life Increased student convenience Increased infrastructure cost
Four-year degrees, briefly	Increased subject matter comprehensiveness, specialization, and departmentalization
Expanded enrollment, faculty, and campus	More students served Increased operating cost

Clarke's successor was Henry B. ("Hal") Eyring, son of the Mormon chemist of the same name. Eyring was a Harvard man, having taken master's and doctoral degrees from its business school. He studied there during the term of James Conant's successor, Nathan Pusey. Like Clarke's long run at Ricks, Pusey's roughly contemporaneous twenty years at Harvard's helm saw little change in the university's DNA. However, it was under Pusey that the modern Harvard came of age. It was also during this time that the full costs of the great research university began to be apparent.

Chapter 9

Harvard's Growing Power and Profile

It would be too strong to say that James Bryant Conant's successor, Nathan Pusey, was his opposite. In choosing Pusey, though, Harvard's governing boards followed their pattern of replacing the outgoing president with a candidate of differing background and strengths.[1] Conant, the distinguished laboratory scientist, Deist, and lifelong Harvard man, was followed by Pusey, a teacher of classics, devout Episcopalian, and educator at female-friendly liberal arts schools. An Iowan who graduated from Cedar Rapids High School and presided for nine years over Appleton, Wisconsin's Lawrence College, he was the first Midwesterner to lead Harvard. His only obvious qualification to succeed Conant was the set of Harvard degrees (B.A., M.A., and Ph.D.) he earned between leaving Cedar Rapids and returning to Appleton. Yet Pusey's family had Boston roots, and he appealed to the Brahmins who had found Conant socially disappointing. In rationalizing his selection, one of them observed, "Mr. Pusey believes in God and he goes to football games. This is progress enough for the present."[2]

Much more important, Pusey brought a sturdy mixture of tenacity and humility to the job. Unlike his three immediate predecessors, all of whom were hired largely for their vision of Harvard's needs, Pusey came with no presumptions about the institution's future. After deliberate study of the workings of the campus, he determined to simply build on the foundation he inherited.[3] He would make no great changes to the DNA of the university that Eliot, Lowell, and Conant created. But he would grow and strengthen it as never before, by raising money to feed the institutional organism his predecessors had designed. That focus on fundraising would become, in its own way, an essential genetic trait of the great research university.

Fundraising Excellence

Pusey had no real track record as a fundraiser when he returned to Cambridge, nor did he immediately distinguish himself as one. Throughout the 1950s, including the first seven years of his presidency, smaller Yale University consistently raised more money than Harvard. Had it not been for the generosity of charitable foundations, most notably the Ford Foundation, Pusey would have been hard-pressed to offset the post–World War II decrease in federal research funding.[4]

In 1957, though, he warmed to a path-breaking proposal by his administrative staff. Rather than raising money on a project or school basis, the university would launch a campaign called "The Program for Harvard College" (PHC). The PHC plan was innovative in two respects. First, it would encompass multiple investment priorities, including new buildings, faculty salary enhancements, and student scholarships. Second, it would be ambitious: the $82.5 million goal was twice the amount ever raised anywhere.[5] If successful, the strategy would not only allow the campus to recover from the relative neglect of the Depression and war years but to realize Conant's ambitious goals of meritocratic excellence.

Pusey proved to be an able pitchman. He took his fundraising activities nationwide, making use of jet travel, and to the national airwaves, appearing on programs such as *Meet the Press*. What had been a discreet gentlemen's game, focused on alumni classes and major individual donors, became a mass market affair of which others took notice. The goal for Harvard College was exceeded, but not before 134 institutions had launched similar drives. Princeton University raised nearly $60 million, MIT $100 million.[6]

The PHC approach worked equally well for Harvard's medical school, which launched a drive for $58 million drive in the early 1960s. In 1963, Pusey set a $200 million goal for the next ten years, but this proved conservative; Harvard raised more than that amount in the first half of the decade alone. In 1955 the university's endowment had stood at $442 million. By 1965, it surpassed $1 billion.[7]

At the same time, federal research funds multiplied, expanding from 8 percent of the university's income to 25 percent. There were also good financial omens from the admissions office: applications were up, allowing for steady increases in tuition. The cost of enrolling at Harvard tripled, to $2,600, during Pusey's term, having doubled under Conant.[8]

Pusey applied this tripartite financial bounty of donations, research grants, and tuition increases to the causes of his predecessors. The size and quality of the undergraduate student body grew. More applicants meant that the entering class could be increased from 1,000 to 1,500 without a lowering of entrance standards. Also, new student aid funds allowed for "need-blind" admission; in other words, Harvard could select students without regard to ability pay.[9] This new student recruiting tool enhanced not only the academic quality of the class, but also its socioeconomic diversity. Conant-style meritocracy in student selection steadily increased.

The university's operations likewise grew in both size and quality. Pusey oversaw the construction of thirty-three new buildings and a doubling in the number of faculty and administrators. As in student selection, meritocracy produced better scholars and scholarship. Harvard systematically increased the reasons for the world's best to come to Cambridge. Those reasons included more endowed chairs, more research positions and research funding, higher salaries and benefits, and greater faculty perks, such as leaves of absence for focused scholarship. The number of Nobel laureates on the faculty increased, a further lure to prospective professors and students.[10]

There was also the draw of the university's political mystique. Alumnus John F. Kennedy built his presidential administration on Harvard talent. Former deans and professors became public figures known not only by name but by face and voice as television broadcasted their policy musings nationwide, much as it did Pusey's fundraising pitches. President Kennedy himself promoted Harvard, hosting a meeting of its board of overseers, of which he was a member, at the White House.[11]

Explosive Expansion and Faculty Autonomy

As Harvard's power grew and its profile rose, its operational complexity and cost expanded. By the 1960s the university comprised fifty departments and schools, with 2,300 subdivisions. The catalog listed 1,614 courses, one for every four undergraduate students.[12] With so many different operating activities (teaching, research, administration, student services, physical plant, and so on) and equally diverse sources of revenue (tuition, research grants, royalties, philanthropy, rents) it was all but impossible to know what anything cost and whether the expense was justified.

Operating expenses grew faster than the endowment, notwithstanding the latter's doubling between 1955 and 1965. Fortunately, healthy growth in government research grants and tuition compensated.[13] Yet some close observers questioned both the sustainability and the justifiability of the growth. Harvard Corporation fellow William Marbury, a Baltimore lawyer, was led to wonder about a pattern of sustaining innovation that, like that of some successful companies, seemed out of control:

> Apart from financial difficulties, has not the time come when we should put the brakes on the explosive expansion which seems to be taking place in every department of the university? Are the demands for more space, more equipment and more personnel

> really justified by the accomplishments? May there not be something in [the] stricture that the Harvard faculty is spending too much money on a kind of intellectual featherbedding?[14]

In the increasingly complex environment, faculty found new sources of power. The decentralization of fundraising gave many schools and departments greater fiscal autonomy. At the same time, they consolidated their control of new faculty appointments and the curriculum.[15] A striking case in point was the new Kennedy School of Government. The Kennedy family agreed to have the school named for John F. Kennedy with the understanding that its emphasis would be practical. The faculty, though, preferred a more scholarly approach and expressed astonishment that the Kennedys might expect anything else. Morton and Phyllis Keller, chroniclers of this period in Harvard's history, described the inevitability of the faculty's strategic triumph: "The essence of the meritocratic University was faculty autonomy; the essence of an autonomous school was its own staff and curriculum. And over time the Kennedy School of Government evolved in accord with its faculty's vision, not that of America's most prominent political family."[16]

In the increasingly complex environment, faculty found new sources of power. The decentralization of fundraising gave many schools and departments greater fiscal autonomy.

Implications for Instruction

Greater faculty autonomy affected the classroom. Things may not have been as bad at Harvard as the situation described in a 1964 Carnegie Foundation Report called *The Flight from Teaching.*[17] Yet it was increasingly difficult to compete for star scholars without promising light teaching loads. That was particularly true in the sciences and medicine, where faculty effectively paid their own way with research grants. A case in point was a chemistry star, one of five in that department at Harvard who would win Nobel Prizes. As his public profile rose, he refused to teach first introductory courses and then any scheduled courses at all.[18] Students drawn to Harvard by such stars often found access to them limited.

However, a national study conducted in 1969 revealed that the so-called flight from teaching could not be explained by faculty preferences alone. More than two-thirds of U.S. professors identified themselves as being at least equally balanced in their teaching and research orientations. Moreover, the data showed that the preference for teaching was significantly greater among older faculty than younger ones: more than 40 percent of professors over age fifty described their orientation as primarily or exclusively teaching focused.[19]

One set of researchers concluded that "men's own interests and values seem to turn away from research and towards teaching with increasing age—and begin to do so fairly early in their careers."[20] Another plausible explanation is that the older generation of professors in the late 1960s had started their careers before the typical university began placing Conant-style emphasis on research in faculty hiring and promotion. Even so, a natural aversion to teaching seems hard to find in this and similar datasets.

A FICTIONAL SCHOLAR'S PASSION FOR TEACHING

The image of an accomplished scholar' interests turning toward teaching is familiar to readers of *The Glass Bead Game.* Having mastered the game, Hermann Hesse's protagonist Joseph Knecht surprises himself by finding less joy in playing it, or in tutoring its most advanced devotees, than in teaching novices. In fact, he begins to dream of working in the academic realms where the game is all but unknown, schooling youngsters at the level where, as he recalls, "teaching and educating were more, and more deeply, a unity."[21] In time, Knecht determines to leave his scholarly community entirely, to devote himself full time to teaching. He steps down from his prestigious academic post with this call to his colleagues: "Above all else we need teachers, men who will bring to our youth the capacity for moderation and judgment and who, by their example, will instill a reverence for truth, obedience to the spirit and service to the world."[22]

A Changing Student Body

By the late 1960s, Harvard's students had changed along with its faculty. In political unrest Harvard lagged Berkeley, where the undergraduate sense of depersonalization and abandonment by the "multiversity" was much greater. But the 1960s also left their mark in Cambridge. Arthur Schlesinger Jr., a Pulitzer Prize-winning Harvard historian who served in the Kennedy administration, described the Harvard College students of the 1950s as "an uncommonly unoriginal, conventional-minded, sloganized, and boring undergraduate generation."[23] That would soon change. A decade later, the successors of this "boring" generation would effectively drive their college president from office.

As the 1960s opened, the typical Harvard undergraduate was a relatively wealthy, white, religious male. He felt no great sense of achievement or entitlement in his admission, given that 1 out of every 2 applicants got in. He took courses from professors who remembered the sacrifices of the war years and expected students to work hard for good grades. He had a concentration in the liberal arts and was planning to write an honors thesis and then go on to graduate school.[24]

This typical student was equally conservative in his life outside the classroom. He conformed to the prevailing preppy dress style and, by written policy, wore a jacket and tie to dinner in his campus house. He also submitted to the university's parietal rules, curfews limiting visits by females to undergraduates' rooms. He read a student newspaper, the *Crimson,* that supported the political establishment. A Republican or political independent, he might turn out for traditional springtime pranks and minor rioting, but not for political demonstrations.[25]

Ten years later the typical student was still male, white, and wealthy. Other than that, almost everything about him had changed. He was less religious and less interested in being taught the kind of values espoused by the Redbook. He was also more aware of having earned his place at Harvard, where admission rates had fallen and tuition had risen. Thanks to grade inflation, he was twice as likely to make the dean's list, an honor shared by 80 percent of his classmates.[26]

Outside of class, he set his own standards. He could dine sans jacket and tie—and, for a time, sans shirt. With the opening of all Harvard classrooms to females, he not only encountered them more often there but could, with the end of parietals, entertain them all night in his room. He was aware of drug dealing and usage on the campus, though he wasn't personally involved.[27]

In addition, the typical student in 1970 lived in a vastly different political environment. He wasn't a member of the campus chapter of Students for a Democratic Society (SDS), but he knew of their confrontational campus protests. He read sympathetic reports of those protests in the *Crimson*, which had adopted a liberal view of social issues such as Vietnam, race relations, and demonstrations at Berkeley.

The *Crimson* had also taken on President Pusey personally. As early as 1962 it ran a series of editorials branding him "conservative" and "look[ing] for sanctuary in history and tradition."[28] This characterization overlooked Pusey's progressive support for civil rights, female students, and academic freedom; his defense of the university community was particularly admirable during the McCarthy era. What the students wanted, though, was greater freedom from moral authority and a university platform for challenging "the establishment." Pusey had been slow to relax moral strictures such as parietals, and he resisted the use of campus for political purposes.

Such administrative heel-dragging provided the ostensible reason for the student demonstration that ultimately triggered Pusey's early retirement. In the spring of 1969 the faculty decided, in the face of SDS-led student pressure, to discontinue Harvard's Reserve Officer Training Corps (ROTC) program, which some considered a symbol of the war in Vietnam. Mercifully for the 345 affected ROTC students, the decision was to take effect after two years, allowing most of them to complete their coursework as planned.[29]

But mercy cut no ice with young student radicals. Citing the ROTC delay, as well as Pusey's relentless expansion of the campus infrastructure, an SDS-led crowd of several hundred demonstrators occupied University Hall, office of the dean of the Faculty of Arts and Sciences; among the group were a handful of junior faculty members. Ejecting the building's occupants, they ransacked files, engaged in minor vandalism, and voted to nonviolently resist attempts at eviction.[30]

The next morning, at five o'clock, Pusey ordered that eviction. Four hundred club-wielding state patrolmen and local police officers cleared the building. Harvard's alumni generally supported the bold move, but the faculty, three-fourths of whom had been appointed since 1960, did not. They voted nearly unanimously to drop criminal charges against the student occupiers, and they protected the junior faculty members from professional sanction.[31] Having lost the support of the faculty and many students, Pusey retired the following year, two years earlier than planned. One year later, in 1971, there would be new presidents at both Harvard and Ricks College.

Chapter 10

Staying Rooted

The political turmoil that led to Nathan Pusey's early departure from Harvard also gripped Stanford, where thirty-eight-year-old Hal Eyring was serving on the faculty of the Graduate School of Business in 1971 when he was selected to take the helm of Ricks College. Bucolic Rexburg, Idaho, had experienced none of the student unrest of either Harvard or Stanford, let alone that of Berkeley. News commentator Paul Harvey, having declared Ricks "as isolated as any major college I have ever seen," went on to observe that "the clear-eyed confidence which used to characterize most American young people is still apparent behind [its students'] wide-open eyes."[1] The commonest social problems on campus were "stomp dancing" and "Beatle Haircuts." Though Ricks College didn't require students to wear jackets and ties, as the Harvard houses did before the 1960s, it mandated hair off the ears for men and "modest" clothing for both men and women.[2]

Eyring faced other challenges. He followed in John Clarke a tireless, beloved champion of the college, a self-described romanticist who over twenty-seven years had made institutional dreams come true, even though the loftiest—four-year status—had been snatched away. In the early 1970s the optimistic spirit of the preceding decade was still much in the air at Ricks. It could be heard in the inaugural charge Eyring received from board representative Marion Romney, a Ricks College athletics hero of 1918 and 1919 and son of the college president of that time. Romney challenged Eyring to "improve upon [the college's] expanded facilities, enlarged student body and erudite faculty."[3]

Rightsizing and Enhancing

The guidance Eyring received from the church board of education's administrative officers, though, was more conservative. For one thing, he was to strongly discourage talk of four-year status. He was also accountable to impose necessary bureaucracy on a multimillion-dollar enterprise still operating with the friendly informality of an extended family.

Like other institutions across the country, the college had been growing at a breakneck pace. Student enrollment expanded by 50 percent between 1967 and 1970; academic offerings and departments likewise proliferated. Eyring quickly consolidated ten academic divisions into five and established communication protocols that historian David Crowder would describe as "fairly rigid—a noted departure from President Clarke's administrative style." In addition, the new president cut nearly a dozen athletic teams, including swimming, tennis, skiing, and rodeo. He also called for the replacement of the historical college logo, which featured the athletic teams' Viking mascot, with something that would give "emphasis to spiritual rather than temporal values." An open competition produced a new logo, a stylized tree symbolic of founding principal Jacob Spori's "mighty oaks," with branches "run[ning] all over the earth."[4]

The more difficult moves came in the 1973–1974 school year, when enrollment fell for the first time in a generation, a sign of the ebbing of the baby boom that had fueled American higher education growth in the 1960s. The board tasked Eyring with bringing employment into line with enrollment, which meant a painful process of identifying faculty and staff members for potential layoff. In the end, the board determined to stay the course, in the hope that enrollments would recover, which they did the following year.

Other frugality measures included reducing the pace of physical plant expansion and creating a salary schedule based solely on academic degree and years of experience, independent of discipline, gender, or any personal achievement. Ricks would have neither contract negotiation by academic stars nor interdepartmental envy among down-at-the-heels humanists and higher-paid scientists and business professors.[5] Everyone on the faculty was paid essentially the same.

In addition to pruning and organizing, Eyring saw opportunities to build on what had come to be known as "the Spirit of Ricks." This abstract notion could be seen in at least two practices. One was the concern that faculty showed for their professorial colleagues and their students. In the extracurricular interest professors took in their mostly teenaged students, Eyring recognized the affection he had felt from Harvard Business School professors such as Georges Doriot. Doriot, considered the father of American venture capital, taught a second-year MBA course called "Manufacturing." During his forty-year teaching career, more than 7,000 students passed through his classroom.[6] Several years after Eyring took the class, the legendary professor learned that this former student, then pursuing a doctorate in an unrelated field, was to be married. Doriot invited Eyring and his fiancée to his office, where he gave his blessing to the union. Similar examples of *in loco parentis* behavior could be seen at Ricks in faculty members who boarded students in their homes, tutored them outside of class, and urged them on to four-year degrees and graduate school.

AN UNRELENTING MENTOR

Georges Doriot, who began teaching at the Harvard Business School (HBS) in 1925, at age twenty-five, was legendary for his attention to his students, whose careers he followed and facilitated throughout his life (Hal Eyring attributed to Doriot three job offers that came in the year before he left Stanford for Ricks College). But Doriot's fealty had to be earned, as described by his biographer Spencer Ante:

> [In 1926] Doriot began to develop a novel education approach. Whereas most professors kept a chilly distance between themselves and their students, Doriot believed strongly in forming a close bond between student and teacher. From the start of his teaching career, he felt that every student deserved personalized attention. He studied each student's history and college grades, and was very attentive to the difficulties in transition from undergraduate to graduate work. Five weeks after his class started, he had seen every one of his ninety-six students at least twice.
>
> A second tenet of his early philosophy, absorbed from his father [a renowned French automotive engineer], was drilling the value of hard work into his students. In a letter to a friend of a colleague, Doriot described with a palpable sense of glee the importance of imparting a strong work ethic. "At least 25 of my students have given me this year at least 10 to 15 hours of work on one course alone," boasted Doriot. "I have several of them working from 9 a.m. up to an advanced hour of the morning. I do believe when these men leave the school they have a definite notion of what an honest day's work means."[7]

In addition to teaching for four decades at HBS, Doriot founded American Research and Development Corporation, the first publicly owned venture capital company, and INSEAD, one of the world's leading business schools.

Eyring observed not only faculty concern for students but also genuine respect for even the most ordinary of them. His predecessor, John Clarke, was famous for the saying, "Ricks was founded upon the firm belief that there are extraordinary possibilities in ordinary people." That egalitarian attitude, reflected in interactive discussions faculty led in the classes he visited, reminded Eyring of the motto of his dissertation advisor, the Harvard Business School's C. Roland Christensen.[8] Christensen, renowned for his skill in discussion-based teaching, declared: "Every student teaches and every teacher learns."[9] That philosophy could be seen at Ricks as well as HBS. Professors knew not only their students' names but also their personalities, capabilities, and learning needs; they used this knowledge to engage the students in teaching one another. The qualifications of the students and faculty at the two institutions were different, but the guiding educational philosophy was much the same.

John Clarke was famous for the saying, "Ricks was founded upon the firm belief that there are extraordinary possibilities in ordinary people."

THE FAITH OF A MASTER TEACHER

C. Roland "Chris" Christensen's teaching career of more than half a century began inauspiciously. A twenty-seven-year-old HBS graduate student with no business experience, he was assigned to teach a course in business policy to eighty second-year MBA students. On the morning of the first class, having sweated through a long weekend's preparation, he entered the classroom coolly, a folder of teaching notes in one arm and a coat draped over the other. Mounting the three steps of a small, high platform replete with brass rail and curtain, he tripped, fell, and sent the teaching notes flying.[10]

Things got better. Christensen became one of Harvard University's most distinguished teachers, named to a university professorship and invited to conduct teaching seminars for his fellow faculty members.[11] But he never lost his feeling of sympathy for teachers and students terrified by the first day of class. Even as he engaged in leading-edge scholarship, pioneering what would become the field of corporate strategy, he made a science of the task of building confidence in learners. He articulated the principles he discovered with pith and power:

Because students relate to one another as peers, they can often communicate more effectively than the instructor in class.

Every student teaches and every teacher learns.

Faith is the most important ingredient in good teaching practice.

I believe that teaching is a moral act.

I believe that what my students become is as important as what they learn. The endpoint of teaching is as much human as intellectual growth. Where qualities of persona are as central as qualities of mind—as is true in all professional education—we must engage the whole being of students so that they become open and receptive to multiple levels of understanding. And we must engage our whole selves as well. I teach not only what I know, but what I am.[12]

Both by exhortation and personal example, Eyring sought to institutionalize the educational benefits that flowed from the Spirit of Ricks and reminded him of his best personal learning experiences. Each semester he team-taught a religion class of eighty or more students. He strove to be known personally by every student, starting with a handshake at fall and winter registrations. Between August 22 and 24, 1973, he shook 5,100 hands; that gave him direct knowledge of the impending enrollment problem.[13] He allowed his personal office to become the court of final appeal for young men reluctant to trim their Beatle haircuts and mustaches.

Eyring felt the importance of keeping the college "close to its roots." His only major curriculum expansion was the creation of programs in horsemanship and crop and beef production, designed to support the ranching and farming operations in the area. He joined in the spirit of staying rooted to Ricks College's past and its local environment by buying a cow of his own. The agricultural programs required the raising of several million dollars to purchase land and build new facilities west of campus, along the banks of the Snake River.[14] On a more modest scale, he approved "self-employment" programs in automotive and electronics servicing, landscape nursery management, and business management.[15] With all of these programs, none of which was mandated by the church board of education, he was not only keeping Ricks close to its roots but effectively moving it back down the higher education ladder.

During Eyring's term a disastrous event brought the college back to its roots in the Rexburg community. On a Saturday morning in June 1976 the newly completed Teton Dam broke, sending 80 billion gallons of water roaring toward Rexburg at 40 miles per hour.[16] Thanks to providential early warning, only eleven people died. But nearly 4,000 homes were destroyed or damaged by water that ran six-feet deep down Main Street. The college, on slightly higher ground, was unscathed except for a house that the flood deposited on the football field. The campus became the center of disaster relief. Student dormitories were opened to 2,400 evacuees, and the college cafeteria served 386,000 free meals in the ensuing months.[17]

"A First-Rate College"

Eyring's three immediate successors, Bruce Hafen, Joe Christensen, and Steve Bennion, each moved Ricks along the path to becoming what Hafen called "a first-rate college." Like Eyring, each accepted two-year status and focused on growing enrollments and program quality.

During the trio's combined twenty-year term, from 1978 to 1997, Ricks became the country's largest privately owned junior college.

In addition to student body growth, the most outwardly visible success came in intercollegiate athletics. The football team finished second in the nation among junior colleges in 1981 and 1986. Men's and women's teams in a half-dozen other sports consistently enjoyed Top 3 rankings. The women's cross-country program in particular dominated its competitors, winning seven straight national titles.[18] Less quantifiable but equally notable progress came in the performing arts. Ricks was renowned for its symphony orchestra, choirs, dance teams, and theater groups, achieving with freshmen and sophomore students a level of quality comparable to that of four-year schools.

The great administrative challenge of this period was enrollment management. A post-baby boom demographic trough in the mid-1980s required a 20 percent tuition reduction to maintain the 6,000-student level reached under Eyring. But the price reduction worked, it turned out, too well. By 1988, the demographic tide had turned, and the board placed a 7,500-student cap on enrollment to prevent the college from exceeding its physical capacity. The next year the college administration began to explore screening mechanisms for what had been, since its founding a century before, an open enrollment institution, requiring just a high school degree and willingness to commit to the school's code of conduct.[19]

Initially, those mechanisms penalized only latecomers: the new-student application deadline was moved, first from August to May and then from May to March. When that proved insufficient to keep the rapidly expanding applicant pool below 7,500, qualification-based screening became necessary. In response to a charge from the board to continue serving "regular" students (that is, graduates not necessarily from the top of their high school classes), the school implemented a mixed system of merit-based and random selection. The top half of the entering cohort was chosen according to academic and other personal qualifications. After the elimination of candidates with very poor academic records from the remaining pool, everyone in it was placed on hold. Then the incoming class was filled by random selection from this hold pool.[20]

When word of a Ricks College admissions "lottery" reached Salt Lake, the board mandated some other approach. Though its members were reluctant to see selectivity become part of Ricks College's DNA, they felt even greater concern about leaving admissions decisions to chance. In response, a new system was devised, by which students in geographic areas of low church membership received preference in getting a Ricks educational and cultural experience. This benefited applicants from regions such as the eastern United States, where a Mormon might have been the only student of that faith in his or her high school. In addition, some students were admitted on condition that they begin in winter semester or during one of the summer terms. The burgeoning applicant pool, however, made it impossible to avoid merit-based selection. In the mid-1990s, Ricks began turning away more would-be students than it admitted, and those who got in looked increasingly less "regular." In the ten years after 1987, the average ACT score went from 18 to 23, and the high school grade point average from 2.7 to 3.4.[21] College administrators and members of the board felt the pain of denying applicants of good character and church standing. They also worried about academic elitism.

Enrollment innovation continued around the margins. The school developed a "fast track" program in 1997. High school students were encouraged to take Advanced Placement or community college courses in anticipation of coming to Ricks, where they could graduate with their associate's degree in two traditional semesters plus one or more summer terms. For every student who did so, another could be admitted within the 7,500-student cap. The goal was to have 3,000 students staying for the summer, in the spirit of the old Ricks Academy summer school and Harvard's year-round operation during World War II. However, course offerings were limited by faculty vacations, making the value of studying in the summer less than advertised.[22]

The board responded to the increased demand by raising the enrollment ceiling first to 8,250 and then to 8,600.[23] That required the appropriation of funds for both additional faculty and new facilities. The members of the board were glad, though, to be investing in an institution rooted in serving freshman and sophomore college students. The educational return on that investment was high relative to what most universities were delivering, thanks to Ricks College's operational efficiency.

Cost effectiveness qualified the college . . . for an expansion of its student body, which had the dual benefit of creating more educational opportunities and preventing academic elitism.

That efficiency derived from Ricks's maintaining its designated place on the higher education ladder in the latter half of the twentieth century. Especially in the two decades after World War II, the college grew bigger and more complex, allowing both its academic departments and its intercollegiate teams to become more specialized. But after a brief flirtation with four-year status, it remained focused on first- and second-year college students, as shown in Table 10.1. It also kept its instructional costs from creeping up, partly by eliminating faculty salary distinctions. That cost effectiveness qualified the college,

TABLE 10.1 Ricks College Evolution, 1972-1996

New Traits	Implications
Return to "roots"	Increased practical training options Decreased academic prestige
Elimination of faculty salary distinctions	Lower salary costs Decreased recruiting incentives Economic equality among the faculty
Enrollment expansion and summer enrollment experiments	More students served Access for "regular" students

in the minds of board members, for an expansion of its student body, which had the dual benefit of creating more educational opportunities and preventing academic elitism.

Through careful management of its DNA—or what Hal Eyring called "staying close to its roots"—Ricks College maintained the confidence of the board and the satisfaction of its growing student body. There were some among the students, faculty, and alumni who continued to long for four-year college status. Each Ricks College president, though, dutifully discouraged such thoughts. That was the instruction of the members of the board, who, though their oversight of Ricks's sister institutions, Brigham Young University and BYU-Hawaii, appreciated the high costs of the traditional university DNA.

PART THREE

Ripe for Disruption

If the cultural level of Castalia were compared with that of the country at large, it became apparent that the two were by no means approaching each other; rather, they were moving apart in a deeply troubling way. The more cultivated, specialized, overbred that Castalian intellectuality became, the more the world inclined to let the Province be and to regard it not as a necessity, as daily bread, but as a foreign body. . . . Without fully grasping the situation, people on the outside attributed to Castalians a mentality, a morality, and a sense of self which was no longer viable in real, active life.[1]

Observation of Joseph Knecht
The Glass Bead Game, by Hermann Hesse

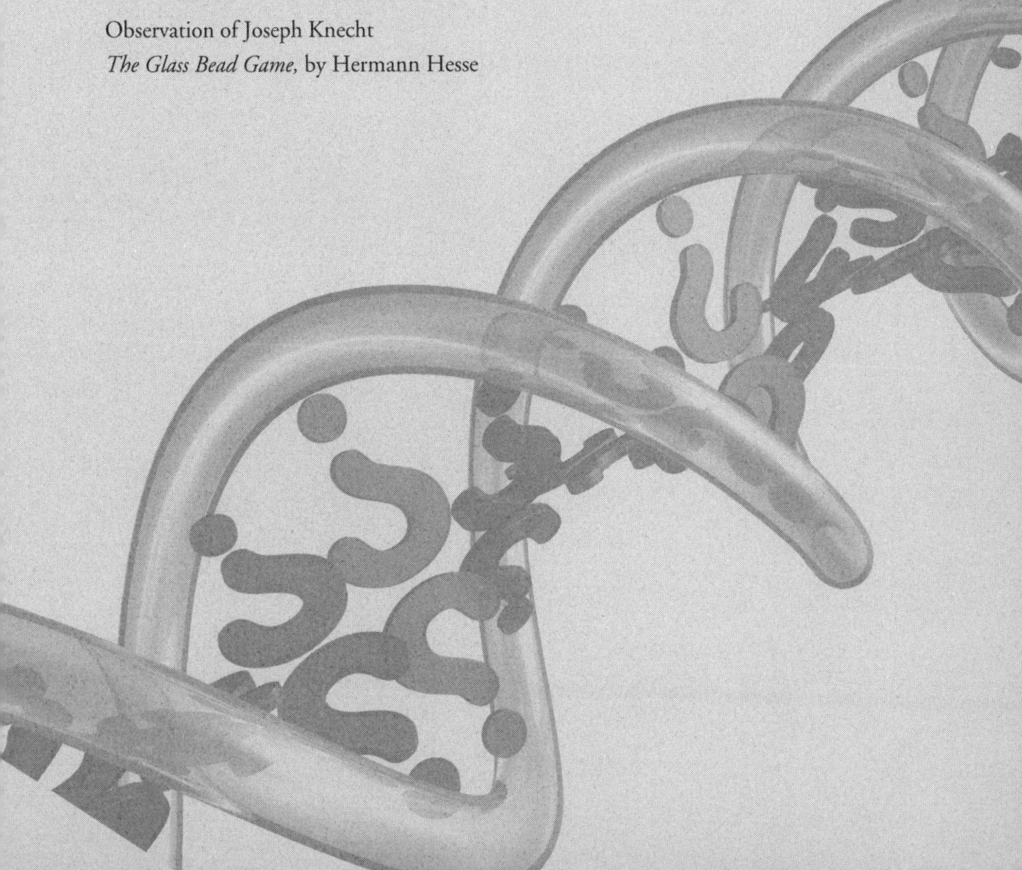

Chapter 11

The Weight of the DNA

When Nathan Pusey stepped down hastily from Harvard University's presidency in 1970, the university had an able successor in the wings, a captain capable of riding out sea change. Derek Bok had been dean of the law school for just three years, but he had already distinguished himself as a thoughtful scholar and steady leader. Like Pusey he was a non-Bostonian, born near Philadelphia. Unlike Pusey—and any president in the preceding three hundred years—he had graduated from a college other than Harvard; Bok was a Stanford undergraduate. But he was tailor-made for Harvard in the 1970s, in many ways Pusey's personality foil: worldly, forward looking, invariably diplomatic. Trained in the adversarial system and seasoned by law school administration, he brought much-needed mediation and diplomacy skills to a fractionating university. He also had an approachability that Pusey lacked. Students could see him driving his VW Beetle around Cambridge and engage him on the basketball court.[1] Faculty would come to appreciate his efforts to reason with them in terms they understood.

In fact, the university Bok inherited was not in crisis. The confrontational demonstrations of 1969 were not a harbinger but the last gasp of a pivotal yet aberrational decade. Though Harvard would remain politicized for most of the ensuing decade, the campus soon resumed relatively normal operations. Bok was blessed to inherit one Faculty of

Arts and Sciences (FAS) dean, John Dunlop, and to appoint another, Henry Rosovsky, who proved to be able academic administrators and diplomats. Also, students and employees alike were the wiser for their unpleasant experiences. When, in April 1972, two dozen black students broke into and occupied Massachusetts Hall, site of Bok's office, he let them remain until they willingly dispersed, six days later.[2]

The confrontational demonstrations of 1969 were not a harbinger but the last gasp of a pivotal yet aberrational decade.

The more persistent legacies of the 1960s were an economic hangover and a university community steeped in individualism. Bok adapted to the fiscal realities of high inflation and a moribund stock market by controlling costs, including faculty salaries, while steadily raising tuition. He also added staff to the traditionally lean central operations of the university, freeing up more of his own time for strategic activity. He excelled particularly as a communicator of vision. While presiding over the university over the next twenty years, he would be a prophetic voice not only to Harvard but to higher education as a whole. His advocacy tools included both policy decisions and public missives. It was no longer possible to control Harvard in the managerial sense, but Bok accomplished much among his complex community of scholars, students, and alumni by way of persuasion.[3]

He consistently advocated three main causes: instruction, diversity, and social engagement. Instructional advances made on his watch included a new core curriculum (the "Core") to replace the old General Education. In creating the Core, Bok leaned heavily on his FAS dean, Henry Rosovsky, a respected economist and capable negotiator who helped win widespread support from the faculty.[4] Unlike the Redbook, the major goal of the new Core was not to ensure a common grounding in knowledge and values but rather to impart common capabilities for acquiring knowledge. This was consistent with Bok's view that the way things are taught matters more than what is taught.[5]

[Bok] consistently advocated three main causes: instruction, diversity, and social engagement.

Openness to specialized rather than cross-disciplinary curriculum produced two practical benefits. One was a broad range of Core courses—350, ultimately—created by faculty who drew from their individual disciplines. Another was senior faculty participation. Ninety percent of Core courses were presided over by senior professors who welcomed the opportunity to teach subjects in which they were expert. Bok further promoted high-quality instruction through curriculum committees that set course standards and via tenure decisions that required serious consideration of teaching ability.[6] He also created a university center for teaching innovation; at his retirement in 1991, the university named the center for him.

On the second front, gender and racial diversity, Harvard made as much progress in Bok's two decades in office as it had in his predecessors' combined century of oversight. The university's soaring prestige produced larger applicant pools, allowing Harvard to recruit minority and female professors and students without lowering standards of merit. No quotas were set for faculty hiring, but a kind of voluntary affirmative action opened doors for blacks and women among the professoriate. Student diversity likewise increased. One of Bok's first moves was to raise the number of female undergraduates by 50 percent; he also oversaw the adoption of gender-blind financial aid policies and concluded a merger agreement with Radcliffe College, Harvard's sister institution.[7]

In addition to promoting diversity, Bok advocated social responsibility and public service, not only in the local community and nation, but worldwide. By the end of his presidency, 60 percent of Harvard College students were engaged in some form of public service.[8] Both undergraduates and students in the professional schools were hearing more in the classroom about ethics and personal conduct. Bok also set Harvard on the road to being more international. He oversaw expansion of the Kennedy School of Government, which increasingly trained foreign government leaders, and the creation of academic programs and research centers addressing such issues as AIDS, poverty, and international security. By the late 1990s, Harvard would have more foreign visiting scholars than any other university.[9]

Harvard's undergraduates were not, however, majoring in international studies or engaging in more international internships, two Bok proposals that the faculty voted down, along with a plan to expand the college to admit more foreign students.[10] Resistance to these proposals evidenced the challenge that even a seasoned and well-respected president faced in leading Harvard beyond the limits of its established preferences and patterns.

Internal Strains

Despite their wide regard for Bok, the faculty over whom he presided were increasingly distanced from his broad university initiatives. For many, the choice to give little attention to causes beyond their own discipline and department was as much a matter of necessity as of preference. The organizational systems that controlled the faculty's professional lives rewarded—and even required—a self-preservation approach to their work. The fight for survival began in graduate school, where the average time to conferral of a Ph.D. was more than nine years and the failure rate as much as 50 percent (compared with 5 percent in law and medicine). For the lucky survivors, the odds of being hired and ultimately tenured at Harvard were low. With the emphasis on scholarly merit, every hiring search became a global one, designed to bring the most-renowned researcher in each field to Cambridge. In a reversal from the A. Lawrence Lowell days, when being an insider conferred an advantage, an internal candidate might reasonably see his or her past commitment to Harvard as a liability. Across the Faculty of Arts and Sciences, three times as many job offers went to outsiders as to insiders. In the Department of History, no internal candidate received tenure for nearly forty years.[11]

At other schools, the star system of faculty recruitment depended on outsized compensation packages, with sought-after newcomers winning pay and scholarly perks in excess of those enjoyed by many faithful old-timers. Bok successfully defended against such inequality by keeping Harvard professors at least on par with their disciplinary peers at other institutions; to this end, the university significantly increased faculty compensation in the 1980s. But salaries still differed greatly across departments. For example, physical scientists made more than professors in the humanities. And the star system couldn't be entirely resisted; standard pay scales for junior faculty ultimately gave way to individual salary negotiations.[12] Pay differentials inevitably reinforced the primacy of research and publication over other forms of contribution. Because higher pay went to those with stronger research credentials, teaching and administrative service to the institution could be seen as financial and even career-threatening liabilities.

Differences in compensation created tensions not only among the faculty but also between the faculty and the administration. With Harvard now a billion-dollar-a-year operation undergirded by a $5 billion endowment, Bok needed professional executives to help him manage its activities and assets. Given the limited capacity of the university to produce such executives from within, it had to recruit them away from jobs in the for-profit sector. Faculty members who sensed their own greater earning potential in the outside world naturally resented administrative pay packages running into hundreds of thousands dollars per year (or, in the case of endowment fund managers, millions). Sensitive to those feelings and to faculty resentment of management intrusions into their affairs, Bok carefully grew the administration at a rate slower than that of the university as a whole during his second decade in office.[13]

A Voice of Warning

In his final years as president and even more upon retirement, Bok became a prophetic voice not only to Harvard but to the higher education community as a whole, advocating change in a way reminiscent of his influential predecessor Charles Eliot. The late 1980s and early 1990s saw rising dissatisfaction with the nation's colleges and universities. With the world in political turmoil, the economy flat, and tuition up, many critics asked why higher education seemed to have lost its sense of social responsibility.

Bok took the issue head-on in his 1988–1989 annual report. He cited a 50 percent decline in public confidence in higher education and referenced a host of critical books, many authored by academics. These missives bore titles such as *The Closing of the American Mind: How Higher Education has Failed Democracy and Impoverished the Souls of Today's Students.*[14] Though Bok decried "flamboyant rhetoric" and "assertions of fact that are flatly wrong," he also warned against "los[ing] sight of the elements of truth in most of the criticisms, truths that even successful universities need to ponder for their own improvement."[15]

Bok became a prophetic voice not only to Harvard but to the higher education community as a whole, advocating change in a way reminiscent of his influential predecessor Charles Eliot.

Among those elements of truth, he felt, were valid concerns about undergraduate instruction. On the one hand, Harvard undergraduates gave the vast majority of their courses passing or better grades. Seventy percent rated the Core "superb," "excellent," or "good," and 80 percent gave those marks to their elective courses and tutorials. But Bok felt the results could have been better. The tendency of senior faculty to avoid undergraduate courses represented one lost opportunity. So did a culture of tolerance for poor teaching, which was rarely confronted. The problem stemmed not only from collegial deference but also from a lack of data on instructional quality. Without broadly accepted measures of what it meant to teach well, subpar performance was hard to address.[16]

Another university challenge was divided attention and, in some cases, divided loyalty. What Clark Kerr, legendary architect of the California higher education system, called the multiversity placed a host of burdens on its faculty: teaching; publishing original research; writing grant proposals and student recommendations; serving on curriculum, hiring, and tenure committees; managing programs; hosting visitors; traveling to other campuses and to academic conferences.[17] In addition to these essential functions, Harvard increasingly sponsored worthy activities that presented potential distractions from its primary mission. For example, many faculty members participated in professional programs sponsored by individual schools and departments; by 1990, 60,000 business executives, newly elected politicians, high school students, and other nontraditional learners were served by such programs. Other university-sponsored programs provided training and expert advice to governmental bodies, foreign universities, and business corporations.[18]

Harvard also gave its faculty one business day per week for outside activities. Many devoted this day to university-related work, such as research, or to public service. Others, though, used it for paid consulting activities that bore little or no relation to scholarship or teaching. Travel became both an educational and a financial drain on the university. There was a Princeton quip that Harvard's professors were like the Strategic Air Command—one-third of them airborne at all times. Expressing regret for the need to impose external control, Bok in 1990 recommended that deans require faculty members to formally account for all of these outside activities.[19]

With so much entanglement in the world beyond the campus, a degree of commercial and even mercenary behavior inevitably crept in. It helped that Harvard was more conservative than many universities in its guidelines for faculty participation in the financial upside of their research discoveries; those who wanted to get rich tended to leave for the private sector. But, thanks to the one-day-per-week policy, it was still possible to lead a kind of economic double life. The university's general counsel, for instance, was surprised by a law school faculty member's response to his request for an opinion on a legal matter. The law professor refused to help on the grounds that the university couldn't afford his standard billing rate.[20]

In addition to calling for better teaching and a tighter focus on the central mission of the university, Bok raised a voice of warning about what he termed "imposed political orthodoxy." He deplored the pressure placed on graduate students and junior faculty to conform to the views of the senior faculty who controlled their professional fates. Students faced a similar risk: to disagree with a professor's opinion was to put one's grade in jeopardy. Bok noted the irony that academic freedom, once threatened by forces external to the university, now faced its most serious risks from within.[21]

[Bok] deplored the pressure placed on graduate students and junior faculty to conform to the views of the senior faculty who controlled their professional fates.

In fact, the increase in Harvard's racial and gender diversity had not been matched by an increase in social and political tolerance. As political science department member James Q. Wilson noted in 1972, "the list of subjects that cannot be publicly discussed [at Harvard] in a free and open forum has grown steadily."[22] Bok, to his credit, resisted pressure to adopt a code of speech narrower than the First Amendment, as had been done at some universities, where political correctness became enshrined in formal policy. But he could do little to help the junior scholar trying to advance an unpopular thesis or the student whose expressions of personal values at odds with the class norm resulted in ridicule.

Nor could Bok do much to stop infighting among faculty members who attacked one another over competing scholarly theories. "Critical studies" proved particularly divisive. Especially in literature and law, a new, more diverse generation of faculty questioned the intellectual underpinnings of past scholarship in their fields. These scholars challenged the great books and the legal precedents of Western civilization as products of politics—attempts by wealthy, white males to dominate less powerful classes and cultures. Bok's law school became a battleground between the "Crits" and traditional "Legal Realists," who sparred over their polar ideologies throughout his presidency.[23]

THE RISK OF SCHOLARLY DISENGAGEMENT

Bok's warnings about "truths that even successful universities need to ponder for their own improvement" echoed those of Hermann Hesse spoken fifty years earlier through his fictional scholar, Joseph Knecht. Confronting his Castalian colleagues on the need for greater social engagement, Knecht declared:

> The average Castalian may regard the man of the outside world, the man who is not a scholar, without contempt, envy, or malice, but he does not regard him as a brother, does not see him as his employer, does not in the least feel that he shares responsibility for what is going on outside in the world. The purpose of his life seems to him to be the cultivation of the scholarly disciplines for their own sake . . .
>
> Granted that every one of us brothers of the Order knows that our supreme and most sacred task consists in preserving the intellectual foundation of our country and our world. That foundation has proved to be a moral element of the highest efficacy, for it is nothing less than the sense of truth—on which justice is based, as well as so much else. But if we examine our real feelings, most of us would have to admit that we don't regard the welfare of the world, the preservation of intellectual honesty and purity outside as well as inside our tidy Province, as the chief thing.[24]

Genetic Constraints

Bok's exhortations were laudable and not without effect. But by the time he assumed the presidency, in 1971, most of the things he lamented twenty years later were already beyond his control, natural and all but immutable products of the university's DNA and the bigger-and-better tendency. Instruction, for example, had been structurally at risk ever since Eliot returned from Germany with his vision of having everything at its best. When Eliot overlaid the German-inspired graduate schools and specialized scholarship on the English-style college, the curriculum inevitably began to narrow and faculty interest in undergraduate instruction to wane. The academic freedom championed by Lowell in some cases had the unintended effect of reinforcing these trends; there was a temptation to see the teaching of undergraduates as a fetter on scholarly freedom. The tendency to neglect teaching grew exponentially when merit-conscious James Conant introduced up-or-out tenure, based foremost on scholarship. Teaching took still more hits with the externally funded research and outside consulting activities Conant pioneered. All roads seemed to lead away from the undergraduate classroom.

These teaching-related problems, as well as the spread and splintering of the multiversity, were exacerbated by Pusey's introduction of big-time fundraising to the system. The new money flowed disproportionately to academic specialists in commercially relevant fields. Competition for financial resources increased among both individual faculty members and departments. In this intensely competitive scholarly system, to be student centered was to cede personal and institutional advantage.

By Bok's time, some scholars considered undergraduate education a diversion from a research university's central mission. That view could be seen in a story Bok told in his 1986 book *Higher Learning.* He reported getting some advice as Harvard's newly appointed president from an experienced man who "headed an academic institution of considerable reputation." This man asked rhetorically, "While you are still in your honeymoon period and people are reluctant to be critical, why not announce your intention to do away with Harvard College?" Doing so, this man reasoned, would

> acknowledge that teaching undergraduates has become an anachronism in the modern university. Professors are equipped to do research and to train their graduate students to do research. Teaching introductory economics to freshmen or European history to sophomores is a waste of talented scholars who should have no responsibilities to divert them from what they do uniquely well.[25]

As far-fetched as this proposal might sound, given that undergraduates comprised a third of Harvard's student body, Bok's presidential peer had a telling point. Like other research universities, Harvard operates two fundamentally different enterprises under a single corporate roof. The resources and activities required to produce world-class scholarly research bear little resemblance to those necessary for teaching undergraduates at an affordable cost. The same faculty can, if so directed, perform both functions. But a first-rate scholar is a tremendously expensive teacher. Moreover, the departmentalization of the university, though it serves the needs of scholars well, tends to produce narrow curriculum; it also leads to high coordination costs in extra-departmental activities, such as the creation of general education programs. Absent countervailing investments in residential houses, tutors, and specially funded curriculum development projects such as those Harvard makes, the result is an undergraduate learning experience of a quality not justified by its high cost.

Like the teaching challenges, the politicization of the university that concerned Bok was also a product of steady evolution. It went all the way back to John Leverett's time, the early 1700s, when Harvard threw off the intellectual shackles of Puritanism. Hard-headed rationality allowed Hollis Professor of Mathematics and Natural Philosophy John

Winthrop to discover the true, natural causes of earthquakes. Such open-mindedness was and is essential to the advancement of science. But the realization that past scholars had attributed too much to divine design produced a skeptical reaction, a groundswell that through the succeeding centuries called into question not only the existence of God but of what Conant would describe as absolute values. Nathan Pusey, speaking at Harvard's divinity school, described the scholarly over-reaction: "Fearing to be victimized we are inclined not to believe at all."[26]

The gradual loss of shared values proved especially costly in the humanities, where knowledge advances via scholarly dialogue rather than the repeatable experiments of the natural sciences. In some academic departments, critically deconstructing the work of past scholars took precedence over contributing to the coherent advance of the discipline. Though there were broader social and intellectual forces at work, publication-based up-or-out tenure and the academic star system created a personal upside to deconstructive scholarship, which offered the advantage of novelty and thus publishability.[27] The growing importance the university placed on diversity also played a part. To the extent that diversity of viewpoints became prized above objectivity and the search for disciplinary consensus, it ceased to be an educational asset. The price of skeptical individualism was intellectually divided departments that failed to speak coherently either to students or to the world at large.[28] By the 1990s neither Bok nor any of his peers had the power to turn this tide by mere exhortation.

The gradual loss of shared values proved especially costly in the humanities, where knowledge advances via scholarly dialogue rather than the repeatable experiments of the natural sciences.

What was truly genetically constrained, though, was the university's cost. The billion-dollar operating budget was one way to measure Harvard's growing financial appetite. Another was undergraduate tuition, which rose from $2,800 to $14,860 during Bok's twenty years.[29] That fivefold increase, which occurred during a period when the stock market rose by just three times, provoked questions and criticism. Bok pointed out that Harvard's tuition covered less than the full cost of education and that need-blind aid reduced the actual price paid by many students. He also noted that, notwithstanding the high cost of enrollment, applicant demand was steady and few graduates complained about the return on their investment of a Harvard education.[30]

But there was little hope for containing tuition increases. Harvard's $5 billion endowment helped close the gap between what it cost to educate a student and what the student paid. Still, by the end of Bok's presidency, tuition covered just 20 percent of the university's $1 billion-plus operating budget, a slightly lower percentage than when he took office.[31] Absent a spike in giving or in endowment investment returns, rising costs would require regular increases in tuition, the one fully controllable source of revenue.

The cost problem had genetic roots. It was one thing to have all at its best in Eliot's day, when academic disciplines were relatively few and the competition for faculty and students was limited to a handful of institutions in the northeastern United States. But as the frontiers of knowledge expanded and the competition to be "the best" took on global dimensions, the price of Eliot's vision skyrocketed. The growth in new obligations was largely beyond the university president's control. Entrepreneurial faculty regularly proposed new programs, often with support from specially cultivated donors. The administration faced three equally unpalatable choices: disappoint the faculty and their donors; leave the quality of the new programs to fate; or prepare to fund the new commitments at the level required to maintain the university's reputation. A university president who hoped to stay in the saddle said yes and then sought to raise new money.

The world's best faculty and students wanted increasingly more from Harvard. The Ivy Agreement spared the university the cost of multimillion-dollar coaching contracts and hundred-million-dollar sports complexes. But super-star faculty recruits required top-of-market pay packages, and even nonathlete prospective students expected comfortable living quarters, workout facilities, and activity centers.

Buildings of all types became more expensive. Much of the cost increase was driven by new information technology, yet that technology did little to increase the instructional productivity of the faculty. Classes were still taught mostly face to face, with student–faculty ratios little changed from those of Eliot's day. The buildings continued to sit largely idle through the long summer break introduced in early 1800s.

The bigger-and-better tendencies in the institution reinforced one another, in a kind of inflationary spiral. New academic programs, for example, predictably led to requests for new faculty, who needed new facilities in which to work. The upward cost pressure was reinforced not only by formal systems, such as salary scales, but by informal traditions. A newly tenured professor could expect not only an increase in pay but also preferences in teaching assignments and office selection. If that professor lacked a doctoral degree from Harvard, one was automatically conferred with the grant of tenure. The genetic preference for "the best" suffused Harvard's culture.

Public criticism of Harvard's cost of attendance would fade with the bull market of the 1990s. But the problems of instruction, faculty division and distraction, and politicization that Bok identified would continue to plague his successors. And, when the financial markets swooned in 2008, the cost problem would return with a force few imagined.

Chapter 12

Even at Harvard

The three presidents who succeeded Derek Bok—Neil Rudenstine, Larry Summers, and Drew Gilpin Faust—led Harvard through two starkly different financial seasons, one ebullient and the other catastrophic. The Rudenstine and Summers presidencies revealed as never before Harvard's financial might. During Rudenstine's term, from 1991 to 2001, Harvard reaped the benefits of an Internet-driven stock market. In 1994 the university's endowment stood at roughly $6 billion. In the succeeding six years, it soared to more than $19 billion.

In addition to the rising market, Harvard benefited from two institutional assets. One of them was Rudenstine's focused attention and skill in cultivating donors. Under his direction, the first Harvard-wide campaign netted $2.6 billion, raising an average of $1 million per day.[1] Another asset was sophisticated, aggressive fund management. Beginning in the early 1990s, Harvard Management Company, the university's investment arm, modified its strategy, shifting away from domestic stock and bonds and into less liquid but potentially higher-returning investment vehicles such as emerging markets, commodities, real estate, and private equity and hedge funds. The more aggressive investment strategy paid off handsomely. In the booming decade and a half that followed, the Harvard style of investment made the university both rich and an object of envy and emulation in the financial asset management industry.

Rudenstine put the money to good use, creating endowed chairs and increasing student financial aid. Both initiatives helped the university increase its preeminence in merit and diversity. He also acquired 350 acres of blighted but strategically located land across the river from Cambridge in Allston, with a fifty-year, multibillion-dollar vision of nearly doubling the footprint of the university.

Harvard's endowment continued to swell under Rudenstine's successor, former U.S. Treasury Secretary Larry Summers; even without a major fundraising campaign, spectacular investment returns increased the endowment by 50 percent in five years. Summers laid plans for the first project in the Allston development, a 500,000-square-foot life sciences laboratory complex. He also launched a review of undergraduate general education, the core curriculum that Bok and his colleagues developed in the 1970s. He aimed to inject into the curriculum more science (especially biology), math, and international content. He also wanted to make general education courses more cross-disciplinary and applied.

A New General Education Program

Summer's presidency ended abruptly in 2006, before either the Allston science complex or the general education overhaul came to fruition. Interim president Derek Bok made the latter project the focal point of the year he served before Drew Faust's appointment. The task force of seven professors and two students he convened proposed a new general education curriculum requiring students to take at least one course in each of eight subject areas. Two of those areas addressed the sciences, and two others issues of globalization, the subjects Summers had considered critical when he undertook the revision of the Core. All of the courses, the task force hoped, would be relevant to "things [students] will be doing for the rest of their lives."[2]

The aspiration to engage real-world tasks and issues was just one way in which the new general education proposal addressed concerns raised by both Bok and Harry Lewis in their 2006 books, *Our Underachieving Colleges* and *Excellence Without a Soul.*[3] In fact, the task force specifically noted having drawn from those books. Bok's influence in particular could be seen in the task force's call for student-engaging pedagogies such as case studies and activity-based learning. Both Bok and Lewis may have taken satisfaction in the task force's recognition of the importance of values. Their final proposal offered hope even for persons of faith. "Religion," it observed, "has historically been, and continues to be, a force shaping identity and behavior throughout the world. Harvard is a secular institution, but religion is an important part of our students' lives." As evidence, a footnote proffered this data: "Ninety-four percent of Harvard's incoming students report that they discuss religion 'frequently' or 'occasionally,' and seventy-one percent say that they attend religious services." The task force suggested that the eight major subject areas include one called "Culture and Belief" and another called "Ethical Reasoning."[4]

Like the Redbook, the task force's proposal passed through a faculty legislative approval process that tempered its ambitions, including some of the emphasis on moral values. However, the faculty overwhelmingly approved the revised proposal. Thanks to involvement of multitudinous constituencies, Bok and his colleagues succeeded in creating something potentially better than what the old Core had become and perhaps even approaching the high intellectual and philosophical standards of the Redbook.

The Harvard Endowment's Ups and Downs

By the time Drew Faust took office in July 2007, the endowment had ballooned to $35 billion. Her greatest financial challenge was not in making ends meet but rather in defending the endowment's gargantuan size. It exceeded Yale's, the second largest, by 50 percent and dwarfed by three times the endowment of the entire California system of ten research university campuses.[5] Given the growth of Harvard's operations during the Rudenstine and Summers years, and the future growth to which they committed the university in Allston, the unprecedented success of the endowment was a godsend. On the other hand, with Education Secretary Margaret Spellings's 2006 call for greater accountability in basic college education, it was an inopportune time for a tax-exempt research university to be so conspicuously affluent.

In her first commencement address, Faust defended the size and uses of the endowment as being commensurate with the scope of the university's mission. Citing endowment revenues as the source of one-third of Harvard's $3 billion operating budget, she declared, "If the endowment were smaller, we would have to do less—less research, less teaching, at a lesser level of quality—or we would have to generate more income from other sources—tuition increases or external funding." Arguing that "in a world where knowledge is increasingly important, our accountability to the future challenges us to do not less, but ever more," she cited the importance of the university's commitment to activities such as stem cell research and "seiz[ing] the Allston opportunity."[6]

With Education Secretary Margaret Spellings's 2006 call for greater accountability in basic college education, it was an inopportune time for a tax-exempt research university to be so conspicuously affluent.

Faust further extolled the virtues of the model of "voluntary accountability" of traditional universities and colleges. "In an era in which large and important financial organizations have been known to disappear over a weekend," she ventured, "universities are durable, proven institutions, here for the long term."[7] What Faust and many of her colleagues didn't know at the time was their own organization's vulnerability to precisely the forces that had caused the first few of a wave of financial institutions to disappear. Harvard's endowment was not only invested in complex instruments that would prove illiquid and overvalued in the ensuing market downturn, it had actually borrowed to make some of those investments.[8] Even its storied managers couldn't unwind the compromised positions fast enough to prevent a catastrophic $11 billion drop.

In the late fall of 2008, Faust's hypothetical smaller endowment, with its associated pressure to do less, became a painful reality. In fact, Harvard's 2007-era wealth, though jaw dropping in terms of financial assets, had always been much less impressive relative to the university's annual operating outlays. The university faced huge recurring expenses—salaries, student financial aid, maintenance of the physical plant—that could be cut only at a great cost in goodwill. It also was committed to new building projects, most notably the Allston science complex.

Even before the market collapse, the university had been living on the edge of its financial means, spending the same percentage of the endowment notwithstanding investment rates of return many times higher than historical averages. It had also used its premium credit rating to borrow for building construction. Thus, when the downturn came, there was little room for maneuvering, even after an increase in borrowing and in the endowment spending rate.[9] Schools heavily dependent on the endowment faced tremendous pressure. The Faculty of Arts and Science, which funded only 50 percent of its annual budget through tuition, research grants, and other non-endowment sources, faced an annual shortfall of nearly 20 percent, or $220 million.[10] The university froze salaries of faculty and non-union staff. It also slowed hiring and offered early retirement packages, which 500 employees accepted. That force reduction, though, proved insufficient; 275 others had to be laid off.[11]

As painful as these cuts were, the more publicly visible sign of the university's misfortune was the Allston development generally and the science complex in particular. Approved in response to rapid developments in fields such as stem cell research, construction on the science complex had begun without the identification of a major donor or other non-endowment funding sources. In February 2009, the university announced a slowdown of the project, with only the foundation to be completed pending a decision of when and how to proceed.[12] Members of the Allston community complained bitterly about the hundreds of acres of vacant Harvard-owned property, an eyesore and a safety hazard that seemed to mock the university's pledge of urban renewal.

For observers of university DNA, the Allston project is similarly symbolic. Even Harvard sometimes struggles to bear the full cost of the Harvard model. It is one thing for a university to have everything at its best. It is another to fund such a strategy in both good times and bad.

It is one thing for a university to have everything at its best. It is another to fund such a strategy in both good times and bad.

Harvard's Recovery

Harvard, like the financial markets, will recover. President Faust and her colleagues face, in her words, the need to "resize and reshape."[13] The task will take time, given the structural rigidity of its financial deficit. The costs associated with the university's 16,000 employees and 600 buildings[14] will be difficult to reduce further. Financial aid to students can be cut, but, though the market would bear more, raising tuition faster than 3 or 4 percent per year is politically inadvisable. Meanwhile, debts must be paid and open projects, such as the Allston science center and the new general education curriculum, funded and finished. As in the case of the economy at large, the university's recovery may be slow.

Yet Harvard has passed through tight financial straits before, notably in A. Lawrence Lowell's early years and in James Bryant Conant's era of Depression and war. Positive signs in the Faust era appeared as early as the fall of 2009. Donations fell in the 2008–2009 academic year, but only by 10 percent. Thanks in part to federal stimulus money, sponsored research rose by 7 percent.[15] Meanwhile, resourceful academic leaders turned their considerable powers of intellect to cost reduction.[16]

Even with the losses of 2008, Harvard's endowment remains huge relative to those of other institutions; by the summer of 2010, it had risen to $27.4 billion.[17] Its brand is still preeminent. Harvard remains the leading choice for the world's most gifted students and faculty. It is also the site of cutting-edge instructional innovations, as we'll see in coming chapters. As in Lowell's and Conant's eras, the university is emerging from the 2008 crisis stronger and more focused.

Other elite private universities and colleges are likewise rebounding. The market demand for positions in their entering classes and on their faculties is so great that no reasonable increase in tuition or paring of salaries will affect their ability to attract the brightest students and scholars. Regulators may continue to call for greater accountability and access, but the power of educational brands such as Yale and MIT and Williams will insulate the elite private schools at least from economic pressure. However, other schools, including some top-tier public research universities, have bigger problems.

Chapter 13

Vulnerable Institutions

In early 2010, the University of California, part of what has been called "the greatest system of public learning the world has ever seen,"[1] was in dire straits. Its flagship Berkeley campus, modeled by chancellor Clark Kerr after Harvard, faced a $1.2 billion gap in state funding for its 2010–2011 fiscal year.[2] Temporary furloughs of all employees, including professors, led to questions about whether Berkeley can maintain its status as the leading public research university.[3] A proposal to increase tuition by nearly a third triggered student protests, one of which turned violent.

The angry chants of those students had been prophesied in the 1960s by Kerr, then president of the UC system. Speaking by invitation at a series of lectures at Harvard, he said:

> Recent changes in the American university have done [undergraduate students] little good—lower teaching loads for the faculty, larger classes, the use of substitute teachers for the regular faculty, the choice of faculty members based on research accomplishments rather than instructional capacity, the fragmentation of knowledge into endless subdivisions. There is an incipient revolt of undergraduate students against the faculty; the revolt that used to be against the faculty *in loco parentis* is now against the faculty *in absentia.* The students find themselves under a blanket of impersonal rules for admissions, for

scholarships, for examinations, for degrees.... [They] want to be treated as distinct individuals.[4]

ACCESSIBLE EXCELLENCE

Reasons for optimism about Berkeley's future can be found in one of the institutions it most closely resembles, the University of Michigan. In Ann Arbor, home to the University of Michigan, the economic disruption manifested in 2008 began thirty years earlier, when a global energy crisis first revealed the vulnerability of the U.S. auto industry to Japanese competition. As the state of Michigan's auto-dependent economy reeled, its largest research university faced the need to innovate. In particular, it was forced to find ways to become more independent of state support while maintaining its commitment to state service.

By 2010, the University of Michigan, led by President Mary Sue Coleman, was receiving just 10 percent of its operating budget from the state. Yet in addition to maintaining world-class research activities, the university remained accessible to Michigan students, who comprised two-thirds of its student body and paid only a bit more than one-third of the out-of-state tuition price. These in-state students also had an even chance of being admitted, thanks to the university's 50 percent applicant admission rate.

Along with success in securing external research funding, Michigan's powerful alumni support, manifested in a $3.2 billion fundraising campaign that Coleman brought to a close in 2008, is key to the university's ability to provide accessible excellence to undergraduates. They enjoy a collegiate living experience similar to the one that Lowell envisioned. Ninety-eight percent of freshmen chose on-campus dormitory life. Ninety-six percent return for their sophomore year, and 84 percent graduate within five years. At any given time, one thousand Michigan undergraduates are participating in faculty-mentored research.[5]

Though Berkeley is likely to rebound, the future of many of California's other public universities is less certain. The genius of the California higher education system designed by Kerr in the 1960s was that it integrated, while keeping distinct, three different types of institutions: research universities, teaching universities, and community colleges. Through Kerr's plan, the brightest one-eighth of California high school graduates were guaranteed a slot at a University of California campus such as Berkeley or UCLA. Graduates in the top third of their classes could go to one of the state universities, which lacked Ph.D. programs and were thus more focused on undergraduate instruction. All high school graduates could attend a community college, with the promise, contingent on performance there, of transferring to a state university.[6]

The genius of the California higher education system designed by [Clark] Kerr in the 1960s was that it integrated, while keeping distinct, three different types of institutions: research universities, teaching universities, and community colleges.

To its great credit, the California system gave every high school graduate a reasonable shot at a college degree while keeping the costs of scholarly research and graduate programs limited to a relatively small number of University of California campuses (initially eight, ten as of 2010).[7] However, Kerr and his fellow designers underestimated the cost of nine state-supported research universities trying to become like Berkeley. At all ten institutions, instructional cost-per-student reflects the high price of giving professors time away from the undergraduate classroom for research and graduate instruction. Yet the relative returns on the State of California's investment in that research and graduate instruction vary. Berkeley can make a good case that its discoveries and stellar reputation justify the state's extra support. The small, lesser-known UC schools have a harder time doing so, though a remarkable fraction rank among the country's leading research institutions.

More significant for the California higher education system is the problem of twenty-three state universities that engage in many activities like those of the research universities, including granting master's degrees and producing scholarship. The burning question highlighted by 2008's downturn is not whether the great research universities, such as Berkeley and UCLA and Harvard, are cost-justified, but whether the less powerful ones, which comprise the vast majority, can continue as they have in the past. The schools most at risk are the more than 700 public and not-for-profit universities that grant graduate degrees but are not among the 200 elite research institutions identified by the Carnegie Foundation, the accepted arbiter of academic standing.[8] Michael Bassis of Westminster College has made the point trenchantly:

> It's likely that the elite institutions will find no shortage of families willing to pay large tuition bills so their children can reap the benefits of a prestigious degree. And the research programs and athletic teams of public flagship universities probably lend enough prestige to their degrees that they will continue to attract students whether or not their instructional systems change. But it's the community colleges, comprehensive public universities, and private colleges without national reputations—schools that enroll 95% of the 19 million students attending accredited institutions across the country—that may be the most vulnerable.[9]

The second- and third-tier schools are largely overlooked by the national media, little known except to those enrolled there or living nearby. They lack the power of large private endowments and the prestige needed to command high tuition rates. Yet though they possess no semblance of Harvard's wealth and reputation, these less prestigious universities' costs are structurally similar to the extent that they have pursued its bigger-and-better strategy. Their classrooms and other expensive physical facilities sit idle through long summer breaks. Their tenure-track faculty split time between research and teaching, effectively reducing their capacity to generate tuition revenue and increasing the institutions' organizational complexity and coordination costs.

These lesser-known schools compete among themselves, Harvard-style, for blue-chip scholars and students. Many also engage in expensive competitive efforts that Harvard does not. Intercollegiate athletics, a money-losing activity for all but a few of the largest universities, is the most visible example. Others include public relations campaigns to boost the university's image, along with outsized scholarships for a relatively small percentage of students whose high SAT scores help in the college-rankings battle.[10]

THE COSTS OF CARNEGIE LADDER CLIMBING

Having helped to architect the State of California's multi-tiered higher education system, Clark Kerr went on to become the first president of the Carnegie Commission. Hoping to make policy recommendations beneficial to America's already world-leading higher education sector, Kerr and his colleagues saw the need for a classification system, one that recognized the great diversity of U.S. institutions. It was they who created the Carnegie classification system, or ladder.

In the California system, Kerr had envisioned a ladder that students could climb—from an associate's degree at a community college to a bachelor's degree at a state university to a graduate degree at one of the California research institutions. It is a great irony that community colleges and state universities would attempt to use the ladder for their own climbs.

The costs of Carnegie climbing go beyond the loss of unique institutional identity and of focus on the constituencies, especially undergraduate students, that institutions were originally chartered to serve. There is also the risk that things easily measured secondhand, such as research funding, degrees granted, breadth of curricular offerings, and student selectivity, crowd out important intangibles, as noted in this 2005 report:

> The data used are all second-hand, and no attempt is made to measure the quality of what institutions do, as opposed to the mere quantity of it. Thus, though moving up the ladder is inevitably expensive, given the costs of scholarly research and granting advanced degrees, it may or may not produce greater value to students and society.[11]

These schools also suffer to varying degrees from the instructional quality problems of the large research universities. Their undergraduate students encounter more lectures than interactive learning experiences, more part-time and graduate student instructors than tenured professors.[12] The courses students take often lack clear connections to one another, to practical uses outside of the academy, or to enduring values. Because these aspiring research universities are both more expensive and less focused on undergraduate instruction than are community colleges and some for-profit educators, students and public policymakers increasingly see the latter as the better educational investment.

Genetic Makeover

These problems of cost and quality are produced not by mistake or happenstance but by design. The roots of the problems are genetic, and the DNA is fundamentally Harvard's. With few exceptions, the smaller and less prestigious universities aspire to be more like the elite research institutions. Referring to this influence, Henry Rosovsky, author of *The University: An Owner's Manual*, has said, "Our finest research universities . . . are the cutting edge of our national life of the mind. They determine the intellectual agenda of higher education. They set the trends."[13]

In emulating the research university model, the trend followers adopt policies and practices that provide de facto answers to a university's three most important strategic questions: (1) What students will we serve?, (2) What subject matter will we emphasize?, and (3) What types of scholarship will we pursue? For these emulators, the answers become (1) graduate students and elite undergraduates over ordinary college students, (2) myriad academic subjects rather than a focused set of practical ones, and (3) discovery research scholarship over more practical forms, such as showing how the discovers of others apply to practical problems or how they can be best taught to students.

The aspiring institutions learn about the policies and practices of the great ones not just secondhand, through published reports, campus visits, and professional interactions but by acquisition of personnel. Graduate students, produced at prestigious institutions in numbers greater than the need for new faculty there, inevitably take employment at less prestigious schools. So do aspiring career administrators, who hope that assuming leadership positions at smaller schools will qualify them for similar opportunities at larger ones. While these career ladder-conscious professors and administrators await a return to the big leagues, they go to work making their new institutions more like the ones from which they came.[14]

As evidenced at early Ricks College, the preferred model is well understood by even the smallest schools.[15] It is not only embodied in the Carnegie ladder and the elite research universities themselves but also encouraged by the standards of accrediting organizations, academic professional associations, publishers of university rankings, and philanthropic organizations. According to this model, getting better means what it did to Charles Eliot—having everything at its academic best. Applied training is dropped in favor of a broad range of scholarly disciplines. Graduate programs are created both to enhance prestige and to provide student assistants for research and teaching support. Faculty get time for research and are rewarded with tenure for doing it well. Full-time professors have doctoral degrees, and salaries are high enough to allow recruitment and retention of scholarly stars.

In this model, size also matters. Climbing the Carnegie ladder requires granting more bachelor's, master's, and doctoral degrees. Many states' funding schemes reward student body growth. For small schools, adding students also creates financial economies of scale (though only up to the point that new classrooms and faculty office buildings must be constructed). Bigger schools can also field stronger athletic teams, a favored cause of students and alumni and a powerful public relations tool.

The model holds tremendous sway in traditional higher education. Some private liberal arts and technical colleges persistently reject its genetic requirements, eschewing in particular graduate programs and faculty emphasis on scholarly research. But in the century and a half since Eliot declared, "We would have them all, and at their best," the bulk of colleges and universities have doggedly tried to make themselves over in Harvard's image. Starting in the late 1900s, institutions such as Ricks Academy, dedicated initially to preparing students for college, undertook the multistage conversion to "normal school," "state teacher's college," "state college," and finally "state university."[16] In the twentieth century, many technical schools and community colleges made the same slow but unrelenting series of moves up the Carnegie ladder. Often, politically

> *Significant problems arise when classification is seen as an adequate representation of an institution's identity or character. Colleges and universities are complex organizations that differ on many more dimensions than the handful of attributes used to define the [Carnegie] classification's categories . . . .*[17]
>
> —Alexander C. McCormick and Chun-Mei Zhao, Rethinking and Reframing the Carnegie Classification

In the century and a half since Eliot declared, "We would have them all, and at their best," the bulk of colleges and universities have doggedly tried to make themselves over in Harvard's image.

connected boosters facilitated the name changes in state legislatures. Always, the curriculum became more advanced; teaching and technical certificates, as well as associate's degrees, dwindled relative to bachelor's, master's, and doctoral degrees. The process has been called by those who lament the loss of basic workforce training "mission creep" or, with reference to its motivating force, "Carnegie creep."

Overstretched and Underfunded Schools

In addition to leaving the original patrons of technical schools and community colleges with fewer public education options, emulating Harvard and the other great research institutions has left many universities underfunded. Legislative grants of name and Carnegie status rarely come with commensurate increases in annual operating budgets. Still, the new university-level expectations have to be met. Satisfying accreditation requirements and Carnegie standards means hiring more Ph.D. faculty and giving them more time outside of the classroom for research. Because the Ivy Agreement typically fails to transfer with the Harvard DNA, there are also higher intercollegiate athletics expectations to meet. Meeting NCAA standards and winning entry into prestigious conferences means large outlays for athletic facilities, coaching staffs, scholarships, and travel. When these investments fail to produce offsetting financial returns,[18] the university has to find a way to close the gap.

Tuition revenues may grow via the admission of more students and price increases. But while the university label commands a modest premium, the newly promoted schools lack the prestige to charge anything like Harvard and the other elite institutions do. In fact, tuition increases sometimes prove the worst of both worlds—insufficient to cover new expenses but enough to drive some students to lower-cost alternatives.

Growing enrollments create a similar Catch-22. The additional students bring incremental revenue, both tuition dollars and, in the case of state schools, public funds. But those students have to be taught. In their first and second years, they can be herded into introductory classes in groups of hundreds. However, as they declare majors and proceed to more advanced offerings, class sizes inevitably shrink. Growth in the number of majors offered, a bigger-and-better tendency that Harvard has avoided but few of its emulators do, means that the larger student body is divided up into small, expensive-to-teach groups.[19]

In fact, the per-student cost of teaching can increase due to university-level standards for scholarly research and the associated reduced teaching loads. Tenure-track university professors teach fewer courses, by half or more, than do their community college counterparts. Particularly in the case of public institutions, enrollment-driven state funding mechanisms catch Carnegie ladder climbers on the horns of a dilemma: to generate more income the institution needs to admit more students, but to satisfy research expectations its professors need to teach less. Often, the solution is to offload the teaching to part-time faculty and graduate assistants and to let class sizes grow.

Almost inevitably, full-time faculty members make personal sacrifices to maintain the new teaching/research juggling act. Professors originally hired by a teaching-focused institution are reluctant to abandon students to lower-quality instruction or, worse, to see them unable to find the classes they need to graduate timely. These good-hearted professors are likely to fill the instructional gaps, new research responsibilities notwithstanding. Some are disadvantaged in these new responsibilities not only by lack of time but also by inadequate scholarly training. At ladder-climbing institutions, they risk becoming second-class citizens, though they may shoulder more than their share of the teaching load.

Elusive Prestige

Even as these institutions experience rising costs, declining quality of instruction, and faculty overwork, the hoped-for prestige of university status proves elusive. That is particularly true in the case of scholarship. The elite research universities continue to win a disproportionate share of article acceptances in the most prestigious academic journals. As more university professors submit papers to a largely fixed number of A-list periodicals, the individual success rate falls. Among those new publication aspirants are not only faculty from the burgeoning ranks of U.S. universities but also a growing body of international scholars. Junior professors at lesser known universities often are left to make the case to tenure committees that their publications in second-tier journals and presentations at minor conferences justify advancement.

Athletic competition likewise yields disappointing returns for most universities. Smaller schools find themselves joining conferences spread out across half a continent or more, requiring extensive travel. Athletic budgets swell not only with rising airfares but also with increased spending on scholarships and facilities. Financially beleaguered schools that propose cutting football, the most expensive program, typically face howls of protests from boosters and back down. Some add football teams, thinking that increased alumni interest and support will cover the cost.

The competition for standout students also comes at a high price. Students with the highest SAT and ACT scores can play the market for the highest bid, which inevitably rises over time. The best-credentialed students expect not only full-tuition scholarships but also money for books and living expenses; it isn't enough to make college free, students have to be paid to attend. Like the push for scholarly and athletic recognition, the effort to manage public image and rankings also proves to be an arms race that leaves all poorer but collectively no further ahead.

Like the push for scholarly and athletic recognition, the effort to manage public image and rankings also proves to be an arms race that leaves all poorer but collectively no further ahead.

Students have paid a price for this inter-university competition for Harvard-style prestige. Since the late 1980s, college tuition and fees have risen 440 percent, four times faster than inflation.[20] Notwithstanding the four-year designation of the institutions they attend, only 35 percent of students nationwide finish in that time frame. In fact, only 55 percent graduate within six years of starting college.[21] Those who do earn bachelor's degrees have a less than one-third chance of being deemed verbally and quantitatively literate, a percentage that is falling.[22]

The problem is that few of the universities that have adopted Harvard's ambitions can match its educational advantages. They are not able to limit their enrollments to the academically most gifted, full-time students, those well prepared for college and able to focus wholly on their studies. They cannot afford a residential house system with live-in tutors or small section supplements to large introductory courses. Nor is their prestige so great that their graduates can easily find places in high-paying jobs or high-quality graduate schools.

> *The model is broken and yet so much that we associate with a college education—that a degree requires four years of study and 120 earned credits, that undergraduate life is also about fraternities and teams and dorm life, and that a faculty member with a terminal degree, usually a PhD, is inherently the best educator—is becoming unsustainable. These assumptions and more have driven up the cost of educating students across higher education, and those costs are now excessive.*
>
> —Paul LeBlanc, president of Southern New Hampshire University

There is also the problem inherent to imitative competition. Even universities that can afford to compete Harvard-style must wrangle over the same limited pool of extraordinary students and scholars. This competition drives up the price of winning without increasing the number of institutional winners. College education gets more expensive, but it does not get better. Hence, universities are subject not only to financial exigency, but to the invective of the Spellings

Commission and other critics. Many state-sponsored institutions find themselves losing support in their state legislatures.

THE CHALLENGE TO KEEP THE STATES IN THE STATE UNIVERSITIES

Even the most dynamic institutions face challenges in overcoming the tendencies of traditional universities. It helps to recognize the dangers of Harvard imitation, as Arizona State's Michael Crow and Ohio State's Gordon Gee have done. But even institutions with these universities' commitment to broad student access and practical higher education face challenges to keeping their costs low and their student accessibility and legislative support high.

Though Arizona State's 2010 resident tuition remained relatively affordable—less than $8,000 per year for an incoming freshman—that price represented a nearly 20 percent increase over the year before. The hike was necessitated by a fall in state support of 26 percent between 2008 and 2010, putting that support at two-thirds of the 1999 level on an inflation-adjusted basis.[23] Ohio State held tuition constant from 2008 to 2010, at $8,406, thanks to the generosity of the state legislature and Gee's success in raising money and holding costs down. However, the university is starting to turn away more applicants: the admission rate fell from 73.7 percent in 2005 to 68.7 percent in 2009.[24]

Keeping quality high, costs low, and access broad will require changes to these institutions' DNA. Crow and Gee have undertaken changes such as streamlining organizational units and focusing them on socially relevant problems.[25] But, having already taken steps to cut $100 million from Ohio State's budget, Gee told his academic colleagues in 2009 that more prioritization—a change to the genetic predisposition to have everything at its best—would be necessary:

> When times are flush, we are apt to spread the wealth around like marmalade. But when resources are tight, our hand is forced, and we must make real, strategic decisions about

> academic direction, about programs for investment and disinvestment, and about how we meet today's enormous challenges. We must finally learn to say the word "no," a word rarely used in higher education.[26]

In addition to facing funding challenges, many institutions are also ripe for disruption by lower-cost providers of higher education. Following a common pattern, traditional universities have let their focus on the most elite students take them beyond the needs and preferences of ordinary ones. These ordinary students are of three types. One is the student who is paying more than he or she would like for a traditional university campus experience. Another is an educationally qualified nonconsumer, a would-be student who cannot afford to attend a traditional university but would embrace a less expensive alternative, even without the usual amenities. A third potential student is one who lacks the educational background to succeed in the typical university but might make it with special help. During the financial downturn that began in 2008, powerful new competitors to traditional universities began to turn their attention to these dissatisfied and left-behind college students.

Chapter 14

Disruptive Competition

For most universities, 2009 and 2010 were difficult years. Even those whose enrollments grew had to serve their new students on tighter budgets. In addition to financial pressure, there was new regulation. The Spellings Commission's 2006 calls for greater accountability stimulated and focused debate as Congress considered the reauthorization of the Higher Education Act, the main body of law through which the U.S. federal government funds higher education. In 2006, the reauthorization of the act was three years overdue. The delay reflected not only partisan politics but also dissatisfaction with the country's return on its higher education investment.

The terms of the reauthorization achieved in 2008, after fourteen temporary extensions, embodied only a portion of the regulatory measures the Spellings Commission recommended. Yet it created additional burdens of reporting and, for some universities, public shame. The most significant new performance-related regulation was a punitive one. The act requires the U.S. Department of Education to publish annual lists of the schools with the highest tuition rates and rate increases. These schools must report their plans for becoming more frugal. In addition, all schools must supply for publication standardized information including student profiles, tuition and expected living costs, average time to graduation, and graduation success rates.[1]

To the relief of traditional universities, the reauthorized act upheld the historical practice of letting schools and their accrediting bodies set their own standards and measures of educational performance. The Department of Education was prohibited from defining and ensuring learning outcomes. Traditional universities also received support relative to an emerging form of competition: the act allows accreditation bodies to hold online educators to the same standards they apply to other institutions.[2]

The Would-Be Academic Raider

Accreditation, though, is no longer the challenging barrier to online education innovators it once was. In the mid-1990s, when former junk-bond king Michael Milken joined Oracle's Larry Ellison in creating Knowledge Universe, the regional accreditation bodies' standards penalized online educators for their relative dearth of traditional curriculum, physical facilities, and full-time faculty.[3] Members of accreditation teams, many of them employees of traditional universities, not only subscribed to the Harvard bigger-and-better model, they also had justified concerns about the quality of online learning technology. To them, it looked the way early ultrasound technology did to General Electric, Siemens, and Phillips—not worthy and not worth investing in.

Milken and his colleagues, however, were among many who saw online technology as having the potential to transform higher education the way he had commercial banking, beginning in the 1970s. In those days, the banking sector fit the Spellings Commission's definition of a mature enterprise: risk averse, self-satisfied, and unduly expensive. The major banks and bond rating agencies assessed credit worthiness on the basis of physical assets and corporate reputation. Companies with large factories and customer bases could readily borrow money; others could not.

Milken recognized that the banks were concerned too much with apparent resources and too little with good business ideas.[4] He sensed that the source of economic productivity was shifting from hard assets and corporate reputation to managerial innovation and agility. He could also prove, down to the hundredth of a percentage point, that the risks of the opportunities he advocated were justified by the investment returns. Armed with this data, Milken raised money and loaned it to corporate "raiders" who bought undermanaged companies and ran them more efficiently. Though the cost to laid-off workers was high, and though Milken is remembered by many only for his criminal conviction, the junk bonds he pioneered revolutionized the financial markets and jump-started the growth of the American economy.[5] Milken showed the value of rewarding ideas rather than already established wealth. It was a disruptive innovation that required the banks and rating agencies to follow suit.

In the 1990s, Milken and others could see a similar pattern in higher education. Regional accreditation bodies, along with many students and employers, put more stock in impressive university campuses and reputations than on demonstrated learning. As a consequence, innovation was being stifled, costs were higher than necessary, and students were being underserved or locked out altogether.

The would-be disruptors of the 1990s failed to ignite a revolution in higher education of the kind Milken sparked in banking. One reason was that they lacked the capacity to prove, as Milken did with junk bonds, that lower-cost educational approaches such as online learning can yield results of comparable quality to those of traditional university study. Some learning outcomes can be measured, but the full effect of a higher education is hard even to define, let alone to quantify with the precision of a financial interest rate.

Even if Knowledge Universe and others could have pioneered compelling learning measures, they would have had to convince the accreditors to adopt those measures in lieu of traditional measure of educational quality. Only students attending accredited institutions can access federal grants and loans for higher education. Trying to sell college courses without a source of financing is like trying to sell cars for cash only—not impossible, but extraordinarily difficult.

Another reason for the failure to revolutionize higher education in the 1990s was online learning's technological immaturity. Many homes lacked Internet access, and data transfer speeds were several orders of magnitude slower than they would be a decade later.[6] Personal computers were likewise relatively slow and expensive. Also, online learning courseware was in its infancy, often resembling the computerized version of paper-and-pencil correspondence courses. To continue with the automobile analogy, launching an online education company in the late twentieth century was analogous to starting a rental car company one hundred years earlier, before the advent of Ford's mass production assembly line and the interstate highway system.

The dot-com boom that funded the education companies and their broadband networks produced a university endowment bonanza, as evidenced by the tripling of Harvard's endowment between 1994 and 2000.

Had everything else been in place—measures of learning, accreditation and financing, mature online technology—there was a fourth reason that the online education companies of the late 1990s would have had little chance of perturbing the incumbents. Those years were a halcyon period for traditional universities and colleges, due to favorable demographic and financial market trends. The dot-com boom that funded the education companies and their broadband networks produced a university endowment bonanza, as evidenced by the tripling of Harvard's endowment between 1994 and 2000. Coffers swelled, as did enrollments.[7]

A Level, High-Speed Playing Field

Today, however, the situation has changed. Accreditation has become more focused on learning outcomes and more accepting of online delivery. That is due partly to pioneering efforts by not-for-profit startups such as a Western Governors University (WGU), a Salt Lake City–based not-for-profit created in 1996 by the governors of nineteen western states.[8] WGU's path-breaking higher education model rests on a combination of two innovations. One is the use of online technology to allow students to learn at their own pace. The other is a competency-based approach to learning certification. WGU does not create curriculum or grant grades. Rather, its full-time faculty specify the things a student should know; they also develop reliable tests of that knowledge. WGU then licenses the best curricular materials from third-party publishers, and its mentors, who fill the role that faculty members do in traditional institutions, guide students as they prepare to pass the competency tests.

AN UNLIKELY PARTNERSHIP

In the early 1990s, two western governors formed a politically unexpected partnership in the cause of higher education. One, Colorado's Roy Romer, was a Democrat who would go on to chair the Democratic National Committee. The other, Utah's Michael Leavitt, was a Republican who would serve as Secretary of Health and Human Services in the cabinet of President George W. Bush. But the two had more in common than just governing adjacent western states. Both came from small rural towns, and both felt a passion for making higher education more broadly accessible. Leavitt, a technophile, was intrigued by the potential for offering college degrees via online learning technology in remote Utah communities. Romer, a licensed pilot and operator of a flight school, wanted to give working adults credit for what they were capable of doing, based on tests like the private pilot's license exam, rather than making them sit in classrooms for a specified number of hours. Both governors saw a coming crisis in public higher education, as recalled by Leavitt:

> Our motivation in building WGU was a belief that a time would come when states would be unable sustain the aggregate funding demands of public education, crumbling

infrastructure, and healthcare. Clearly, higher education would be a victim. Specifically, we believed that Medicaid would erode the states' capacity to subsidize the-brick- and-mortar, time-based model. Inevitably, we reasoned, states would be forced to raise tuition beyond the reach of the average student and/or they would begin limiting enrollment. In such an environment a state's long term economic prosperity would require a more efficient model that could deliver high quality at a lower cost and in a scalable way.[9]

Their combined political connections and bold vision of competency-based online degree programs allowed Romer and Leavitt to assemble a broad coalition of nineteen governors and business and philanthropic supporters including AT&T, IBM, Microsoft, Oracle, the Bill & Melinda Gates Foundation, and the Lumina Foundation. The institution they founded, Western Governors University, drew upon the talents of innovative higher education scholars and consultants, who helped WGU develop tests of students' competence.

At the time, winning accreditation for such a doubly innovative model of higher education seemed a long shot. But with the help of its sponsoring governors, WGU successfully urged accrediting bodies and the federal government to give it the benefit of the doubt in accreditation and in access to federal financial aid for its students. Its combination of pedagogical rigor and political backing carried the day.

WGU not only won accreditation but did so with an unprecedented four regional associations. It admitted its first applicant in 1999 and just over a decade later enrolled 20,000 students in all fifty states. One of the best represented of those states was Indiana, whose governor, Mitch Daniels, championed an articulation agreement guaranteeing graduates of the state's public community colleges admission to an entity called WGU Indiana. Though WGU continues to receive public and private grants, it fully sustains its educational operations on the basis of annual undergraduate tuition of $5,780.[10]

Like WGU, many for-profit online universities can now boast of regional accreditation and federal aid access. In fact, their struggle to overcome past accreditation barriers has given them an advantage in demonstrating learning outcomes. Such proof of learning was a leading agenda item of the Spellings Commission and is akin to the interest rate calculations that Michael Milken used to shake up the banking industry of the 1970s.[11] Going forward, increased insistence by accreditors and regulators on demonstrations of student learning will play to the online companies' strengths.

Disruptive Innovation

On two other dimensions—technology and wealth—current trends likewise favor online educators, particularly the for-profit ones. The increasing speed of Internet communication has been mirrored by enhancements in online instruction technology; online courses are getting demonstrably better, now equaling or exceeding the cognitive outcomes of classroom instruction. At the same time, the economic downturn that has forced cost cutting at traditional universities has given the financial edge to the for-profit educators, many of which have strong balance sheets and access to the capital markets.

ONLINE LEARNING 3.0: INDIVIDUALIZED, DATA DRIVEN, AND SOCIAL

The University of Phoenix, founded in 1976 to serve working adults, was among the leaders in applying many of the innovations now common in for-profit higher education. Among those are standardized courses focused on learning outcomes, year-round operation, and programs for faculty training and development. The University of Phoenix was also a pioneer in online education, beginning in 1989.

In 2010 Phoenix undertook another innovation: the creation of a new learning system. This software-based system has capabilities similar to those of commercial websites that infer what an individual Web surfer is likely to buy based on his or her online behavior. In addition to surveying a given student directly, Phoenix's new platform infers the ways that the student learns best, based on his or her interactions with course materials and performance in the course.

The system facilitates remedial learning opportunities when the student is struggling and enriched ones when the student is succeeding. It can also make recommendations to both student and instructor about the types of content and the instructional strategies likely to work best; for example, a student who learns better from video than text can be offered more of that learning medium. In addition, the system can connect students working on similar problems, allowing them to share experiences and learn from one another.

Online educators, for-profit and not, also enjoy access to a growing body of skilled instructors who know how to make the most of the medium, in terms of both learning quality and serving many students at once. Traditional universities' overproduction of master's and Ph.D. degree holders relative to their own needs for new faculty members has created a pool of qualified online instructors who are willing to work for a few thousand dollars per course.[12] By contrast, a tenured professor who teaches four or five courses per year and has no outside research funding may cost ten times that amount, on a per course basis.[13] The only way for such a professor to compete, costwise, is to teach hundreds of students at a time. The cost disparity may grow as English-speaking advanced degree holders in less developed countries join what is becoming a global online instructional workforce.

Online educators, for-profit and not, also enjoy access to a growing body of skilled instructors who know how to make the most of the medium, in terms of both learning quality and serving many students at once.

Adjunct instructors give the online educators two other advantages. Rather than receiving an annual salary, as full-time faculty at traditional universities do, online instructors are paid by the course. This means that the online university can match teaching supply to student demand—an instructor is hired, or contracted for, only when a class is likely to have enough students to generate an operating profit. Also, an online instructor's teaching performance is easily monitored, and an underperformer has no contractual right to further employment. Along with well-defined learning outcomes, the ability to cull ineffective instructors may be another reason why online courses have achieved average cognitive outcome parity with their face-to-face counterparts.

In addition to their instructional cost and quality advantages, the online educators have the benefit of lower physical facilities costs. They also enjoy the competitive advantage of being focused purely on student instruction. Rather than operating two enterprises, a scholarly solution shop and an instructional value-adding process, they organize their activities entirely around the latter. (See Table 14.1.) They have no graduate schools or scholarly activities to attend to. There are no traditional faculty departments, no tenured faculty, and no rank-related salary distinctions.

THE ONLINE COST ADVANTAGE

A bit of simple math highlights the problem for institutions practicing the traditional model of face-to-face instruction by full-time faculty members. Advanced degree-holding adjunct instructors teach online courses for less than $1,000 per credit hour.[14] These courses have been shown to achieve cognitive learning outcomes comparable to those of traditional classroom-based courses.[15] If thirty students are taught at once, the instructional cost per credit for each student is less than $35. At this rate, the cost of delivering 120 credit hours, the amount typically required for a bachelor's degree, is $4,200. There are non-instructional expenses, such as course development, computer infrastructure, and academic advising. But the advising can be hired out at low market rates, like the instruction is, and course development and computer infrastructure costs fall as they are spread over a large number of students. Even if these overhead expenses amount to twice the direct cost of instruction, the cost of delivering a full four-year degree is less than $13,000.[16]

This compares with a four-year price of $28,000 and $106,000 at the typical public and private institutions, respectively.[17] In other words, the price of an online degree could be less than half the price of a traditional college education, even with the latter's public and private subsidies. The differential would be even greater for a student who made the most of the online program's convenience by living at home, saving an additional $32,000 or more.[18] This is the kind of price differential that has led to disruption of other industries, such as computer technology, steel mills, and newspapers.

For-profit online educators operate year-round, avoiding the cost of a long summer recess. They offer fewer majors and courses than traditional universities do, focusing on those in greatest demand. They have the capacity to admit all qualified applicants. Instead of granting honors and grades based on a forced curve, they increasingly evaluate students on the basis of learning outcome achievement. Of course, they operate no athletic teams.

These advantages of low instructional cost and tight focus have allowed many for-profit educators, especially those with strong online programs, to achieve great market success. Their lower total cost also allows them, should they choose, to price their accredited degrees at a fraction of the traditional cost. Historically, the leaders have preferred the high-margin adult education segment, where online students often receive tuition support from their employers. However, as the diploma mill stigma of online education fades and the high end of the market becomes saturated with competitors, the premier online companies have the option of lowering price to attract even brand-conscious young students. With each passing year, the learning preferences of these digital natives, raised in a world of texting, Facebooking, and

TABLE 14.1 Traditional versus Online University Traits

Traditional University Trait	Online University Copied?
Face-to-face instruction	No
Rational/secular orientation	Yes
Comprehensive specialization, departmentalization, and faculty self-governance	No
Long summer recess	No
Graduate schools atop the college	No*
Private fundraising	No
Competitive athletics	No
Curricular distribution (GE) and concentration (majors)	Focused offerings
Academic honors	No
Externally funded research	No
Up-or-out tenure, with faculty rank and salary distinctions	No
Admissions selectivity	No

*Note: Online universities that operate both undergraduate and graduate degree programs do so without creating the separateness and competition for resources typical of research universities.

computer gaming, will favor the online educators. The trend is already evident: the Sloan Foundation reports that online enrollments grew by 17 percent in 2009, compared to overall higher education growth of just over 1 percent.[19]

The online education companies are not without their shortcomings; many deserve the heightened regulatory scrutiny they began receiving in 2010. Yet the weaknesses and outright abuses of some should not be taken as indictment of the power of online education. When the regulators have finished their culling and standard setting, the survivors will be stronger for the special scrutiny, just as their battle for accreditation and market credibility has given them an edge in demonstrating learning outcomes.

FOR-PROFIT INSTITUTIONS' STUDENT SUPPORT

More than many traditional institutions, for-profit educators spend heavily to recruit students. That is true of DeVry University. Of DeVry's roughly $1.5 billion 2010 operating budget, nearly $225 million, or 15 percent, went to advertising its programs and name.[20] For-profit institutions make these investments in awareness and image partly to compensate for their lack of academic prestige and high-profile athletic teams.

A student acquired at such high cost receives concomitantly high levels of help in staying in school. The risk of failure to finish is great, because many students are working adults with heavy out-of-school responsibilities; many also come from economically and educationally disadvantaged backgrounds. Even with special attention from academic counselors who employ automated performance tracking systems, DeVry's bachelor's degree-seeking students graduate at a rate below the national average.[21] Yet DeVry's cost of conferring a bachelor's degree, even accounting for those who do not graduate, is $40,128, compared with a peer average of $74,268.[22] This is possible because of the efficiencies inherent in DeVry's organizational strategy and design, particularly its tight focus on student instruction (rather than student amenities and faculty research), year-round operation, and effective use of online learning technology.

The chairman of DeVry's board, former Princeton and University of Michigan president Robert Shapiro, describes the institution's philosophy of student service:

> If you have a Ph.D. and you enter most universities and colleges, they assume you know how to teach and so on. We don't assume that. We have a training program. We have an

evaluation program; we have feedback on this, so we're constantly evaluating—almost month by month—the quality of what we're doing.

. . .

I was president of the University of Michigan. It's not going out of business anytime in our lifetime. DeVry could go out of business in a year—not in decades—if it wasn't serving its students. So it has to pass a much tougher test than traditional higher education does. I hardly think we do it perfectly; I'm sure we have many improvements that we could make, but we're always on the trail, always trying to do something.[23]

This disruptive new form of competition will require traditional universities to change fundamentally. Belt tightening and incremental enhancements will not be enough, as Babson College president Leonard Schlesinger has warned:

> This "more and better" attitude toward managing the college or university may appear to be gone in this environment, but it hasn't disappeared. A prevailing view among college leaders is to batten down the hatches and cut costs on multiple fronts for the short term, assuming a return to the "old" normal. But there is ample evidence the old normal may never return. Thus cost-cutting is an incomplete solution. We must recognize the ground is shifting in fundamental ways for higher education. We must reframe our approach to managing colleges and universities in the face of a new normal.[24]

Schlesinger's warning is echoed by Ohio State's Gordon Gee:

> The first instinct in responding to this sudden economic crisis is to hunker down and wait for the storm to pass. That is the instinct, but acting on it would be a grave mistake.

> . . .
>
> Our challenge today is radical reformation. Change at the margins will not do. The choice, it seems to me, is this: Reinvention or extinction.
>
> If we think it cannot happen to us, we ought to recall the fate of the Swiss watchmakers. Fabulous craftsmen, certainly, but the world has moved on, technologies have advanced, habits have shifted.[25]

It is necessary to step back, as Charles Eliot did a century-and-a-half ago and rethink the traditional university. A decade before the downturn of 2008, that kind of rethinking was occurring at Ricks College.

PART FOUR

A New Kind of University

As every flower fades and as all youth
Departs, so life at every stage,
So every virtue, so our grasp of truth,
Blooms in its day and may not last forever.
Since life may summon us at every age
Be ready, heart, for parting, new endeavor . . . .[1]

From the poem "Stages"
The Glass Bead Game, by Hermann Hesse

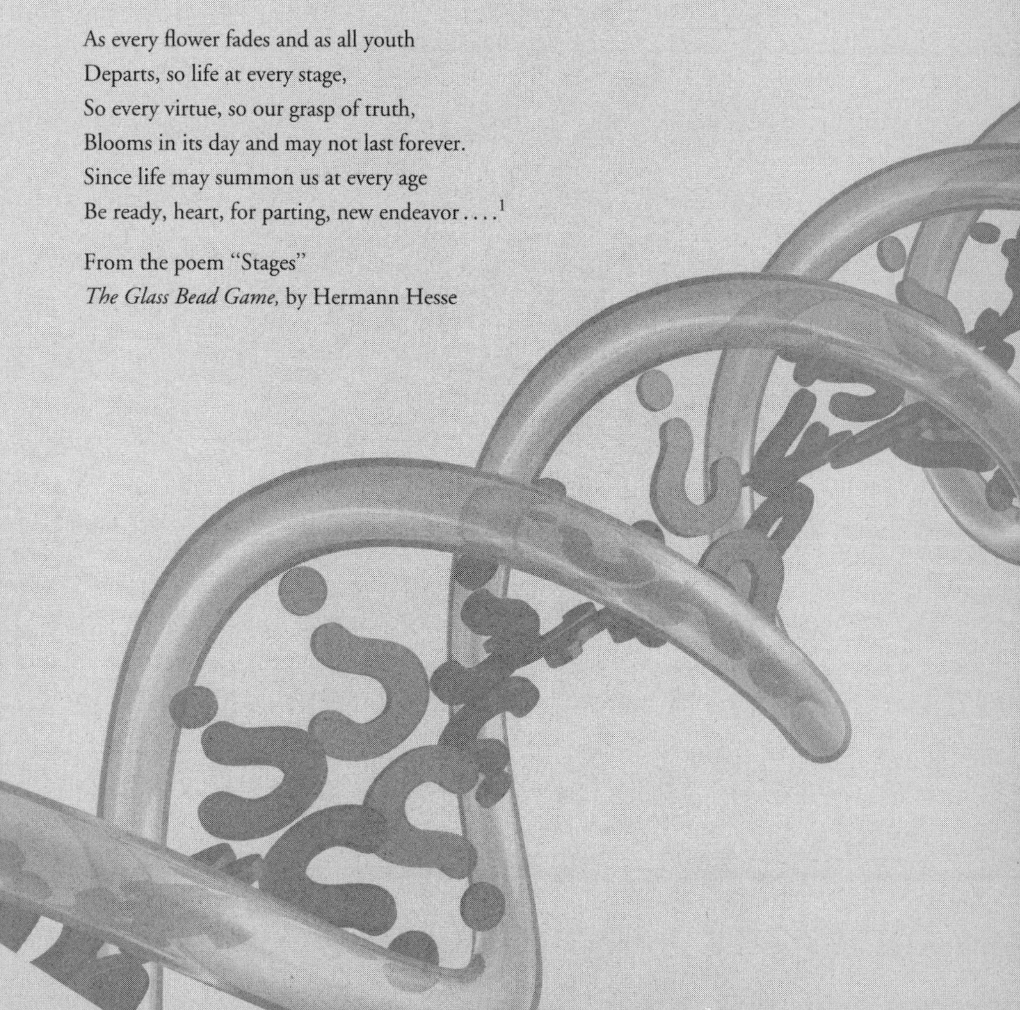

Chapter 15

A Unique University Design

David Bednar assumed the presidency of Ricks College in 1997, succeeding previous president Steve Bennion. Like Hal Eyring, Bednar came from a business school; since 1981 he had been at the University of Arkansas, where he served for a time as an associate dean. Bednar also resembled Eyring in his emphasis on teaching. Upon arriving in Rexburg he declared "educational leadership" his top priority. His statement of guiding principles for the college included the assertion that every person is a teacher. He introduced himself to faculty members as "a teacher who is now working as a president, not a president who used to be a teacher."[1]

Notwithstanding his passion for teaching, Bednar's management and decision-making training would prove, in the long run, more vital to the evolution of the college than he or anyone else could have guessed. In fact, he quickly began to make his mark administratively. From the beginning he challenged conventions, especially those rooted in academic tradition. In an early staff meeting his vice presidents received the assignment to "tear apart the summary of Ricks' mission and goals, rewrite it, and make recommendations." Arriving at a time when the college was turning away nearly half of all applicants, Bednar particularly wanted his colleagues to think about how to serve more students at an affordable cost.[2]

He built teams, delegated freely, and gained a reputation for responsiveness, typically replying the same day to email and phone messages. All-employee meetings and departmental breakfasts became a tradition, as did visits by the president to individual faculty offices and monthly Q&A sessions open to the entire campus community. Bednar and his wife Susan entertained students each Monday night; on Sundays they made unannounced visits to student apartments. Early administrative initiatives included reemphasizing the Ricks College practices of presidential participation in each faculty hire and of a common pay scale for all faculty members. With regard to the former practice, Bednar stated his belief that faculty hiring was the university's most important decision.[3]

Bednar also took a hard look at Ricks's marquee intercollegiate athletic teams. Paradoxically, winning national championships increased the athletic department's fiscal deficit, as it required tournament travel that wasn't fully offset by the incremental revenues. Proposals to reduce the financial shortfall through corporate advertising and sponsorships worried his administrative team, though they ultimately granted approval. They also agreed to the elimination of the men's and women's track teams; while both of those teams would take third place nationally a few months later, they involved too few students and cost too much money to justify.[4]

Even as he challenged his colleagues to think about serving more students, Bednar preached the board's new "zero-standard" for growth. The board had implemented this policy in response to continual requests from its higher education institutions for more faculty and physical facilities. Unable to alter the bigger-and-better tendencies of its universities and colleges, the board determined to at least contain them by capping both faculty positions and building square footage.

Unable to alter the bigger-and-better tendencies of its universities and colleges, the board determined to at least contain them by capping both faculty positions and building square footage.

At his first all-employee meeting, Bednar vowed that the college would honor the zero-standard and still find ways to admit more students. He invited his colleagues to "think about how we think" and to "set goals so high that we cannot imagine achieving the results through our existing processes." He cited the success of Sam Walton, whose Arkansas-based company, Wal-Mart, he had worked with for more than fifteen years as a business school professor. Walton met with derision when he initially proposed to double the industry standard of $50 in sales per square foot of retail space. But, Bednar reported, Wal-Mart had since achieved $300 per square foot and aspired to reach $1,000.[5]

In that spirit, Bednar challenged Ricks's employees to think about how its educational offerings might "impact the entire Church and its membership worldwide." The key was to do it with existing resources, probably through the use of information technology. He spoke of the potential to serve 50,000 students globally or, in the alternative, to serve just 8,600 and be "irrelevant." "You can't get there," he warned, "by thinking the way you do now."[6]

Before the turn of the millennium, the college had taken a few faltering steps along the path to serving more students not only in Rexburg but elsewhere. All students were required to take at least one online class to graduate. By 1999, the college had mapped out fifty-one "fast track" majors, with emphasis on highly enrolled ones such as English and business, which would allow a student to make progress to graduation during not only fall and winter but also during the traditional summer break; these included articulation agreements with state universities in Idaho and Utah where students could continue in pursuit of bachelor's and master's degrees.[7]

Particularly promising was a proposal to admit students on one of three academic calendar "tracks." For example, rather than being admitted in the fall and staying for winter, a student might be invited to come on the condition of attending winter semester and the spring and summer terms, or those two terms plus fall semester. The effect of this system, if those not admitted on the traditional fall-winter schedule could be convinced to accept a nontraditional track, would be to fill the spring and summer terms to a level closer to that of the fall and winter semesters, thereby increasing the college's annual enrollment without the need to hire additional faculty or build more classrooms.[8]

There was also a fledgling attempt to serve students internationally. Working with a church-owned high school in Mexico, Ricks began offering technical certificates to Mexican students recently returned from voluntary mission service. The initial emphasis, on welding, was broadened to include specially developed certificates in automotive repair, English as a second language, and computer usage. A rotating set of faculty members from Rexburg provided onsite instruction of students and training of local instructors. In the summer of 1999, 101 certificates were awarded.[9] Like Hal Eyring's agriculture-related initiatives, these technical certificate programs represented an effort to keep Ricks rooted in its historical mission. The certificate programs offered the prospect of educating many more students, all of them nonconsumers of traditional higher education.

However, at what appeared to be the heights of success, the board directed that the effort be turned over to the local Mexican high school. Before Ricks could grow outward, it would have to grow upward. That was soon to happen, to the surprise of all but church president and board chairman Gordon Hinckley.

An Unexpected Announcement

On Tuesday, June 20, 2000, the employees and students of Ricks College received an invitation to a meeting scheduled for the next morning at 8 o'clock. A crowd of several thousand gathered at the appointed time in the school's basketball arena. David Bednar opened the meeting and introduced ninety-year-old church president Gordon Hinckley, who appeared via audio/visual feed from Salt Lake City, where he stood before the news media. Hinckley made a startling announcement:

> The First Presidency of The Church of Jesus Christ of Latter-day Saints and the Board of Trustees of Ricks College announce that Ricks College will change from its present two-year junior college status to a four-year institution.

At this news, the throng in Rexburg erupted. Bednar, a former football quarterback, drew on that experience as he waved to quiet the crowd. Hinckley paused before proceeding, but when he continued his voice could hardly be heard in the arena over the slow-to-subside roar of approval.

> The new four-year school will be known as Brigham Young University-Idaho, with the name change designed to give the school immediate national and international recognition. The memory of Thomas E. Ricks will continue to be appropriately honored and perpetuated.
>
> This change of status is consistent with the ongoing tradition of evaluation and progress that has brought Ricks College from infant beginnings to its present position as the largest privately owned two-year institution of higher education in America. With some additions and modifications, the physical facilities now in place in Rexburg are adequate to handle the new program. Undoubtedly, some changes to the campus will be necessary. However, they will be modest in nature and scope.
>
> BYU-Idaho's move to four-year status will be phased in over a period of time and accomplished in such a way as to preserve the school's autonomy and identity. Adjustments to its mission will be minimal. The school will have a unique role in and be distinctive from the other institutions of higher education within the Church Educational System.

By this time, the crowd was more subdued. The loss of the Ricks name surprised everyone and disappointed many. They listened more intently as Hinckley went on.

> BYU-Idaho will continue to be teaching oriented. Effective teaching and advising will be the primary responsibilities of its faculty, who are committed to academic excellence.
>
> The institution will emphasize undergraduate education and will award baccalaureate degrees; graduate degree programs will not be offered. Faculty rank will not be a part of the academic structure of the new four-year institution.
>
> BYU-Idaho will operate on an expanded year-round basis, incorporating innovative calendaring and scheduling while also taking advantage of advancements in technology which will enable the four-year institution to serve more students. In addition, BYU-Idaho will phase out its involvement in intercollegiate athletics and shift its emphasis to a year-round activity program designed to involve and meet the needs of a diverse student body.
>
> Of necessity, the new four-year institution will be assessing and restructuring its academic offerings. Predictably, the school will need to change and even eliminate some long-standing and beneficial programs as the school focuses upon key academic disciplines and activities.
>
> Specific programmatic details about and time lines for the change are presently being worked out. These details, which will be discussed with and approved by the Board of Trustees, will be announced at appropriate times in the future.[10]

After Hinckley signed off, Bednar said to those gathered, "Now it would be appropriate to cheer." They did so, but not uniformly. The athletic coaches sat stunned, wondering if they had just been fired en masse. No one had been briefed in advance. Bednar himself had known for only a matter of weeks. Everyone had questions about what would happen next, and there were few answers.

THE WEIGHT OF HINCKLEY'S PRONOUNCEMENT

As Gordon Hinckley announced the creation of BYU-Idaho, he was perceived by its employees both as their boss and as their ecclesiastical leader. For the faithful, to argue with the proposed design of the institution would have been to question more than just an administrative decision. Few academic leaders, if any, could make institutional pronouncements with such authority. Yet Hinckley had more than ecclesiastical authority on his side. His plan for BYU-Idaho made it, for all but the athletic staff, a more attractive employer. That was obviously true relative to what Ricks College had been—BYU-Idaho would offer new intellectual opportunities and enhanced institutional prestige. But the new university was also designed to be a more stable employer than its peer institutions. Hinckley didn't cite that selling point, though it was built into the university's DNA. The economic efficiencies attendant to year-round operation and the application of online learning technology would allow BYU-Idaho not only to grow its student body at low cost but also to pay its faculty better. In 2010, McKinsey would find that those faculty members made an average of $92,439 in total compensation, compared with $80,867 for their institutional peers.[11] Hinckley's ecclesiastical mantle and the faithfulness of Ricks College employees decreased his need to make the rational, self-interest-stimulating case for change. However, it was there to be made in economic terms all the more convincing now, with disruption at the door.

Hinckley's Innovative Vision

Hinckley himself didn't have an implementation plan for the university. But he knew that the genetic structure was right. The exigencies of the Great Depression and an offer of employment from the church kept him from pursuing his boyhood dream of a graduate degree in journalism. Still, he had gained a thorough understanding of the traditional higher education model through twenty-five years as a member of the board. He particularly knew the university tendency to expand and climb.

It was Hinckley who had implemented zero-standard, realizing that the only sure way to contain the costs of a university or college is to limit faculty hiring and office space. Yet while Hinckley was concerned about creeping costs, he desperately wanted more young church members to have the opportunity to attend one of its higher education institutions, especially the flagship, BYU. In the mid-1990s, as both Ricks and BYU turned away applicants in record numbers, he tasked a team of analysts to study options for serving more students. One of the scenarios analyzed was building an entirely new campus. The required capital investment staggered the board, and the option of building a new university was quickly ruled out. At the same time, however, the study team produced unexpectedly compelling data on the value to the church of its higher education system. The team found that, relative to church members who went to other universities, students who attended its sponsored schools graduated at higher rates, earned more, and donated more time and tithes.[12] Even in purely financial terms BYU and Ricks generated a positive return on investment, in the way that states hope their higher education systems will do.

The question in Hinckley's mind, though, was how to serve the most new students at the lowest possible cost. He knew that BYU, with its faculty committed to scholarly research, had a substantially higher cost per student than Ricks. He was impressed by the recent innovations at Ricks, especially the proposed track system for operating on a year-round basis. He also admired David Bednar's leadership skill and commitment to thinking outside of the box. In fact, Ricks College had held a special place in Hinckley's heart for years. At Bednar's inauguration in 1998 he had said:

> Of the very many problems with which the Board deals . . . very, very few concern Ricks. This school just seems to go along

> with its wonderful responsibility of educating those who come to learn. We do not hear of difficulties with the faculty or with the students. Both bodies know why they are here, and they steadfastly pursue their objectives to accomplish that purpose.[13]

One day in early 2000, after a meeting of the board, Hinckley asked Hal Eyring to come to his office. Eyring was then the commissioner of education, directing all church schools the way Ernest Wilkinson had done. After inviting Eyring to close the door, Hinckley said, "Hal, couldn't we serve more students at a lower cost by making Ricks a university?" Caught off guard, Eyring fumbled for a moment and then began enumerating the additional costs of granting bachelor's degrees at Ricks. Even if the new year-round program worked, he pointed out, adding junior and senior level classes would require more faculty. They would need offices, and that would mean adding buildings; so would providing classrooms for the additional students. "No, President Hinckley," Eyring concluded, "it will cost you more, not less."

"No it won't," Hinckley shot back, "it will cost me less *per BYU graduate*." Hinckley's reply revealed that he'd been thinking deeply about the matter. Already, before consulting with Eyring or anyone else, he had the idea of applying the much more recognizable BYU name to Ricks College. He also demonstrated in the "per BYU graduate" phrase his understanding of marginal economics, a concept about which Eyring had known nothing before arriving at the Harvard Business School. Ricks College faculty members, whose professional activities centered on the classroom, could provide instruction less expensively than BYU faculty because they spent more time doing it. Therefore, each new salary dollar invested in Rexburg would yield, on the margin, a greater return in terms of students served. That would be especially true as the school added online learning opportunities to its traditional face-to-face classroom instruction.

But that conclusion about the economic efficiency of Ricks revealed another of Hinckley's presumptions about the DNA of the new university: there would be no typical research mission, and no up-or-out tenure or rank based on scholarly publication. In going from junior college to university status, the institution's educational mission would not change in the way typical of the Carnegie climb. BYU-Idaho's faculty members would stay focused on student instruction, just as they had been in Ricks College days. BYU-Idaho would be a single-minded enterprise, serving students exclusively in its teaching and scholarship.

BYU-Idaho would be a single-minded enterprise, serving students exclusively in its teaching and scholarship.

The new university would also award only associate's and bachelor's degrees; there would be no graduate programs. Hinckley knew the price of graduate programs through his oversight of the main BYU campus in Provo. Its professional schools were well regarded but increasingly more expensive to operate at a high level of quality. Maintaining top-fifty rankings for its MBA program and law school required large annual outlays in support of faculty scholarship and student career placement. Graduate programs in arts and sciences were likewise expensive, because of their low student–teacher ratios and high research costs, including capital outlays for scientific laboratories and equipment.

Having considered the full cost of graduate programs and the alternative means for reaping some of their benefits, including engaging BYU-Idaho undergraduate students in mentored research with their professors,[14] Hinckley determined to confine the graduate education mission to the church's flagship BYU campus. In so focusing BYU-Idaho he followed the lead of Clark Kerr, effectively designing it as the Carnegie equivalent of California's four-year colleges (which later became its state universities). BYU would pay the price of selective admissions, scholarly research, and competitive athletic teams and professional schools. The campus in Rexburg would benefit from these brand-building investments while keeping its costs lower and its access wider.

TABLE 15.1 BYU-Idaho and Traditional University Traits	
Traditional University Traits	**BYU-Idaho Copied?**
Face-to-face instruction	Mixed with online learning
Rational/secular orientation	No
Comprehensive specialization, departmentalization, and faculty self-governance	Yes, though with focus on "key" disciplines
Long summer recess	No
Graduate schools atop the college	No
Private fundraising	Yes
Competitive athletics	No
Curricular distribution (GE) and concentration (majors)	Yes
Academic honors	Yes
Externally funded research	No
Up-or-out tenure, with faculty rank and salary distinctions	No
Admissions selectivity	No

Hinckley's proposal for the new university built on much of the DNA of Ricks College but also changed some of it dramatically, especially in the case of intercollegiate athletics. As shown in Table 15.1, his design represented a substantial reengineering of the DNA of the traditional university.

Eyring's Exhortations

In his role as church commissioner of education, Hal Eyring expounded on Hinckley's design for the new university, both privately in the succeeding days and publicly in the months and years to come. In a 2001 address in Rexburg, he reminded those affiliated with the new university of the shortest sentence in the public announcement of Ricks College's becoming a university: "Adjustments to its mission will be minimal."[15] He noted with approval that the mission statement submitted that year to the school's regional accreditation body remained unchanged. Referring to that statement, which emphasized undergraduate education, he said, "These could be the words of Thomas Ricks or Jacob Spori or any of the leaders from the beginning." This was a compliment to the fledgling university for staying close to its roots rather than embarking immediately on a ladder climb.

Of course, Eyring knew that the move to university status would require adding faculty and facilities; he and the other members of the board had already approved substantial outlays for both. Appreciating the tendency of such expansion to become habitual in higher education, he applauded David Bednar's commitment to frugality, as manifested in a motto Bednar often cited, "Use it up, wear it out, make do, or do without."[16] Eyring identified institutional and individual frugality as not only financially commendable but also a source of advantage in "turbulent times." "We will depend more upon inspiration and perspiration to make improvements than upon buildings and equipment," he declared. "Then hard economic times will have little effect on the continuous innovation that will not cease at this school, even in the most difficult times."

Eyring also knew the academic tendency to measure excellence mainly in terms of research publications; he had felt the publish-or-perish pressure as a tenure-track professor at Stanford in the 1960s. Thus, he quoted and commended a post-announcement statement Bednar made about scholarship, one that defined the term in an untraditional way:

> We should be excellent scholars, and our scholarship should be focused on the processes of learning and teaching. We will not be a recognized and highly regarded research institution in the traditional sense of that term. We will, however, emphasize a wide

> range of scholarly endeavors and excel in and play a pioneering role in understanding learning and teaching processes with faith and hard work, and in the process of time.[17]

A Focus on Key Disciplines

Finally, Eyring recalled the announcement's reference to "focus[ing] upon key academic disciplines." "Now," he explained, "President Hinckley has long experience in education—long experience—so he knew how remarkable it was to pay such a tribute to this place. He said there would be focus, not a growth and spread in the academic offerings." In fact, Eyring may have spoken these words less by way of commendation than of exhortation. Just one year after the announcement, the first BYU-Idaho course catalogue made reference to nearly forty bachelor's degrees, and more were planned.[18] The bigger-and-better tendency was already at work in the new university's curriculum.

Eyring had hoped there would be, at least in the beginning, no more than a dozen majors; having relatively fewer majors would help the university keep its costs low and educational quality high. In hindsight, a rapid expansion of four-year offerings may have been inevitable, given that Ricks College had 125 associate's degrees and that many of these were being eliminated in the transition to university status.[19] Also, there was a good argument that educational quality required a sufficiently broad range of majors for students to choose from.

However, the plan for BYU-Idaho had actually been to be more Harvard-like than the traditional university in terms of the number of majors offered. Harvard, ironically, has been more careful in its management of subject matter than most of the universities that emulate it. Though the size of its course catalogue might still provoke James Conant to declare, "This is ridiculous," the college has managed to keep its majors, or concentrations, to less than fifty.[20] The typical research university has several times that number; even BYU-Idaho now has more. Moreover, Harvard concentrations typically require fewer hours than their equivalents at other universities. These choices—to have fewer majors and require fewer major hours—spare the institution and its students significant cost.

Both Eyring and Gordon Hinckley appreciated from experience that undergraduate majors are a powerful driver of increased intellectual and organizational fragmentation as well as financial cost. Some new majors are interdisciplinary, but most represent a slice of an existing one. The subdivision of majors allows for greater specialization and depth of subject matter. Faculty members favor this, as they do a growing number of required major hours, because it facilitates introduction of their specialized research into the undergraduate curriculum. As Eliot, champion of the elective system, knew, that makes instruction more engaging for them and their students.

But greater subject matter depth comes at the expense of breadth, as Lowell, creator of Harvard's distribution system, recognized. While the increased specialization of majors serves future academics well, these students comprise a small fraction of the undergraduate population. Even at Harvard only 5 percent of seniors report the intention to immediately pursue doctoral studies in the arts and sciences; more than half, by contrast, plan on graduate study in business, medicine, or law.[21] Specialized majors can leave students underprepared both for this kind of graduate study and for entering the workforce with just a bachelor's degree. Additionally, they make four-year graduation more difficult.

Eyring had also seen how new majors and graduate programs can create increased institutional costs. Astute proponents of a new major or program will tout their ability to create it with few new courses and no new faculty or physical facilities. But these requests almost invariably come later, as the proponents—who in the meantime may have won independent departmental status—argue the need for increased quality, in the form of specialists to teach cutting-edge classes and offices and lab facilities to house them. The "bigger" request, which leads to the introduction of a new major, often presages a subsequent plea to make the major better.

THE EASY-TO-CREATE AND HARD-TO-ELIMINATE MAJOR

Majors tend to proliferate in universities for the same reasons that courses do. They are easily proposed—the main hurdle is a demonstration that the faculty are qualified to teach the courses that comprise the major at other institutions. Questions such as what the degree will cost the university to confer and what economic return a graduate can expect to make receive only secondary consideration.

As with new courses, fellow faculty members and academic administrators are reluctant to challenge their colleagues' proposal of a new major. In the academic spirit of collegiality and experimentation, the inclination is to "give it a try," particularly because programmatic comprehensiveness correlates with Carnegie ladder status. Yet eliminating a major is immeasurably more difficult than dropping a course from the catalog. Not only are many faculty members invested, rather than a few or only one, there are students in the pipeline who must either be allowed to finish or forced to choose another specialty. There are also graduates of the major who might find the value of their degree impaired by the major's elimination. Even more than courses, majors must be created with care.

Eyring had hoped that BYU-Idaho would, like the for-profit educators, eschew such major-driven cost creep by offering a limited range of practical majors, such as business and teacher education, that could be delivered at high volume—in other words, with double-digit student–teacher ratios even in the advanced courses. This would not only produce low instructional cost per student but also increase the likelihood of placing graduates in good employment. Subject matter focus was a critical element of the BYU-Idaho DNA that the new university could not afford to lose. It was one of many elements of Gordon Hinckley's unique design that would require both innovative implementation and careful preservation.

Chapter 16

Getting Started

There was no question that David Bednar was the right man for the job of turning Ricks College into BYU-Idaho. Psychologically, the new university president and his colleagues were working from a standing start. However, they had already built the essential foundation for the unique four-year university that Hinckley envisioned. The three-track system of admissions necessary to fill the spring and summer terms and operate year-round was already under development. So was much, though not all, of the necessary building program.

Fulfilling some of the more radical mandates of the new university's strategy, such as eschewing graduate programs and faculty rank, was simply a matter of resisting the bigger-and-better tendency. For this Bednar and the board could thank Ernest Wilkinson and his successor administrators of the church system of higher education. Had it not been for their vigilance in defining Ricks in community college terms, by the year 2000 it likely would have acquired two of the defining characteristics of the research university, Charles Eliot's graduate programs and James Conant's research-driven, up-or-out tenure. That neither existed at Ricks meant BYU-Idaho enjoyed a genetic advantage in undergraduate education like that of academically modest liberal arts colleges. The faculty would engage in scholarship "focused," as Bednar said, "on the processes of learning and teaching." They would do it with the help of undergraduates rather than graduate students and would not feel driven to please the editorial boards of traditional scholarly journals and university presses.[1]

Heavyweight Teams and Administrative Engagement

Even new university responsibilities, such as designing bachelor's degrees and winning four-year accreditation, were accomplished in short order. Provisional accreditation came in 2001 and full accreditation just three years later. This success came in part because of Bednar's creation of a "heavyweight team" to oversee the effort.[2] The members of this team included faculty members and administrators with intimate knowledge of both the Ricks College curriculum and the standards of the Northwest Commission on Colleges and Universities, the regional accreditation body. This team was given authority to cross organizational boundaries and create standard processes for designing curriculum and gathering the information required by the accreditors.

HEAVYWEIGHT INNOVATION TEAMS

One of the things that Clayton Christensen found as he did the research that led to *The Innovator's Dilemma*[3] is that disruptive innovations rarely come out of established enterprises. Even when a truly new way of doing things occurs to someone in a successful organization, the established systems and standards take over. A new idea that isn't dismissed entirely is almost inevitably modified to fit the ways things are traditionally done, losing its innovation impact in the process.

The simplest solution to this problem is to create an autonomous organizational unit to develop the idea, as IBM did when it decided to build a personal computer (PC) in the early 1980s. Knowing that IBM's sophisticated salesmen and marketing managers would consider the PC a toy and try to either soup it up or kill it, the senior executive team put the developers in Florida. That was far enough from IBM's New York headquarters that they could focus on meeting the needs of price-sensitive nonconsumers of computers, without regard for the main organization's fixation on high profit margins and corporate image. The result was breakthrough new product for IBM.

Under the right circumstances, major innovation can be fostered within an established organization. A critical tool for doing so is a *heavyweight team* made up of experts who represent all of the necessary organizational functions and can speak for their departments without feeling beholden to them. Ideally, they are located in physical proximity to one another and led by someone with substantial organizational authority. If members of a heavyweight team take collective responsibility for finding a better way to do things—with awareness but not overriding concern for potential impacts on their individual departments—established organizations can move nimbly in new directions, as BYU-Idaho did in turning itself into a university.

Though accreditation came in record time, other changes took longer to settle out. One was the dropping of the Ricks College name in favor of BYU-Idaho. Descendants of Thomas Ricks, who numbered in the thousands, felt the sting of this loss keenly. The board approved Bednar's recommendation to name a large classroom building then under construction in honor of the school's founder.

Worries about what would become of the beloved Spirit of Ricks plagued more than just members of the Ricks family. With academic offerings and student enrollment projected to grow significantly, many of the institution's supporters feared that it would lose its intimacy and informality. For years after the announcement Bednar spoke publicly of how the university would continue to embody the Ricks College tradition of caring and concern; the formal tagline for the new BYU-Idaho alumni association became "Preserving and Enhancing the Spirit of Ricks."[4] Bednar also continued with his traditions of formal and informal communication, such as regular all-employee meetings and campus-wide Q&A sessions. Efforts such as these notwithstanding, university employees grew accustomed to having students, parents, alumni, and other patrons attribute their disappointments in its policies to a loss of the old college ethos. One angry alumnus called Bednar a "killer of the Spirit of Ricks."[5]

For some, even more painful than changing the school's name was eliminating its intercollegiate athletic programs. The announcement not only caught all of the coaches and athletes completely off-guard, it came at a time of unprecedented success. The women's and men's cross-country teams were in the midst of winning, respectively, seven and three consecutive junior college national championships. The football team had lost the national championship game by just three points in 1998 and was a perennial Top 10 performer. The athletes were also successful in the classroom: in 1999, six Ricks teams had finished first in the national academic rankings.[6] The situation could hardly have been more different from that of Harvard at the time of the Ivy Agreement. Ricks was winning, and its reputation outside of Rexburg rested heavily on athletics.

In the Salt Lake press conference following the announcement, the first question asked of President Hinckley was about the football team's future. In response to a subsequent question, "Why do away with athletics?" he replied, "It takes too much money."[7] Hinckley knew what top-flight athletic teams cost at BYU, and it was easy to imagine how coaches and players who consistently won at the junior college level would strive for similar success in the NCAA. He could foresee the problem NCAA president Myles Brand would identify in 2008: "Athletics spending has increased in recent years at a pace that ultimately is unsustainable."[8] That would almost certainly be true for the church if it operated two independent programs, particularly with one of them in a rural community with a limited fan base.

The burden of implementing the decision to eliminate intercollegiate athletics fell to David Bednar. He determined to honor Ricks College's scholarship commitments by operating all existing teams through two additional seasons, during which time the school won two more cross-country national championships and finished with a number 5 ranking in football.[9] The ongoing athletic success only added to the pain and indignation of those involved, and Bednar bore the brunt of their efforts to reverse the no-athletics decision. He stood firm, declaring his door to be open but categorically refusing to revisit the university's position. Nearly all coaches and other athletics support personnel were offered continuing positions at the university; a few qualified for retirement packages.[10] In the end, some chose to take coaching positions elsewhere. Most, though, stayed and focused on the physical education classes they had previously taught part-time.

THE END OF INTERCOLLEGIATE ATHLETICS

The day after Gordon Hinckley announced the creation of BYU-Idaho and the end of Ricks College's intercollegiate athletic programs, the region's largest newspaper, the *Idaho Falls Post Register,* ran the headline "So long Vikings." The lead article on the subject described the news as "personally and professionally devastating to everyone in the athletic department." The photos of eight coaches, along with their Ricks College career records, appeared under the heading "The Coaching Casualties." Football coach Ron Haun's record was listed as 160–32–2. Women's basketball coach Lori Woodland was recognized for 243 wins against 40 losses.[11]

The *Post Register,* noting Ricks's success in two premier athletic conferences, said, "It was the broad range of those leagues, which include teams from Idaho, Utah, Colorado, Oregon, and Arizona, and the expense that it took to travel in order to compete, that ultimately led to the decision to eliminate Ricks' athletic program."

Notwithstanding the personal and institutional pain associated with such decisions, economic realities have led other schools to look hard at the costs and benefits of their intercollegiate athletics programs, especially football, the most expensive one. Hofstra and Northeastern universities both eliminated football at the end of the 2009 season. At Hofstra, $4.5 million was thus freed for other purposes, including need-based student aid.[12] In 2010, the University of California, Berkeley eliminated five sports, including baseball, affecting some 20 percent of its student athletes and thirteen coaches, but producing a much needed savings of $4 million in the year immediately following.[13]

A New Approach to Student Activities

One former Ricks coach who stayed was the school's athletic director, Garth Hall. He became chair of a committee—another heavyweight team—tasked with creating what Bednar called in his post-announcement press conference "a wide-ranging and extensive activity program, including athletics."[14] Hall approached the task with the perspective of having coached football at the NCAA Division I level for more than two decades at six universities. He appreciated the rationale for taking a different path at BYU-Idaho. He had seen the high institutional cost of intercollegiate athletics, especially as a head coach at a regional university in a city several times larger than Rexburg; its athletic program's revenues covered only 25 percent of its nearly $5 million cost.[15]

Less than sixty days after the announcement of BYU-Idaho's creation, Hall's team of faculty, administrators, and students proposed a wide-ranging set of programs, including activities in the categories of sports, fitness, outdoor recreation, visual and performing arts, hobbies and crafts, service, entertainment, and academics.[16] What proved to be most significant for the university in the long run was the proposed principle that "students who advance

Hall's team of faculty, administrators, and students proposed a wide-ranging set of programs, including activities in the categories of sports, fitness, outdoor recreation, visual and performing arts, hobbies and crafts, service, entertainment, and academics.

will be given the opportunity to serve in teacher, coach, and supervisor capacities."[17] The team envisioned a student leadership pyramid. For example, a freshman might start as a participant on a volleyball team and in the ensuing years rise to team captain, team coach, and ultimately league organizer. The last of these positions might come with a scholarship or stipend, but the other leadership responsibilities would be filled on a volunteer basis. All of the positions would allow students to teach other students.

Involving students via what would become known as the student leadership model was significant in two respects. In addition to offering hands-on leadership training beneficial to students in their personal and professional lives, it would also allow for cost-efficient growth. The entire cost of the new activities program, including the non-athletic categories, was funded at one-third the cost of the old athletics budget.[18]

By 2009, the university sponsored 192 unique activity programs that were run by more than 7,500 students. The former intercollegiate athletic teams were more than replaced, at least in terms of student involvement. Where there had been a single football team before there were eight, playing in full pads on a field that experienced so much wear that the natural grass had to be replaced with artificial turf. Where there had been no competitive swimming team in Ricks College days, BYU-Idaho had four. Non-athletic activities such as musical performance and community service also multiplied.

Internships and Career-Oriented Majors

Much as the end of intercollegiate athletics made possible greater benefits for the bulk of students, so did the institutional name change that initially piqued champions of The Spirit of Ricks. Those benefits became apparent as BYU-Idaho students sought employment. The new name provided recognition and a measure of credibility with employers, many of whom had BYU graduates already on the payroll. Most who hired a BYU-Idaho student found that students from Rexburg could perform on par with those from Provo.

The beneficiaries of the BYU-Idaho name included not only graduates but also junior and senior students served by an internship program created under David Bednar's direction by another heavyweight team of faculty and administrators. The goals of this internship team were twofold. One was to supplement the new university's "integrated" bachelor's degrees. Many of the departments offering the new four-year degrees were initially too small—in some cases only three or four faculty members—to teach the typical range of specialized junior and senior-year courses. The solution was an integrated degree, one with a major of no more than 45 credit hours, less than the typical 50-plus hours. In addition, the integrated degree required a 24-credit minor or a set of two 12-credit "clusters" in complementary fields. For example, a construction management major might take a minor in business, and an English major one cluster in graphic design and another in computer technology. This would not only solve the problem of limited upper-division offerings but also increase the employability of graduates. The simple, low-cost solution might also be one of higher quality for the ordinary student.

In fact, the rationale for the integrated degree was only secondarily to make up for lack of curricular depth, which was a problem that would soon be solved by the hiring of additional faculty, the majority of them Ph.D. holders. Given BYU-Idaho's mission of serving undergraduates of diverse academic abilities, the emphasis on employment preparation made sense regardless of the university's capacity to provide advanced courses.[19] Though some graduates would proceed immediately for further study, the majority would be looking for jobs.

David Bednar had a keen sense of the kind of education required to win those jobs, thanks in part to his work at the University of Arkansas. While on the faculty there, he had helped design the curriculum for the Walton Institute, Wal-Mart's in-house provider of management education. He had also led Arkansas students in consulting project work for Wal-Mart and many of its supplier companies. From these experiences, he had seen the value of integrating classroom and workplace-based learning. Though Rexburg lacked the natural learning laboratories provided by the myriad corporate offices in the area of Northwest Arkansas around Bentonville, Bednar believed that the right kind of university-sponsored internship program might provide even greater educational opportunities for BYU-Idaho students.

Creating internship services for undergraduate students amounted to another alteration of traditional university DNA. With Eliot's placing of Harvard's graduate programs atop the college, undergraduate curriculum designers began to presume that the primary purpose of a bachelor's degree was to prepare a student for graduate school. Especially as Harvard's selectivity and prestige rose in the second half of the twentieth century, professors and students alike took it for granted that the latter were either gaining a liberal education in anticipation of studying business, law, or medicine, or that they were taking the introductory coursework required for admission to a Ph.D. program. Expecting to spend at least six years at the university, undergraduate students felt little pressure to become acquainted with professional environments, let alone to prepare for a career immediately upon college graduation. Rather than viewing summers as an opportunity to augment their classroom studies with workplace experiences, they treated them as they did in high school, as vacation time. Unfortunately, that attitude of "time to spare," which is unwise even for the students at elite colleges who are likely to attend graduate school, carries over to typical college students, who may face a greater likelihood of failing to graduate at all than of earning a graduate degree.

The BYU-Idaho team tasked with creating the internship program recommended that an internship be required as part of each integrated major.

Hoping to avoid this problem, the BYU-Idaho team tasked with creating the internship program recommended that an internship be required as part of each integrated major. Though academic credit would be granted, the requirement would be fulfilled in a student's semester away from classes; a student attending the spring and summer terms and the fall semester, for example would perform the internship in winter. Along with this recommendation, the university implemented the team's proposal to create an internship office and establish formal relationships with major employers in a dozen "hub cities" spread from Seattle, San Jose, and Los Angeles on the west coast to New York and Washington, D.C., in the east.[20]

The track system gave the new university's interns an advantage over their competitors from other schools. The internship office encouraged employers to think of their interns not as mere future recruits, for whom special projects would have to be manufactured each summer, but as a steady stream of real workers available year-round. The idea found especially warm reception with the major accounting firms, which could plan on having BYU-Idaho students working not only in the summer but also in the much busier fall and winter seasons, when most clients close their books and finalize their taxes. This year-round availability, combined with the brand recognition provided by BYU's well-regarded undergraduate programs, quickly opened doors in places where the name Ricks College had never been heard.[21]

Though valuable to students, the internship program proved expensive to implement. Establishing employer relationships required five full-time administrators to travel heavily, especially in the early years. They were often joined by faculty members, who sought to understand what employers wanted and to ensure that the academic curriculum provided it. The university also found it necessary to subsidize students' travel to the hub cities for hiring interviews. Many students failed to see the value of an internship at all. As the internship program matured, the emphasis shifted from creating new employer relationships to convincing students to take advantage of the opportunities already available.

David Bednar presided over all of these developments (see Table 16.1)—the creation of four-year curriculum featuring integrated

TABLE 16.1 Innovations of the David Bednar Era, 1997-2004	
New Traits	**Implications**
University program and accreditation	Advanced study opportunities Potentially increased cost
Integrated majors	High customizability Low cost of curriculum creation Limited opportunities for advanced study
Activities program and leadership model	Increased student involvement Low operational cost Decreased spectator interest relative to competitive athletics
Internship program	Enhanced career placement Increased cost

majors, the securing of university-level accreditation, and the development of student activities and internship programs—with confident patience. He could feel the power of the institution's design and people, and he knew that both were independent of him. He spoke often of feeling honored to be "only laying a foundation" for BYU-Idaho.[22] The president who would build on that foundation was yet to come.

Chapter 17

Raising Quality

On the first Monday in June 2005, the faculty members of the Harvard Business School (HBS) were called by their dean, Kim Clark, to an unscheduled meeting. It was a season of success for HBS. In the ten years since Clark had taken the helm, the school had seen a significant increase in its faculty and a tripling of its endowment.[1] Its century-old Georgian-style campus showcased four new donor-funded buildings and had been extended by the creation of six research centers around the world, helping Neil Rudenstine characterize Harvard as a "far flung empire on which the sun never sets."[2]

Clark, holder of bachelor's, master's, and doctoral degrees in economics from Harvard, was admired as both a scholar and a leader. His administration's initiatives included bringing a more global perspective to the curriculum and raising the behavioral standards of the student body, particularly regarding their treatment of female classmates and professors. Both on campus and in the news media, he became a respected evangelist for ethical leadership and values. In addition to making the school more ethics oriented and global, he also brought it to the forefront of information technology usage. As Clark's tenure neared its close, Harvard President Larry Summers, a fellow economist and friend, described him as "an extraordinarily effective leader of Harvard Business School."[3]

Clark's colleagues expected him to turn the deanship over to a successor sometime in his tenth year; he had promised that publicly, arguing that a great institution needs "fresh eyes" at least every decade. They knew that in addition to having the option of staying on as a professor, he would, at just fifty-six, have his pick of leadership positions in both the private and public sectors. Clark's colleagues did not expect, though, to hear him announce his departure from HBS at a hastily called faculty meeting just a few days before graduation ceremonies. Nor could they fathom his new destination: BYU-Idaho. Few had heard of the place, and fewer thought it deserving of such a leader. Yet as Clark strode from his final faculty meeting, his colleagues rose in ovation.

Presidential Interregnum

David Bednar left BYU-Idaho in October 2004 to assume another leadership position in the Mormon Church. The church board of education waited until the end of the academic year at HBS to approach Kim Clark. During the resulting presidential interregnum, many university employees, weary from the fast pace of change under Bednar, expected that the new president would give them time to catch up and even rest a bit. That would have been consistent with the presidential succession pattern at Harvard in the last half of the twentieth century. After James Conant's introduction of a radically new general education program and meritocracy-enhancing systems such as up-or-out tenure, Nathan Pusey prudently decided to enhance the new status quo, mainly through fundraising. Neil Rudenstine did much the same after Derek Bok introduced the Core and agitated for diversity and social engagement. Harvard's governing boards apparently saw virtue in a period of institutional consolidation after one of great change.

But in picking Bednar's successor, Gordon Hinckley had in mind someone more like an A. Lawrence Lowell to follow Charles Eliot—a strong, innovative leader who could enhance the DNA of the new university while building on its basic structure. When Hinckley introduced Kim Clark as the new president of BYU-Idaho, it was clear to those who knew him that the university was not going to lie fallow after its season of unprecedented change. Larry Summers, speaking in

Rexburg at Clark's inauguration, foreshadowed the change yet to come at BYU-Idaho: "In the classrooms and corridors of Harvard Business School, which I'm afraid to say are not jargon-free, it is often said that a certain organization stands at an 'inflection point'—a special moment of opportunity and potential transformation . . . . [T]his proud institution stands at such a moment in its history."[4]

Before ever setting foot in Rexburg, Clark had begun to study BYU-Idaho's history, all the way back to the founding of the Bannock Academy. He recognized the genetic reengineering inherent in BYU-Idaho's creation from Ricks College. He also comprehended the Spirit of Ricks, which in many respects reminded him of the learning-driven, student-engaging ethos of HBS. With his background in globalization and information technology, he saw the potential to take BYU-Idaho's innovative educational model to a new level.

Happily, David Bednar felt none of the discomfort at Clark's appointment that Eliot did at Lowell's. In fact, the two would become fast friends, sharing not only a love for the university but a passion for golf. More important, Clark and Bednar found that they shared a vision for the university that went beyond the innovations undertaken at its creation.

Three Imperatives

Clark outlined that vision in his inaugural address. He spoke of three imperatives. The first was to "raise substantially the quality of every aspect of the experience our students have," the second to "make a BYU-Idaho education available to many more [students]," and the third to "lower the relative cost of education." Personally well acquainted with the bigger-and-better tendency, Clark conceded that higher education tradition treats these three goals as mutually exclusive. It is generally assumed that reducing the cost of instruction is antithetical to increasing its quality. Likewise, tradition holds that more students can be served only if cost goes up or quality goes down. "But," Clark declared, "we are not bound by tradition."[5]

Clark acknowledged that the quality of a BYU-Idaho education was already high.[6] That was statistically evident in the university's faculty recruitment record. In its first two years BYU-Idaho had hired 67 new faculty members, 45 of them net additions to the existing complement. Those 67 postings drew more than 1,100 applications, a sign of professorial interest in the new institution and also an indication of the quality of the new hires.[7]

More significant, Clark could see what Hal Eyring had at Ricks College in the early 1970s: professors who went beyond merely teaching, becoming mentors to students in the spirit of Harvard's Georges Doriot and C. Rowland Christensen. Clark appreciated the importance of that above-and-beyond professorial service from his teaching and administrative experiences at Harvard Business School. In fact, he was fortunate to have learned the principle as a young college student. While setting his class schedule, he asked his uncle, a university dean, what courses he should take. The uncle replied, "Don't take courses. Take professors."

While setting his class schedule, [Clark] asked his uncle, a university dean, what courses he should take. The uncle replied, "Don't take courses. Take professors."

Taking professors rather than courses served Clark well as a Harvard student. In his sophomore year he recognized his interest in economics; he was particularly drawn to the work of Alexander Gerschenkron, a renowned economic historian. Before graduating from Harvard College, Clark had taken two full years' worth of courses from Gerschenkron and was well on his way to a Ph.D. in economics.

In graduate school Clark forged a lasting relationship with John Dunlop, Derek Bok's first Faculty of Arts and Sciences dean. By then Dunlop had returned to teaching economics, with the distinguished title and special prerogatives of University Professor, the faculty honor created by James Conant in the 1930s. Clark took a class from Dunlop in the latter's specialty, labor relations, and subsequently received an invitation to serve as his research assistant. A year later, when President Gerald Ford appointed Dunlop as Secretary of Labor, Clark went with him to Washington. Upon returning to Harvard, Dunlop took up residence at the business school, from which he served as Clark's dissertation advisor. When Clark completed his Ph.D., Dunlop encouraged him to join the HBS faculty.

Clark was glad to see that BYU-Idaho students could "take professors," as he had done. Yet he also recognized several opportunities to enhance the quality of the students' learning experience. One, a recommendation of the administrative team he inherited from David Bednar, was to create a new academic calendar with a true third semester. BYU-Idaho technically operated a full spring and summer schedule, but did so via two eight-week terms. Faculty members could choose which of the two terms they would work, taking the other off as a typical academic break.

The system was difficult to administer, as most faculty wanted to work the first term and take the second one off. Worse, it disadvantaged the students. They had access to their assigned faculty advisor for only half of the nontraditional semester. Also, their classes were taught twice as quickly as they would be in the fall or winter semesters. A student taking a four-credit biology or calculus course, for example, would spend eight hours per week in class rather than the usual four. Even carrying one-half of the traditional fall and winter semester course load, spring and summertime students found it difficult to learn a new subject in just eight weeks; there was too little mental "soak time."

On top of that timing problem, many of these students labored under the disadvantage of lower high school grades and test scores. As the track system then operated, applicants with the highest grades and scores got to choose their track first. The majority chose the traditional fall–winter schedule, leaving the less well prepared students to run the gantlet of the less forgiving spring and summer terms.

Resetting the Academic Calendar and Clock

Clark's team proposed and ultimately won acceptance of two fundamental changes to the university's DNA that equalized the quality of the summer experience. One was a three-semester academic calendar with an employment contract by which faculty members would teach year-round, except for a short summer break. The other was a system for track assignment that gave no special preferences and built each track to be academically comparable in terms of student qualifications.

The proposed year-round calendar preserved a significant block of uninterrupted time, roughly six weeks, for faculty professional development and personal vacation. This was possible because of an innovation in the daily class schedule. Historically, the university had run classes for the usual fifty minutes, and its semesters had lasted sixteen weeks. By lengthening class times to sixty minutes, Clark's team created a fourteen-week semester with total classroom time equivalent to the old approach. The student and faculty workload during each week would be greater, but the total time in class during the shortened semester would remain the same.[8] The faculty would naturally receive a pay increase for the greater workload and the additional weeks worked in what would become the new spring semester.

When first mooted before the faculty in the fall of 2005, just a few months after Clark's arrival, the proposal triggered widespread debate about how the three semesters should fall out across the twelve-month calendar. Some, for example, preferred having August off, while others wanted December. In an Eliot-esque way, Clark's team invited broad input. Facultywide electronic discussion boards were created and meetings held with departments. Ultimately, eight unique calendar proposals were put forward for full faculty vote. In a lighthearted attempt to distinguish and personalize the proposals, each was named as the National Weather Service does hurricanes, but with a biblical leaning: Abigail, Boaz, Claudia, Daniel, and so on to Hezekiah.[9] A large majority of faculty supported an August break and separating the fall and winter semesters with the traditional Christmas and New Year's break. Only a relative handful opted for less than full-year contracts.

Even with the pay increase, the new contract delivered both a better experience for students and reduced cost per unit of instruction. With virtually all of the faculty teaching a full spring semester, it was now possible to fill that semester to the same level—11,600 full-time students—as fall and winter. No new buildings were required, and faculty benefits, roughly a quarter of salary compensation, remained the same. On the margin, the pay increase yielded a greater than 1-for-1 return in the university's ability to serve more students at higher quality and lower per student cost.

Clark's team also recognized an opportunity in the break between the end of spring semester, in late July, and the beginning of fall semester, in early September. That was enough time to offer two- and three-credit courses to ambitious students who decided to stay in Rexburg during the break. Faculty, both full-time and adjunct, could be paid to work on a per course basis. Here again, the marginal returns far exceeded the costs. With no additional fixed investment, the filling of the summer break had the potential to increase the university's annual instructional capacity by almost 15 percent, just as creating the spring semester had increased it by 50 percent.

With no additional fixed investment, the filling of the summer break had the potential to increase the university's annual instructional capacity by almost 15 percent

Incoming students adapted to cohort-equalizing track assignments with little more concern than the faculty had expressed over the year-round contract. It helped that the three semesters were now truly equal in the proffered learning experience and that the out-of-the-ordinary spring semester offered better weather in chilly Rexburg than the other two. A small minority of students and parents voiced opposition to nontraditional track assignments, and some chose other schools.

However, even high-ACT and high–grade point average students who received a non-fall–winter track assignment accepted at nearly the same rate as before. By late 2007, BYU-Idaho would operate year-round at a constant level of instructional and student body quality.[10]

HURDLES TO YEAR-ROUND OPERATION

At first blush, the great hurdle to year-round use of the expensive college campus may appear to be faculty support. The academic summer break is more than a cultural expectation—for scholars, it provides focused time for vital research and writing. Yet the growing prevalence of adjunct instruction (both face to face and online) means that fewer tenure-track faculty are needed to provide robust summer curricula. Moreover, if summer offerings are sufficiently enrolled, the additional tuition revenue may allow for handsome faculty compensation, given that the incremental non-instructional costs are limited. But there's the real rub: convincing enough students to take classes during the summer.

California's higher education leaders recognized the potential benefits of summer operation in the late 1960s, when booming demographics strained the state's system of colleges and universities. A formal study projected savings of hundreds of millions of dollars, all from using existing physical facilities rather than constructing new ones.[11] It wasn't until 1999, when the demographic cycle and the state's magnetic economy brought a new wave of would-be students, that the legislature seriously pursued this strategy, creating special financial incentives for public universities and colleges to operate year-round.

The results were mixed. In the ten years after 1999, summertime enrollments at the University of California campuses nearly tripled, but even at that increased level those campuses were operating at less than a quarter of fall semester levels. The relative summer utilization of the state university and community college campuses declined slightly.[12]

The problem was one that the study of thirty years earlier had foreshadowed: getting students to change their schooling patterns. A 2006 legislative analysis suggested several innovative methods for enticing students to enroll in summer courses, in addition to requiring students at high-demand campus such as Berkeley and Los Angeles to attend some summer terms. Proposed incentives for voluntary participation included reducing summer tuition rates, offering popular courses that fill quickly in the fall and winter, and giving fall registration and housing priority to students who enroll in the summer.[13] Though the budget battles attendant to economic hard times steal attention from such nuanced marketing strategies, they hold great potential for serving more students at reduced cost.

A Model for Learning

Another innovation Clark proposed to the faculty in his first year in Rexburg was a common framework for instruction and learning, soon dubbed the "Learning Model."[14] In his nearly three decades of teaching at the Harvard Business School, Clark had come to appreciate the power of a shared instructional framework. The foundation of that framework at HBS is preparation by students and professors to engage in classroom discussion where the learning is "participant centered." Often but not always, the focus of preparation is a case, the story of a company or executive facing a business dilemma. Students read the case and other preparation materials and discuss them in small groups before coming to class. Professors make similar preparations, using a teaching note created by the case's author. Those who teach sections of the same course meet weekly to debrief their past weeks' classroom experiences and to prepare for upcoming ones.

Clark proposed to the faculty in his first year in Rexburg . . . a common framework for instruction and learning, soon dubbed the "Learning Model."

Though Clark felt strongly about having a common, campuswide framework for instruction, he knew that it would have to be unique to BYU-Idaho. Thus, he did not prescribe the principles or the pedagogical approaches of the Learning Model; when asked, he was quick to point out that case-based discussion is only one of many ways to be participant centered in the learning process. To launch the effort, he convened a daylong meeting of the faculty. The result of their discussion was a list of more than two hundred principles. That list was turned over to a committee of volunteers who worked for more than a year to aggregate and whittle the two hundred principles down to half a dozen.

The deliberative process of this committee was, in the words of one member, "herky-jerky" and "non-linear."[15] The self-nominated group of nearly twenty dwindled over time to a core cadre who debated intensely and sought input from the faculty at large. Clark's contribution at the end was to consolidate two of the committee's six principles in which he saw some overlap, creating a final list of five.[16] He also suggested adding a process component, a recommendation for the *way* in which learning occurs. When ultimately approved by the committee, the Learning Model included the five principles and a proposed cycle of (1) preparing to learn, (2) teaching one another, and (3) pondering and proving one's learning.

Among the principles that emerged were the simple notions that students are responsible for their own learning and for teaching one another. These patterns of learning had long been a part of the Spirit of Ricks and of the new university that David Bednar had often described as student centered. Clark also recognized them as jibing with the method of teaching at the Harvard Business School. The best-known champion of that method was C. Roland Christensen, Hal Eyring's dissertation advisor and an instructional expert on whom Derek Bok drew in his efforts to enhance teaching at Harvard.[17] Christensen argued that great teaching not only engages students but makes them partners with the instructor in the learning process.[18] That partnership requires a teaching and learning "contract" running both between instructor and student and also among the students themselves.[19] The contract includes the course syllabus, with its assignments and grading standards, but goes much further. It embodies the expectation that students and instructors will come to class prepared to teach one another in an environment of mutual trust and respect.

This model of learning requires more than just moving beyond the traditional lecture. Instructors become responsible for dual competency, mastery of both the subject matter and the art of conveying it for maximum student learning.[20] The latter necessitates not only understanding how to engage students, such as by initially deflecting a question from one student to another; it also means sensing the capabilities and needs of each individual well enough to determine which student ought to receive the deflected question. In this style of learning, teaching success depends as much on knowing the students as on knowing the subject matter.

Instructors become responsible for dual competency, mastery of both the subject matter and the art of conveying it for maximum student learning.

Keys to Implementing the Learning Model

As Eyring had at Ricks College in the 1970s, Clark found that this kind of student-engaging instruction was already occurring to a significant degree at BYU-Idaho.[21] Still, when it came to broader application of these techniques, some faculty worried that putting more of the teaching responsibility on students would lead to what some called "ignorance swapping." Clark saw the need to formalize and raise awareness of the best teaching practices on campus and to provide tools for faculty and student use. He tasked a team with codifying and disseminating the best of what was occurring at BYU-Idaho, Harvard, and other innovative schools. The team organized seminars and developed a learning resource website that included tools for creating cases and problems, concept tests, and systems of peer mentoring.[22] By 2008 students as well as faculty members were using many of these tools and could recite from memory the three procedural steps of effective learning: "Prepare, teach one another, and ponder and prove."

The Learning Model team included former Harvard MBA director and longtime Kim Clark colleague Steve Wheelwright, who came to BYU-Idaho in 2006 after retiring from HBS. Wheelwright worked with faculty members both in groups and one on one, demonstrating discussion-based teaching techniques and observing classes. He encouraged professors to make reciprocal visits to one another's classrooms, a standard HBS practice, with the purpose of learning from and teaching one another as instructors.

In 2007, Steve Wheelwright was appointed president of BYU-Hawaii, a BYU-Idaho sister institution established 1955 to meet the higher education needs of Mormon students in the Pacific Isles. A BYU-Idaho faculty development committee continued to sponsor activities similar to those Wheelwright had encouraged, such as brown bag lunches and conferences where faculty members shared instructional tips and curricular innovations. The committee's chair, Spanish professor Steve Hunsaker, enjoyed describing his conversion to the new style of instruction. "I always dreamed of being a teacher," he would say, "but I taught for a long time before I realized the difference between teaching and creating learning experiences."

Though appealing in theory, the Learning Model presented challenges in practice. Initially, the greatest difficulty was promoting adoption. Some faculty members resisted the apparent attempt to systemize and standardize their teaching. Talented lecturers particularly resented the implication that classroom discussion is a superior form of instruction in all situations. In time, they found encouragement in the idea, taught by Steve Hunsaker and others, that a skillful lecture can provide a valuable foundation for classroom discussion.[23]

As adoption of the Learning Model progressed, there was also the converse problem: teachers relying too much on students to instruct one another without first having conveyed enough foundational information or having established the necessary framework for class discussion. Some students complained of their professors' abdication of teaching responsibility. The balance between too much control and too little proved difficult to strike, a problem familiar to those with experience in discussion-based teaching and learning.

These challenges highlighted the need for enhanced evaluation of what was occurring in the classroom. Notwithstanding the strong Ricks College and BYU-Idaho commitment to teaching, formal assessment of instruction and curriculum had occurred only infrequently. That was particularly true for faculty members with "continuing status," the university's version of tenure; those continuing status professors had their courses evaluated only every ninth semester, or one semester every three years.

Part of the problem was lack of confidence in the evaluation process. Many faculty members viewed student evaluations as subjective and shallow, more a measure of popularity than of instructional effectiveness. To address this concern, faculty members and academic administrators jointly developed a more comprehensive assessment system, including an evaluation form that not only reflected the principles and practices of the Learning Model but also required students to assess their own performance.[24] The first four items on the BYU-Idaho course evaluation form read:

1. I was prepared for class.
2. I arrived at class on time.
3. I was an active participant in online or face-to-face class discussions.
4. I sought opportunities to share my learning with others outside of class.

The form applied similar Learning Model standards to the course and the instructor. Students evaluated the degree to which "The course provided opportunities to learn from and teach other students" and "The instructor responded respectfully and constructively to student questions and viewpoints." In addition to the revised course and instructor evaluation form, there was an increase in assessment frequency: every third year, continuing faculty members received student evaluations for three consecutive semesters, giving them not only three times more feedback but an opportunity to attempt enhancements, see their impact, and make further refinements.

COSTS AND BENEFITS OF A COMMON LEARNING MODEL

For years after its initial introduction, the Learning Model continued to provoke debate. One faculty member, a highly rated teacher, expressed a sentiment share by others when he described the Learning Model as ''an oxymoron'' and a deterrent to instructional ''autonomy, mastery, and purpose.'' Others further argued that the specification of learning outcomes, already an accreditation requirement, obviated the need to also specify learning processes; they predicted an unhealthy shift in emphasis from outcomes to mere means. Academic administrators, observing resentment among some faculty members and self-doubt among others, spoke of the need to ''demystify the Learning Model.''

Maryellen Weimer, Professor Emeritus of Teaching and Learning at the Pennsylvania State University, has documented both the benefits of what she calls ''learner-centered teaching'' and the reasons that many faculty members and students resist it. Some students, she has found, like being spoon-fed and criticize instructors who use anything other than ''teaching-as-telling'' methods; they particularly resist pedagogical changes that create grading uncertainty. Faculty members, for whom the transition to learner-centered teaching initially means more work, and who worry about the risk of failing to cover essential course content, may see this student immaturity and recoil.[25]

As the BYU-Idaho Learning Model gradually came to be viewed as a tool rather than a taskmaster, its individual and institutional benefits became more apparent. Students began rise to the occasion, and classroom learning improved. With continually refreshed pedagogical frameworks, case studies, learning objects and other tools at their fingertips, faculty could better manage the up-front costs of transitioning to the Learning Model; these tools also helped them find more time to focus on incorporating new developments in their disciplines into the curriculum. With its emphasis on preclass preparation and teaching one another, the Learning Model likewise helped in setting expectations and providing peer support for the many BYU-Idaho students whose efforts in high school hadn't prepared them for the academic rigors of college. Finally, the Learning Model proved to be a valuable starting point for designing university-wide online and general education, or "Foundations," courses.

Foundations: A New Approach to General Education

Clark recognized another opportunity to enhance the quality of learning in the university's long-standing but yet-unfulfilled commitment to its accreditors to revise the general education (GE) program. He had observed at close range Larry Summer's unsuccessful attempt to overhaul Harvard's Core. Still, he felt that Lowell, Conant, Bok, and Summers were wise to put Harvard College's General Education curriculum among their leading curricular priorities. He agreed with Bok's reasoning in launching the effort to create Harvard's Core in the early 1970s:

> A residential college occupies a predominant share of the time, energy and experience of students during four vital years in their development, years that fall immediately prior to important choices of role and career. Having assumed this position, the college must pay attention to those critical choices insofar as it is capable of doing so. Such decisions require that students gain a developing awareness of their values, capacities, limitations and interests together with an understanding of the various roles and opportunities available for spending a useful, productive life.[26]

Clark recognized that students and faculty alike view the typical GE program as a low point of college study. Too much breadth in the choice of courses and lack of integration robs most GE programs of their intellectual and social value. For many students, GE requirements are hurdles on the way to more focused and engaging major offerings. For faculty, they can be exercises in educational mass production preferably delegated to graduate assistants and adjuncts.

Yet Clark hoped that BYU-Idaho could create a general education program capturing not only the science and globalization content to which Summers aspired but also the common courses, cross-disciplinary perspectives, and moral values called for by the Redbook. He saw in the revamping of general education, which he renamed "Foundations," more than just a chance to upgrade the curriculum for freshmen and sophomores. As Eliot had done in introducing the elective system, he recognized potential second- and third-order benefits to the quality of the students' learning experiences. By infusing these new courses with Learning Model pedagogy, for instance, the university could set the standard for its application in the majors. The rising generation of BYU-Idaho students would be trained as well-prepared, active classroom learners, and they would expect to be challenged accordingly in non-Foundations courses as they progressed toward graduation.

Clark also envisioned intellectual and social benefits going beyond the formal curriculum. For example, he imagined informal, out-of-class discussions at dinner tables and in study halls, the kind that Lowell had sought to recreate—and that Clark had enjoyed as a college student—in Harvard's house system. BYU-Idaho couldn't replicate the house system, with its students and teachers from related academic disciplines all living under one roof. But by specifying commonly required courses and teaching according to a common model of learning, the university could increase the likelihood of impromptu learning experiences occurring among students who were taking the same courses from different professors.

A similar benefit might be realized by faculty members. Clark knew firsthand that outstanding professors at HBS succeed in the classroom not by virtue of individual talent or personal preparation alone but by participation in teaching groups. In the first year of the Harvard MBA program, 900 students divided into ten sections take the same courses. Each section is taught by a different professor, but the subject to be discussed each day is the same. Not only students in a given section but also faculty members from different sections can help one another prepare for class; later, they can debrief what went on there.

The faculty collaboration occurs in formal teaching groups. An assigned group leader, typically someone with long experience in teaching the course, guides colleagues in discussing their common teaching challenges and strategies. The process has the dual benefit of disseminating best practice and also educating less experienced faculty in the art and science of teaching. Teaching groups both enhance the learning experience of students and serve as a vehicle of professional development for professors. The system is particularly powerful for new faculty members, who learn from the experiences of their more seasoned colleagues.

Finally, Clark hoped through Foundations to stimulate the sort of interdepartmental collaboration identified by his predecessor, David Bednar, as vital to the university's success. Bednar had warned of the tendency of university departments and majors to proliferate and become intellectually narrow in the process. As a new university, BYU-Idaho had a rare opportunity to avoid that fate. Effective integration across traditional academic boundaries would be valuable not only to students in their intellectual development and career preparation but also to faculty members in their scholarship. "Our success as an institution," Bednar predicted, "will be determined in large measure by how well we facilitate the integration of curriculum and pedagogy across traditional boundaries. If we focus exclusively on departmental development and fail to achieve this overarching objective of effective integration, then we will have bungled one of the greatest educational opportunities of [our time]."[27]

Effective integration across traditional academic boundaries would be valuable not only to students in their intellectual development and career preparation but also to faculty members in their scholarship.

Designing the Foundations Curriculum

The development of Foundations courses did serve the purpose of integrating faculty from different departments. Nearly a quarter of the faculty, 110 professors representing every one of the university's 39 departments, participated in the creation of 25 new courses. They worked from a charge written by a faculty committee that had spent a year, from 2006 to 2007, negotiating the outlines of the program. Foundations would comprise forty credit hours, or one-third of a student's graduation requirements. Students would take courses in nine subject areas: English, math, science, American history and government, international affairs, humanities, family relations, religion, and analytical thinking and moral judgment. All but the religion courses, which embodied a design shared by BYU-Idaho's sister institutions, would be specially developed for the Foundations program.[28]

The faculty committee that produced this proposal drew upon Derek Bok's newly published book, *Our Underachieving Colleges*, which not only identifies the deficiencies of traditional general education but also offers proposals for making it better. Bok's call for "learning to think" and "building character" influenced the committee's view of the analytical thinking and moral judgment course, as his call for "preparing for a global society" did the international affairs course.[29]

The committee also found inspiration in a teaching principle enunciated by Charles Eliot at his inauguration and cited by Bok: "The lecturer pumps laboriously into sieves. The water may be wholesome, but it runs through. A mind must work to grow."[30] An informal survey conducted the year before revealed that BYU-Idaho was little better than the typical university on this score: according to students, lectures consumed nearly 80 percent of class time.[31] Clark had suggested that this ratio be inverted, with professors lecturing only 20 percent of the time.[32] In Foundations courses, the committee hoped, students would spend the other 80 percent of class time "work[ing] to grow" under the professor's direction, particularly according to the Learning Model principle of teaching one another.

On a related note, the committee took to heart the notion expressed by Bok that the content of Foundations courses would matter less than the way they were taught: "One cannot assume that students will retain most of what they are taught merely because they have taken a course, however important its content may be. Instead, the residue of knowledge and the habits of mind students take away from college are likely to be determined less by *which* courses they take than by *how* they are taught and *how well* they are taught."[33]

Bok's position supported Kim Clark's belief that the new Learning Model would be critical to the success of Foundations, and vice versa.

Creating the Foundations Courses

Once the Foundations committee's recommendation for courses had been approved, each of the twenty-five course development teams met with Clark for an initial briefing. He challenged them to build on the academic diversity designed into their team roster and to apply the Learning Model in developing the new courses. Textbooks were to be avoided (not necessarily burned, as he had been quoted as saying) in favor of originally authored online materials. Though Lowell's name was not invoked, the courses were to meet his standard of being more than merely introductory to a particular discipline; the charge was to make them cross-disciplinary and applied to real-world problems.

The initial update meetings three months later revealed signs of stress and apprehension. Beyond the significant time and effort required, there were valid concerns that ran the gamut from curriculum content to organizational dynamics to teaching philosophy. Many teams, for instance, expressed the worry that crossing disciplines and adding real-world applications would make it difficult to cover the essential material; they reported struggling to decide what traditionally taught content to omit.

Other teams were working through the awkwardness inherent in their cross-disciplinary composition. A humanities department member wondered how he could contribute to the American history and government course team, which was staffed mainly by historians, political scientists, and economists.[34] Among all teams there was sensitivity to the potential loss of individuality inherent in teaching to a standard curriculum, the more so because of the Ricks College tradition of faculty connecting personally with students.

With each quarterly update, convergence of content and teaching strategy became more apparent. The breakthrough for many teams came when they stopped negotiating over disciplinary content and began thinking more holistically. For example, the science team, comprising faculty from physics, chemistry, biology, geology, and psychology, hit on the idea of teaching science fundamentals through the lens of important systems such as the human brain. Abandoning the traditional survey approach of most introductory courses, they determined to take students deeply into a few personally relevant topics, teaching ad hoc the essential principles of science. They embraced the challenge of finding the essence of their individual disciplines, the precondition to combining them.

Some of the most effective teams actually celebrated their lack of disciplinary expertise. A group that chose to develop an elective international affairs course on Pakistan had no one with a formal research background in it. Their leader quipped, "The makeup of our team sounded like the beginning of a bad joke: 'You've got a geographer, a linguist, an economist, and a religion professor all in the same room . . . .'"[35] This team had the benefit, though, of a clear purpose: helping students to understand a little known but globally important country.

The team let their lack of subject matter expertise and disparate backgrounds unite them. They divvied up themes according to individual interest and comfort level. The Russian professor studied the societal effects of Pakistan's language, tribes, culture, and education system. The religion professor, a former attorney, analyzed subjects ranging from faith to foreign relations. Each team meeting began with an informal presentation by one or more of these experts-in-the-making. The team designed their course to engage students in a similar process of discovery. They trusted that their relative lack of scholarly expertise would be made up by their ability to say, "Here's what I know, and here's how I learned what I know." Effectively, they redefined the meaning of bigger and better, to accord with the needs of their students. They reasoned that deep subject matter expertise might be less valuable to first-time learners than empathetic perspectives on how to engage the subject matter.

The majority of the new Foundations curriculum was rolled out in the fall of 2008, with the remainder the following semester. The initial results were mixed. Many teams were still writing curriculum as they taught, and some faculty expressed concern about being taken too far beyond their disciplinary expertise. Student evaluations of those first semesters were lower than hoped and in the case of some courses indicated the need for substantial overhaul. One, a novel course that attempted to meld both verbal and visual communication, was scrapped altogether in favor of a more traditional advanced writing course, without which, academic administrators had learned, BYU-Idaho's associate's degree would not meet the transfer requirements of other universities.[36]

The transferability issue was just one of the challenges created by these cross-disciplinary Foundations courses. Another was convincing students who were already committed to a major of the benefit of taking relatively rudimentary Foundations courses related to that major. Why, for example, make a physics major take the "Foundations of Science" course? Some of these students appreciated the value of teaching their peers and exploring the connections among the disciplines, along with the real-world applications of science. Others, though, complained about being required to retake "high school science."

The management of Foundations curriculum, from course creation and updating to the staffing of classes, also proved difficult. Most of the problems stemmed from Foundations existing outside the university's departmental structure. For one thing, ensuring an adequate supply of sections for a single course could mean enlisting faculty from half-a-dozen departments. A similar problem presented itself when courses needed revision: Would the departments commit the faculty resources?

Clark responded by naming a dean of Foundations. It was a step short of the separate general education faculty for which Conant had argued. However, Clark hoped that the BYU-Idaho faculty would, in the spirit of David Bednar's call for effective integration, transcend the departmental structure of the university when it came to Foundations. He encouraged the Foundations course development teams to pursue a spirit and process of unified continuous improvement of the type he had studied as a young academic researcher in the auto assembly plants of Japan. In the semesters following the Foundations launch, all teams engaged in significant revision, and most students and faculty reported increased satisfaction.

TEACHING WHAT YOU DON'T KNOW

The notion of a professor's teaching a course unlike any he or she has taught or even taken as a student isn't as uncommon or dangerous as it might sound. As Therese Huston argues in *Teaching What You Don't Know*,[37] it happens often and will do so more often as the percentage of tenure-track faculty members at many universities falls and as learning outcomes-enhancing programmatic initiatives such as Foundations become more common.

Huston suggests that teachers without deep subject matter expertise can do more than just compensate; there are ways to convert the apparent liability into a teaching asset. As in the case of BYU-Idaho's Pakistan course, instructors who have struggled to master course content before teaching it are more likely to sense students' learning roadblocks and less likely to "over-answer" technical questions. They may also rely more on teaching and learning tools, which, once mastered, can be taken from one new teaching assignment to the next.

> Huston notes that teaching what you don't know can enrich the professorial experience, providing variety and stimulating new disciplinary insights.

Raising Quality Outside of the Classroom

Clark also recognized the need to better serve BYU-Idaho students outside of the classroom. He appreciated the fact that students have customer service experiences not only with their professors but also with a host of other university employees: academic advisors, financial aid and registration officers, cashiers, sales clerks, telephone operators, custodians, parking enforcers. Both through heavyweight teams that operated for a year or more and also through shorter-term initiatives, he and his colleagues sought to systematically improve students' experiences with representatives of the university.

Some of the initiatives were as simple as screening form letters for courteousness; the bursar's office, for example, was encouraged to find ways to show increased respect and concern in billing notices, even in the case of past due accounts. Likewise, telephone operators and office receptionists (most of them student employees) received etiquette training. The standard for answering inquiries went beyond being respectful and well informed about one's own sphere of operation. Front-line representatives of the university were taught to stay with inquirers until their questions were answered, even if that meant escorting them to another office.

Students also received formal training in helping one another honor the university's standards of conduct and achieve their personal goals. Through a new Student Living program, the university offered case-based curriculum for roommates to apply in their apartments. The first of four lessons was called "Helping Roommates Become More: Moving beyond 'sharing the same roof' to a positive learning experience." Another lesson addressed conflict resolution. A third was titled "Honor and Integrity: Keeping commitments and encouraging others to do the same."[38] Each of these lessons began with a true-to-life case of roommate struggles, followed by principles and other cases for follow-up discussion. The Student Living office enlisted student volunteers in taking this curriculum to the apartment complexes, where they demonstrated it and trained others in its use.

The Necessity of Sacrifice

In most of their quality-enhancing initiatives, Clark and his BYU-Idaho colleagues could claim to have defied higher education trends: the quality of the student experience generally increased, per student costs stayed the same or dropped, and the way was opened to serve more students. That was clearly true of the new calendar, with its full-fledged third semester requiring few new faculty or facilities. It was less obviously but similarly true of the Learning Model and Foundations, which operated symbiotically to increase the number of students a professor could teach at once. When applied effectively, the Learning Model, with its discussion emphasis, allowed for effective instruction of at least ninety students, the size of a first-year MBA section at the Harvard Business School. Clark set the limit on Foundations courses at eighty-five, with a targeted average of thirty to forty. That eighty-five-student limit meant reducing the section size of a few general education courses that had operated with two hundred or more students. But it also allowed the typical Foundations course to accommodate more students than had been served by its general education predecessor. Through the Learning Model, the university was on a path teaching more students at higher quality and lower cost.

All of these achievements required individual sacrifice. The faculty in particular shouldered extra burdens, some temporary and others permanent. During the eighteen-month period of Foundations course development, most of the faculty release time[39] granted was tied to that effort, preempting scholarship and other individually determined projects. That made the faculty's high teaching load of four three-hour courses per semester feel even heavier. Also, sabbatical leaves were temporarily reduced in number.

The sacrifice of working year-round for the sake of creating a third semester truly equivalent in quality to the other two was permanent. So was supporting the university's decision to raise average class sizes. Though the Learning Model and the carefully designed Foundations courses allowed this to occur without negative impact on the student learning experience, it increased the faculty's burden in grading and student advising. Defying tradition required more than just innovation; it also required working harder.

Defying tradition required more than just innovation; it also required working harder.

Clark's administrative team found that the essential quid pro quo for this kind of personal sacrifice was increased communication and institutional support. From the beginning of his tenure at BYU-Idaho, Clark had advised his administrators to apply the following rule: "Take the amount of communication you think is necessary and double it; then, take that amount and triple it." Notwithstanding this standard of communication and the broad involvement of the faculty in the new calendar and curriculum initiatives, the pace of change left many wanting both more information and more involvement in the decision-making process.[40]

Clark and his team responded with ad hoc departmental meetings in which what some faculty members had called "administrative monologue" could be supplemented with faculty–administration dialogue. The administration and faculty also collaborated in the creation of five-year development plans for all full-time professors, by which they were assured of opportunities for personal scholarship in addition to their course development activities.

An Auditorium to Grow Into

Not all of BYU-Idaho's quality enhancements came through innovation or individual sacrifice. Some had to be paid for the traditional way: with more money. That was true of the university's doubling the size of its student center, a key element of enhancing the student experience outside of the classroom.

It was also true of a new auditorium. In spite of Gordon Hinckley's statement in announcing the creation of the university that the physical additions to the campus would be "modest in nature and scope," he later authorized a gathering place that was anything but modest in size. At Clark's inauguration, where fewer than 4,500 guests could squeeze into the university's basketball arena, a visiting member of the board said, "You need something bigger than this." Clark took that observation as a directive and made a new auditorium part of BYU-Idaho's campus master-planning activities.

Clark and his facilities team reasoned that if something larger were to be built, it ought to accommodate the entire student body, then capped at 11,600 full-time students per semester. The need went beyond inaugurations and graduations, which involved only a portion of the student body. The primary use for the auditorium would be the university's weekly devotional, the equivalent of chapel at Eliot's Harvard. Like Harvard's chapel, BYU-Idaho's devotional was optional rather than compulsory. But attendance ran as high as three-fourths of the student body, and it likely would increase if the half-dozen overflow sites around campus were replaced with a single large facility.

Within several months Clark took to the church board in Salt Lake a proposal for an auditorium to accommodate roughly 12,000; also included was a multipurpose foyer area the size of ten basketball courts to be used mainly for athletic play. His sense of relief at winning the board's approval turned to amazement one week later, when Hinckley called to say, "I've been thinking about your auditorium; you need to make it bigger and build it sooner than planned." Though Clark and his colleagues wondered at the directive to expand the facility beyond the size of the student body, it took little time to reconfigure the auditorium's design to seat 15,000.

Unfortunately, the construction process bogged down from the start. Detailed design for the one-of-a-kind facility required more effort than expected, and preliminary excavation revealed a hash of lava rock similar to the ground beneath the old Ricks Academy gym building. As construction stalled, the price of raw materials, especially structural steel needed by China for its Olympic building boom, soared. The auditorium's general contractor revised its cost estimate up by 50 percent. Pioneer frugality and innovative product design had met its match in brick-and-mortar reality.

Clark spent the unusually harsh winter of 2007–2008 watching, from his office window, the tedious efforts to blast and level the hole from which the auditorium's foundations were slowly rising. Fortunately for BYU-Idaho, its sponsoring institution had the wherewithal to keep the auditorium project going. In fact, Gordon Hinckley's instruction to start construction immediately seemed prescient, as the project was fully funded before the market crash. Yet the auditorium served as a reminder of the dangers of the traditional university's reliance on physical facilities and of the virtues of a zero-standard for further expansion.

Through the long winter Clark felt comforted by the knowledge that the auditorium would be finished, come what may. He also found encouragement in the thought that another project was in the works, one with the potential to further reduce the university's costs of instruction and increase its ability to serve enough additional students to fill the auditorium.

Chapter 18

Lowering Cost

At his inauguration, Kim Clark had shared a vision of reducing costs and increasing access to the university. He began by noting that the year-round academic calendar, with its three-track system for admitting students, was a major step in this direction. However, he stated the imperative to do more, referring specifically to information technology and innovative teaching techniques. He spoke of "breaking down the barriers of time and space" and of finding "new ways of learning and teaching that will yield a higher quality experience while requiring relatively fewer resources per student."[1]

Clark's point man in this effort to reduce cost and expand access through technology was a former HBS colleague, Clark Gilbert, whom Clark invited to join the university's administration. By academic training and professional business experience, Gilbert was an expert in technology-driven innovation. He had done his doctoral dissertation on the disruption of the newspaper industry by online publications. He had also developed a popular course on new business ventures at HBS and was a consulting partner of innovation specialist Clayton Christensen.

Gilbert also had a unique connection to BYU-Idaho that predated his 2006 arrival in Rexburg and would prove unexpectedly valuable in expanding the university's use of instructional technology. As a volunteer mentor of economically and educationally disadvantaged young people in the Boston area, he had discovered in 2004 a BYU-Idaho scholarship program designed specifically for that population.

With Gilbert's mentoring, these "at-risk" youths, who otherwise might have been nonconsumers of higher education, qualified as Heber J. Grant Scholars.

From Roxbury to Rexburg

Heber Grant, who never attended college, was born in the Utah Territory in the 1850s. His father died nine days after his birth, leaving Grant's mother alone to raise her son in a time before social welfare systems. Grant became known for overcoming economic and social disadvantage and for serving twenty-six years as president of the Mormon Church. The BYU-Idaho Heber J. Grant Program, created just prior to Kim Clark's arrival, provided financial support to disadvantaged applicants such as children of single parents or students who would be the first in their families to attend college.[2] Continuing assistance was conditioned on participation in life and study skills courses when they got to Rexburg; to remain a Grant Scholar, a student had to spend time studying financial budgeting, time management, and academic and career planning. These courses were taught by fellow Grant Scholars who had been at BYU-Idaho for a year or more. That was the other part of the scholarship bargain: giving back by mentoring others. The mentoring system reflected the student activities model, with volunteers rising through a leadership pyramid from one semester to the next, and the mentoring itself embodied the principles and practices of the Learning Model, especially students teaching of one another.

The Grant Scholars Program allowed even troubled youths from Boston's roughest neighborhoods to take advantage of BYU-Idaho's commitment to serving more students. The university opened its doors to anyone with a high school grade point average of 2.0 (a C average) and an ACT score of 16 (the equivalent of 790 on the SAT); the only condition was abiding by the school's code of honor. Gilbert and his fellow church volunteers built a pipeline from Boston to BYU-Idaho, helping dozens of at-risk youngsters, most of them from ethnic minorities and many of them second-generation immigrants, become Heber J. Grant Scholars.

Kim Clark gave Gilbert responsibility for both the Grant Scholars and the student activities program when he arrived in Rexburg the summer of 2006. The two programs operated on similar principles, and Gilbert systematized the operations of both; in particular, he and his colleagues explored and refined the processes by which student teach one another.

A year and a half later, Clark moved Gilbert into a new assignment: the creation of online courses and degree programs. Gilbert immediately recognized the opportunity to apply his pre–BYU-Idaho experiences to this new challenge. As he had studied and consulted to major newspapers in their attempts to create online editions, he had seen the tendency of successful incumbents to apply the new technology to the old processes without altering them. For example, newspapers tended to simply put their traditional print version online rather than adapting it to the unique capabilities of the new electronic medium. At the same time, Gilbert observed the lack of meaningful content and quality standards in many dot-com publications. The incumbents often couldn't see the full power of online technology because of the way they had been doing things. Conversely, the newcomers seemed to think that technology alone was enough. Both, Gilbert's research and consulting work showed, were wrong.

The Challenge to Create High-Quality Online Courses

In early 2008, when Kim Clark tapped him to lead the university's online learning efforts, Gilbert was prepared to help bridge a similar conceptual gap in education. On the one hand, he knew from watching stodgy newspapers try to make the Web conform to their conventions that simply putting an existing university course online would fail to create a meaningful student learning experience. On the other hand, he knew both from the financial failures of most dot-com publishers and from the poor reputations of many online universities that good online courses would require innovative, first-rate course designs and strategies for engaging students. Thanks to his first eighteen months' work at BYU-Idaho, with Grant Scholars and student activities leaders, he had new ideas for doing that.

Gilbert and his team appreciated the aversion to online courses of some BYU-Idaho faculty members; many justifiably viewed online learning askance. Shortly after the creation of the university in 2000, and in response to the requirement that each student complete at least one online course before graduating, nearly fifty offerings had been quickly created. Like most online courses of the time, these offerings allowed students to work at their own pace and provided no student-to-student interaction. They were, in the words of one course developer, "flexible from a schedule standpoint, but not the best learning experience."[3]

In addition to providing no interaction among students, the earliest BYU-Idaho courses also reflected the assumption that instruction is either/or, either all in the classroom or all online. Gilbert and his colleagues were intrigued by mounting evidence that the best form of learning is a hybrid of both.[4] A combination of both online and in-class instruction allows the various learning activities to be conducted via the more effective medium. For example, many activities traditionally done in the classroom, such as listening to a lecture or taking a test, can be effectively conducted online. Even an instructor-led discussion may be better if it occurs both in class and online, allowing shy students to make their points in the more anonymous online setting. Blending the online and in-class environments lets both students and instructors make more focused use of their time, potentially producing a learning experience of both lower cost and higher quality. A hybrid course also more effectively reaches students with differing learning styles.[5]

Blending the online and in-class environments lets both students and instructors make more focused use of their time, potentially producing a learning experience of both lower cost and higher quality.

"STUDENT-CENTRIC" USE OF ONLINE LEARNING TECHNOLOGY

One of the major recommendations of Clayton Christensen's *Disrupting Class* is to take a "student-centric" approach to education, one that responds to students' unique learning styles and preferences. This is difficult in face-to-face settings, especially when class sizes are large. By contrast, hybrid online learning allows students to choose among multiple paths for achieving a specified outcome. The key, as Christensen and his *Disrupting Class* colleagues point out, is not to simply to "cram" computers into existing educational models, as has too often occurred in the public schools, where $60 billion has been spent with little impact on student learning behavior.[6] A similar phenomenon can be observed in many college classrooms, where an expensive "tech station" and Internet wiring may be more often used to augment a lecture than to change the way students engage in learning.

As computers became pervasive tools for work in the 1980s, businesses faced a similar temptation, as then-Harvard Business School professor Shoshana Zuboff pointed out in her book *In the Age of the Smart Machine: The Future of Work and Power.*[7] Zuboff warned of a fateful choice between using computers to simply automate tasks for the sake of increased efficiency, potentially marginalizing workers, or using computers to inform workers, making them more valuable. Today, effective companies apply computational power to achieve both purposes. Many universities are doing something similar, using online technology not just to make learning more efficient, but to enhance it by allowing students and professors to better prepare for face-to-face learning experiences.

Under Charles Eliot and A. Lawrence Lowell, Harvard had invoked a form of hybrid instruction, albeit entirely face to face. As course sizes grew into the hundreds, Eliot created small sections led by junior instructors, who in small-group settings could answer questions difficult for the "course head" to address in large lectures. Lowell took the intimacy to a deeper level with tutorials, another module in Harvard's hybrid system of instruction. Gilbert's team saw the long-term potential to create, by marrying online and face-to-face instruction, the intimate, immersive learning environment that Lowell dreamed of, but without the cost of his tutorial and house systems.

The Power of Peer Instruction

The team also recognized the online potential of the teach-one-another principle. Building on processes developed for the Grant Scholars and student activities programs, they made student-to-student interaction an essential element of the courses they created.[8] They found additional inspiration and guidance in a mounting body of scholarly evidence that sometimes the best learning occurs peer-to-peer.

That was being proven not only in rarefied graduate school environments like the Harvard Business School but in undergraduate universities and community colleges.[9] It works not just in business and other "soft" sciences but in quantitatively precise fields such as math and physics. In fact, one of the highest-profile advocates of peer instruction is a Harvard physics professor, Eric Mazur. As Ricks College was becoming BYU-Idaho, Mazur was proving what Gilbert had seen among Grant scholars and BYU-Idaho activity leaders, namely that a student who has just mastered a complex concept, such as Newton's third law of motion or financial interest rate compounding, can often explain it more effectively to a fellow novice than can a professor who may have long since taken the concept for granted. This finding supports the conclusion of BYU-Idaho's faculty team that created the international affairs course on Pakistan—in some cases, the lower-cost, less-specialized learning peer can be a more effective teacher than the highly credentialed scholar.

Mazur began exploring peer instruction out of concern that even some of his brightest physics students couldn't make the connection between the equations they had mastered in the classroom and real-world physics problems, such as what happens when one moving object collides with another. That kind of application gap was demonstrated in a painfully humorous way by a film crew that interviewed newly graduated Harvard and MIT engineering students, still in caps and gowns, and asked them to light a bulb when given a battery and a wire. Most failed.[10]

Mazur brought such conceptual tests into his classroom. He used innovative techniques, including polling via electronic clickers, to identify which students could make the real-world application of the physics problems they were studying. He invited these students to explain to their mistaken or confused colleagues how they had arrived at the right answer. His research showed that with help from their peers even less competent students can make great gains, equal to what well-qualified ones do in traditional lecture environments.[11] Gilbert and his team saw the potential value of this kind of peer instruction in all BYU-Idaho courses, both face to face and online. But it proved particularly beneficial in the online environment, where well-structured peer-to-peer interactions helped to compensate for the more limited contact between student and instructor.

A SUCCESSFUL TEACHER'S WILLINGNESS TO INNOVATE

In the early 1990s, Eric Mazur was a successful professor in the Harvard Physics Department. His performance in both the laboratory and the classroom was superior, enough to earn him tenure. But then he came across work by Arizona State's David Hestenes showing that even after passing a physics class most students didn't understand the fundamentals of Newtonian mechanics. At the time, Mazur's lectures were getting positive feedback from students, who were passing what he considered difficult exams. Still, he remembered his own stultifying years as a physics undergraduate student, when rote memorization was the price of survival and he considered dropping out to become an artist or photographer. He wondered whether his students would have to wait, as he did, to get into the laboratory before they could really understand and love physics.

To Mazur's chagrin, administering Hestenes's tests of conceptual understanding to his Harvard undergraduates revealed that about half couldn't apply what he had taught them. Looking at the test, one student asked, "How should I answer these questions? According to what you taught me? Or according to the way I usually think about these things?"

"That was the moment," Mazur would later say, "I fell out of my ivory tower. It was then that I began to consider new ways of teaching."[12] With the tenure hurdle behind him and more than enough research to occupy his time, Mazur could have justified standing pat. Moving himself—and his students—out of the comfort of the standard pedagogy would be more than just time consuming. Until they could collectively find better ways to learn physics, deviating from the rote, predictable approaches risked student dissatisfaction and even diminished learning. But Mazur enlisted his students in the exploration process with the promise that their grades wouldn't suffer and they would learn more.

> *Children start life full of curiosity, they are all scientists—people ask "Why, why, why?" all the time. At some point in their middle school years . . . their curiosity gets turned off. From that point on, rather than ask "Why, why, why?" people concentrate on facts. They want to know the fact, or the answer, so that they can memorize it.*[14]
>
> —Eric Mazur

Mazur's experiments in the classroom proved as successful as those in his laboratory. By 2010 he not only supervised one of the largest research groups in Harvard's Physics Department but was one of the leading authorities on helping students teach one another. Mazur authored *Peer Instruction: A User's Manual,*[13] in which he explains how to teach large classes interactively. Particularly as the Learning Model was being developed and implemented, Mazur frequently welcomed faculty entourages from BYU-Idaho to his office and classroom.

An Online Course Production System

In creating online courses of higher quality than those BYU-Idaho had been operating, Gilbert and his team enjoyed more than just the benefit of understanding peer instruction. They were also ahead of the game thanks to the steady advance of computational and communication technology, which allowed for more interactive and engaging learning without increased expense. For example, students could talk to and see one another via laptops at a level of quality possible only with expensive video-conferencing equipment just a few years before.

The BYU-Idaho team also applied principles of production management to the process of course development. Its instructional design specialists collaborated with faculty members in creating online courses not only suffused with peer instruction but also outcome driven.[15] They began by specifying what students were to learn, a fundamental step often overlooked in the development of face-to-face courses. That omission is one likely reason that online offerings produce equal or superior cognitive learning outcomes.[16]

RIO SALADO COLLEGE

BYU-Idaho faced a momentous decision in creating its online course production system. Rather than establishing an autonomous organization for the purpose, the university determined to rely on heavyweight teams, developing each course via faculty appointees and instructional design professionals who brought the expertise of thier various domains to bear in a team effort. Given the university's commitment to serving all of its students—both those in Rexburg and those at a distance—via online courses that needed to be consistent with their face-to-face equivalents, the benefits of collaborating across organizational boundaries outweighed the costs.

An institution that exemplifies the benefits of organizational autonomy in online course development is Arizona's Rio Salado College, one of the eight schools featured in *Winning by Degrees.*[17] Rio Salado, which calls itself "the college within everyone's reach" was created in 1978 by the Maricopa County Community College District, the largest such district in the U.S. Of Maricopa's ten colleges, Rio Salado is the only one with no traditional campus. Its charter specifies an emphasis on "distance delivery," and in 1996 it became a pioneer in Internet-based education.

With limited campus operations to account for in the innovation process, Rio Salado was able to focus fully on the possibilities inherent in online learning. Students, mostly working adults, can choose from more than 500 online and hybrid courses and 40 degree programs. A "block calendar" offers 48 start dates each year, with a combination of 16-week and 8-week courses; an automated learning management system, RioLearn, allows students to take the first seven days of study to choose between the 16- and 8-week paths.

Rio Salado's emphasis on centrally developed online courses and part-time faculty keeps its costs relatively low, while the quality of student learning is relatively high: Rio Salado students score above the national average on Educational Testing Service's (ETS) Proficiency Profile, a measure of abilities in critical thinking, reading, writing, math, humanities, social science, and natural sciences. The combination of low cost and high quality has helped Rio Salado become the community college with the largest online enrollments in the U.S.[18]

BYU-Idaho's standardized production process for online courses required ongoing modification. For example, the university's faculty association president made the case for more intense faculty involvement than originally planned, not only in course development but in the hiring and training of online instructors. He argued persuasively that the investment of time and effort by the full-time faculty was critical to assuring common course content and high quality across on-campus and online offerings.[19] By early 2010, more than 40 percent of full-time faculty members had participated in online course development.

BYU-Idaho's full-time faculty members also participated in the screening of specially recruited and trained online adjunct instructors.[20] As had been the case in recruiting full-time faculty for the new BYU-Idaho, the supply of online instructors far exceeded the need; in one round of recruiting, 39 were hired from a pool of 765 applicants. Unlike traditional adjunct faculty, who had to live within a few hours' drive of Rexburg, these online instructors could be drawn from anywhere in the world. Each had a master's or doctoral degree in the relevant discipline. All completed an online training program and subsequently participated in ongoing teaching groups that met virtually, employing the same online technology used in student instruction.[21]

Well staffed and more systematically structured than typical traditional courses, these online offerings produced comparable outcomes notwithstanding the lack of face-to-face interaction. On average, online courses nearly matched face-to-face offerings in student satisfaction and measurable learning outcomes. Significantly, the distribution of results was tighter: the best online courses couldn't match the best face-to-face experience, but the lowest-rated online course was better than the poorest of what was occurring in the classroom; the constant correcting and culling of low-performing online instructors meant that the "lower tail" of the online performance distribution was relatively short.[22] Gilbert trusted that the average quality of the online courses would steadily improve through innovation, as predicted of new technologies in *The Innovator's Dilemma*[23] and as he had seen in the online publishing industry.

The fully online offerings enjoyed an across-the-board cost advantage over traditional instruction. Many of the online adjunct faculty were working professionals or homemakers for whom the pleasure of teaching was as great a motivator as financial compensation. The university paid new online instructors $2,500 per course, an amount consistent with the market rate, but still only about a third of the cost of a full-time faculty member.[24] The size of the pool of qualified applicants ensured that the university would be able to provide low-cost, high-quality online instruction to far more than the 11,600-plus students studying at any given time in Rexburg.

THE EXPANDED ROLE OF CAMPUS-BASED FACULTY IN ONLINE LEARNING

Campus-based faculty members, especially those working full-time, may see online courses as a competitive threat. The online instructor makes less and works on short-term contract while providing a product that, in purely cognitive terms, offers comparable value. In head-to-head competition, that has an ominous feel.

In reality, the expansion of online learning, which allows many more students to access college education and thus increases the overall demand for instruction, creates valuable new roles for full-timers on campus. The most obvious need is for online course development: the best courses are the combined product of instructional designers and faculty subject matter experts. In addition to specifying what to teach and how, these experts may also add content modules that include video clips of their own lectures, effectively becoming course heads. There is also the need for leadership of online course delivery teams and of professional mentoring for individual instructors. The cost effectiveness of online offerings means that an institution is well served to free full-time faculty members from a percentage of their face-to-face teaching duties to perform these roles.

The expanded instructional roles for faculty might be likened to those of a professional singer.[25] At the core, there is a focus on personal performance before the live audience. But the singer's influence can be multiplied as he or she writes and publishes music (designs online courses), records performances for electronic delivery (creates personal video clips), and organizes choral groups and provides voice coaching (leads teaching groups and mentors individual instructors). The campus-based faculty member's scholarship can enhance the performance of all of these functions.

As long as an overall institutional balance can be achieved, individual faculty members can be more or less involved in online learning support; some could move deeply into this new realm, while others might seek no change to their face-to-face teaching load. Online learning is disruptive at the institutional level—very few universities and colleges will be able to ignore it. However, gifted face-to-face teachers within innovative institutions may be able to continue much as before.

Graduation Delays

Even as BYU-Idaho's cost-reducing and access-expanding online learning initiatives progressed, a hidden cost problem in the university's curriculum required attention. By 2008, the typical graduate was finishing not in the minimum-required 120 hours but in 139, or nearly two extra semesters. For several years after the first bachelor's degrees were granted, it was assumed that BYU-Idaho graduates were finishing with more than the minimum credit hour requirement because of delays in the university's getting the necessary courses up and running. The expectation was that, with the passage of time and the completion of the third- and fourth-year curriculum, the number of hours at graduation would drop to something closer to 120. But five years after the university began offering bachelor's degrees, the trend was still up.

BYU-Idaho was not alone in its hours-at-graduation problem. College students who graduate with only the minimum required number of hours are the exception everywhere except at Harvard and similar elite private schools.[26] At those institutions, which can accept only a small fraction of applicants and must subsidize their students' education via endowment funds, academic planning and counseling receive top priority. Also, the basic requirements are limited. For example, a Harvard student seeking a bachelor's degree in computer science is required to take fewer than one-third of his or her total courses in that field.[27] With such careful upfront planning and relatively limited major requirements, only a few percent of students need more than four years to graduate, in most of those cases usually for reasons of personal health or family crisis.

Elsewhere, though, the converse tendency operates. Especially at public universities whose state funding is based on enrollment, every student, including the one in his or her fifth or sixth year, is a source of incremental revenue. In an under-enrolled public institution, such a student may be seen not as a financial drain but a boon. There is not only limited economic incentive to speed students to graduation, but, if anything, a mild temptation to ignore their curricular meanderings. The federal government facilitates the dynamic, granting financial aid to students until they have earned 180 credits, or the equivalent of a bachelor's degree and a half.

At the same time, genetic tendencies deep within the university operate to increase the course requirements of a college degree. The number that hangs up the typical student is not the university's overall graduation requirement, which typically is set at an amount readily achieved in four years of study. Rather, the trouble lies in the required number of major hours, a determination made by the sponsoring department. The two requirements, hours-to-graduate and major-hours, must both be satisfied, but they operate independently. The typical college student hits the graduation requirement level but still has major hours left to complete and thus must continue at school beyond the expected four years.

Several factors combine to make the major hours requirement the more difficult to satisfy. One is underinvestment in academic counseling at most universities. Even when that counseling is adequate, though, there are two other behavioral tendencies that predominate. First, students inevitably change their minds. Even a well-advised student who has completed a general education program is likely to change majors at least once; many students change two or more times as they try to align their interests, capabilities, and career plans with a primary course of study. That becomes problematic when the combined requirements of general education and the major too nearly equal a four-year program. The student who changes to one of these majors after having pursued another one finds that the previous major credits are, quantitatively speaking, wasted. No matter how effective the efforts of academic advisors, such a change means taking more than four years to finish, as 65 percent of U.S. college graduates do.[28]

The Creeping Major

As nearly predictable as the student tendency to change majors is the tendency of major requirements to grow. One reason for the growth is the educational background of university faculty. Ph.D.-trained professors naturally want those students who aspire to following in their professional footsteps to succeed in graduate programs. Thus, even majors that few students will pursue at the graduate level may be designed to cover all of the content necessary to prepare them for graduate study. In the words of Pulitzer Prize-winning Harvard faculty member Louis Menand, "The undergraduate major is essentially a preparation for graduate work in the field, which leads to a professional position. The major is set up in such a way that the students who receive the top marks are the ones who show the greatest likelihood of going on to college and becoming professors themselves."[29]

The process has been at work since the early 1900s. That was when the elite Association of American Universities, which Charles Eliot helped found, began, in the words of historian Arthur Cohen, "effectually accrediting other institutions by listing those whose bachelor's degree holders could be deemed ready for graduate study."[30] That graduate school orientation, along with the growth of new knowledge in most fields, often leads university curriculum committees to add major hours so as to ensure student readiness for advanced degrees.

Much of the growth occurs in highly specialized elective offerings, no one of which must be taken; rather, students are required to choose at least so many courses from a diverse group of electives, making their best guess as to what will contribute most to their postgraduation goals.

Growth in majors can also be encouraged by employers of graduates. When asked by faculty curriculum developers, employers may express preferences for more advanced training of students. The tendency to seek product enhancements, or sustaining innovations, is a trait typical of customers in all industries. But it is especially pronounced in the case of employers of college graduates, because it is the students, not the employers, who bear the cost of the enhancements. Satisfying the preferences of these secondary customers of the university, which seems like good competitive practice, can lead to over-engineering of the major—producing a college degree of potentially higher quality but at too high a price to the student. A bachelor's degree holder can't depend on being paid substantially more than the going rate for a four-year degree, even if he or she has taken five years to earn it.

Such growth and narrowing of majors wasn't planned at BYU-Idaho. The integrated bachelor's degree envisioned at the university's creation had between 36 and 45 major hours. The idea was to add complementary courses from one or more different disciplines to this relatively small core, creating a degree with both depth and breadth. Combined with one or more internships, such a degree was intended to provide high workplace relevance.

By 2009, though, most of the integrated majors required 55 hours, along with the originally envisioned minor or set of two "clusters" totaling 24 hours. Many specialized majors required 80 hours. When added to the 40 hours of Foundations, none of these 79- and 80-hours programs allowed room for students to change majors more than once, or take even a single elective class, and still graduate in four years.

The additional major hours were added as the faculty grew in numbers and specialized expertise. In part, the intent was to increase the quality of students' graduate school and career preparation. More hours were also added with the implementation of Foundations. The old general education program, essentially a system of distribution, had allowed the majors to dip into GE by requiring students to take, for example, a particular introductory science or humanities course. When the discipline-specific GE options were replaced by the more cross-disciplinary Foundations courses, the majors had to expand to include the introductory courses they had formerly borrowed.

The trend not only reflected the bigger-and-better tendency, it also represented a failure to make good on David Bednar's challenge to "facilitate the integration of curriculum and pedagogy across traditional boundaries." When organized into departments, even the most student-centered professors naturally design majors reflective of the departmental structure. That was true of many of BYU-Idaho's specialized majors, such as mechanical engineering, where 69 of the required 80 credits were delivered by members of the mechanical engineering department.[31] Even the integrated majors were essentially the combination of a department-centric major with a similarly department-centric minor. Integration of curriculum across the boundaries of the departments and their disciplines was limited. The goal of cross-disciplinarity realized in the Foundations curriculum did not naturally emerge in the majors.

The costs of the trend toward specialization and deepening weren't apparent for several years, when students subject to the new requirements began to graduate. Those costs were both institutional and personal. The university bore its share, given that tuition covered less than half of its annual operating costs and none of its capital outlays for new buildings. The extra 19 hours at graduation meant that the average student was receiving this 100 percent-plus tuition subsidy longer than necessary. Another way to count the cost was to consider the additional students who might have been served if graduation occurred uniformly at 120 hours. With a student body of 11,600, there was the potential to admit roughly 1,800 more at no additional cost if four-year graduation could be achieved uniformly.

Other costs were borne by the students. Those included more than just the additional two semester's worth of tuition. There was also the opportunity cost of the income they could have been generating as graduates and the additional cost of borrowing, which was likely to be more necessary in the later college years. Another potential cost was failure to graduate. BYU-Idaho's 62 percent graduation rate exceeded the national average of 55 percent.[32] But lengthening the time to graduation undoubtedly increased the risk of students' failure to finish.

Innovative Responses to the Creeping Major Problem

The university responded by enhancing the quality of student advising. In addition to assigning each student a faculty advisor, a program already in place before the discovery of the hours-at-graduation problem, the university advising office developed a computer-based "drag-and-drop" planning system. A student with a declared major could sit down at the screen and see icons representing all of the courses required for graduation. As the student attempted to drop each of these courses into an eight-semester template, the computer program would identify the prerequisites courses and allow completion of the graduation plan only if all curriculum policies were satisfied.

Though this system clarified the planning process, it highlighted the problem that no amount of planning could cure, namely the difficulty of finishing in four years after a change from one deep, narrow major to another. The computer-based planning program helped students foresee and avoid the mistake of taking courses that would not count toward their major requirements. However, changing majors meant starting over—literally putting a new name into to the "major" field of the planning program and seeing a new set of requirements, totaling eight semesters in itself.

The university's answer to this structural barrier to timely graduation was to begin to modularize its curriculum, drawing on principles developed by Kim Clark and his academic colleagues before his move to Rexburg.[33] Modularity is the principle that has allowed the computer industry, among others, to provide ever-higher-performing and more customizable products to users at ever lower costs. The various components of the computer—memory chips, disk drives, software, printers, and so on—are created as modules. Each is a unique but integrated component of the larger system. Specialists focus on making their particular component at the highest possible quality and lowest possible cost, taking advantage of the latest innovations. All the while they know that common design principles will allow their component to work effectively with the others. Purchasers can then customize a world-class machine at the lowest possible cost.

The university's answer to [the] structural barrier to timely graduation was to begin to modularize its curriculum.

In fact, the principle of modularity was critical to Eliot's elective curriculum. In creating courses with specified content and assigned instructors known in advance to students, he established a competitive market based on modular curriculum. Faculty strove to develop specialized courses that would attract students; the effect was to increase the quality of all offerings. For Eliot, the course was the only module of instruction necessary. In his purely elective system, students could create bachelor's degrees from any combination of courses. Lowell later recognized the need for larger modular units to ensure a proper balance between general and specialized knowledge. His system of distribution and concentration led to two meta-modules, general education and the major. At many universities, a scaled-down major would become a smaller modular unit, the minor.

Modularity had also been the inspiration for BYU-Idaho's integrated majors, with their associated minors, clusters, and internships. But with the growth of the largest module—the major—the integrated design became a liability relative to graduating in four years, especially if a student changed majors. Clark asked his academic leaders and faculty members to make four-year graduation a realistic goal for all diligent students, including those who changed majors more than once. They adopted the slogan "No Credit Left Behind."[34]

The principles of modular design facilitated the goal of leaving no credit behind on the path to graduation. The first step in modularizing a major was to make a minor optional; the student who, because of major changes or the desire to take an eclectic mix of nonmajor courses, accumulated 120 hours without filling the requirements of a minor could graduate without one. The next step was to pare back the requirements of each major and to ensure that prerequisite courses were kept to a truly essential few. For example, the number of mechanical engineering course credits required of students in that major was reduced from 68 to 54.[35] Collectively, the elimination of the minor requirement and the scaling back of major hours meant that fewer courses were required and that more could be taken in parallel rather than sequentially. The effect was to allow graduation in less time, as measured both by the credit hour and the calendar. Making minors optional, for example, was expected to reduce the time required to graduate by at least one semester.

To accompany the scaled-back major, the faculty began to create more-advanced modules designed to prepare students for particular careers or for graduate school. Significantly from a delivery cost standpoint, these advanced modules had few courses that weren't shared among many other modules; they were not, in other words, traditional specialized emphases, comprised of esoteric courses from a single academic department.

Here again, Harvard has been doing something similar for future academics since Eliot's day, when courses were designated as Primarily for Undergraduates, Primarily for Graduates, or For Undergraduates and Graduates. The basic requirements for a Harvard bachelor's degree comprise mostly courses from the Primarily for Undergraduates category. Those minimum requirements typically amount to only about one-third to one-half of the total credits required for graduation, substantially less than other schools' average majors. However, students bound for graduate school can add advanced courses from the other two categories, For Undergraduates and Graduates and Primarily for Graduates.

At Harvard College, Kim Clark got a jump on his master's and Ph.D. training while still an undergraduate concentrator in economics. He made the most of Harvard's allowing great depth for some students while not requiring it of everyone, a key factor in graduating nearly all of its students in just four years.

BYU-Idaho began to apply the spirit of this flexibility, effectively reintroducing into its DNA a Harvard trait that most universities had lost. It applied modular design principles Clark had written about, particularly the need to design modules to serve specific purposes and to connect meaningfully to other modules. For instance, the faculty added to many majors introductory modules meant to help students decide whether the major was for them. Other modules linked theory with practice, helping students prepare for specific jobs. Mechanical engineers, for instance, could choose application-specific modules such as product development or supply chain management; many of the courses in these advanced modules were major requirements, already offered to students in large numbers, in fields such as business management and accounting.

Rather than leaving it to students to guess which specialized offerings to choose from after completing the core requirements of their majors, as is the case with the traditional major, the faculty created collections of courses, such as the product development module for mechanical engineering majors, to support chosen career paths, including but not limited to graduate school. Helping students to focus on a particular career or graduate school path meant that the total number of required courses could be reduced without sacrificing the quality of a student's education relative to their career needs. With this guidance in designing well-integrated modules of curriculum, students could customize their education, like their computers, to be both more valuable to them personally and also less expensive.

Clark also encouraged the creation of interdisciplinary majors. For example, a new web technology degree was developed by faculty from a half-dozen departments, including computer science, graphic design, and communications. In addition to agreeing upon a collection of specialty courses from those departments, they collaborated in the creation of new courses that crossed disciplines.

As with the move to the year-round calendar, trimming back specialized majors and creating interdisciplinary ones meant altering the genetic tendencies of the university and asking the faculty to break with tradition. Their interest in deep, specialized majors was more than personal. They felt justified concern for the preparedness of students for graduate study and—in fields such as accounting, engineering, and teacher education—professional certification requirements. Most faculty members recognized, though, that the answer to meeting the specialization needs of a minority of students was not to require deep specialization of all. The new modular majors allowed for subject matter depth without making it the default design.

A University Report Card

Given the long cycle time for earning a college degree, as well as the time required to create modular majors the university standard, it would take several years for these curriculum streamlining measures to bring down BYU-Idaho's average hours-at-graduation to something close to 120. In fact, all of the university's initiatives to raise the quality of its education while reducing the cost would take not only time but also ongoing assessment. The challenge grew as members of heavyweight teams created to launch initiatives such as the Learning Model, Foundations, and online curriculum development stood down and returned full time to their regular responsibilities in the organization. Though the goal was to have every member of the faculty and many administrators implementing these initiatives, the press of daily responsibilities and the lack of a specially tasked, cross-functional oversight body could, without some countervailing mechanism, lead to a loss of momentum.

Clark's response was to create a university report card. The concept was an adaptation of the balanced scorecard popularized by his HBS colleague Robert Kaplan in the 1990s. Kaplan, an accounting professor, recognized the inadequacy of purely financial data in informing efforts to improve the performance of an enterprise. He proposed a combination of financial and nonfinancial measures, such as customer satisfaction, with target values established for each measure and linkages identified among causes and effects. The combination of different types of data means that users of the balanced scorecard must make subjective judgments about what matters most to the performance of the enterprise. Kaplan argued that this apparent quantitative weakness is actually a virtue because it requires the members of an organization to develop a shared definition of success.

DETAILED FLIGHT INFORMATION

In advocating a balanced mix of institutional success measures, Robert Kaplan and his colleague David Norton, a professional consultant, drew upon a persuasive aviation analogy:

> Think of the balanced scorecard as the dials and indicators in an airplane cockpit. For the complex task of navigating and flying an airplane, pilots need detailed information about many aspects of the flight. They need information on fuel, air speed, altitude, bearing, destination, and other indicators that summarize the current and predicted environment. Reliance on one instrument can be fatal.
>
> [T]he scorecard guards against suboptimization. By forcing senior managers to consider all the important operational measures together, the balanced scorecard lets them see whether improvement in one area may have been achieved at the expense of another. Even the best objective can be achieved badly.[36]

Another virtue of a balanced scorecard is the potential to simplify measurement systems by defining priorities and focusing attention on the handful of measures that are most critical. As Kaplan and Norton noted:

> The balanced scorecard minimizes information overload by limiting the number of measures used. [Institutions] rarely suffer from having too few measures. More commonly, they keep adding new measures whenever an employee or a consultant makes a worthwhile suggestion. One manager described the proliferation of new measures at his company as its ''kill another tree program.''[37]

The university's institutional research and assessment officer, Scott Bergstrom, took the assignment to develop a BYU-Idaho report card encompassing all of the university's major initiatives and day-to-day operations.[38] Working with more than fifty administrators, deans, and department chairs, he added important measures of educational quality, such as students' satisfaction with classes and graduates' success in finding employment or winning graduate school admission. Measures of employee development were included, as were estimates of the degree of Learning Model implementation. Hours-at-graduation, the litmus test for curriculum modularization, also appeared prominently.

Bergstrom invited department chairs to set their own target performance levels for university-wide measures and to add measures of their own. The report card was posted online, where it could be continuously updated and accessed by all university employees. It proved valuable not only in broadening awareness of the university's key initiatives and objectives but also in preparing for periodic events such as annual budgeting and regional accreditation.

The report card was posted online, where it could be continuously updated and accessed by all university employees.

Though the report card revealed persistent challenges and unexploited opportunities, the effectiveness of BYU-Idaho's unique design and innovative approaches could be seen in the university's financial bottom line. Thanks to year-round operation, the elimination of intercollegiate athletics, a growing number of online courses, and a continued focus on undergraduate education, the cost of educating students at BYU-Idaho was essentially the same as it had been at Ricks College—roughly $8,700 per year in 2010 dollars, including an imputed charge for the capital invested in the physical facilities. Deviations from the traditional university DNA had offset the introduction of upper-division courses, student activities, and the internship program, allowing BYU-Idaho to avoid the cost increase typical of institutions that make the move from two- to four-year status. Observing these trends in 2007, Kim Clark decided it was time to explore ways to serve more students.

Chapter 19

Serving More Students

In his inaugural address Kim Clark set the expectation that BYU-Idaho would accommodate more students on its Rexburg campus. He spoke of finding "creative ways to organize, schedule, and calendar the educational experiences of our students so that more of them may come."[1] But he also stated a goal of taking higher education to students "all over the world." He expressed his conviction that "this university is in this valley where our pioneer heritage is deeply ingrained, where the people are humble and faithful, so that we can be a proving ground of great fidelity [relative to global education needs]."

Clark's ambition was shared by others, including several of his predecessors. David Bednar recalled a day in 1997 when education commissioner and former Ricks College president Hal Eyring came to survey the construction of a campus chapel. Eyring had just returned from a two-week tour of South America, where he had met with church members, many of them poor even by local standards. Standing beneath the chapel's lofty ceiling and grand pipe organ, he privately noted to Bednar that tithes offered by those people had helped pay for the new building, the like of which they would never see. Of the church's higher education system, he soberly observed, "We do so much for so few and so little for so many."

High-Fidelity Higher Education

From the founding of the university, Bednar and his colleagues had built the curriculum to serve a broad constituency, not just traditional bachelor's degree-seeking students. That commitment was evident in his declaration to the faculty that associate's degrees would not be "cannibalized," in his words, to speed the creation of bachelor's programs.[2] Rather than climbing the Carnegie ladder and eliminating the rungs beneath, BYU-Idaho would be a "two-tiered institution," offering both associate's and bachelor's degrees.

Clark built on the principle of serving a broad population with his reference to pioneer heritage and "a proving ground of great fidelity." The word *fidelity,* as he used it, has formal meaning in the realm of product design. When an innovative new product, such as a pharmaceutical drug, is tested in the laboratory and in clinical trials prior to mass distribution, the tests are evaluated for their fidelity. A test of good fidelity is one that yields results on a small scale that accurately predict a medication's performance in the broader market.

Clark's goal was to apply BYU-Idaho's heritage of frugality and student focus to developing forms of higher education that would provide good results not only in Rexburg but also in the rest of the world, especially in less-privileged places such as Latin America and Africa. The university's new online courses seemed to satisfy some of the tests of global fidelity. Their measurable quality matched that of on-campus courses and was independent of location. Their cost met Clark's target of one-tenth the on-campus amount, accounting for the expense of physical facilities.

Clark's goal was to apply BYU-Idaho's heritage of frugality and student focus to developing forms of higher education that would provide good results not only in Rexburg but also in the rest of the world, . . .

But there was still the question of whether foreign students could succeed in these online classes, which presumed English fluency and graduation from an American-quality high school. Clark directed his colleagues to continue testing the new curriculum on campus. They sought to enhance it while serving more students in Rexburg and eyeing possibilities in the rest of the world. The team constituted to expand campus enrollment beyond 11,600 students per semester called itself "Enrollment Expansion I," a name presaging a second initiative to grow enrollment away from the campus.

Enrollment Expansion I and the Fishbone

Serving more students via a fixed resource base is a classic operations management problem, a matter of optimizing a production system's efficiency. Steve Wheelwright, Clark's colleague of twenty-five years at Harvard, had been studying such operations problems since taking his Ph.D. at Stanford's business school under the direction of Hal Eyring. As a member of the Enrollment Expansion I team, Wheelwright introduced a time-tested analytical technique to his BYU-Idaho colleagues. He showed them how an Ishikawa, or "fishbone," diagram can clarify the relationship of a desired outcome to the host of causes that produce it. Kaoru Ishikawa was a Japanese engineering professor and former naval officer who translated the pioneering work of J. Edwards Deming and fathered the quality movement in Japan. Building on Deming's work, Ishikawa created the fishbone and demonstrated its power in first in the Kawasaki shipyards and then in Japan's state-owned telephone company and other large enterprises.

Like all operations management scholars, Steve Wheelwright was well versed in the Ishikawa technique, which was reimported with the rest of Deming's quality movement to the U.S. in the 1970s. Having sat quietly in the team's first disjointed discussion of factors such as classroom capacity, faculty–student ratios, and student dropout rates, Wheelwright came to the second meeting with an initial pass at a fishbone diagram; it showed the connections among these factors and the university's key output, college graduates. The team spent the next several months refining the diagram, applying a technique initially proven by Japanese shipyard engineers to BYU-Idaho's Rexburg campus.

KAORU ISHIKAWA AND THE JAPANESE QUALITY MOVEMENT

Ishikawa's fishbone, or cause-and-effect diagram, was part of a broader set of tools, some borrowed from U.S. colleagues including J. Edwards Deming, that he used to pioneer the quality movement in Japan. Ishikawa was ahead of his time—on both sides of the Pacific—in seeing ways to engage not only administrative leaders but rank-and-file employees in assuring product quality and customer satisfaction. He observed that the root causes of quality problems are often known only to those with hands-on exposure to the manufacturing process. He also recognized that these lowest-level employees may fear bringing bad news forward. Thus, even in enterprises that invest in quality control, such as by hiring specialists to track outcomes, the root causes of quality problems persist.

Ishikawa's answer to this organizational problem was a ''quality circle'' comprised of self-directing front-line employees. These employees would be volunteers, assuring that none felt compelled to run the risk of punishment for reporting the root causes of problems. The company would give them time during the normal workday to do their analysis, as well as the necessary authority and resources to address the problems identified. A significant ancillary benefit would be an increase in their collective autonomy and individual job satisfaction.

A respected university researcher, Ishikawa proved equally influential among Japan's industrial leaders, whom he persuaded to test his techniques.[3] Armed with his fishbone and other analytical tools, along with his philosophy of making customer satisfaction the end goal of all activities, Ishikawa's quality circles helped propel Japanese manufacturers to the fore of global competitiveness. They shattered the long-accepted belief in a cost/quality tradeoff by producing cars and consumer electronics that were both affordable and reliable. Among those inspired by their example was Kim Clark, who as a young Harvard Business School professor studied the Japanese auto companies.

One of the first things highlighted by the fishbone diagram (presented in part in Figure 19.1) was the significance of BYU-Idaho's hours-at-graduation, or throughput, problem. The registrar's office had that number at its fingertips, and the team immediately discovered how producing graduates with more than 120 hours decreased the university's ability to serve additional students. Another factor was average class size, which correlated directly with the number of graduates produced. Quantifying the effects of class size gave the team greater appreciation for discussion-based learning, peer instruction, and other aspects of

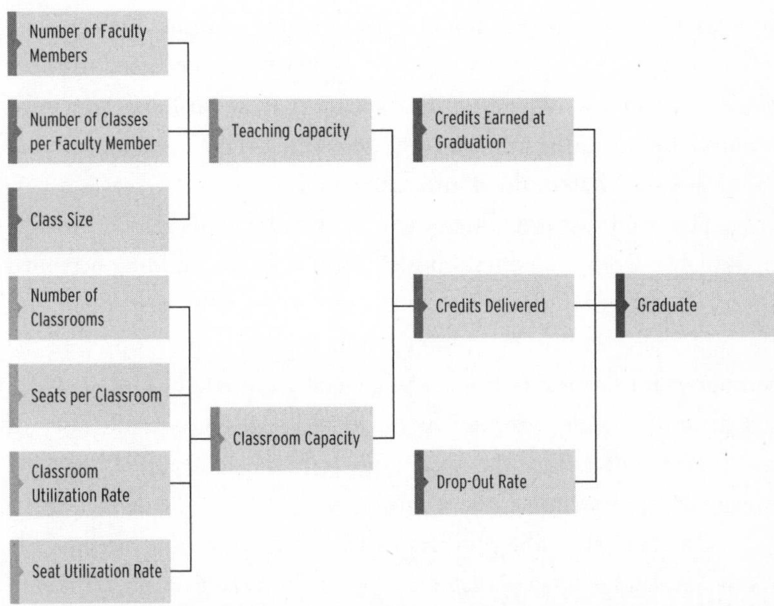

FIGURE 19.1 Fishbone Analysis of Graduate Production[4].

the Learning Model that allow students to learn more effectively even in groups as large as eighty or ninety. It focused the team on classes with small enrollments, including a surprising number with five or fewer students.

It was far more difficult, though, to determine how many more students the university could serve without adding new classrooms. The anecdotal evidence, provided by the department secretaries who matched instructors with classrooms, indicated no excess capacity. The task of testing that conclusion, which some team members doubted, required a visual inspection of every classroom on campus to determine its practical seating capacity.[5] That data then had to be manually matched with the secretaries' classroom assignments and the registrar's record of the number of students in each class.

When all of the data collection and number crunching was done, the results surprised even those who had doubted the reports of scarce space. It turned out that between 7:45 a.m. and 5:30 p.m. each weekday the typical classroom was occupied 70 percent of the time, a reasonably high figure but not one discouraging of future growth. The telling statistic, though, was the percentage of seats occupied in those classes—again just 70 percent. That meant that, at what appeared to be a university operating at peak efficiency, any given classroom seat was in use less than half of the normal school day.

The team discovered that each department secretary's knowledge of available rooms was often limited to those in the building occupied by the department; that created a disconnect between perception and the underlying reality. In addition, some faculty members pressed the secretaries for favorite rooms at the generally preferred times, between 9 a.m. and 2 p.m. Working with an artificially constrained set of classrooms and times, the secretaries naturally concluded that the university was bursting at the seams.

One answer to the problem came in the form of a campuswide room-scheduling process that drew upon the new data on classroom capacity. The process helped department secretaries meet faculty preferences while achieving greater classroom utilization. Further relief came from renovations and consolidations of chronically underutilized rooms such as laboratories and computer rooms. The latter were an anachronism in the age of laptops, which were mandatory for BYU-Idaho students.

Through the report card, as well as regular face-to-face updates from the Enrollment I team and other task forces, Clark and his colleagues could see the university's gradual progress in raising quality and lowering costs. They also saw the success of the year-round calendar and three-track system. By mid-2008 the spring semester was full to more than three-fourths of the 11,600 target level for fall and winter. More than sixty online courses were being delivered by a cadre of eighty adjunct instructors, with more of both in the pipeline. Due to the low marginal cost of adding students, tuition dollars covered the new growth; the church's total financial cost of supporting the university went down as the student body grew. Thanks to the fishbone, Clark knew that low-cost growth via online learning and improved classroom utilization was sustainable up to at least 15,000 students per semester or 22,500 on an annual, three-semester basis. Armed with this data, he sought and received from the board authorization to increase the on-campus student body by 900, to a total of 12,500 students per semester, with the prospect of going to 15,000 by 2015. It was a confirmation of the success of the new university's unique model, a blend of the traditional university and a set of disruptive innovations (see Table 19.1).

Enrollment Expansion II: From Rexburg to Manhattan

For several years, Clark and his BYU-Idaho colleagues had talked about the possibility of moving beyond the Rexburg campus to deliver college-level education to "nontraditional" students, in the spirit of A. Lawrence Lowell's extension program at Harvard. This was already happening in the form of an online Bachelor of University Studies (BUS) program launched in 2007. Through it, students who had begun a degree in Rexburg but had not finished could do so entirely online. The BUS

TABLE 19.1 Innovations of the Kim Clark Era, 2005–Present

New Traits	Implications
Full year-round operation	Reduced cost-per-student More students served Reduced flexibility for students (track assignment) Increased faculty workload
The Learning Model	Enhanced learning experiences Increased student responsibility Increased faculty preparation effort
Foundations	Broad, common learning experiences Opportunities for faculty teaching groups Challenges of integrating across disciplines Constraints on student course selection
Student Living program	Enhanced apartment environment Reduced cost of supervision Increased cost of instruction
Online courses and degrees	Low-cost, convenient learning New costs of course creation and support Challenges of faculty involvement and quality assurance
Modular majors	Increased customizability Decreased cost of changing majors Increased complexity of academic planning One-time costs of reconfiguring majors

degree was a boon to many former students, especially mothers who had dropped out of school to raise children. However, the program lacked the intimacy of the on-campus experience: though these students enjoyed interacting online with their BYU-Idaho colleagues, they had no face-to-face learning opportunities. The program presumed a degree of self-sufficiency and motivation greater than that of the typical college-aged student. It was also limited to four emphases: business, English, communications, and marriage and family studies.

Clark wanted to overcome the limitations of the BUS program, with its exclusively online curriculum and narrow range of specializations. He hoped to create a learning outreach model that would work not only for adults with some college experience but also for young people with no prior exposure to higher education, especially those whom traditional institutions might consider unfit for college. He of course wanted them to have a broad range of study options. In early 2007, he challenged Clark Gilbert and his online team to experiment with gathering online students to a common location for weekly face-to-face interaction. They did so in two places, BYU-Idaho (in Rexburg) and its sister institution BYU-Hawaii, where Steve Wheelwright had taken the helm. They chose two introductory-level courses, one in English and the other in math.

The weekly face-to-face gathering in each location was presided over by a peer mentor, a student who had taken the course recently and been specially trained in facilitating classroom discussion according to the BYU-Idaho Learning Model. Students in both classes and on both campuses performed well, but the face-to-face gathering worked better for the English students. Their online instructor had created special learning exercises just for that gathering, rather than simply viewing it as an opportunity for unstructured tutoring and socializing. The Hawaii experiment taught the online team that these distant-site courses needed to be hybrids, a combination of online and traditional classroom instruction.

Clark's next challenge to the team was more ambitious and required board approval. In three U.S. cities—Boise, Phoenix, and

Manhattan, New York—they recruited a total of fifty young people not currently enrolled in college, including some with no college experience. After a fashion similar to that of the Hawaii experiment, each cohort would take semester-long online courses and meet in person weekly. In this case, though, the meeting would occur not on a university campus but at a local church institute building, similar to those over which Ricks College president John Clarke had presided before coming to Ricks College.

Each institute had a full-time director, but the church board of education made it clear that institute directors were not to be diverted from their existing responsibilities, primarily organizing and teaching church religion classes to college-aged students. To keep the hybrid model of online and face-to-face instruction affordable, the team sought out volunteer retired couples to meet with the students each Thursday night, playing the role of supportive coaches and mentors rather than teachers. Students led discussions and helped each other, using the Learning Model, while completing the bulk of their course work online. This model allowed students to have the benefits of a face-to-face gathering without BYU-Idaho's incurring the costs of hiring remote teachers at each site.[6]

Customized Higher Education Pathways

Because nearly all of the students in the new program had jobs, the curriculum for the first semester was light. Each student took three courses. Two were taken online, and the third, a religion class, was taught face-to-face at the institute by its director. This first semester's curriculum, along with the two to follow, assumed the need to reproduce the college preparation that Charles Eliot and the Redbook's authors expected to occur in high school. The students differed dramatically from their counterparts in Rexburg, even most of the Heber J. Grant scholars. Of the twenty-two in Manhattan, for example, only ten were native English speakers. Thirteen had some previous college experience, the others none. Their average age was twenty-six.

Though the program required a high school degree or its equivalent, most of the students had been out of school long enough that college readiness couldn't be taken for granted; at least in a limited way, it would be necessary to vertically integrate, a la Henry Ford and his steel plant. Fortunately, an Academic Start suite was readily assembled from existing components. One of the online courses, called "Life Skills," was adapted from the Grant scholars program; it addressed subjects such as time and money management. The other online course, called "College Success," was developed by specialists from the tutoring center in Rexburg.

To the team's satisfaction, eighteen of the twenty-two Manhattan students completed the first semester's requirements. The specially tailored curriculum and peer interaction allowed nearly all who made a serious effort to succeed. Fifteen reenrolled for the second semester, in which they took college math and a second religion course. Similarly encouraging results came in Phoenix and Boise.

The second semester, though, revealed new challenges. Many students struggled in the first real academic course, college math. The team recognized that, notwithstanding the peer-to-peer interaction built into the online course and the support of the volunteer couple at the institute, more academic advising support was needed. They recalled the observation made by several online university administrators that effective online learning requires one-and-a-half to two times as much "out-of-class" student support as face-to-face courses do.

> *Through . . . increased support, as well as ongoing course redesign and refinement, success rates of the students in Manhattan, Phoenix, and Boise were brought up to levels comparable to those in Rexburg.*

Drawing upon the students-helping-students principle embedded in BYU-Idaho's activities program and Learning Model, the team both beefed up its professional support, hiring more academic advisors, and also injected several forms of student leadership into the distant-site pilot programs. Those included enlisting volunteer students in Rexburg to provide online assistance; they acted as one-on-one mentors. In addition, BYU-Idaho students on their semester away from the Rexburg campus were recruited to work as volunteers under the direction of the couples at the institutes. Through this increased support, as well as ongoing course redesign and refinement, success rates of the students in Manhattan, Phoenix, and Boise were brought up to levels comparable to those in Rexburg.

The Next Steps

Before launching these initial experiments, the team had considered what might come next for the students. One option was enrollment in the BUS online degree program, to which the university planned to add subject matter–specific bachelor's degrees. Yet this path, though appropriate for adult learners who had spent a year or more on the Rexburg campus, seemed less than ideal for most of these fledgling students. Some hoped to transfer to Rexburg, others to local community colleges. Still others wanted professional training instead of traditional bachelor's degrees. All needed a meaningful credential in the near term, given their age and need to make a living as they studied.

The team, which dubbed its new program "Pathway," determined to accommodate as many of these individual paths as possible. (See Figure 19.2.) The need for near-term employability in particular required significant modification to the traditional bachelor's degree. A conventional general education program seemed like the wrong next step for Pathway students. Applying the modularity principle, the team designed a special curricular pathway by which most of the university's Foundations courses would be preceded by a technical certificate. They recognized that this putting of specialization before general study was effectively turning on its head the traditional model of curriculum, established by Lawrence Lowell. Lowell's approach of distribution before concentration makes sense only if a student is very

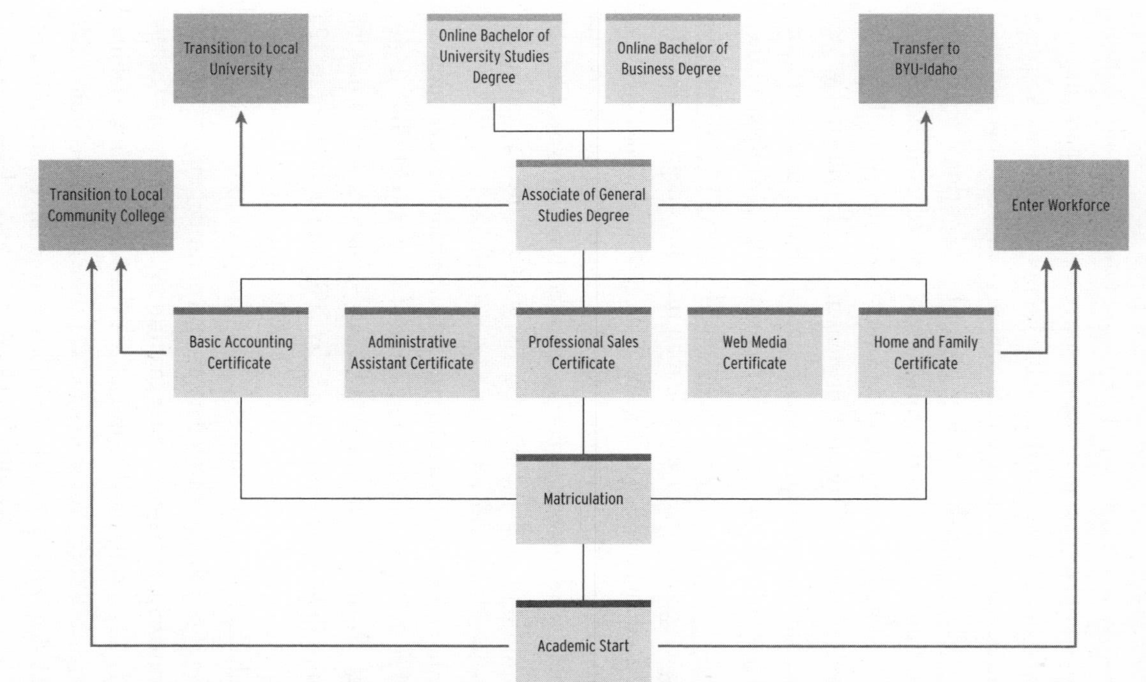

FIGURE 19.2 Pathway Program Curricular Options.

likely to graduate, as is the case at Harvard. If the risk of dropping out before completion of a bachelor's degree is significant, as it is at most universities, then delaying the start of focused study disserves the student, leaving a college dropout with training little more valuable than a high school degree. It also underserves the first- and second-year students who need to work part-time but cannot convert their learning from a general education program into more gainful employment.

For students at risk of failing to finish a bachelor's degree, the better design puts the technical certificate first, embedded in subsequent associate's and bachelor's degrees like a Russian nesting doll. From his days of working with Clayton Christensen, Clark Gilbert saw this new curriculum as a disruptive innovation. The elite universities and colleges rightly focus their efforts on increasing the percentage of their students who graduate. They know that associate's degrees and technical certificates are generally less valuable than bachelor's degrees; they also know that students come to college with the goal of graduating, not of being employable after dropping out. Yet those two goals are not incompatible. The value of achieving them both becomes apparent by seeing the world through the eyes of at-risk students and nonconsumers of higher education whose needs have been overlooked.

Having conceived this nested structure, the team was disappointed to learn that the university had lost most of its non-bachelor's degree credentials. Notwithstanding David Bednar's commitment to making BYU-Idaho a "two-tiered institution," by 2009 only a dozen of its 125 associate's degrees remained; it offered no technical certificates at all. The cannibalization of which Bednar had warned occurred naturally in the process of creating a full-blown university curriculum.

Fortunately, a two-year sister institution, LDS Business College in Salt Lake City, continued to specialize in basic professional training. Courses such as Office Procedures and Customer Relations from LDS-Business College filled gaps in five certificate programs created primarily from first- and second-year BYU-Idaho offerings. The certificates ranged from traditional office functions such as administrative assisting and basic accounting to newer fields such as web media development. Each was designed as a front piece to a related associate's degree, which would be created by the faculty in Rexburg in time for continuing students to transfer in as sophomores. Those associate's degrees would, in turn, fit by design within specifically designed bachelor's programs.

In fact, the Pathway team found one accommodating bachelor's degree already on the books. Students who had completed an associate's degree in a field such as architectural or automotive technology could earn a bachelor's of applied management degree with only 24 credits' worth of business-related courses. This bachelor's degree had been created in 2003 to help former Ricks College students who were working toward associate's degrees in applied fields complete bachelor's degrees quickly. With the introduction of traditional bachelor's degrees at BYU-Idaho, student interest in the applied associate's degrees waned; as a result, the applied management bachelor's degree was all but forgotten. For Pathway students, though, it proved to be a boon.

A Tremendous Cost Savings

Though the members of the team appreciated the importance of giving Pathway students a cost-effective means for coming to Rexburg, they knew that continuing students were at least as likely to transfer to a local community college or to continue studying online. The great financial advantage of the program was not just its low tuition ($65 per credit hour, half of the price in Rexburg and less than or roughly equal to community college tuition in the three pilot areas). The real savings for students came from staying in their current living and work settings. Of the roughly $12,000 total annual cost of attendance in Rexburg, only a little more than $3,000 was tuition;

Taking courses online in Manhattan, Phoenix, and Boise could mean a total education savings not of 50 percent, but something closer to 90 percent.

most of the remainder comprised rent, food, and transportation. Particularly for students living with their parents and working jobs paying more than they could make in Rexburg, taking courses online in Manhattan, Phoenix, and Boise could mean a total education savings not of 50 percent, but something closer to 90 percent.

The economic advantages of this new program, with its modular openness to multiple endpoints, hearkened back to Clark Kerr's system of community colleges that feed state universities. Rather than taking up expensive residence in a distant city and immediately facing the rigors of a bachelor's degree program, Pathway students could start at home in a low-cost, low-stress academic environment. They could sample college at a price of a few hundred dollars, plus transportation costs for the weekly trip to the local institute building, rather than BYU-Idaho's all-in first-semester cost of $6,000. If things went well, they had the option of transferring to BYU-Idaho or an unaffiliated community college or other four-year university with which credit articulation agreements would be created. They could also stay with the program long enough to earn a certificate and then to go straight to work with a technical certificate and the advantage of having little or no financial debt.

Pathway's use of online technology made it more cost effective than not only traditional community colleges but also purely online universities. Part of the reason was the preexisting investment in BYU-Idaho's residential campus. Whereas an online university must invest in curriculum development, computer infrastructure, and student advising and administrative systems, all of these were already in place in Rexburg. Though the Pathway program created incremental costs for human services such as academic advising, much of the fixed cost of a Pathway education was covered by the tuition of Rexburg-based students, who were still getting a bargain relative to the average cost of a traditional university education. In effect, BYU-Idaho's on-campus instructional activities, which were supported by a full-time faculty who had developed online courses that were already running on established computer systems, allowed the university to price its Pathway courses to cover only the relatively low marginal costs.

At $65 per credit, the cost of a year's worth of study could be reduced from the $8,700 of the Rexburg program, for which students paid less than half that amount, to roughly $1,950. Pathway students could also save the cost of room and board, which might total another $8,000-plus per year. A Pathway student could, under the right conditions, earn a four-year degree for a total of less than $8,000, with no subsidy by the church.

Reciprocal Benefits

The Pathway program produced unexpected benefits back on the campus. The need to create certificates and associate's degrees for Pathway students had the effect of accelerating the modularization of the four-year curriculum for on-campus students. Modularization was further inspired in the upper division, as faculty members anticipated the transfer of Pathway students to Rexburg; their goal was to provide modules that would allow a technical certificate or associate's degree holder to complete a bachelor's degree, with no credit left behind. The achievement of that goal would benefit not only transfer students from other universities but also BYU-Idaho students who changed majors to graduate in the hoped-for four years.

Another benefit to BYU-Idaho's traditional students accrued when a committee was created to enhance the experience of freshmen students. One of the committee's objectives was to give new students assistance in making the academic transition to college—picking a major and learning time and money management were leading concerns. This committee looked to the Pathway program's Academic Start suite of courses in designing a new course for freshman in Rexburg.

The benefits of reaching beyond the campus flowed back in ways that hadn't been foreseen when the Pathway program was created. Disruptive innovation often has that effect. Innovations designed initially to serve nonconsumers ultimately change and enhance the ways high-end consumers are served. BYU-Idaho's efforts to serve students at a distance had the effect of increasing the quality and decreasing the cost of education for its on-campus students.

BYU-Idaho's efforts to serve students at a distance had the effect of increasing the quality and decreasing the cost of education for its on-campus students.

This success was predicated partly on attention to two rules of managing disruptive technological change.[7] One is to give responsibility for disruptive technologies to organizations whose customers need them. Kim Clark did that by putting Clark Gilbert in charge of both online learning and the Pathway program. Rather than applying online technology only to traditional students and classroom environments, Gilbert and his team had the incentive to adapt it to the needs of higher education nonconsumers. Serving these nonconsumers required rethinking the traditional higher education model and thus produced disruptive learning innovations.

The other rule Kim Clark observed is matching the size of the organization to the size of the market. Gilbert's small team was well matched to the similarly small group of Pathway students. He and his colleagues became the de facto academic advisors and parental figures to the fifty young people in the initial cohort. They took the students' phone calls and texts round the clock during that first semester. As a result, they were able to respond quickly to unforeseen needs. Their strategies for serving the Pathway students evolved more quickly than would have been possible had they not been organized as a semi-autonomous team.[8]

International Pathways

Seeing the low cost and relative success of the Pathway pilot, Kim Clark sought the board's approval for a new test. In addition to its 230 institute buildings in North America, the church operated 324 overseas.

Each of these had a full-time director, and nearly all had high-speed Internet access. Finding volunteer couples to serve as onsite mentors would be difficult in some countries, but otherwise the essential Pathway infrastructure was in place.

The church also had a financial aid program called the Perpetual Education Fund (PEF), established by Gordon Hinckley in 2001, less than a year after the creation of BYU-Idaho. The PEF, a kind of educational microlending program, took its name from Brigham Young's Perpetual Emigration Fund. The Perpetual Emigration Fund aided nineteenth-century Mormon pioneers in their trek from the east coast of the United States and various European countries to the Utah Territory. The church and individual benefactors created a financial corpus from which qualifying émigrés could draw, on the condition that they repay the amount borrowed, with minor interest, upon settling on the western frontier. All told, some 30,000 pioneers made use of the Perpetual Emigration Fund.

Hinckley established the Perpetual Education Fund on similar principles, with international institute directors identifying qualified students. Those students used the borrowed funds to pursue certificates and degrees from local trade schools and colleges. In its first eight years of operation, the Perpetual Education served more than 40,000 students who realized, on average, a three- to fourfold increase on their pre-education incomes.[9] The amounts borrowed were similar to the cost of obtaining a technical certificate or associate's degree through the Pathway program. Thus, Clark could see not only the educational infrastructure to take Pathway international but the financial infrastructure as well.

Even with the essential pieces in place, it was a bold moment to propose international expansion. At the time, early 2009, the church had a hiring and budget freeze in effect, due to the 2008 economic downturn. But the Pathway model conformed to Commissioner Hal Eyring's prediction about the university's frugality being a source of advantage in turbulent times. As Eyring foretold, relying "more upon inspiration and perspiration to make improvements than upon buildings and equipment" had allowed for "continuous innovation . . . even in the most difficult times."[10]

With board approval, Clark charged the Pathway team to explore the potential for pilots in two new countries, Mexico and Ghana, which were chosen as relatively easy entry points into Latin America and Africa. The team would need to develop online English as a Second Language courses for both Mexico and Ghana, but BYU-Idaho's more international sister institutions in Provo and Hawaii had language instruction experts who offered assistance. In both countries the church institute system, including online communication infrastructure, was strong.

Realizing the Benefits of the New DNA

By 2010, a decade after the announcement that Ricks College would become BYU-Idaho, the university had realized many of the benefits inherent in its new DNA. (For a graphic representation of the evolution of the DNA of Ricks College and BYU-Idaho, see Figure 19.3.) More students were being served: 18,355 versus 10,160.[11] The institutional operating cost of serving each student had increased slightly, from $5,771 to $6,155. However, in light of the inherently higher cost of providing a four-year degree, with its specialized course offerings, that could be considered an efficiency victory.[12]

The sources of the university's efficiency could be seen in other statistics. Whereas the student body had grown by 80 percent, the full-time faculty had grown by only 50 percent. In spite of the addition of the 400,000-square-foot auditorium, the university had only 126 square feet of building space per student, compared with 153 in Ricks College days. Efficiency could also be seen in the academic catalog. The number of courses in the catalog had grown, from 879 to 1293, but that 30 percent growth was, like the increase in faculty, small relative to the student body growth. The number of degree programs and academic departments had shrunk. Whereas Ricks College had

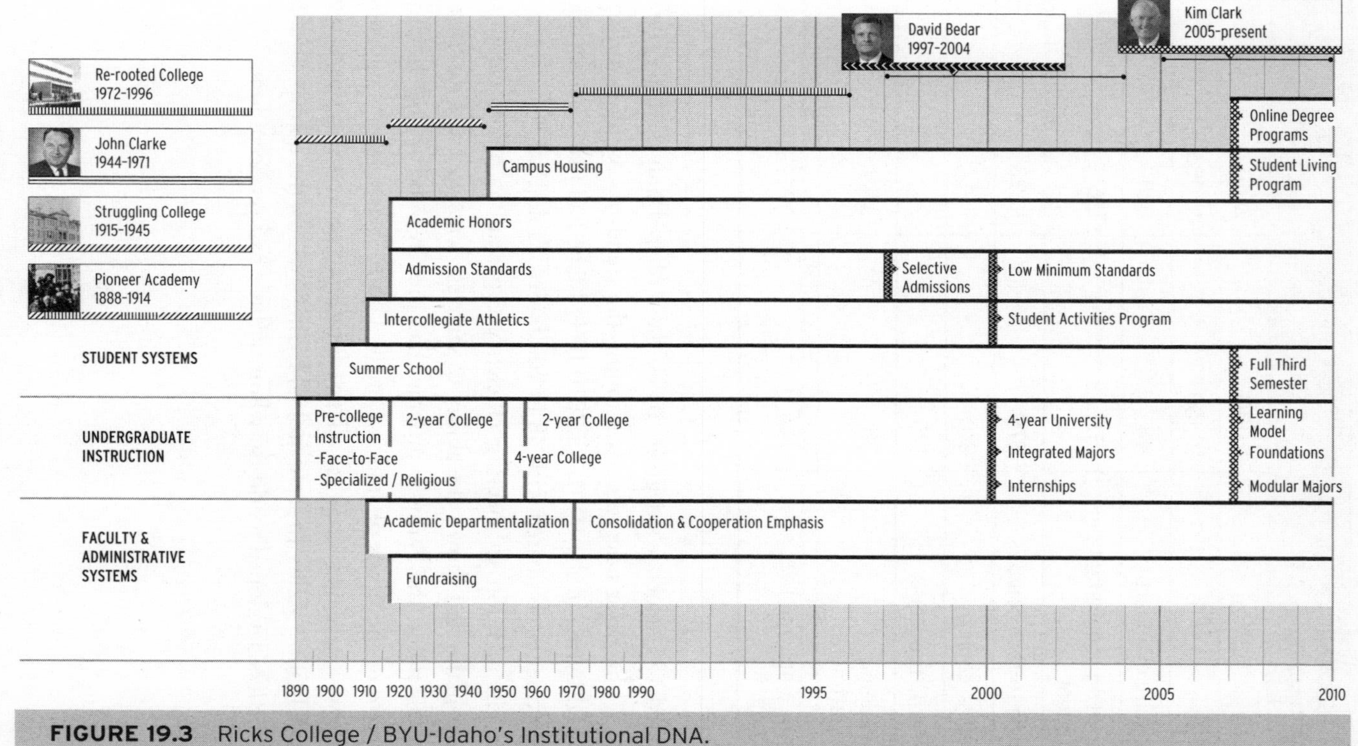

FIGURE 19.3 Ricks College / BYU-Idaho's Institutional DNA.

TABLE 19.2 A Comparison of Ricks College and BYU-Idaho, 2000–2010		
	2000	**2010**
Students	10,160	18,355
Faculty members	411	628
Building square feet per student	153	126
Face-to-face courses	879	1,293
Online courses	20	104
Degree programs	125	94
Academic departments	38	33
Operating cost per student	$5,771	$6,155

offered 125 associate's degrees, BYU-Idaho offered only 17 associate's and 77 bachelor's degrees. Continuing the trend of consolidation set by Hal Eyring in the 1970s, in 2010 BYU-Idaho had just 33 academic departments, compared with 38 in 2000. (See Table 19.2.)

In addition to meeting efficiency expectations on its campus, BYU-Idaho had shown the ability to serve students well at a distance. To this point, the Pathway program had proven to be of high fidelity relative to the needs of students in the United States who would not otherwise have had access to college education. The next step was to test BYU-Idaho's ability to serve, in Hal Eyring's words, the many students in the less developed world for whom so little had yet been done.

PART FIVE

Genetic Reengineering

If we accept a home of our own making,
Familiar habits make for indolence.
We must prepare for parting and leave-taking
Or else remain the slaves of permanence.[1]

From the poem "Stages"
The Glass Bead Game, by Hermann Hesse

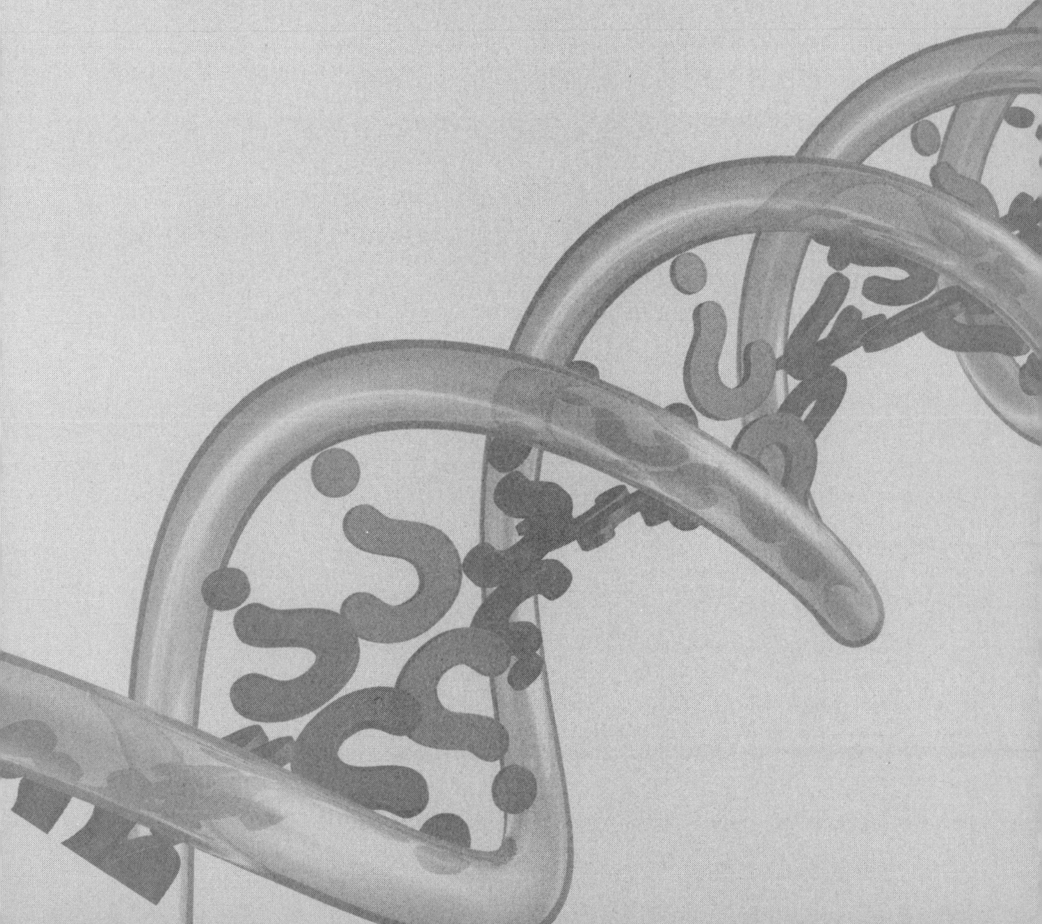

Chapter 20

New Models

As we've seen in the stories of Harvard and BYU-Idaho—and as media reports make clearer every day—technological and social change threatens to undermine the traditional university's dominance. The delivery of higher education to students is set to change in ways that will make the innovations of Charles Eliot and his Harvard successors pale by comparison. Moreover, the timetable will be measured in years rather than the decades that they had to work with. In the near future, high school students will receive promotional messages like this one:

- Instead of taking hyper-competitive AP courses and not-so-valuable electives next year, why not earn real college credit before you graduate from high school? You can start your college degree now, taking online courses that will make you feel like you're on Facebook instead of sitting in a classroom listening to a lecture or reading a textbook.
- When you graduate from high school, you'll have a wide range of options. You can continue to live at home and take online courses, ultimately getting your degree that way; we have a study center near your home where you can go to get tutoring help, meet with other students, or just have a quiet place to study. You can also take face-to-face courses there.
- You can come to one of our traditional campuses, which have all of the features of the best colleges: on-campus dorms with private rooms, live tutors, and good food choices; off-campus housing where

you can cook your own meals and park your car; social clubs; athletic teams anyone can join; and great entertainment.

- Your decision about when and where to study doesn't have to be all-or-nothing: every semester you can choose whether you want to study at home or "at college"; you can also take any semester off for an internship or a vacation.
- You can customize your courses to fit your preferred learning style: most of our courses come in three varieties: fully face to face, fully online, or a mix of the two, a "hybrid" that meets less often than the traditional face-to-face course.
- We'll also help you design a degree program that will ensure your employability whenever you choose to graduate. You can take job-specific courses first and later add the liberal arts and specialized courses required for a bachelor's degree and graduate school, if you want. Our technical certificates and associate's, bachelor's, and master's degrees fit together so that no one has to "drop out" before they're finished. Whenever you decide to finish your college education, you'll have a credential to show for it. You'll also have received help finding an internship that has the potential to lead to a full-time job.
- You don't need to worry about the problem that most college students have in graduating in just four years. Our degrees are modular, which means that you can change majors without having to "start over." We have special bachelor's degrees that take just three years to complete. With careful planning and consistent effort, you can graduate quickly, with a degree that will take you where you want to go.
- You can graduate without a mountain of debt. Our fully online courses cost about as much as a typical textbook, and our hybrid courses, where you work both online and in the classroom, are much less expensive than the traditional kind that require you to be in class two, three, or even four time each week. Depending on the mix of courses you take, your bachelor's degree could cost a fraction of what you would pay at most universities.

This promotional message may seem futuristic, but its essential elements are in place; innovative institutions in addition to BYU-Idaho provide many of them already. For example, Southern New Hampshire University's SNHU Advantage program, a "no-frills" associate's degree program, allows students to live at home while taking morning classes at one of SNHU's five satellite centers. Advantage students pay just 40 percent of the price of the university's regular associate's degree programs. They are also free in the afternoons and evenings to work part-time jobs. The combination of living at home and generating income while earning an SNHU degree brings its effective cost down to a small fraction of the traditional cost of going to college. Like students in BYU-Idaho's Pathway program, participants in SNHU Advantage take all of their credits with them as they proceed toward a bachelor's degree, which they can pursue either through online courses or at the main residential campus.

In addition, SNHU is making pioneering efforts to reduce the time required to earn a bachelor's degree from four years to three. Since 1996, it has operated what it calls a "3-Year Honors Program in Business Administration." Students take courses in interdisciplinary, semester-long modules that merge business, technology, and the liberal arts. Each of the six semesters includes a weeklong integrative project, and the third year includes a consulting project for organizations outside of the university.[1] A new field-based, experiential bachelor's degree program, College Unbound, also allows students to graduate in three calendar years.[2]

Transcending the Dichotomy

BYU-Idaho, SNHU, and others like them are pioneering new models of higher education, blending elements of Eliot's traditional university and the fully online model. The universities pursuing this blended approach lack the prestige of the great institutions and thus cannot fund that expensive model via gifts, grants, and high tuition rates. At the same time, their commitment to face-to-face instruction—manifested in expansive physical facilities and full-time faculty—prevents them from competing cost effectively with the fully online specialists. Rather than feeling trapped, though, these institutions have recognized an opportunity between the genetically entrenched past and the online disruption that seems to be the inevitable future of higher education. They are challenging the either/or dichotomy and proving it to be false.

The key to doing so is to embrace the learning advantages to be found across the spectrum that runs from fully face to face to fully online instruction. Though the power of face-to-face learning is undeniably great, so is the disruptive potential of online education. It cannot be dismissed as inferior in quality to traditional classroom-based instruction. In addition to being much less costly than their face-to-face equivalents, well-designed and -managed online offerings tend to increase in quality more systematically.

The systematic improvement of online learning has many sources. One is the steady advance of computational and communication technology, which allows online courses to be made more interactive and engaging without increased expense; for example, students can now talk to and see one another via laptops at a level of quality possible only with expensive video-conferencing equipment just a few years ago. They can also engage in computer simulations of laboratories and hospitals and businesses. Thanks to learning software created with the aid of cognitive scientists and psychometricians, the sophisticated successors of the early developers of aptitude tests such as the SAT, computers themselves are getting "smarter," better able to judge a student's performance and respond with tailored tutorials.

Another source of online course improvement is market competition among instructors. Teaching performance in the online environment is easily monitored, and course-by-course contracting creates a Darwinian incentive to improve. A third source of improvement is the oversight role played by professional course designers. These specialists not only have training

Teaching performance in the online environment is easily monitored, and course-by-course contracting creates a Darwinian incentive to improve.

and experience in enhancing learning outcomes, they have that goal as their sole objective, without the mixed motives of the full-time professor who favors a particular teaching style or subject matter emphasis.

To make an automotive analogy, online courses are comparable to the cars rolling off the line of a Toyota factory. The online course equivalent of this factory continually upgrades its technology and its workforce. In addition, it operates under the direction of educational "engineers" who are scientific about learning outcomes. These engineers minimize the use of nonstandard processes, such as professor-specific sections of the same course, which create unnecessary costs (*muri*, in Japanese). They also reduce the likelihood of inconsistent performance, such as deviating from a syllabus (*mura*), and of wasted effort, such as inefficient grading procedures (*muda*). The result is a system that continuously improves, providing ever-higher quality at low cost.

In competition with such an educational production system, a tenure-track professor at a traditional university, whose professional advancement depends more upon research than instruction, faces a challenge in some ways like that of a weekend and evening enthusiast who builds custom cars. Of course, this is yet another inapt higher education analogy: the face-to-face instructional craftsperson can create experiences difficult and perhaps even impossible to replicate in the purely online environment. Still the typical instructor, even one without pressing scholarly duties, will find it hard to compete without the support of teams and technologies like those behind the best online courses.

Administrators and faculty members of traditional universities may understandably respond to this view of the future with a mix of incredulity and fear. Many BYU-Idaho faculty members felt some of both emotions. Like other experienced teachers, they had seen online courses consistently underdeliver on promises of revolutionizing the learning process. At the same time, they naturally feared the implications of one-for-one replacement of face-to-face instruction by online learning.

Time is revealing both the potential of online learning and the importance of hybridizing it with face-to-face experiences. Not only for-profit educators but also traditional institutions such as BYU-Idaho, SNHU, and Cornell, which we will encounter again shortly, are operating online production systems that apply the efficiency principles of the Toyota production system. Traditional universities have all of the assets needed to compete effectively in the online environment. The subject matter expertise of their full-time faculty members and their existing campus computer systems give them a potential quality and cost advantage in delivering online education.

The real advantage of the traditional universities, though, is their ability to meld online and face-to-face learning experiences. Face-to-face learning goes beyond formal classroom instruction; it includes the important informal learning that comes when students interact with one another in campus activities. The combination of online technology and the college campus has the potential to take traditional universities to new levels.

Online learning is proving to be a classic example of a disruptive technology. . . . New and powerful digital technologies with the potential to transform the online experience in ways that significantly reduce costs and enhance student learning are now driving online learning upmarket into some of the best institutions in the country.[3]

—Michael Bassis, Westminster College, Utah

Vital Jobs to Be Done

Visualizing the opportunity open to traditional universities requires recognizing an irony, which is that the very changes that threaten them also make them potentially more valuable than ever before—valuable enough to justify a price premium over today's online disruptors of the higher education status quo. The thing for members of university communities to remember is that it is not only they who feel threatened. So do individuals, companies, and governments.

Three trends feel particularly intimidating. One is increasing economic competition, which requires perpetual reinvention; if quality does not increase even as costs are reduced, workers lose their employment and enterprises fail. At the same time, making good decisions is becoming more difficult: knowledge seems impossible to wring from a surging sea of data. Finally, social relationships are becoming more complex. The digital world is simultaneously more connected and more fragmented and impersonal.

These threats—obsolescence, disorientation, and depersonalization—imply three vital jobs to be done, jobs that traditional universities can do uniquely well. The jobs sound familiar to those who know universities at their best: (1) discovering and disseminating new knowledge, (2) remembering and recalling the achievements and failures of the past, and (3) mentoring the rising generation. Understanding these jobs is the first step for universities seeking to establish a sustainable competitive position in the new higher education environment.

The notion of an organization's doing a "job" has roots in the work of a Harvard Business School professor named Theodore "Ted" Levitt, who arrived there in 1959. Just one year later, he published a seminal article called "Marketing Myopia,"[4] in which he accused business managers of focusing more on the things they make than on the customers those things are ostensibly designed to serve. Throughout his twenty-five years in the classroom at HBS, Levitt preached the importance of distinguishing means from ends. The purpose of a business, he taught, is not to make products or services, but to "create and keep a customer." The key to doing so is to be "wedded constructively to the ideal of innovation."[5]

But innovating on behalf of a customer is difficult, Levitt warned, because of the tendency to think of improving the product or service that the customer buys, rather than addressing the job that it is bought to do. "People don't want a quarter-inch drill," he reminded his students, "they want a quarter-inch hole."

Drawing that means/ends distinction has never been more important in higher education. As in so many industries, the higher education bigger-and-better emphasis has been on product features: the range of courses offered, the prestige of the institution, the campus accommodations. Now, with a college education becoming simultaneously more expensive and a precondition to earning a living wage, there is a temptation for students and policymakers to focus on making the fundamental product—a degree—more affordable; in the face of today's wrenching economic and social pressures it is natural for not only marketers of higher education but also customers to become myopic.

Yet the job that students and policymakers need done is the bestowal of the insights and skills necessary not to just make a living but to make the most of life. A college degree creates its significant wage-earning advantage because it is designed with more than mere economic goals in mind. Among those extra-economic goals are the jobs of discovery, memory, and mentoring, jobs that traditional colleges and universities perform as few other institutions can.

The job that students and policymakers need done is the bestowal of the insights and skills necessary not to just make a living but to make the most of life.

What Universities Do Best

The first job that universities do uniquely well—discovery—was a leading objective for Harvard's Charles Eliot when he placed graduate programs atop the college, strengthened the academic departments, and broadened the university curriculum. Discovery was also the primary reason for James Conant's up-or-out tenure system. Together, these systems have produced powerful results. University discoveries have helped shape the modern world, as detailed by Columbia's Jonathan Cole in *The Great American University*. Even with private industry spending much more on research, universities still play the leading role in basic, or discovery, research: in 2008 universities performed roughly 60 percent of basic research in the U.S.[6]

Ironically, some of the university's discoveries now threaten its historical mode of operation. Online technologies such as computer chips and Internet search engines are the products of university professors and their students. So are the instructional and business strategies that allow for highly efficient delivery of a college degree. That fact bodes well for traditional universities. As seen in innovations such as BYU-Idaho's fishbone and report card, they can develop technologies and ideas that will take themselves and those they serve to new heights, just as they discovered the tools that are now causing disruption in the higher education industry. At many universities, students are playing an increasing role in that discovery process.

A HIGH RATE OF RETURN ON DISCOVERY RESEARCH

In 2008 the University of Utah, the state's largest public university, tied MIT in producing the most new companies via research discoveries—twenty. Utah, the recipient of only one-fifth as much research funding as MIT and seventieth among all universities, was an unlikely contender for this title. Yet the feat was no fluke: Utah was second on the list behind MIT in each of the preceding two years, ahead of such research giants as Cal Tech, Michigan, and Harvard.[7]

Utah's strategy for commercializing research holds hope for universities trying to do the job of discovery without the financial clout of the largest research institutions. In 2005 the university determined to build upon its existing advantages of an entrepreneurship-friendly state and a successful research park. It created a technology commercialization office that established working relationships with local angel investors and venture capital firms. The office also developed in-house capabilities such as a new business "accelerator," Venture Bench, that sponsors an entrepreneur-in-residence program and assists with market analysis, website development, and accounting and legal services.[8] To bridge the gap between company inception and funding by external investors, the university created a Virtual Incubator Program, which gives a potential spin-off company up to $50,000 (free of overhead charges) for continued research and development.[9]

Though these supportive systems are important, according to university president Michael Young, Utah's greatest competitive asset in commercializing research is its students. "Our advantage," Young says, "comes from connecting our research scientists to students from disciplines ranging from business and law to engineering and medicine, who can help these scholars realize the full potential of their discoveries." In 2010, more than 900 students and 88 percent of the university's academic units participated in this commercialization work. In addition to involving students in Venture Bench and related activities, the university operates an $18 million student-raised and managed venture capital fund, which prepares students for careers in venture investing. The benefits accrue not only to students and scholars but to the surrounding community: in the first six years after Young and his colleagues established these linkages, the University of Utah helped found 109 companies, 90 of which continued to operate in the state at the end of that period.[10]

Like discovery, memory is also built into the university's DNA. Beginning with his or her freshman year of college, the future university scholar moves to the cutting edge of knowledge only after thoroughly probing its foundations. A college general education program exposes young students to a broad range of disciplines, with emphasis on the historical development of those disciplines. A major course of study then brings students from past to present, fundamental to advanced, before they win the right, in graduate school, to assume the scholar's role of adding to the body of knowledge in their field.

This intellectual grounding, or memory, allows university scholars to perform a critical memory-related function today. They can help learners gain their footing in the flood of information that might otherwise overwhelm them. Thanks largely to universities, the sum of knowledge has exploded. Via tools such as Stanford-spawned Google,[11] learners now have this knowledge at their fingertips. Yet they lack an understanding of what to search for and what to make of it when they find it. Traditional institutions of higher education are uniquely qualified to help learners do what they might otherwise struggle to do on their own. These scholarly communities have the collective insight and experience to answer a learner's most vital questions: How can I achieve proper breadth and depth in my formal education? What books should I read? What sources of information can I trust? What new information matters? What principles don't change? What works and what doesn't?

Along with discovery and memory, mentorship is another traditional strength of the university, one that goes back to its earliest evolutionary state, when colonial colleges were little more than boarding schools for teenagers. These students learned as much from living with their tutors and studying with one another as from the formal pedagogy. James Garfield alluded to the power of academic mentoring in a statement about his former teacher, Williams College president and moral philosopher Mark Hopkins: "The ideal college," Garfield said, "is Mark Hopkins on one end of a log and a student on the other."[12] Appreciating the truth of that remark, Lawrence Lowell invested heavily in a residential housing system to allow more students to sit on the collegiate "log" with their own Mark Hopkinses. Though few universities could replicate Harvard's house system, most built dormitories and created campus activity centers. Thanks to the postwar expansion of traditional university campuses, several generations of young people have literally grown up at college.

Given the importance of the jobs of discovery, memory, and mentoring, the vulnerability of traditional universities lies not so much in their growing costs but in their relative performance of these jobs. Even in an increasingly competitive world, the traditional university has a unique, vital role to play. That is recognized by its external supporters. Government agencies and corporations are still willing to fund productive university research. Taxpayers and legislators appreciate, at a reasonable cost, the social benefits of the university's memory. Many students and their parents are willing to pay a premium price for a university experience with face-to-face instruction and personal mentoring. There are complementary roles for community colleges, technical institutes, and for-profit institutions to play; these institutions are especially critical in serving students who would otherwise be non-consumers of postsecondary education. But universities of the kind that Harvard's Eliot, Lowell, and Conant envisioned are vital to the cause of higher learning.

Unique Assets

The traditional university has two unique assets for performing the jobs of discovery, memory, and mentoring. Each must be recognized as an asset of both great potential value but also great cost.

The first of these unique assets is the university's physical campus. Paradoxically, the trend toward technology-based learning and communication that threatens to undermine the university's traditional approach to instruction is also one reason that its campus is so valuable. Now more than ever, parents want to send their texting and video game-dependent children to settings where face-to-face interaction is unavoidable. Many relish the thought of their children facing professors who demand preparedness for class. They also see value in their children's living with roommates, the most worthy of whom may serve as role models and the worst of whom at least provoke self-introspection. Even in the days of cohesive high schools and family farms and businesses, the traditional university was valued as a place for young people to mature into adulthood. Today it may be one of the few places where that can happen systematically.

> *Ironically, and thankfully, the glorious abundance of the virtual has created an even greater longing for the real.*[13]
>
> —Mary Sue Coleman, president of the University of Michigan

The other unique asset of the university is its professoriate. The Ph.D.-trained professor who has survived the tenure process is a rigorous thinker with a deep memory. That professor also has the potential, thanks to long teaching experience and the campus setting, to be not only a discoverer of new knowledge but also a life-changing mentor. The traditional higher education setting provides a still unmatched opportunity to "take professors, not courses." Though online pedagogies continue to improve and are likely to produce cognitive learning outcomes superior to those of the traditional classroom lecture, the most lasting, transformative learning is personal, the result of an intimate, lasting connection with a great teacher. What James Garfield said of Mark Hopkins and his log, Eliot would undoubtedly have said of Josiah Cooke and his makeshift basement laboratory. So would Lowell of Benjamin Peirce's help in publishing a math paper and Conant of Charles Jackson's mentoring and his personal introductions to the great German chemists.

A measure of personal intimacy can be achieved at a distance. Caring instructors can reveal their personalities online, offering collective and individual encouragement and inviting introspection that transcends the formal curriculum. Likewise, online mentors can form lasting bonds with students. That is true, for instance, of Western Governors University's mentors, who talk by phone with their assigned students for at least thirty minutes each week throughout the degree program. WGU students and mentors are unlikely to meet face to face until graduation, but by that time they may have become fast friends.

Still, the life-changing professor puts the traditional university on a different plane than its low-cost competitors. Things happen face to face, especially outside of the classroom, that are unique. To enter a professor's office and discuss matters unrelated to a particular course is to join a special scholarly community. The value of the transcendent, personal learning experiences possible in such communities is great enough that students who have the financial means will pay the price not only of the professor's salary, but of the campus setting, today's "log."

Not coincidentally, the university's most unique assets relative to the jobs of discovery, memory, and mentoring are also among its most expensive assets. Efficiency-minded educators generally eschew the costs of large brick-and-mortar campuses and of full-time faculty who engage in student mentoring, curriculum development, and discovery research. These assets are valuable because they are unique. But because they are so expensive, the university must deploy them parsimoniously and strategically.

The Efficiency Imperative

The typical university must decrease the cost of each degree it grants. As pointed out by McKinsey in *Winning by Degrees*, there are two main ways of doing that. One is to increase the percentage of students who graduate, and who do so in a timely manner. Modularizing the curriculum so that students are more likely to finish with the minimum number of required credit hours is key. So is the academic advising and personal tutoring needed to sustain students who would otherwise drop out.

The other way to reduce the cost of obtaining a college degree is to decrease the costs of the institutional resources that go into it, especially the costs of facilities and instruction. Year-round operation and efficient classroom scheduling have the potential to increase the utilization of physical facilities, for many institutions their second-largest cost after faculty salaries and benefits. The concept of year-round instruction is as foreign in traditional universities as it is taken for granted by for-profit organizations. Though a BYU-Idaho-style three-track system may be a bridge too far for many traditional institutions of higher education, the successful ones will find incentives for both faculty and students to make better use of campus resources during the summer.

The most powerful mechanism of cost reduction is online learning. All but the most prestigious institutions will effectively have to create a second, virtual university within the traditional university, as BYU-Idaho and SNHU have done. The online courses, as well as the adjunct faculty who teach them, should be tightly integrated with their on-campus counterparts; this is an important point of potential differentiation from fully online degree programs. To ensure quality, universities may also decide to limit online class sizes or pay instructors more than the market rate. Even with such quality enhancements, online courses will allow traditional universities not only to save instructional costs but also to admit more students without increasing their investment in physical facilities and full-time faculty.

The most powerful mechanism of cost reduction is online learning.

AN ELITE UNIVERSITY'S ONLINE SUBSIDIARY

It was an all too common scenario in 2000. An established institution, a leader in its industry, creates an Internet subsidiary—complete with a name starting with a small *e*—in hopes of catching the dot-com wave. An initial investment of $30 million seems a modest price to pay, with $100 million initial public offerings (IPOs) of newly started companies a common occurrence.

In hindsight, this story reads like the script of an investment tragedy, particularly with the added detail that the would-be Internet entrepreneur was a university. But eCornell has been making a profit for its parent, Cornell University, since 2005. Though the profits are great enough that a dividend could be paid to the Cornell endowment, which staked the $30 million investment, the university's trustees have opted to allow eCornell to reinvest those profits into new programs and infrastructure for continued growth.[14]

Cornell created eCornell as a for-profit subsidiary, not for the purpose of maximizing financial returns but to facilitate flexibility in governance and ensure attention to marketplace performance. The connection to eCornell's not-for-profit parent is strong. Full-time faculty members author eCornell's courses, with the support of professional online curriculum developers. Faculty members may also participate in web conferences with students and contribute face-to-face instruction to hybrid offerings.[15]

By 2010, the online eCornell within the traditional Cornell University annually enrolled more than 10,000 students in twenty-six certificate programs. Nearly all students are working adults retooling for new or enhanced careers, in fields such as business, health care, and hospitality and food service management. The combination of high-quality online curriculum, independence in time and place of study, and the Cornell name have produced sustainable growth achieved only by the most successful few of the dot-com companies that survived the bursting of the Internet bubble early in the twenty-first century. eCornell's 24 percent growth in students served in 2010 exceeds the online learning industry average of 21 percent. Its year-over-year revenue growth of 25 percent would make for only a modest dot-com-era IPO, but one likely to yield a handsome return on investment. The real return on investment, though, is the capacity that eCornell gives its parent institution to serve new students with low-cost, high-quality learning technology that potentially benefits its on-campus students as well.

Most traditional universities already manage their instruction costs by employing lower-cost adjunct faculty and graduate students; more than half of the instructors at the typical not-for-profit institution fall into one of these two categories.[16] But this faculty pool is geographically limited, just as the classroom is limited by space and time. Moreover, few of these adjunct instructors work within quality assurance systems like those of the best online educators. To be cost competitive, a university must develop high-quality online courses that can be taught by qualified instructors from around the world.

Before long, even the best-taught face-to-face courses will be hybridized, suffused with online components.[17] Lectures and other non-interactive activities such as in-class quizzes are being put online, allowing full-time faculty instructors to focus on high-value pedagogies such as case discussions. Customized online tutorials and simulations of real-world environments will increasingly be added to the curriculum. The number of face-to-face sessions per course will diminish as more is done online; specially trained teaching assistants and mentors will facilitate online discussions and grading. Full-time faculty instructors will thus be able to teach more students without an increased workload, in a way analogous to the large-section model devised at Harvard in Eliot's day. Those instructors will have the ability to stay connected to what is happening under the direction of others by following the online conversations and participating at their discretion.

"Work That the World Wants Done"

Though cost reduction is necessary for the typical university, it will not be enough. Operational efficiencies notwithstanding, BYU-Idaho and similar innovators with full-time faculty and expansive campuses still expend more per student than their fully online counterparts. The real challenge for traditional universities is to justify the greater cost in the minds of students and their parents. That is one reason why Kim Clark's initial emphasis was on quality rather than cost; before seeking cost competitiveness, he wanted to ensure a clear quality advantage via innovations such as the Learning Model and Foundations.

Lawrence Lowell likewise emphasized quality as he assumed Harvard's presidency. It was 1909, and his university was struggling under the weight of Eliot's vision of having everything at its best. Then as now, costs ran ahead of revenues, and critics questioned the relative value of a college education. Some wanted to see it reduced from four years to three. Lowell, however, raised their sights. In rallying his Harvard colleagues, he asked a rhetorical question appropriate to our day:

> May we not feel that the most vital measure for saving the college is not to shorten its duration, but to ensure that it shall be worth saving? Institutions are rarely murdered; they meet their

> end by suicide. They are not strangled by their natural environment while vigorous; they die because they have outlived their usefulness, or fail to do the work that the world wants done; and we are justified in believing that the college of the future has a great work to do for the American people.[18]

In his balanced, golden-mean way, Lowell would sense both opportunity and vulnerability on today's higher education landscape. He would see the traditional university's opportunity to excel in the jobs of discovery, memory, and mentorship—"work that the world wants done." At the same time, though, he would recognize the need to change the traditional university's DNA. By studying the history of higher education since his day, Lowell would see that most of today's universities are congenitally predisposed to committing "suicide."

Suicide by Imitation

For all the nimbleness and cost advantages of for-profit competitors, most universities' fundamental problems are of their own making. They are engaged in genetically driven, destructive rivalry with their own kind—other institutions trying to be the world's best according a single, narrow definition of excellence. Much of the trouble is rooted in Conant's push to make Harvard excellent. His tools for finding the best students and scholars, the SAT and up-or-out tenure, presumed that Harvard and its peers would educate only a tiny fraction of the U.S. populace. In Conant's time, only 1 out of 20 Americans earned a college degree.[19] He wanted to find the few of these college-bound students who would benefit most from a Harvard education. He also felt driven to return the institution to academic preeminence. Focusing on only "the best" served both purposes.

The strategy worked fantastically well, partly because Conant underestimated the future demand for college education. As the typical high school graduate became more likely than not to enroll in college,[20] Harvard went from accepting 2 out of 3 applicants to denying 9 out of 10. The supply of candidates for faculty positions likewise mushroomed. Excellence-assuring mechanisms that in the 1930s helped Harvard become less clubby and mediocre made it, seventy years later, unforeseeably elite.

At the same time, the excellence-driven Harvard became more expensive and less capable of serving its share of college-bound students. As its prestige and costs soared, its relative capacity to educate the masses plummeted. Because many students could afford to pay only a fraction of the full cost of their education, the university had to make up the difference; even with its unusually large endowment, there was a limit on the financial aid Harvard could supply and thus the number of students it could admit. The universities that followed Harvard's lead likewise became more expensive and less accessible. In institutions unable to generate sufficient new revenues, through sources such as fundraising and sponsored research, the quality of undergraduate education also suffered, as they were unable to finance both their new scholarly activities and historical levels of faculty–student interaction.

Across higher education generally, the result has been a decrease in the value of a diploma relative to its cost and the closing of doors to would-be students.[21] But it is not only students who have suffered by the broad adoption of the elite university model. So have scholars. The current system of academic meritocracy, in which tenure depends on publishing via elite journals and academic presses, limits the activities and potential contributions of junior faculty members. Learning innovation is undervalued, as are other forms of scholarship that do not result in traditional publication. Many individual faculty members and even whole departments fail to win due recognition for their contributions to the university and its students.[22] The genetic tendencies that drive universities up the Carnegie ladder underserve the majority of both students and faculty.

Making Choices

Fortunately, the number of students worldwide seeking education is growing, as is the potential for knowledge discovery and the need for cultural memory. The world needs more university education, not less. However, there are too many universities trying to be like Harvard without fully understanding the costs of what Harvard does. To perform the jobs of discovery, memory, and mentoring at a competitively sustainable cost, the strategy of the university must reflect firm choices about what it will and will not attempt to do.

To perform the jobs of discovery, memory, and mentoring at a competitively sustainable cost, the strategy of the university must reflect firm choices about what it will and will not attempt to do.

The concept of making tradeoffs is easy to articulate, but hard even for for-profit enterprises to consistently apply. The bigger-and-better tendency tempts successful organizations to want to do everything for everyone. Two decades after Ted Levitt argued the importance of remembering the job for which a product or service is created, one of his junior colleagues at the Harvard Business School, Michael Porter, showed by rigorous research that long-term success requires not just satisfying customers' needs but doing so consistently better than one's competitors. Though Porter's analysis was complex, the guiding principles that flow from it are straightforward. They

We decided this year to buck a trend and not pursue AACSB accreditation for our School of Business . . . . Our analysis revealed that it would redirect more than $2 million per year to activities and priorities that showed no demonstrable improvement in the experience of students.[23]

—Paul LeBlanc, Southern New Hampshire University

include the ideas that competitive success requires being different, making unique choices about what an organization will and will not do.[24]

Porter's challenge to make tradeoffs and be different indicts the traditional higher education strategy, as it does the bigger-and-better strategies of many successful businesses. It strikes at the heart of Eliot's vision of everything at its best and at a century of bigger-and-better Carnegie climbing by American colleges and universities as well as Harvard imitation by many international universities. Yet it also offers hope of success through unique strategic choices. Rather than climbing the same ladder as all other institutions, a university can succeed by being selectively different.

To succeed in an increasingly competitive world, even the best universities must find a strategy that transcends Harvard imitation. It isn't necessary to entirely forego graduate programs and discovery research, as Gordon Hinckley and David Bednar did at BYU-Idaho. But universities must step off of the traditional ladder in defining themselves. That means thinking about what they do, not solely in terms of the course taken by Harvard and the other elite research universities that pursue excellence across the full academic spectrum.

AN INNOVATIVE COLLEGE AT THE TOP OF ITS NICHE

When Leonard "Len" Schlesinger arrived at Babson College as its new president in 2008, he was surprised to encounter thoughts to deemphasize the entrepreneurship curriculum for which the school was famous; the concern was that other schools with substantially greater resources were entering that realm. *U.S. News* had ranked Babson's MBA program number 1 for entrepreneurship for fifteen consecutive years, and its undergraduate business program was similarly renowned. Yet some of Schlesinger's new colleagues suggested that this entrepreneurship-focused strategy pigeon-holed Babson and made it vulnerable to competitors. Better, they argued, to push for a rise in the school's general ranking relative to the most elite schools.

Schlesinger, a former faculty member and administrator at both Harvard and Brown as well as a senior executive with Limited Brands, owner of such distinctive marks as Victoria's Secret and Bath and Body Works, disagreed strongly with this idea. He knew from personal experience in both higher education and retail marketing how difficult and expensive it is to create a unique brand. He also knew the value of having one, as Babson did.

Rather than agreeing to step from the top of a small but important academic niche onto the Carnegie ladder, Schlesinger held a series of strategic discussions among the community that helped focus his colleagues on deepening and broadening Babson's entrepreneurship capabilities and reputation. The members of the Babson community agreed on three goals: (1) being known as *the* educator for entrepreneurship of all kinds; (2) extending Babson's capabilities to the world, via initiatives such as expanding programs for working professionals, developing curriculum for small business owners, and helping to create a school of management and entrepreneurship in Abu Dhabi, and (3) ensuring a sustainable financial model for the college.[25]

The Babson strategy also includes plans for expanding its use of blended face-to-face and online instruction, which will both extend Babson's reach and reduce its costs of instruction. A collaborative agreement with nearby Wellesley and Olin colleges, the one a premier liberal arts institution and the other a leading engineering school, will allow Babson students and faculty members to enjoy the benefits of academic diversity while preserving the college's strategic focus.[26]

Like Babson and many others, successful institutions will develop their own models, eschewing wholesale adoption of either the Harvard or the purely online models but incorporating elements of both. While making the most of online technology, they will limit themselves to particular aspects of the work the world wants done by universities; that will allow them to do what they do at competitive levels of quality and cost. They will choose based on what jobs they can do uniquely well. The critical choices relate to students, subject matter, and the definition of scholarship.

Chapter 21

Students and Subjects

The first critical dimension of choice for universities is the range of students to serve and the credentials to offer them. The new university Charles Eliot created served both undergraduate and graduate students, an apparently broad choice that has been widely emulated. Harvard undergraduates, though, are unusual. They are more capable than typical college students. They are also more likely to pursue graduate education; that allows them to be more satisfied with a liberal education rather than technical preparation for a career.

This system worked well at Harvard, thanks largely to A. Lawrence Lowell's special investments in the college. James Conant's predicating tenure on research put the undergraduates at an inherent disadvantage relative to graduate students, but Harvard compensated for diminished faculty attention by feeding Lowell's expensive system of undergraduate houses and tutors. Harvard also benefited from Conant's use of the SAT, which soon produced an average admitted freshman so bright and motivated as to be able to transcend almost any weakness in the educational program.

Harvard, in other words, succeeds not only because of its wealth, but because it has limited its choice of students to serve to only the most elite graduate and undergraduate students. In its professional schools, the choice is narrower still—graduate students only. That may partly explain their greater immunity to economic downturn and public criticism than the Faculty of Arts and Sciences (FAS), which has responsibility for both graduate programs and Harvard College. Given its commitment to these fundamentally different types of student, the FAS would be in truly financial dire straights were it not for the relatively small size and elite quality of the college.

The challenge for nearly all other universities, in addition to having less to spend than Harvard, is that their undergraduates are much more diverse in both educational objectives and academic abilities. Many of these students will not attend graduate school, so their college experience must include practical career preparation. Some also need remedial education to be ready for college courses. With the research university's additional commitments to graduate programs and faculty scholarship, even Harvard could not fund all of the degree programs and special tutoring necessary to serve such a broad range of undergraduate students.

A Focused Choice of Students

That is why the most successful schools make careful choices about the types of students they serve. Focused liberal arts colleges, for example, differentiate themselves by granting only bachelor's degrees. Students at these schools do not get the kind of head start on graduate coursework that Harvard College students can through courses for both undergraduates and graduates. Nor can they finish after two years with an associate's degree or take bachelor's degrees in applied fields, as they might at public universities. But students at the best liberal arts colleges receive unusually focused faculty attention and intellectual stimulation. They also get the full attention of the school's career placement officers, who at large universities often give disproportionate support to professional school students.These liberal arts colleges have made tradeoffs that give them a unique competitive advantage relative to a particular kind of student, one who places high value on intimate undergraduate instruction and will pay a high price for it. In a world of growing demand for higher education, there is likely to be a

The most successful schools make careful choices about the types of students they serve.

place for these institutions, particularly as they make innovative use of online technology to enhance instruction and keep costs from escalating.

BYU-Idaho has chosen a broader but similarly differentiated range of students to serve. Like the liberal arts colleges, it eschews graduate education. But while serving typical graduate school-bound college students, it has also reemphasized associate's degrees and technical certificates. It meets the needs of students of diverse abilities and interests by helping them teach one another; the college-ready are enlisted in teaching those who are not, a valuable educational experience that is less common at elite universities. BYU-Idaho also reaches out via low-cost online learning technology to students constrained by finances or geography. These distance learners, who would otherwise be higher education nonconsumers, meet periodically with one another and interact daily, online, with their Rexburg peers. The combination of low-cost and relatively high-quality learning fills a heretofore unmet need for this group of students.

Community colleges are more focused still, serving only two-year degree seekers. This focus helps them meet the needs of students burdened by poor academic preparation and bearing work and family responsibilities. It is for their focus and resulting low cost that community colleges are seen as attractive public investments relative to traditional universities. Even so, their future success depends on reducing their instructional costs via online learning and providing the student support necessary to increase their graduation rates.

Institutions granting only certificates have shown the power of focus in helping students persist to graduation. Nationwide, only 43 percent of students who enter a two-year public institution seeking a certificate achieve that goal within five years. However, institutions that focus solely on certificates, rather than both associate's degrees and certificates, achieve a 72 percent graduation rate.[1] That is approximately the average rate for the twenty-six free-standing Tennessee Technology Centers, which McKinsey highlighted in *Winning By Degrees.*[2] Tennessee legislation separates the production of certificates and associate's degree, foreclosing any consideration of a ladder climb. Instead,

Tennessee Technology Centers distinguish themselves through superior service to certificate seekers; six of these centers achieve graduation rates in excess of 80 percent. Students can earn certificates in areas such as architecture and construction, business management, health science, and information technology. The McKinsey team observed, "A focused mission allows these institutions to improve their execution while allowing their delivery model and processes to be tailored to meet the objectives of their student population."[3]

The Student as Primary Constituent

In addition to choosing which students to serve, the university community must recognize students as primary constituents and the job of mentoring them as being equally or more important than any other, including discovery research. Except in the case of the most elite research institutions, the university that does not view serving students as its primary mission is doomed to decline. The problem is not just the lower instructional costs of the for-profit educators. It is also the rise of focused research enterprises. Employees of purely discovery-focused corporate R&D groups and government research institutes are inherently more cost effective than university scholars, who must split their time between research and instruction and whose explorations are not market driven. Given these lower-cost alternatives, the knowledge discovery function of the university has become comparatively too expensive to justify public and private subsidies absent a compelling educational purpose. Lowell's test of the university's social usefulness can only be met as it was in his day—with an emphasis on mentoring students and educating society in uniquely valuable ways. Otherwise, the university cannot justify the inevitable expense of combining research and instruction under one roof.

The university community must recognize students as primary constituents and the job of mentoring them as being equally or more important than any other.

As university professors know well, students have new tools for demanding attention to their preferences. The online technology that allows them to learn at lower cost also allows them to express their opinions as never before. Popular websites such as Ratemyprofessors.com and Facebook, the latter created in a Harvard dorm room, portend a social network-driven world in which third-party rankings and even accreditation may become irrelevant. A university's fate is more likely to be determined by the balance of its constituents who consider it benevolent rather than self-interested. Today's elite universities are likely to be academically well regarded one hundred years from now. The question, though, is whether some of them will have been acquired as the premier label in the portfolio of a for-profit education company. Their independence will depend on whether their constituents—the faculty, the alumni, and especially the students who consume their services rather than merely admire them from a distance—love them or abandon them.[4]

The students in particular will be crucial. None can be considered a customer; as with the doctor's patient and the lawyer's client, the wise student trusts the professor to know his or her best interest. However, if traditional universities do not treat students as their most critical constituents, the for-profits will have the advantage in winning them over, particularly those students considering less prestigious institutions. Many of the for-profits have found great success in catering to working adults. This market segment offers better profit margins than do the younger ones served by traditional universities. But as the overall market matures and competition at the top end intensifies, the for-profits will seek new opportunities among younger learners, including those with the academic preparation and financial means necessary to attend traditional institutions. The for-profits' low marginal cost of instruction allows them to drop their prices far below those of even public universities and colleges. It is only a matter of time before this market segment becomes their primary target for growth. Even prestigious universities will be affected by competitors, for-profit and otherwise, that put the needs of students first. The student-centered university is the exception today. In the future, no other kind is likely to succeed.

Helping Students "Achieve the Dream"

Though universities have a broader educational mission, they can benefit from practices such as those being applied by the 130 community colleges participating in Achieving the Dream (ATD): Community Colleges Count, a Lumina Foundation-funded initiative.[5] Achieving the Dream institutions use student achievement data to focus their efforts on student success. One ATD school, Valencia Community College, achieves a graduation rate of 35 percent, 15 percentage points higher than its peers nationwide. It does so with a 32:1 student–teacher ratio, almost 50 percent higher than the peer average of 22:1. The combination of a higher graduation rate and lower costs of instruction and other student services allows Valencia to confer an associate's degree for $22,311, compared to an average of $56,289.[6]

Valencia's success flows from innovations that include a cohort model and a for-credit "student success" course for freshmen in which they learn study skills. They also use an academic and career planning tool called "LifeMap," which helps them connect their personal goals with the Valencia resources vital to achieving them.[7] LifeMap recognizes and serves students differentially, based on their particular points on the path to graduation.[8]

Valencia's staff are also committed to "seeing the college through the eyes of the student." That means streamlining and automating processes that affect students; in many cases, students can serve themselves, completing transactions such as accepting financial aid online. The result is faster service at lower institutional cost. Cost efficiencies in some student services allow Valencia to make greater than average investments in others, such as academic counseling and career services. The efficiencies inherent in the higher student–teacher ratio similarly allow for greater investment in measuring and maintaining the quality of instruction.[9]

The State of Florida likewise does its part in seeing the college experience through the eyes of students. Florida policies encourage dual high school and college enrollment, Advanced Placement (AP) and International Baccalaureate (IB) programs, and generous acceptance of transfer credits. For example, associate's degree graduates are guaranteed admission to a state four-year institution and the transferability of at least 60 credits.[10]

Subject Matter Focus

To survive increasing competition, most universities need to be both more student focused and more narrowly focused in their academic offerings. Eliot's ideal of having all subjects at their best was always expensive. Now, with for-profit educators focused on the subjects in greatest demand, it is competitively untenable. Undergraduate majors in particular must be rationalized from a cost standpoint. Majors that are chronically under-enrolled and fail to place graduates in careers or graduate programs are candidates for elimination or combination. The number of elective courses offered even in many highly enrolled majors must be reduced. This process has already begun in earnest at many universities.[11]

> *Colleges need to move away from the more and better approach and position themselves for the new economic reality by focusing on what they can do best.*[12]
>
> —Len Schlesinger, President of Babson College

The culling should be undertaken with care. Breadth of study options differentiates traditional universities from the for-profits and facilitates performing the jobs of memory and mentoring. Outright elimination of too many majors and courses could be damaging to the institution not only intellectually but also competitively. The typical university major, though, needs to be trimmed back and modularized to allow students to combine the most essential major courses with offerings from other fields and still graduate in four years. The upshot in many majors is likely to be a reduction in the number of advanced, specialized courses or at least a decrease in the frequency with which they are taught.[13]

Most of the schools cited by McKinsey in *Winning by Degrees* make focused choices of subjects as well as students, creating benefits of both low cost and high completion rates. For example, Indiana Wesleyan University (IWU) serves roughly one-third of its 15,000 total students via a Center for Adult and Professional Studies, or CAPS, that specializes in college education for working adults. Unlike many adult degree seekers, who tend to study at their own pace, often independently, IWU's CAPS students pursue bachelor's degrees as part of an assigned cohort. Cohort members take three-credit courses lasting six weeks each, and the majority of courses taken are required rather than elective. Because of the importance of cohort collaboration, only one absence is allowed per course. According to McKinsey:

> Initial assignments serve the double purpose of having students get to know each other on a personal level while getting students accustomed to the learning environment either on campus or online. University leaders cite the cohort model and clear structured degree pathways with few electives as an important factor driving their graduation rate—65 percent compared to a peer average of 46 percent.[14]

In addition to achieving high completion rates, IWU-CAPS spends just $40,851 per degree granted—one-third less than average—even while investing 10 percent more in student support.

Beyond the Rational Curriculum and the Formal Classroom

In at least one respect, though, the university must consider broadening its subject matter. For the sake of both its own survival and society's good, the traditional university needs to reengage on the subject of values and renew its commitment to character development. The moral void created by the secularization of higher education is a critical weakness. As Derek Bok noted in *Our Underachieving Colleges*, "Two-thirds of all freshmen consider it 'essential' or 'very important' that college help them develop their personal values."[15] But because of "the reluctance of the faculty to teach material in which the methods of analysis and validation are so subjective," he observed, many undergraduates "gain more in developing their values and principles from bull sessions with friends than from the classes they attend. To this extent, they fail to gain as much enlightenment as they might about subjects that deservedly form a vital part of their development."[16]

Bok is right. Students go to college for more than narrow academic training. In addition to cross-disciplinary general education, they need access to mentors who can speak both from academic training and also from personal experience to what makes for long-term welfare, what is right and what is wrong not only for societies but for individuals. Introducing moral views into higher education requires a delicate balancing act.[17] It is an act of intellectual asymmetry: How does one decide to introduce some ideas not subject to scholarly methods of analysis while omitting others? Yet it is precisely that kind of judgment that separates the university graduate who is merely technically competent from one trusted to make the most important decisions. Society pays outsized rewards to those who can make high-stakes judgments not subject to purely analytical methods.

Tenured university professors are implicitly expected to make such judgment calls, as manifested in their being paid many times more per student taught than their untenured counterparts in the for-profit world who can produce, on average, the same cognitive outcomes. If they continue to be paid that premium in the future it will be not just for bringing new discoveries into the classroom but also for transmitting cultural memory and for mentoring. Their ability to perform those jobs will be vital to the traditional university as it increases its percentage of courses taught online; as that occurs, it will be all the more important to have face-to-face offerings rich in the value-laden and concern-manifesting conversations that are more difficult to have at a distance.

The expectation that a professor make delicate decisions in teaching moral values and cultivating character in students is not unreasonable. As Derek Bok has declared, "It is perfectly possible to teach moral reasoning or prepare students to be enlightened citizens without having instructors impose their personal ideologies or policy views on their students."[18] One of the most important values for students to be taught is one that university faculty members embody by their choice of profession: the value of imparting knowledge to others for the sake of lifting them. The Harvard Business School's C. Roland Christensen, master of discussion-based instruction, described teaching as a "moral act." He expressed supreme confidence in its efficacy. His confidence rested in a noble view of student potential and a dedicated teacher's ability to develop it:

> *"It is perfectly possible to teach moral reasoning or prepare students to be enlightened citizens without having instructors impose their personal ideologies or policy views on their students."*
>
> —Derek Bok

> I believe in the unlimited potential of every student. At first glance they range, like instructors, from mediocre to magnificent. But potential is invisible to the superficial gaze. It takes faith to discern it, but I have witnessed too many academic miracles to doubt its existence. I now view each student as "material for a work of art." If I have faith, deep faith, in students' capacities for creativity and growth, how very much we can accomplish together. If, on the other hand, I fail to believe in that potential, my failure sows seeds of doubt. Students read our negative signals, however carefully cloaked, and retreat from creative risk to the "just possible." When this happens, everyone loses.[19]

Christensen reserved the final hour of his landmark Business Policy course for a rare lecture. He lectured his class of future managers and executives on the most powerful motivating force in business: genuine concern for employees and customers. He had research to support the point, but his students had felt the real proof in the way he treated them throughout the semester.

In addition to moral authority and personal concern, students need a measure of guidance *in loco parentis.* Though they may not appreciate it fully in the moment, they often look back gratefully on the professors who held them accountable not only for their academic performance but for their conduct and demeanor and ambitions. They appreciate mentoring in personal matters, as a Hal Eyring did Georges Doriot's unsolicited approval of his marriage. The would-be life-changing professor cannot be value neutral or laissez faire. The university community that expects parents to pay the high cost of its expansive campus cannot entirely refuse to act *in loco parentis.*

Few institutions are likely to choose the kinds of strictures accepted by BYU-Idaho students or those that applied to residents of the Harvard houses in the 1950s. Yet each campus should make a conscious choice about the ethical and social environment it intends to promote. Students and their parents are interested in the differences among schools, as evidenced by the popularity of "party school" rankings. Given the relatively high cost of attending a traditional university, it cannot afford to let the quality of its campus social environment be determined randomly. Schools that set and meet an expectation, whatever that may be, will have an advantage over those that do not.

Chapter 22

Scholarship

The third critical dimension of choice for the traditional university is scholarship-related activity. Because our story of BYU-Idaho didn't show a university wrestling with issues of traditional scholarship, we'll delve into those issues more deeply here than we did the choices of students and subjects.

Along the dimensions of students served and subjects pursued, Charles Eliot's design for Harvard vastly broadened its scope of activity. By contrast, his call to have all subjects at their best ironically presaged a pronounced narrowing of university scholarship. The irony is that, in calling for scholarship at its best, Eliot did not necessarily mean just cutting-edge research. Though he admired the original discoveries and literary compositions of the German and French scholars, he also valued scholarship for its tendency to "promote the material welfare of mankind" and to advance "truth and right."[1] In fact, if anything he had an administrative bias not for research but for instruction, as evidenced by his statement, "The only conceivable aim of a college government in our day is to broaden, deepen, and invigorate American teaching in all branches of learning."[2]

Today even the most research-oriented universities reference the importance of teaching and service in their tenure standards. But particularly since James Conant's introduction of up-or-out tenure, scholarship—defined as original research and publication—has been the overriding factor in tenure and rank advancement decisions.[3] Just as Eliot lost the Rumford Chair in 1863 to a superior researcher, notwithstanding being an innovative teacher and the indispensable assistant to Harvard's then-president, today's tenure aspirants know that no other success or sacrifice can compensate for failure to publish.

It can be argued that publication is the determining factor in tenure and rank advancement because the other forms of contribution are difficult to measure reliably. The quality of a professor's teaching, for example, is not easily assessed; students are the only ones who fully experience it firsthand, and their ability to judge its worth is limited. Yet the quality of a given piece of original research or writing likewise is not easily measured. Confidence in the ability of an academic journal or a university press to judge one submission superior to another rests on an elaborate system of blind peer review that is both complex and expensive. Similar investments in measuring the amount and quality of a professor's contribution in the classroom would undoubtedly allow distinguishing the great from the good.[4]

An administrator of Conant's genius for measurement could have designed such a system. Conant's goal, however, was to make Harvard not just great in the absolute sense but great relative to all others: "the best." Outstanding instruction can occur anywhere. But Nobel Prize-winning scholarship is, by definition, unique. Harvard's system of up-or-out tenure was designed to promote that one-of-a-kind research scholarship.

Many of the institutions that copied Harvard soon found themselves producing neither great instruction nor noteworthy research. As Derek Bok observed in 1989, a majority of faculty members at these institutions reported feeling that quantity of research matters more than quality.[5] Bok declared that such quantity-driven approaches to scholarship are "hard to defend, as they beggar instruction to promote research of dubious worth."[6]

A Scholarship Model Inherited from a Golden Age

Part of the problem of research quality that Bok observed is a product of changed circumstances. Conant experienced research scholarship under nearly ideal conditions for university professors in his field, organic chemistry. He took his Ph.D. during a time when the basic structure of the atom and the mechanisms of atomic bonding were being discovered. These discoveries shed powerful new light on phenomena that preceding generations of chemists, including Charles Eliot, had studied in relative darkness.

Conant enjoyed the collaborative support of senior members of Harvard's chemistry department, several of whom had mentored him since college days (and one of whom, department chairman and Nobel laureate Theodore William Richards, had become his father-in-law). He also corresponded and collaborated with the cutting-edge European chemists of the day, especially the world-leading Germans. In addition to the favorable climate for discovery created by recent scientific breakthroughs and strong collegial support, Conant enjoyed an advantage in publishing his work. In the U.S., a relative laggard in organic chemistry at the time, his world-class research drew special attention from one of the premier domestic periodicals in his field, the *Journal of the American Chemical Society.*[7]

These environmental advantages propelled the talented and hard-working Conant to a level of research and publication success difficult to replicate today. In the six years before he assumed Harvard's presidency, in 1933, Conant published three books and an average of nearly ten papers per year, all but a few in the *Journal of the American Chemical Society.*[8] If he had remained in the laboratory, his research and publication productivity might well have increased. As Harvard's president, he observed from a distance the scientific paradigm shift attendant to the application of quantum mechanics to chemistry. Had he not been bound up in administrative responsibilities, he could have applied insights from the new discipline of quantum chemistry to explore one of his personal specialties, chemical reaction rates.

Given his personal experience, it made good sense to Conant to emphasize research publication in his up-or-out tenure system. In fact, that system, which quickly took hold at Harvard and other U.S. research universities, undoubtedly contributed to the country's rise to scientific preeminence. Yet in the coming decades, as research science became more expensive and research scientists more numerous, few tenure-track faculty members would experience anything like Conant's success. That would be especially true in the inevitable periods of more modest scientific advance in a given field, when researchers mostly fill the gaps in sweeping work done by predecessors, like Conant, who were lucky enough to start their careers during times of great change.

The Scholarship Challenge for Modern-Day A. Lawrence Lowells

With the steady advance of technology, physical scientists can be assured that more change is coming sooner or later, and with it the opportunity for new discoveries. There is no similar assurance, however, in many other academic fields. A. Lawrence Lowell, for example, would find today's world of scholarship far more competitive and confining than the one in which he made his name. The 1896 publication that secured Lowell's position on the Harvard faculty, his two-volume *Governments and Parties in Continental Europe,* assessed the workings of political parties in six countries: France, Italy, Germany, Austria, Hungary, and Switzerland. He reviewed each country's political institutions and recent history, showing the effect of these factors on party life.[9]

Lowell emphasized the narrow scope of his book, prefacing it with the disclaimer, "The present work deals only with a very small part of the great subject of political parties." He also noted having chosen countries with more than two main parties so as to avoid duplication of other scholars' work. The political systems of his six nations, he observed, had been "far less studied than . . . the bi-party system that prevails generally in Anglo-Saxon countries."[10]

Even with this careful delimitation of a field of inquiry, Lowell found his work partly duplicated before he could get it to press. While he was still in the midst of researching and writing, a French scholar published a two-volume analysis of politics and governance in the great constitutional monarchies and republics, including Lowell's big three, France, Italy, and Germany. In the preface to his book, Lowell took pains to distinguish his work as being different in its causal perspective. The French scholar, he asserted, looked primarily at government officials and analyzed parties only for their impact on those officials. *Governments and Parties in Continental Europe* took things the other way around, focusing on parties and identifying the effects of officials on the parties.[11]

Had Lowell been seeking tenure as a political historian fifty or so years later, in the middle of the twentieth century, the need to focus his inquiry to avoid preemption would have been far greater. By then the passage of time had added to the body of political history, but it had also brought many more university scholars to study it. To make original, publishable observations, Lowell would have needed to narrow his subject. He might, for example, have made comparisons between two countries rather than six. He also might have focused on just one aspect of political parties in those countries.

By the beginning of the twenty-first century Lowell's road to tenure would have been more difficult still, due to the expanded body of existing work and the many more university scholars seeking original intellectual territory. Today, publishing in fields such as Lowell's requires more than just a narrow focus of study. Seeking tenure now, a young Lowell would need to consider strategies such as critically analyzing his predecessors' work or reinterpreting political history from the standpoint of particular interest groups. He might even be tempted to join in analyzing the value of his own academic discipline, asking questions such as whether anyone can draw generally valid conclusions about the past.[12]

The Growing Challenge of Discovery Research

For outsiders, there is a tendency to see scholars as intellectually self-interested—inordinately prestige conscious; captivated by specialized research interests; averse to real-world performance standards; uninterested in ordinary students. The reality is that a university professor's activities are as organizationally driven as any other professional's. The typical tenured professor is as likely to have chosen academic life based on a desire to teach as on passion for a narrowly defined field of scholarship. But, since his or her early twenties, that professor has been required to run a scholarly gantlet that at multiple points presents a better than even chance of failure: gaining admission to graduate school; completing a dissertation; securing a tenure-track position; winning tenure. At every stage, survival is a long shot dependent on conformance to a research-publication model of scholarship. That model requires gunning for the top journals and university presses, narrowing one's field of inquiry, meeting exacting and sometimes arbitrary performance standards set by academic peers, and minimizing teaching responsibilities. Being the rare survivor of every stage of the professorial gantlet requires mastery of the research scholarship system that defines and drives the traditional university.

The gantlet is getting steadily more difficult to run. Since the late 1960s most academic fields have produced an oversupply of Ph.D. holders relative to the available tenure-track university positions.[13] Clark Kerr, whose University of California system graduated far more Ph.D.s than it could begin to consume, saw the problem coming more than four decades ago.[14] The post–World War II boom in college graduates produced a related increase in applications to Ph.D. programs across the country, which admitted candidates in numbers well beyond their own need for future faculty. It was one thing for Berkeley and Harvard to do this, but another for the less prestigious universities, which had less-accomplished students and more-limited resources with which to work. The result was an academic market swamped with competitively undifferentiated professorial candidates.

In recent years, the difficulty of winning a university tenure-track position has been compounded by a trend away from offering such opportunities. Between 1997 and 2007, the percentage of tenure-track instructors at four-year universities fell from more than 50 to 39 percent.[15] At research universities, fewer than 30 percent of instructors are on the tenure track. Against this shrinking demand, the growing supply of candidates requires many to work in temporary and part-time teaching positions.

Since the late 1960s most academic fields have produced an oversupply of Ph.D. holders relative to the available tenure-track university positions.

Those fortunate enough to get on the tenure track face new challenges in surviving the up-or-out, publish-or-perish process. The number of scholars trying to publish via the elite journals and academic presses is growing. The competition has become global, with prestige-conscious Asian universities and their sponsoring governments increasingly targeting the best English-language publications.[16] A proliferation of new journals helps tenure-track faculty only at the less elite universities, where the number of articles published may count for more than the quality of the publication. The cutting of budgets and outright closure of university presses makes it harder for scholars to publish books even through less prestigious channels. This matters especially to tenure-track faculty in the humanities, for whom publishing books is the ultimate test of scholarship.

This perspective suggests that it is the DNA of the university that produces its scholarship-related problems today, not the inherent preferences of professors.[17] Personal preference alone does not explain the choice of research over teaching or the selection of esoteric inquiries over more broadly practical ones. Those decisions are also driven by experience and by an instinct for professional survival and advancement in an increasingly competitive environment. The apparent inclination to favor the library and the laboratory over the classroom reflects a self-preservation calculus rather than a natural aversion to instruction and mentoring. The desire to research and teach specialized, advanced subjects rather than broader ones reflects years of narrow inquiry, not inherent inability to integrate and apply knowledge.

A Broader Definition of Scholarship

As Derek Bok lamented the diversion of scholarly effort into research of "dubious worth," he conceded that "universities that lack distinguished scholars are unlikely to stop putting undue emphasis on publication only when there are credible, attractive models of excellence other than that of the research university."[18] As it happened, an alternative model of scholarship was proposed just one year after he made this statement. Writing with a group of colleagues in 1990, Carnegie Foundation president and former U.S. Commissioner of Education Ernest Boyer suggested a fourfold definition of scholarship. In addition to what he called the scholarship of discovery, which encompasses traditional academic research, he added three other categories: integration, application, and teaching.[19] These latter three types would expand the traditional definition of scholarship to include putting discoveries into context, showing their application to practical problems, and sharing them with students.[20]

> *We must justly prize those faculty who are truly gifted . . . .We will never totally forsake recognition for publishing in the usual academic journals, but we must be brave and wise enough to appreciate and reward other forms of scholarship as well.*[21]
>
> —Gordon Gee, president of The Ohio State University

Boyer made it clear that all faculty need to establish their credentials as researchers, something they do in producing master's theses and Ph.D. dissertations. However, Boyer and his colleagues argued that "it is unrealistic, we believe, to expect *all* faculty members, regardless of their interests, to engage in research and to publish on a regular timetable. For most scholars, creativity simply doesn't work that way."[22]

Boyer suggested both a broader, fourfold definition of scholarship and a broader definition of peer review, with an emphasis on writing but not necessarily on publishing in refereed journals. He proposed that faculty be given credit for textbooks and "popular writing," assuming review by qualified peers.[23] Today these recommendations seem all the more sensible, given the feasibility and ubiquity of electronic publication.

Boyer suggested . . . a broader definition of peer review, with an emphasis on writing but not necessarily on publishing in refereed journals.

Boyer's definition of scholarship is modular: an academic institution can use the definition to customize its mix of scholarly activities.[24] Under David Bednar, for example, BYU-Idaho chose to focus on the scholarship of teaching. Kim Clark's call to create cross-disciplinary courses with practical relevance expanded the school's definition of scholarship to include, in a modest way, integration and application.

Clark's former employer, the Harvard Business School, has the financial and faculty resources to emphasize all four dimensions of scholarship. Like Harvard's other graduate schools, it is a leader in discovery scholarship. But HBS does not limit its definition of *better* to only this form of scholarship. The school's faculty members also engage in integrative, applied, and instruction-related scholarship. For example, Michael Porter's path-breaking insights into competitive strategy stemmed from the integration of discovery research from many distinct fields. Developing a theory of how institutions create and sustain competitive advantages required him to integrate insights from many traditional disciplines, including economics, finance, accounting, operations management, organizational behavior, business policy, public policy, law, and military strategy.

HBS faculty members also engage in the scholarship of application and instruction. Clayton Christensen's initial discoveries in just one industry, computer disk drives, have been applied in many others (such as, in these pages, higher education).[25] C. Roland Christensen's scientific approach to discussion-based learning contributed to a body of teaching scholarship that includes the 350 new HBS cases created each year, which are used for classroom discussion by universities around the world.[26]

All three of these well-recognized contributors to Harvard's mission deviated from the prevailing university approach to scholarship, which is to seek to prove something entirely new. Instead, they followed their intellectual instincts and did, to paraphrase Lowell, useful things the world wanted done. In the process, they created not only great practical value for society but new intellectual platforms for scholars in their fields. A similar case can be made for Eliot. He was an undistinguished researcher but an administrative genius and the creator of the world's most powerful paradigm for higher education. Any university, including Harvard, would do well to have a path to tenure for such a uniquely valuable scholar.

A NEW TYPE OF CARNEGIE CLASSIFICATION

In 2006, having reassessed the effects of its classification system, the Carnegie Foundation introduced a new, elective category, a "Community-Engagement Classification." All institutions remain subject to the standard system, but they may also decide to seek this new status, which recognizes "diversity of institutions" and seeks to "engage institutions in a process of inquiry, reflection, and self-assessment."[27]

More than giving higher education institutions a new badge of distinction, the purpose of Community-Engagement Classification is to focus their scholarly, teaching, and learning activities on the communities in which they reside, with the intent of producing mutual benefit—work the world wants done. Ernest Boyer's broad definition of scholarship, especially the knowledge application and teaching categories, potentially facilitates this kind of interconnection of faculty members, students, and members of the external community.

The application process for Community-Engagement Classification requires institutions to make explicit the connection between what they say they want to achieve and what they do in practice, an exercise amounting to thorough genetic reengineering, as suggested in a 2008 Foundation report:

> One of the major strengths of the institutions that were classified as engaged with their communities was a compelling alignment of mission, marketing, leadership, traditions, recognitions, budgetary support, infrastructure, faculty development, and strategic plans—the foundational indicators of community engagement.
>
> For example, Portland State University's motto, "Let knowledge serve the city," was translated into budgetary priorities, an office of community/university partnerships, a consistent message from institutional leadership, and promotion and tenure guidelines that reward Boyer's "scholarship of application."[28]

Diversity of scholarship at the Harvard Business School calls into question the public stereotype of the university scholar and illustrates the potential power of a broader definition of scholarship. In fact, great teachers at all universities practice the scholarship of integration, application, and teaching every time they engage a learner, whether a graduate student or an undergraduate. To effectively convey an idea they must first answer at least three questions:

1. How does this idea relate to other ideas?
2. How does it apply in practical settings?
3. How can I best communicate it?

Unfortunately, the world at large rarely hears from these great university teachers. They are not given time or incentives to publish what they know about integrating, applying, and teaching the new discoveries of their colleagues. Even those research discoveries get limited circulation: they are likely to be shared outside of the academy only to the degree that they show economic value.

The Need for New Scholarship Incentives

Changing that reality will require modifying the research- and graduate program-favoring incentives built into the university's organizational DNA. Columbia English professor James Shapiro, a former hero of a great books course in the undergraduate core curriculum there, has trenchantly voiced the need to recognize more than one form of scholarly contribution. When asked about his decisions to stop teaching the course, he replied, "When you acknowledge this course and reward faculty accordingly, then I'll be glad to teach it again. But in universities today salaries and resources are built on the star system, and everyone knows that."[29]

To perform the critical jobs of discovering and sharing knowledge, universities need a diversity of tenure paths and faculty contracts that provide the essential acknowledgments and rewards. The tenure process is particularly determinative. As Louis Menand has observed, "Until professors are produced in a different way, the structure of academic knowledge production and dissemination is unlikely to change significantly."[30]

A form of diversity in faculty promotion and compensation already exists at most universities, but it reflects the haves-and-have-nots rationale of the traditional tenure system. Non-tenure-track faculty often make less than their peers even when carrying outsized teaching and administrative loads. Universities and their faculty members are better served by customized contracts that reflect a professor's unique mix of instructional, administrative, and scholarly activities, with scholarship defined to include research related to discovery, integration, application, and teaching.[31] These forms of scholarship can be weighted differently based on institutional objectives. Still, all institutions need to ensure that their promotion and compensation systems do not have the effect of making instruction a stepchild.

Harvard Business School has shown the potential for altering the traditional scholarship DNA. For example, its course development path to tenure recognizes the focused scholarship of teaching required to keep the institution at the forefront of business education, just as its research and publication track creates incentives and opportunities to produce traditional scholarship. Course development was, in the beginning, the main path to tenure at HBS. In the 1920s, when Dean Wallace B. Donham encouraged adoption of the case method of instruction, he challenged members of the faculty to develop classic instructional cases such as those he had studied as a Harvard Law School student. Most full-time faculty members engaged in both case writing and course development.

Course development means just that: not merely effective classroom teaching, which is a point of pride for HBS and a requirement of all faculty, but the creation of intellectual content to guide and facilitate the instruction process. The standard of excellence on the course development track to tenure is similar to that of the research-and-publication track: the creation of powerful new ideas, rigorously supported and peer-reviewed.

The difference for course development faculty is that their ideas are published in the form of instructional materials—cases, case teaching notes, technical notes for students, course overview notes—rather than articles in scholarly journals. While most other top-flight business schools base tenure primarily on research scholarship, like the rest of academia, HBS has both stayed in the forefront of research and maintained its ability to cultivate instructional genius in the model of C. Roland Christensen. No school at Harvard is considered more relevant by the nonacademic world or is more esteemed by its academic competitors. The Harvard Business School's success suggests that Lowell-style usefulness in scholarship is not limited to discovery research, nor does it detract from scholarly reputation.

The Tenure Debate

The notion of diverse forms of scholarship and types of scholars raises the question, "What about tenure?" From the standpoint of the university's ability to do things the world finds useful, the question may be less important than it seems. Both those who decry tenure as an anticompetitive labor practice and those who argue its vital role in protecting scholars often fail to distinguish the process from the outcome. The main outcomes of tenure, job security and intellectual self-determination for competent professors, are not necessarily a net liability to the university. Nor are they things unique to higher education. To the extent that tenure is problematic, the problem lies more in the way tenure is granted than in its outcome.

Universities are not alone in applying a tenure ethos. Honoring the value of experienced employees is a hallmark of high-performing institutions; whether universities or businesses, they seek to retain their proven people.[32] That is particularly true of knowledge-dependent enterprises such as law firms and management consultancies that, like universities, invest in creating a core group of carefully trained and vetted partners.[33] Such stalwart contributors do not normally slack off or suffer diminished capacity with time. Nor, in a country where free speech is both legally protected and recognized as a competitive asset, do longtime employees often find themselves terminated merely for expressing opinions about what is best for the organization. Well-managed companies, like universities, honor long service and intellectual honesty not only

The notion of diverse forms of scholarship and types of scholars raises the question, "What about tenure?"

out of legal and moral obligation but also because of the competitive value of individual experience and collective openness.

> *The essence of [creating a great company] is to get the right people engaged in vigorous dialogue and debate, infused with the brutal facts. . . .*[34]
>
> —Jim Collins, author of *Good to Great: Why Some Companies Make the Leap... and Others Don't*

In this respect, the typical tenured university professor is little different from his or her for-profit company counterpart. It is true that the tenured professor enjoys a high degree of intellectual autonomy. He or she can make unfettered choices of what to study and what to say in the classroom, based only on demonstrated expertise.[35] This is not so different, though, from the various forms of employee empowerment practiced by high-performing companies, including factory floor job rotation and self-directing work groups.

What is most unusual in the typical university is the publication-focused, lengthy, and too often uncertain process for winning tenure. This process has at least two potentially self-defeating effects on the institution. One is to artificially skew faculty preferences away from teaching and to foster unproductive anxiety and a sense of second-class citizenship among untenured professors.[36] Another is to create the risk of entitlement feelings among those who survive the protracted, stressful process. The result can be a reduction in individual commitment to the institution and its students, both pre- and post-tenure. It is the tenure process, not necessarily the university's guarantee of employment and intellectual self-determination to those who win tenure, that can disadvantage the institution.

That may explain Gordon Hinckley's having omitted reference to tenure in his announcement of the creation of BYU-Idaho. Hinckley focused not on tenure but on the issue of rank: "Faculty rank," he said, "will not be a part of the academic structure of the new four-year institution."[37] Hinckley's concern about Ricks College professors becoming members of a university faculty was neither that they would grow lazy nor that they would face greater threats to their academic freedom. What Hinckley wanted was to preempt the creation of different professorial classes based primarily on research productivity. Such scholarship-based class distinctions, he felt, would distance faculty from one another and ultimately from the institution and its students.[38] Thus, in addition to keeping compensation the same across all disciplines, with differentials based only on lengthy of service, Hinckley reinforced the tradition that each member of the faculty be called simply "professor." He recognized that it was not tenure per se but its grounding in a narrow view of producing "the best" scholars and its manifestation in multiple academic ranks that was to be avoided at the teaching-focused university he was creating.

The Right Kind of Tenure

Hinckley felt comfortable with BYU-Idaho's pursuing the same approach to faculty employment that had worked well for Ricks College. That approach resembles what good companies do: work hard to identify people with good long-term potential to contribute; give them incentives consistent with the organization's goals; invest in their development; and hang on to them.

The BYU-Idaho hiring process, which culminates with what David Bednar called a college president's most important decision, begins with a global search that must produce multiple qualified candidates.[39] Vetting of these candidates occurs in the classroom, where teaching capacity is observed, and in personal interviews that begin with departmental and college representatives and end with the president.

For three years after being hired, a BYU-Idaho professor has probationary status that, in the large majority of cases, produces "continuing status." The decision is based on a review conducted by academic leaders and the president. The primary criteria are teaching and other instruction-related contributions to the university, such as curriculum development and student advising. These criteria square with the university's choices of students, subjects, and scholarship.

As in most professional organizations that hold their employees to clearly stated objectives, dismissals of faculty with continuing status at BYU-Idaho are rare. That comports with the exhortation of the American Association of University Professors (AAUP): "In the effective college, a dismissal proceeding involving a faculty member on tenure, or one occurring during the term of an appointment, will be a rare exception, caused by individual human weakness and not by an unhealthful setting."[40]

Continuing status at BYU-Idaho does not foster a sense of professional invincibility. In fact, no tenured professor should feel immune to ongoing performance assessment and potential dismissal for failure to meet threshold standards of productivity. The AAUP has made that clear, saying, "The faculty must be willing to recommend the dismissal of a colleague when necessary."[41] Institutions are expected to set their own definitions of adequate cause for dismissal; these may include incompetence and neglect of duty.[42]

Though the AAUP allows for post-tenure review, fewer than half of four-year institutions surveyed by the Harvard Graduate School of Education have policies for conducting such reviews.[43] Herein lies another process flaw that is unrelated to tenure's main outcome, employment security. Many university communities presume that tenure is an immutable decision; for them, the presumption becomes self-fulfilling, and they may find themselves employing unproductive faculty members who cannot be

Though the AAUP allows for post-tenure review, fewer than half of four-year institutions surveyed by the Harvard Graduate School of Education have policies for conducting such reviews.

dismissed. This can be particularly problematic in the United States, where anti-age discrimination laws create a high bar for dismissing older workers.

Tenure granted by the wrong kind of process can impose debilitating costs on a university, including decreased instruction quality, faculty disunity, and diminished productivity. Yet the flaws are in the process rather than the concept of employment security. A flawed process is one that grants tenure for activities such as mediocre research that does not substantially contribute to the institution's mission, one that is opaque and perceived to be arbitrary, or one that creates a presumption of immunity to post-tenure performance review. An institution that operates such a process has itself—not tenure—to blame.

Universities may benefit from more of the right kind of tenure, as BYU-Idaho does from its continuing faculty status. Those benefits include (1) incentives for tenure-track professors to innovate in ways that help the university, such as contributing to general education courses; (2) less dividedness among the faculty, the majority of whom will either have tenure or be confidently on their way to earning it; and (3) fewer courses taught by potentially unqualified instructors.[44]

A form of tenure might be extended even to adjunct faculty, including those working online. An adjunct instructor who has successfully passed through a well-designed probationary process represents an asset of far greater value than the current market rate for such services implies. Universities that rely on these "contingent" faculty will benefit from contracting with the best of them on terms designed to increase their long-term commitment to the institution and its students. An outstanding adjunct instructor might, for example, be guaranteed a certain annual course load and paid a premium rate. This is the compensation model of some for-profit institutions.

Even a well-designed and managed tenure process is not without its potential risks. Among those is an increase of faculty power, which can be used to thwart administrative efficiency measures or even call for the removal of a president.[45] But as Richard Chait of Harvard's Graduate School of Education has noted, "The degree of professional autonomy varies more as a function of institutional prestige, culture, and ethos than is suggested by a faculty member's tenure status."[46] In other words, tenure is more likely to strengthen a particular an existing faculty view of institutional authority than to create one.

This suggests that tenure can also work in favor of a skillfully led institution. A faculty member who enjoys a sense of employment security may be more likely to support a well-reasoned and communicated administrative proposal for change. Charles Eliot created tenure for his faculty and trusted them to act in the best interests of the institution, treating them as "the most intelligent and fair-minded body of men in the world, for his purposes."[47] His power to lead Harvard was the greater because it ultimately rested with self-confident faculty members who chose to support his institutional initiatives. The tenure debate, to the extent it focuses on reasonable employment security and intellectual freedom, is misplaced. A high degree of individual security and self-determination are good for all organizations that depend on human insight and commitment for their success, including and especially universities.

The Scholar's Out-of-Class Activities

As in the case of tenure, questions about professors' connections to the world outside the classroom require nuanced analysis that is sensitive to the needs and welfare of the university community. These out-of-class connections can benefit not only individual scholars but also students and the institution as a whole. For example, high-quality research can both burnish the university's reputation and expose students to cutting-edge thought. Even a student-centered university with limited graduate programs may be justified in performing traditional scholarly research, especially as it enlists undergraduate students in the effort.

Likewise, the so-called commercialization of universities is not a problem per se. Institutional research contracts with private sector companies and individual faculty consulting activities need not come at the expense of students. Properly managed, they can make a net contribution to the educational mission of the university, including its job of mentoring. Students benefit from professors' connections to the world outside academe, particularly as they are invited to participate in those external activities. That is borne out, for example, in the one-day per week given by most leading business schools to their faculty members, whose connections to the corporate world yield rich dividends for MBA students in the form not only of insights brought back to the classroom but also student consulting projects and career connections.

Of course, university administrators and faculty members must recognize the high cost of their combined scholarly and instructional activities. Performing these two fundamentally different activities under one roof, in a way that research laboratories and for-profit educators do not, inevitably creates coordination costs that must be justified by their benefits. The benefits of scholarly activity will outweigh those costs only if the activity is motivated by a true quest for knowledge and a hope of some ultimate good to students and society at large. It is all right that a given line of research may have no immediate practical purpose, on the one hand, or that it be funded by a for-profit company on the other. But the goal of the scholar must be the advance of knowledge, not the bolstering of a tenure portfolio or the acquisition of university overhead reimbursements.

The student-conscious scholar is uniquely valuable, capable of performing the jobs of discovery, memory, and mentoring like no one else. Thus, the university is justified in assuring such a scholar employment security and in encouraging him or her to explore the boundaries of knowledge not only in the laboratory and library but in the world at large. Of course, this presumes that the university has defined *scholarship* more broadly than just discovery research and in a way consistent with its unique choices of students and subjects. It also presumes that the policies of the university align with and reinforce these choices. Given the genetic tendency to imitate the great research universities, which aspire to having everything at its scholarly best, creating alignment around unique choices isn't easy. The choices cannot be made only tacitly or on paper. The university must have its strategy reflected in its institutional DNA: its program offerings, organizational structures, policies and procedures, and other systems that guide and support its activities. In particular, the university's strategic choices must be reflected in its success measures. We explore what it takes to accomplish that in the following chapter, the next-to-last in our journey.

Chapter 23

New DNA

The things we've seen in our exploration of higher education's past and current competitive realities indicate the need for most traditional universities to genetically reengineer themselves. In the roughly seventy-five years during which Charles Eliot, A. Lawrence Lowell, and James Conant presided over Harvard, its DNA was set. Since the 1950s, when Conant left to help in the reconstruction of Germany, that DNA has remained largely unaltered, even as it has been widely copied. Universities have grown larger, more complex, and more expensive, but their basic character still reflects decisions made in the late nineteenth and early twentieth centuries. The times now require additional evolutionary adaptation. Because of the pace of change around them today, university communities must respond quickly.

Assessing Capabilities and Making Choices

The starting point is an honest assessment of a university's most valuable assets: its faculty and its physical campus. With these assets in mind, the question to ask is, "How good are we *really*—not just relative to other institutions, but in terms of meeting the needs of the students, governments, and other constituencies we serve—at doing the jobs of discovery, memory, and mentoring?"

The starting point is an honest assessment of a university's most valuable assets: its faculty and its physical campus.

To the extent that the answer vis-à-vis any of the three jobs is "not very good," the members of a university community need to assess their choices of students, subjects, and scholarship. Because so many institutions have adopted the Harvard DNA without the financial resources to sustain that model, in many instances it will be necessary for the university community to make tradeoffs, hard choices about shifting the emphasis of their activities and even ceasing some things altogether.

The prospects for making such decisions in higher education have historically been poor. Faculty members reasonably expect to have a say in matters that affect the quality of the university's activities. Many have chosen academic life and a particular academic institution over higher-paying opportunities and with a sense of commitment that goes beyond what the typical company can expect. The quid pro quo for this faculty commitment is voice in the decisions that affect not only their work but their professional lives.

Historically, faculty members have sought to preserve institutional support for their individual activities and for the traditional university model that has proven so successful in performing the jobs of discovery, memory, and mentoring. The university's departmental structure has—in a way analogous to the federal structure of American government, in which even a small state has some say—ensured the university's commitment to a broad range of academic disciplines.

Now, however, the external pressures on universities require many to respond in ways that go beyond incremental, across-the-board budget reductions. The viability of the whole institution is at risk, and with it the ability of individual faculty members to make the kinds of contributions for which they joined the academy—or simply to keep their jobs. Realizing their collective and individual ambitions will require all members of the university community to consider changes in the ways they pursue the mission of higher education.

Prerequisites for Successful Conversations about Tradeoffs

Each institution will need to make unique tradeoffs, and some members of the university community will be affected more than others. Several principles for success, though, apply generally. One is that the institution must put questions of people ahead of questions of strategy. That may sound un-businesslike, but it is in fact a key conclusion reached by business researcher Jim Collins in the study that led to his book *Good to Great: Why Some Companies Make the Leap . . . and Others Don't.* Likening a business organization to a bus and its strategy to the destination of the bus, Collins says, "Leaders of companies that go from good to great start not with 'where' but with 'who.'"[1] According to his research, the most successful businesses make sure that they have the right people on the "bus" before they decide where the company is going. These must be people who are both capable and committed to "A-plus effort."

Traditional universities benefit from having invested heavily in getting the right people on the institutional bus. The tenure process ensures intellectual capacity and work ethic, and the compensation level means that most professors have put the love of discovery, memory, and mentoring ahead of financial wealth. Though organizational structures and systems may promote defensive and even self-serving behavior, the typical university has a team of remarkable capability and commitment. Its potential for innovation is vast.

However, maintaining individual commitment while changing fundamental aspects of the university's DNA requires an equally high level of commitment from the institution. Particularly with tenured positions in many fields at a low ebb, faculty members cannot be expected to vote themselves "off the bus." Innovation may require them to alter their activities, but no meaningful discussion of change can be undertaken without assurances that capable members who commit to innovating can remain with the community.

That principle guided Charles Eliot, who implemented tenure at Harvard, as he undertook the innovations that established the great American university. It has likewise been a principle of innovation at BYU-Idaho. Throughout its history of ups and downs, including the reversion in the 1950s from four- to two-year status and the elimination of intercollegiate athletics in 2000, the institution has protected the employment of individuals capable of and committed to its mission. No one's seat on the bus is guaranteed, and some, such as the coaches who left BYU-Idaho instead of taking teaching positions, have chosen to get off rather than change seats. But the institution's innovations have been premised on the bus being big enough for its current riders.

Taking that position, especially in difficult times, requires university leaders to have faith not only in their people but in the institution's future. But even if the faith in the future is nothing more than that—an inchoate sense of what the institution is capable of—there is no other place for university leaders to start. The university's people, especially its faculty members, are both the bus's engine and its brakes. Before any new direction is charted, they must be assured of their voice and safety in the journey.

Different Types of Tradeoffs

The choices that each university community makes should be unique, driven by its aspirations and capabilities. In general, though, universities need to become more focused and realistic about what they can achieve. Most need to narrow their choice of students and subjects and to deemphasize discovery scholarship in favor of other forms.

Consider the case of a regional university that has ascended quickly to that status and is financially overextended by the costs of its new graduate and athletic programs, as well as decreased faculty teaching loads designed to allow time for scholarship. To increase its prospects for long-term success, this school might choose to refocus on its undergraduate students and on subjects leading to employment in fields such as business and teaching. The university will also benefit from modular curriculum that decreases the time its students take to graduate and increases their employability. Its general education module should be designed with liberal ambitions but a practical bent, to serve students who have come with poor college preparation or might be inclined to view their higher education as purely vocational. Given the likelihood of its graduates' going straight to work, this regional university could benefit from an alumni-supported internship program.

Consistent with those choices of students and subjects, this university might emphasize the scholarship of integration, application, and instruction; given its relative lack of institutional prestige and inability to draw new students on the basis of its name alone, this university could benefit particularly from scholarly efforts to demonstrate learning outcomes. To the extent that discovery research continues, undergraduate students should be involved.

Very likely, this regional university will need to reduce its operating costs by consolidating or eliminating some departments, majors, graduate programs, and athletic teams. It should explore the potential to serve students more cost effectively through year-round operation and online learning. It should also scale back its investment in merit scholarships and higher-than-average pay packages for faculty scholars.

Obviously, faculty members will be impacted by these changes, and their support and leadership will be crucial. In addition to shifting the focus of their research—and perhaps having less time for it—some will need to accept assignments to teach a greater proportion of introductory courses than before. However, there will be opportunities to play challenging and potentially rewarding new roles in developing new curriculum, especially online courses, and in mentoring online faculty in their teaching and students in research. As the university's summer offerings fill, the university may be able to increase faculty compensation. And, as the size of the student body grows, there will be increased opportunities to teach advanced courses.

A STRATEGICALLY FOCUSED REGIONAL UNIVERSITY

Few institutions have climbed the Carnegie ladder with the speed and success of Utah Valley University (UVU). Founded in 1941 as a state vocational school, the institution took a new name at the rate of nearly one per decade—trade tech, technical institute, community college, state college, and finally state university. In the process, its student body grew to nearly 33,000 students, equaling in size the state's flagship research institution, the University of Utah. To the technical certificates originally offered have been added associate's, bachelor's, and master's degrees, and a school that started with no athletic program currently competes at the NCAA Division I level.

In 2010, though, the UVU community and its new president, Matt Holland, stood at a crossroads. Holland's academic résumé includes the names Duke and Princeton, creating the natural expectation among many faculty and alumni of a continued Carnegie climb. But in addition to double-digit enrollment growth, UVU had been hit by double-digit state funding cuts. Rather than competing head-to-head with the five Utah universities on the ladder ahead of UVU, Holland and his colleagues determined to create a university that is both academically "serious" and "inclusive" of all types of students and the surrounding community.

UVU's strategy for pursuing serious scholarship while still remaining open to all high school graduates is built on the new Carnegie classification, Community-Engagement. UVU has used a $400,000 Carnegie grant to stimulate programs for student internships, community projects, and faculty research collaboration. That faculty research emphasizes the nontraditional elements of scholarship suggested by Ernest Boyer: integration, application, and instruction.[2] UVU is also expanding its online curriculum, the key to serving more students in its resource-constrained environment.

The choices of an elite liberal arts college could be different. Its lack of graduate programs and Division I intercollegiate athletics, along with its higher tuition, might reduce the need for efficiency measures such as year-round operation. Likewise, its selectivity may produce a student whose solid preparation for college and intention to attend graduate school diminishes the need for an integrated GE program and modular majors tied to internships and professional certifications. Still, the high tuition of elite liberal arts colleges creates an expectation that every activity will be student oriented. Faculty scholarship, for example, should involve students.

The hundreds of less well-endowed private colleges need to take another tack. For them, online learning is a critical tool, particularly in hybrid form. For example, a course with four face-to-face classroom sessions per week can be redesigned to have only half as many professor-led discussions, the balance being replaced with online student-to-student learning led by a skilled but less expensive adjunct instructor. The full-time professor is thus freed up to serve more students or engage in more scholarship.

At the same time, all liberal arts colleges must preserve their advantages in memory and mentoring, two of the primary reasons for which students and their parents are willing to pay a premium price. The instruction of the liberal arts college should remain predominantly face-to-face and its curriculum cross-disciplinary, like that of Salt Lake City's Westminster, where online learning is part of a "high-tech/high-touch" education. The liberal arts college should also encourage interactions among professors and students that are personal and inspiring, like those between Mark Hopkins and James Garfield during the time they shared as teacher and student at Williams College.

General Genetic Recommendations

Though unique choices are critical, because many universities have overextended themselves in a common climb up the Carnegie ladder, in pursuit of Harvard and its peers, many of the genetic changes they need to make are similar. Table 23.1 shows the changes that most institutions should consider.

Some of these genetic alterations could be made at a stroke, as was the case when the new BYU-Idaho eliminated competitive athletics. More realistically, the changes will take time, as they did when Kim Clark called for a new learning model and general education program. Particularly in the case of academic programs, the faculty must lead the effort, and their deliberative process will be time consuming.

TABLE 23.1 Recommended DNA Alterations

Traditional University Traits	Recommended Alterations
Face-to-face instruction	Mix of face-to-face and online learning
Rational/secular orientation	Increased attention to values
Comprehensive specialization, departmentalization, and faculty self-governance	Interdepartmental faculty collaboration Heavyweight innovation teams
Long summer recess	Year-round operation
Graduate schools atop the college	Strong graduate programs only Institutional focus on mentoring students, especially undergraduates
Private fundraising	Funds used primarily in support of students, especially need-based aid
Competitive athletics	Greater relative emphasis on student activities
Curricular distribution (GE) and concentration (majors)	Cross-disciplinary, integrated GE Modular, customizable majors, with technical certificates and associate's degrees nested within bachelor's degrees

continued

TABLE 23.1 *(Continued)*

Traditional University Traits	Recommended Alterations
Academic honors	Increased emphasis on student competence vis-à-vis learning outcomes
Externally funded research	Undergraduate student involvement in research
Up-or-out tenure, with faculty rank and salary distinctions	Hiring with intent to train and retain Customized scholarship and employment contracts Minimized rank and salary distinctions, consistent with a student-mentoring emphasis
Admissions selectivity	Expansion of capacity (for example, via online learning and year-round operation) to limit the need for selectivity

The same principle of gradual, faculty-led implementation applies to changes such as offering more summer courses and creating new faculty contracts. An across-the-board changeover to a three-semester academic calendar and year-round employment contracts for faculty may be unavoidable for institutions in dire financial straits. For many, though, the shift can be gradual, with summer offerings increased incrementally and contracts changed voluntarily or altered as new faculty are hired.

The important thing to remember, from a compensation standpoint, is that the cost efficiency of these summer offerings is great. There is no new cost for buildings or faculty benefits, and the incremental costs of student support, such as academic advising, is relatively small. This means that faculty compensation can be generous, as long as classes can be filled. At the same time, because a BYU-Idaho-style track system is impractical for most schools, summer offerings will need to be rolled out gradually, with tuition discounts and other preferences given to attract students.

The Benefits of Growth and an Emphasis on Quality

The university's faculty members hold the key to successful institutional change. One lesson we can infer from the BYU-Idaho experience is that change is more palatable for all members of the university community, especially faculty members, when it occurs in the context of institutional growth rather than shrinkage, and when the innovation emphasis is on quality rather than mere cost reduction. For example, the addition of third- and fourth-year students at the creation of BYU-Idaho helped ensure that former Ricks College athletic coaches could be employed as physical education instructors and student activities leaders; the emphasis in these areas was on improving the quality of the student experiences through application of the Learning Model. The continuing growth of the university and its emphasis on learning quality likewise eases concerns as online course are added. Full-time faculty members need not feel concerned about being replaced by online adjunct instructors, because the demand for face-to-face courses remains high. Moreover, the full-time faculty have a vital role to play in ensuring quality in the course design and delivery process.

For a university facing declining enrollments, the idea that change is easier to effect as part of an overall strategy of growth and quality enhancement appears to present an organizational Catch-22. However, there are opportunities for such a school in a strategy that includes simultaneously focusing its choices of students, subjects, and scholarship and also reaching out to nonconsumers of higher education, as BYU-Idaho and many for-profits are doing, and as Lowell did in creating Harvard's extension programs. In particular, online courses designed to serve students who are not fully prepared for college, such as the Academic Start suite of courses in BYU-Idaho's

Pathway program, create expansion possibilities even in geographic regions of apparently low higher education growth. High schools and community colleges are potential partners in this outreach to nonconsumers of university education, especially the many students who currently do not continue after completing a high school or associate's degree.

As noted in the story of BYU-Idaho's Pathway program, established universities have inherent cost efficiencies in serving students via online degree programs. Much of the educational infrastructure—courses, computer systems, advising systems—may already be in place. In addition, traditional universities have the benefit of their faculty subject matter experts and established reputations, giving them the potential to save costs in course creation and marketing relative to purely online educators. Particularly as the overall demographic trend turns down, strategies for serving college nonconsumers at high levels of quality present an invaluable opportunity for growth and the institutional innovation that will be easier because of it.

Our greatest partnership here at Ohio State should be with the community colleges. We're all part of the same mission, which is education from pre-K through life.[3]

—Gordon Gee, president of Ohio State University

You Get What You Measure

Whether a university is growing or not, a crucial step in changing its DNA is choosing supportive success measures. It will make little difference, for instance, to declare a focus on undergraduate students and hire outstanding teachers if faculty tenure and promotion continues to hinge primarily on research and publication. The university's strategic choices must be supported by the success measures it applies to itself and to its employees, particularly the faculty. Like other organizations, universities produce the results they do by design. They do not always get what they want, especially when their competitive environment changes significantly, as it is doing now. However, what they want—as manifested by the activities they measure and reward—largely determines what they get, for better and for worse.

In many respects, the traditional university has chosen success measures that are not only inconsistent with the jobs of discovery, memory, and mentoring but work in opposition to them. Traditional institutions of higher education are in dire straits today not just because of the general tendency to emulate the activities and copy the traits of the elite research universities, which themselves struggle under the financial burden. The typical university both organizes itself like these hard-to-copy standouts and also adopts their success measures and incentive systems. The result is a higher education sector enacting poor strategic choices with uniformity and dogged consistency.

Much of the problem lies in the chosen indicators of success. For too long, traditional universities have been more concerned with measures of what they do and what they consume than with measures of what they produce. Accreditation teams, for example, historically worried about the percentage of faculty holding doctoral degrees, the adequacy of physical facilities and financial reserves, and the number of classroom hours required to graduate. Ranking agencies still reward the universities that turn away many applicants, pay their faculty well, keep classes small, and win the respect of peer institutions. Tenure committees count publications and seek stars in narrowly defined fields. Alumni expect bowl and tournament berths.

Only recently have government regulators demanded accountability for the educational benefits universities produce and the efficiency with which the produce them: What does college cost? How many students are admitted? How many graduate? How long does it take them to graduate? How many get good jobs? At the same time, accrediting bodies have changed their measurement emphasis from inputs and activities to outcomes. This plays to the strengths of the for-profit educators, who have made a science of measuring learning outcomes.

Meaningful Success Measures

To compete in this environment, the traditional university must change what it has historically valued and measured. At a minimum, that will mean voluntarily embracing many of the criteria that the Spellings Commission would have forced on it, such as creating performance benchmarks for productivity and efficiency.[4] The successful university will take its measurement efforts further, by developing a report card like BYU-Idaho's that is customized to the university's strategic choices and incorporates performance statistics defined with those choices in mind.

> *By . . . establishing new criteria for success, we are choosing not to participate in a race that has already been lost.*[5]
>
> —Michael Crow, president of Arizona State University

As in the case of reengineering the DNA, the emphasis on various success measures will differ among institutions. However, several general guidelines apply. One is to shift the emphasis from things that matter to scholars and ranking agencies to things that matter to students and governmental bodies; increasingly, the latter define bigger and better differently than the former do. In the past, students and governments placed great value on prestige. They were also willing to let presumed experts, academicians and the creators of rankings, determine the meaning of prestige for them. Today, with higher education costs escalating and academic prestige becoming more difficult to trade on in a competency-oriented marketplace, students and governments want to draw their own conclusions about what their universities are doing for them rather than what scholars and ranking agencies have valued.

Rankings, for example, reward schools for enrollees with high SAT and ACT scores. Students, by contrast, pay tuition with the expectation of earning a degree that can be completed in four years with a bearable debt load; they also expect to receive a credential meaningful to employers and graduate schools. In their "ranking," the measures that matter are time-to-graduation, tuition cost, and career placement or graduate school admission rates.

There is a similar disconnect between the success measures of scholars and those of governments. Scholars value publications and prizes. Governments, by contrast, fund universities primarily to produce capable, civic-minded graduates and economy-stimulating innovations. These outcomes are manifested in high salaries and rates of civic participation among graduates, as well as company creation. Publications and prizes may correlate with these outcomes, but they do not ensure them.

Another guideline for measuring success in this new environment is to invest in qualitative assessments as opposed to purely quantitative ones. Many of the things that matter most to students and employers can currently be assessed only qualitatively. For example, the highest forms of student competence, such as creativity and judgment, are hard to quantify. That may change as learning measurement technologies advance. However, in the near term universities need to invest in making qualitative assessments of their students' performance, just as they do in peer reviews of faculty scholarship. Though it is easy to identify the number of majors and courses a university offers, more important to students and society is the quality of those offerings. Likewise, a professor's academic credentials, which can be assessed with relative certainty, matter less than his or her ability to create effective learning opportunities.

An additional measurement priority is ratio analysis. For example, the cost of a traditional university education has grown so great relative to new alternatives that the discerning student and legislator must consider not only how good an educational offering is, but how good it is for what it costs. That kind of price-to-value analysis has long been applied by prospective students as they decide whether to attend a public university or a private one. Today, with the potential to obtain an online degree at a fraction of the cost of one offered even by a public institution, the price/value tradeoff becomes all the more relevant. Students want not just high-paying jobs, but an acceptable ratio of starting salary to student debt. Governments likewise care not just about the number of graduates but the total cost of producing each graduate. In other words, efficiency measures matter.

Efficiency measures matter.

One way to envision the kind of success measures needed in the future is to compare them with those of the past and present. Depending on the strategic choices of an institution, the shift may look like this:

Students
Traditional Success Measures

- Number of students enrolled
- Average SAT/ACT Score
- Number of National Merit Finalists
- Number of Rhodes/Marshall Scholars
- Number of advanced degrees granted
- Ratio of undergraduates to graduate students

Additional Success Measures

- Number of graduates per year*
- Percentage of students graduating within six years*
- Institutional cost per degree granted*
- Student cost per degree earned*
- Average time to graduation*
- Average debt load of graduates*
- Graduate school admission rate*
- Board certification pass rate*
- Job placement rate*

---

*Note: An asterisk in the list denotes the need to track a measure by major and/or department

- Average starting salary of graduates*
- Alumni satisfaction*

Subjects

Traditional Success Measures

- Number of courses offered
- Number of majors offered
- Number of graduate programs
- Number of academic centers/departments/colleges
- Number of tenure track faculty
- Percentage of faculty holding terminal degree in field
- Number and size of libraries

Additional Success Measures

- Quality of general education program
    - Integration of disciplines
    - Practical applications
    - Values orientation
- Quality of majors
    - Modularity
    - Cross-disciplinarity
    - Connection to the workplace
- Degree of student engagement in learning*
- Degree of curricular outcome orientation*
- Student learning outcomes*
- Percentage of courses offered both face to face and online*
- Quality of internship and other extracurricular learning opportunities*

Scholarship

Traditional Success Measures

- Number of publications via prestigious journals and presses
- Number of scholarly citations
- Number of Ph.D. students supervised
- Number of scholarly prize-winning faculty
- Regional and discipline-based accreditation

- Membership in the Association of American Universities (or similar domestic organizations outside the United States)
- Quantity of external research funding
- Number of patents and quantity of revenue derived from university intellectual property

Additional Success Measures

- Degree of student involvement in scholarly activities*
- Degree of inclusion of scholarship in the curriculum*
- Tendency of scholarship to strengthen interdisciplinary and interdepartmental ties*
- Influence of scholarship on practitioners*
- Influence of scholarship on teachers*
- Number and strength of new company spinoffs

Notable in these lists of success measures is a shift from quantity to quality and from simple outputs to efficiency and effectiveness ratios; the words *number* and *quantity* are often replaced with the words *degree* and *quality*. Also pronounced is the shift from what students give the university to what they get from it. In the case of scholarship measures the movement is toward an inclusion of forms of scholarship other than discovery research.

Many of these additional measures are likely to require new data-gathering efforts; an example is the influence of a university's scholarship on practitioners, an outcome of secondary concern to many scholars today. Some other measures will resist efforts at precise quantification; the degree to which students are actively engaged in learning is one example. However, the value of these measures lies as much as anything in the conversations they trigger. In the beginning, they require members of the university community to agree on what measures matter most and what level of success is acceptable. On an ongoing basis, they provoke debates about whether success is being achieved. It is the measurement process more than the measurements themselves that shape the institution and guide its members' activities. The right success measures provoke the right kinds of conversations. Ultimately it is those conversations that keep the university evolving adaptively.

Chapter 24

Change and the Indispensable University

Given the demand for the university's indispensable services, there is good reason to feel now as A. Lawrence Lowell did one hundred years ago: that the college of the future has a great work to do. The need for universities' discoveries, memories, and mentoring is greater than ever, and their capacity to perform those functions is unique.

Yet Lowell would also see in traditional higher education now what he did then, the need for change. It is not just that online technology is producing competitive disruption and threatening universities from without. American universities rose to preeminence by voluntarily embracing innovation. They changed when the great European universities of the day did not. Innovation was not a defensive reaction but a strategy for success. Lowell, like his predecessor Charles Eliot, believed that Harvard's most persistent tradition was the tradition of change.[1]

Today the traditional university's challenge is to change in ways that decrease its price premium and increase its contributions to students and society.

Today the traditional university's challenge is to change in ways that decrease its price premium and increase its contributions to students and society. Its expensive campus and professoriate must be deployed innovatively against the jobs of discovery, memory, and mentoring. It won't be enough to change superficially, such as by cutting budgets or working faculty harder. Tough choices about students, subjects, and scholarship must be made. These choices must be reflected in the university's institutional DNA and in its success measures.

Enhanced Freedom and Usefulness

Administrators and faculty should not fear a loss of freedom in this process. Though the new technological and competitive environment threatens the higher education status quo, it also holds the potential to make universities not only more appreciated by students and society but also freer. Competition is increasing, but success no longer depends on imitation, and more universities can "win." Institutions need not be subject to one-size-fits-all, hierarchical classifications and rankings. Faculty need not be bound by the narrow constraints of the publish-or-perish system.

As university communities make the choices necessary to win their constituents' loyalty, they can succeed regardless of the opinions of third parties. In the future the most successful institutions will be those that lift their students furthest and fastest and that share their scholarship most broadly. Universities will be recognized for the learning they impart rather than for admitting the smartest students. The impact of their scholarship will be judged by not only those who cite it but those who integrate, apply, and teach it. Traditional academic classifications and rankings will mean less in a world of satisfied students and external supporters. Every university that satisfies its chosen constituents can be indispensable.

NOT A LADDER BUT A LANDSCAPE

Successful universities and colleges view themselves as competing not on a higher education ladder but a landscape. Such a landscape can be seen—literally—on the western slopes of Utah's Wasatch Mountains. High on the foothills above the Salt Lake Valley sits the sprawling 1,500-acre campus of the University of Utah. Visible from any point on the valley floor are its research park, medical complex, and distinctive football and basketball stadiums, the former host to the 2002 Winter Olympics and the latter a frequent regional venue for the NCAA Basketball Tournament.

The university serves a large undergraduate population, including many Utah students, and its hospital and research activities make a significant contribution to the local economy. Many students and faculty members come from outside the state, drawn by the opportunity to do world-class research in an attractive recreational and residential environment.

Farther down the hill, Westminster College fills both a literal and a figurative niche. Its campus comprises just 27 acres, but every square foot supports a dedicated student-learning environment. Two-thirds of Westminster students live either on or adjacent to the campus. Still, thanks to the college's innovative teaching and learning strategies, its campus extends in a virtual sense into the surrounding city and, via online learning technology, to the world.

Lower in the valley, Western Governors University (WGU) operates its entirely virtual and truly global campus from a multistory glass building in a commercial office park. The closest that any WGU student is likely to get to this headquarters building is the University of Utah's Kingsbury Hall, a performing arts center where WGU's semi-annual commencement exercises are held for graduates hailing from all fifty states and many overseas military stations.

Farther south, the campus of Utah Valley University (UVU) straddles Interstate 15, an ideal location for an institution with more than 30,000 students and no dormitories. UVU represents the high road for young students seeking a face-to-face learning experience of good quality and low cost. Like the University of Utah, Westminster College, and Western Governors University, UVU's focus on strategically chosen students, subjects, and scholarly endeavors allows it to compete not against those other institutions but against its own definition of success.

Our Cautious Optimism

We, the authors of this book, are cautiously optimistic about the future of traditional institutions of higher education. The caution stems from Clayton's research, which shows how difficult it is for established organizations to respond to disruptive innovation of the kind occurring now. If traditional universities and colleges can change their DNA quickly enough to avoid serious disruption they will have defied a huge amount of experience and data.

Our optimism flows from personal experiences in higher education that can't be quantified but are powerfully felt. Universities—and especially university professors—changed our lives for the better when we were students. We both left business careers to return to academic life. We believe that if anyone can beat the odds against being disrupted it is our remarkably capable and committed colleagues in higher education.

> *What an opportunity it is to have the privilege of being a teacher, the greatest of all vocations, for it keeps us anchored in the world of youth, ideas, and research.*[2]
>
> —C. Roland Christensen

The world desperately needs its university communities. They can and should be its teachers and meaning makers. Of all institutions they are best positioned to integrate new discoveries with the wisdom of the past and to show how those discoveries can improve current practice. They can be conservators and promulgators of great ideas, including moral truths. Above all, they are uniquely positioned to mentor students on their campuses.

In addition to performing the tasks of discovery, memory, and mentoring in the university environment, traditional universities can wield greater influence beyond their walls. They can create curriculum that will help high schools prepare their students for college. They can help technical and community colleges improve their liberal education offerings and increase the percentage of students who continue for a four-year degree. They can export higher education opportunities to less developed countries. They can invite the world to join their learning communities and share in ideas for solving pressing social and economic problems. Their scholarly activities can, as Conant hoped they would, continue to have great relevance.[3]

The technology necessary to accomplish these things has been discovered, much of it in universities. Though it threatens the old order, it vastly expands the university's capacity. Eliot's view of technology, as expressed in his 1869 inaugural address, suggests that he would have jumped at the opportunity to use it:

> The revolutions accomplished in other fields have a lesson for teachers.... In education, there is a great hungry multitude to be fed.... It is for this American generation to invent, or to accept from abroad, better tools than the old; to devise or transplant... prompter and more comprehensive means than the prevailing, and to command more intelligent labor, in order to gather rapidly and surely the best fruit... and have time for other harvests.[4]

Pruning and Focusing

At his inauguration Eliot also prophesied, "It will be generations before the best of American institutions of education get growth enough to bear pruning."[5] Some five generations later, the time for pruning has come. Even the strongest universities will do well to refocus their activities. Most university communities will need to go further, asking fundamental questions about what they can do well and abandoning much of what they have undertaken in a spirit of imitation. Those that continue to imperfectly imitate Harvard's strategy will find their costs increasing and their market share shrinking, whether they like the logic of the marketplace or not.

> *If . . . there are no trade-offs [institutions] will never achieve a sustainable advantage. They will have to run faster and faster just to stay in place. . . . The essence of strategy is choosing what not to do.*[6]
>
> —Michael Porter

On the other hand, those communities that commit to real innovation, to changing their DNA from the inside out, may find extraordinary rewards. One key is to understand and build upon past achievements while being forward-looking. Lawrence Lowell spoke of looking fifty years into the future as he led Harvard.[7] The universities that survive near-term challenges will be those that recognize and honor their strengths while innovating with optimism.

> *The universities that survive near-term challenges will be those that recognize and honor their strengths while innovating with optimism.*

University communities that focus their activities and measure success in terms of absolute performance rather than relative rank can enjoy a bright future. If they suppress the compulsion to have everything and instead play to their unique strengths they can achieve much more than they do now. They can be "the best" in the eyes of their own students, faculty members, and public and private supporters. They can serve more of their chosen students at higher levels of quality. They can become more expert in their chosen subjects and practice more individually customized and more influential scholarship. They can contribute more to the intellectual, economic, and moral vitality of the country and the world. If they embrace innovation and give up the ambition to have it all, they can have much, much more.

Notes

Preface

1. The four institutions are Brigham Young University (BYU), in Provo, Utah, which grants bachelor's degrees and a limited range of master's and doctoral degrees; BYU-Hawaii, a four-year university; LDS Business College, a two-year school in Salt Lake City; and Ricks College.
2. Harry R. Lewis, *Excellence Without a Soul: How a Great University Forgot Education* (New York: Public Affairs, 2006).
3. Byron G. August, Adam Cota, Kartick Jayaram, and Martha C. A. Laboissiére, *Winning by Degrees: The Strategy of Highly Productive Higher-Education Institutions* (n.p.: McKinsey & Company). http://www.mckinsey.com.

Introduction

1. According to data published by the National Center for Higher Education Management Systems in 2009, the graduation rate is higher than 50 percent for bachelor's candidates (http://www.higheredinfo.org) but varies substantially according to the selectivity of the institution, as demonstrated by Frederick H. Hess et al., *Which Colleges Actually Graduate Their Students (and Which Don't),* American Enterprise Institute (June 2009). http://www.aei.org.
2. Henry Rosovsky, *The University: An Owner's Manual* (New York: W.W. Norton, 1990), 29.
3. http://www.arwu.org.
4. Rosovsky, *University*, 29.
5. http://www.aaup.org.

6. A survey of more than 500,000 full-time faculty found that the majority feel that teaching should be the primary criteria for academic promotion. David W. Leslie, "Resolving the Dispute: Teaching Is Academe's Core Value," *Journal of Higher Education* 73, no. 1, (January–February, 2002): 56–57; see also Ernest L. Boyer, *Scholarship Reconsidered: The Priorities of the Professoriate* (Princeton, NJ: Carnegie Foundation for the Advancement of Teaching, 1990), 43–44.
7. See Leslie, "Resolving the Dispute." Leslie concludes, "Given a reasonable level of security and compensation, faculty—on the average—would prefer to teach and be rewarded for teaching than to seek opportunities for pay if it means doing more research and publication." 70.
8. See *Digest of Education Statistics*, 2008, Tables 186 and 234. http://nces.ed.gov.
9. Clayton M. Christensen, *The Innovator's Dilemma* (New York: HarperCollins, 2003).
10. For a summary of the theory of disruptive innovation, see Clayton Christensen, Michael Horn, and Curtis Johnson, *Disrupting Class: How Innovation Will Change the Way the World Learns* (New York: McGraw-Hill, 2008), 45–51. For a fuller treatment, see Christensen, *Innovator's Dilemma*.
11. http://www.mindingthecampus.com.
12. Institutional variety in higher education is great. See, e.g., Burton Clark, *The Academic Life: Small Worlds, Different Worlds* (Princeton, NJ: Carnegie Foundation for the Advancement of Learning, 1987). However, among universities granting at least bachelor's degrees, the diversity of aspirations is less than the diversity of actual condition.
13. http://www.umich.edu/pres.
14. http://vpf-web.harvard.edu/annualfinancial, 4.
15. Byron G. August, Adam Cota, Kartick Jayaram, and Martha C. A. Laboissiére, *Winning by Degrees: The Strategy of Highly Productive Higher-Education Institutions* (n.p.: McKinsey & Company), 14, 15, 49, 51, 55. http://www.mckinsey.com.
16. The relatively high per year cost of the two-year associate's degree is a function of lower completion rates.

Part I

1. Hermann Hesse, *The Glass Bead Game*, trans. Richard and Clara Winston (New York: Henry Holt, 1990), 363. Thanks to Jon Lindford of BYU-Idaho for suggesting the applicability of Hesse's story to today's universities.

Chapter 1: The Educational Innovator's Dilemma

1. U.S. Department of Education, *A Test of Leadership: Charting the Future of U.S. Higher Education* (Washington, DC: U.S. Department of Education, Education Publications Center, 2006), xii.
2. http://www.acenet.edu.
3. Department of Education, *Test of Leadership*, 8–16.
4. Hermann Hesse, *The Glass Bead Game*, trans. Richard and Clara Winston (New York: Henry Holt, 1990).
5. Ibid., 14–16, 38–39, 69, 377.
6. Derek Bok, *Our Underachieving Colleges* (Princeton, NJ: Princeton University Press, 2007), 6.
7. Ibid, 8.
8. Harry R. Lewis, *Excellence Without a Soul: How a Great University Forgot Education* (New York: Public Affairs, 2006), xii.
9. Ibid, 18.
10. Drew Faust, 2008 commencement speech. http://www.president.harvard.edu/speeches; http://www.hmc.harvard.edu/pdf/2009_HMC_Endowment_Report.pdf; http://www.president.harvard.edu/speeches.
11. "Higher Education and the Federal Government," presentation by Dr. Terry Hartle to the Northwest Commission on Colleges and Universities, February 18, 2010 (unpublished).
12. http://www.washingtonpost.com; http://chronicle.com; Jennifer Gonzalez, "For-Profit Colleges, Growing Fast, Say They Are Key to Obama's Degree Goals," *Chronicle of Higher Education*, November 8, 2009. http://chronicle.com.
13. http://www.apollogrp.edu/Annual-Reports, 6.
14. Ibid.; http://www.ucop.edu/acadaff/swap, 2.
15. http://www.southmetroed.org.

16. http://earlyaviators.com.
17. http://www.devry.edu.
18. Byron G. August, Adam Cota, Kartick Jayaram, and Martha C. A. Laboissiére, *Winning by Degrees: The Strategy of Highly Productive Higher-Education Institutions* (n.p.: McKinsey & Company), 14, 15, 49, 51, 55. http://www.mckinsey.com. Six Sigma is an operations management certification program originally developed by Motorola.
19. The terms *disruptive innovation* and *creative destruction* were introduced into popular parlance by Clayton Christensen and Joseph Schumpeter, respectively. See *Innovator's Dilemma* and Joseph Schumpeter, *Capitalism, Socialism and Democracy* (New York: Harper & Row, 1950).
20. See, e.g., Christopher J. Lucas, *American Higher Education* (New York: St. Martin's, 1994), 194–195, 227–228, 233; Arthur M. Cohen, *The Shaping of American Higher Education: Emergence and the Growth of the Contemporary System* (San Francisco: Wiley, 2009), 107–108; Frederick Rudolph, *Curriculum: A History of the American Undergraduate Course of Study Since 1636* (San Francisco: Wiley, 1977), 225–226.
21. http://www.carnegiefoundation.org.
22. Ibid.
23. http://nces.ed.gov/FastFacts/; U.S. Department of Education, National Center for Education Statistics, *The Condition of Education 2008* (NCES 2008–031), Table 20-1. http://nces.ed.gov.
24. http://www.aaup.org/.
25. Toni Mack, "Danger: Stealth Attack," *Forbes,* January 1999. http://www.forbes.com.
26. In addition to regulatory pressures and increased competition from for-profit institutions, public universities also face the prospect of dramatic changes in the way states fund them. For example, proposals for higher education vouchers have been made. See Richard Vedder, *Going Broke by Degree: Why College Costs Too Much* (Washington, DC: AEI Press, 2004), and James C. Garland, *Saving Alma Mater: A Rescue Plan for America's Public Universities* (Chicago: University of Chicago Press, 2009). Voluntary action is preferable to these various forms of external pressure.
27. There is great variation among types of higher education institutions. Technical colleges, community colleges, and liberal arts colleges, for example, differ fundamentally from one another and from universities.

Also, many of the most elite universities and colleges explicitly try to differentiate themselves from Harvard. For example, the elite liberal arts college develop undergraduate-focused curriculum and can make valid claims to offering an undergraduate experience in some respects superior to that of Harvard College. Other schools offer unique work and travel-study experiences. The relative commonality of the elite institutions, though, can be seen in the similarity of the students they admit and the prices they charge.

28. Louis Menand refers to the reproduction function of the academic disciplines in *The Marketplace of Ideas: Reform and Resistance in the American University* (New York: W.W. Norton, 2010), 105. He writes, "The most important function of the system is not the production of knowledge. It is the reproduction of the system."
29. CT, MRI, and PET stand for computerized axial tomography, magnetic resonance imaging, and positron emission tomography, respectively.
30. Harvard president Charles Eliot paid this tribute to Johns Hopkins University: "I want to testify that the Graduate School of Harvard University, started feebly in 1870 and 1871, did not thrive, until the example of Johns Hopkins forced our faculty to put their strength into the development of instruction for our graduates." Christopher J. Lucas, *American Higher Education* (New York: St. Martin's, 1994), 179. Historian Frederick Rudolph similarly noted Harvard's debt to other institutions: "There on the banks of the Charles River in Cambridge [Harvard] shaped itself into a university, unlike Cornell, unlike Johns Hopkins, but owing much to both." Rudolph, *Curriculum*, 155. The University of Chicago, founded in 1892, provided models for departmentalizing, dividing faculty into ranks, and rewarding scholarship over teaching. See Lucas, *American Higher Education,* 180, 185–186.
31. http://asunews.asu.edu; http://www.osu.edu.
32. David Von Drehle, "The Big Man on Campus," *Time,* November 11, 2009. http://www.time.com.
33. http://www.thecrimson.com.
34. 7 United States Code, Section 304.
35. http://president.osu.edu.
36. August et al., *Winning by Degrees*, 16.
37. http://www.snhu.edu.
38. August et al., *Winning by Degrees*, 13.

Part II: The Great University

1. Hermann Hesse, *The Glass Bead Game*, trans. Richard and Clara Winston (New York: Henry Holt, 1990), 15.

Chapter 2: Puritan College

1. Andrew Schlesinger, *Veritas: Harvard College and the American Experience* (Chicago: Ivan R. Dee, 2005), 3–4.
2. The Charter of the President and Fellows of Harvard College under the Seal of the Colony of Massachusetts Bay, May 31, 1650, in Samuel Eliot Morison, *The Development of Harvard University Since the Inauguration of President Eliot* (Cambridge, MA: Harvard University Press, 1930), xxv, cited in Harry R. Lewis, *Excellence Without a Soul: How a Great University Forgot Education* (New York: Public Affairs, 2006), 25.
3. http://www.president.harvard.edu; Schlesinger, *Veritas,* 100.
4. Lewis, *Excellence,* 26.
5. Samuel Eliot Morison, *Three Centuries of Harvard, 1636–1936* (Cambridge, MA: Belknap Press of Harvard University, 2001), 25.
6. Schlesinger, *Veritas,* 7.
7. Lewis, *Excellence,* 26–27.
8. Morisson, *Three Centuries,* 35.
9. Lewis, *Excellence,* 26–27
10. Ibid., 74–75.
11. Ibid, 27–28.
12. Frederick Rudolph, *Curriculum: A History of the American Undergraduate Course of Study Since 1636* (San Francisco: Wiley, 1977), 42.
13. *Corporation Records,* vol. 1, p. 246; UAI.5.30.2, Harvard University Archives, cited in Lewis, *Excellence*, 28.
14. Morison, *Three Centuries,* 78.
15. Schlesinger, *Veritas,* 36.
16. Lewis, *Excellence,* 28.
17. Rudolph, *Curriculum,* 44.
18. Morison, *Three Centuries,* 100, 161–162.
19. Ibid., 190–191.
20. Lewis, *Excellence*, 29.
21. Ralph Waldo Emerson, in *The Works of Ralph Waldo Emerson, vol. 10: Letters and Biographical Sketches* (Boston: Houghton, Mifflin, 1883), 312, cited in Lewis, *Excellence,* 30.

22. John Y. Simon, Harold Holzer, and William D. Pederson, eds., *The Lincoln Forum: Abraham Lincoln, Gettysburg, and the Civil War* (New York: Da Capo, 1999), 41.
23. Letter from Charles Sumner to Joseph Story, September 24, 1839, quoted by David Herbert Donald, *Charles Sumner* (New York: Da Capo, 1996), part I, 14 (emphasis in original), cited by Lewis, *Excellence,* 29.
24. Andrew P. Peabody, *Harvard Reminiscences* (Boston: Ticknor., 1888), 202, cited in Lewis, *Excellence,* 29.
25. http://oasis.lib.harvard.edu/; http://www.thecrimson.com.
26. Lewis, *Excellence,* 30.
27. An analogous dynamic has developed in general hospitals, as described in Chapter Three of Clayton Christensen's *The Innovator's Dilemma* (New York: HarperCollins, 2003). Note that we use the term *cross-disciplinary* distinctly from *interdisciplinary*. The former implies study and scholarship that transcends disciplinary boundaries. For example, a cross-disciplinary general education course on the human mind might draw unequally from many disciplines, such as molecular biology, anatomy, psychology, and ethics, without an explicit exploration of the different views and methods of those disciplines. A more interdisciplinary course, by contrast, would compare and contrast the approaches of two or more disciplines in their treatment of a common subject. Louis Menand offers an enlightening definition and critique of interdisciplinarity in *The Marketplace of Ideas: Reform and Resistance in the American University* (New York: W.W. Norton, 2010), 119–121. Menand is himself a cross-disciplinary scholar, an English professor who won a Pulitzer Prize for History.
28. Lewis, *Excellence,* 127.
29. In a report titled *On the Clock: Rethinking the Way Schools Use Time*, Elena Silva notes that the public school calendar has likewise evolved to address concerns other than agricultural necessity. She writes, "In large cities, long school calendars were not uncommon during the 19th century. In 1840, the school systems in Buffalo, Detroit, and Philadelphia were open between 251 and 260 days of the year. New York City schools were open nearly year round during that period, with only a three-week break in August. This break was gradually extended, mostly as a result of an emerging elite class of families who sought to escape the oppressive

summer heat of the city and who advocated that children needed to 'rest their minds'." 2. http://www.educationsector.org.

30. Lewis, *Excellence,* 31.
31. Rudolph, *Curriculum,* 77–78.
32. Lewis, *Excellence,* 32; Rudolph, *Curriculum,* 184–186.
33. Rudolph, *Curriculum,* 62.
34. See, e.g., Hugh Hawkins, *Between Harvard and America: The Educational Leadership of Charles W. Eliot* (New York: Oxford University Press, 1972), 218–219.
35. Drew Faust, 2008 commencement speech. http://www.president.harvard.edu/speeches.
36. Morison, *Three Centuries,* 306.
37. Rudolph, *Curriculum,* 87.
38. Morison, *Three Centuries,* 35, 324.

Chapter 3: Charles Eliot, Father of American Higher Education

1. Keith Sheppard, "From Justus Von Liebig to Charles W. Eliot: The Establishment of Laboratory Work in U.S. Schools and Colleges," *Journal of Chemical Education* 83, no. 4 (April 2006): 567.
2. Hugh Hawkins, *Between Harvard and America: The Educational Leadership of Charles W. Eliot* (New York: Oxford University Press, 1972), 15–16.
3. Quoted in Andrew Schlesinger, *Veritas*: *Harvard College and the American Experience* (Chicago: Ivan R. Dee, 2005), 108.
4. Hawkins, *Between Harvard and America,* 18.
5. Ibid, 26.
6. Ibid, 32.
7. Ibid, 31.
8. http://www.news.cornell.edu.
9. Charles W. Eliot, "The New Education," *Atlantic Monthly*, February–March 1869, reprinted in Richard Hofstadter and Wilson Smith, *A Documentary History of Higher Education* (Chicago: University of Chicago Press, 1961), 636–637.
10. Samuel Eliot Morison, *Three Centuries of Harvard, 1636–1936* (Cambridge, MA: Belknap Press of Harvard University, 2001), 327–328.
11. http://president.harvard.edu.

12. Schlesinger, *Veritas,* 123.
13. Charles William Eliot, Inaugural Address, in Samuel Eliot Morison, *Development of Harvard University, 1869–1929* (Cambridge, MA: Harvard University Press, 1930), lix (emphasis added).
14. See Hawkins, *Between Harvard and America,* 90–92.
15. See Frederick Rudolph, *Curriculum: A History of the American Undergraduate Course of Study Since 1636* (San Francisco: Wiley, 1977), 137.
16. Harry R. Lewis, *Excellence Without a Soul: How a Great University Forgot Education* (New York: Public Affairs, 2006), 34.
17. Hawkins, *Between Harvard and America,* 93.
18. See Rudolph, *Curriculum,* 137.
19. Hawkins, *Between Harvard and America,* 99.
20. Ibid., 99–101.
21. Ibid., 92.
22. Rudolph, *Curriculum,* 135; Harvard had, by this time, followed the lead of pioneers such as Brown University in allowing students to choose some courses.
23. See Hawkins, *Between Harvard and America,* 94.
24. There were still two subject matter requirements to satisfy, one in English and another in foreign language, but no one course was required of all students. See Derek Bok, *Our Underachieving Colleges* (Princeton, NJ: Princeton University Press, 2007), 15.
25. Hawkins, *Between Harvard and America,* 94.
26. Rudolph, *Curriculum,* 196
27. Eliot, "The New Education," reprinted in Hofstadter and Smith, *Documentary History of Higher Education* and cited in http://opac.yale.edu/president/message. In addition to looking to European universities, Eliot also admired Yale's postgraduate program.
28. Until 1890, the Graduate School of Arts and Sciences was called the Graduate Department.
29. Hawkins, *Between Harvard and America,* 276.
30. Ibid., 58–61.
31. Ibid., 204–205; Frederick Rudolph, *The American College and University: A History* (Athens: University of Georgia Press, 1961), 291.
32. See Hawkins, *Between Harvard and America,* 117–118, 272–273.
33. Lewis, *Excellence,* 35.

34. Ibid., 37.
35. Ibid., 39.
36. Hawkins, *Between Harvard and America,* 65, 67, 71–72. The 1940 tenure statement of the American Association of University Professors (AAUP) specifies that a tenured professor can be dismissed only for "adequate cause, except in the case of retirement for age, or under extraordinary circumstance because of financial exigencies." http://www.aaup.org.
37. Hawkins, *Between Harvard and America,* 66–67.
38. Ibid., 67–68.
39. Ibid., 74.
40. Ibid., 77.
41. Ibid., 111. The story of this truant son's discovery by his irate father is humorous. The boy had carefully written a series of post-dated letters and left instructions with a friend to post them at appropriate intervals. The friend put them all in the mail simultaneously. When the father came to campus looking for his son, no university officer was aware of his absence. Class attendance checking became mandatory as a result. Samuel Eliot Morison, *Three Centuries of Harvard, 1636–1936* (Cambridge, MA: Belknap Press of Harvard University, 2001), 368–369.
42. Hawkins, *Between Harvard and America,* 110.
43. Ibid., 106–107.
44. Morison, *Three Centuries,* 419.
45. Hawkins, *Between Harvard and America,* 113.
46. Morison, *Three Centuries,* 369.
47. Hawkins, *Between Harvard and America,* 109.
48. Report to the Overseers, 1883–1884, quoted in Andrew Schlesinger, *Veritas: Harvard College and the American Experience* (Chicago: Ivan R. Dee, 2005), 134.
49. Lewis, *Excellence,* 232, 237.
50. http://pds.lib.harvard.edu.
51. Hawkins, *Between Harvard and America,* 225–226.
52. Ibid., 227.
53. Ibid., 229.
54. Ibid., 240.
55. Ibid, 92, 102.
56. Ibid., 237–238, 246, 248.

57. Ibid., 243.
58. The challenges of American secondary education are beyond the scope of this book. They are addressed in Clayton Christensen, Michael Horn, and Curtis Johnson, *Disrupting Class: How Innovation Will Change the Way the World Learns* (New York: McGraw-Hill, 2008). Also, the 2006 report of the New Commission on the Skills of the American Workforce, *Tough Choices or Tough Times*, makes bold recommendations, including the preparation of high school students to begin college at age sixteen, as they did during Harvard's first two centuries. The report also recommends a system by which high schools could remain comprehensive but also facilitate focused preparation for career training and university study. http://www.skillscommission.org/executive.htm.
59. U.S. Department of Education, National Center for Education Statistics, *The Condition of Education 2008* (NCES 2008–031), Table 20-1.http://nces.ed.gov.
60. Christensen et al., *Disrupting Class*, 11.
61. Ibid., 53.
62. Ibid., 54.
63. Ibid., 55–56.
64. http://nces.ed.gov; William M. Chace, *One Hundred Semesters* (Princeton, NJ: Princeton University Press, 2006), 14, 54.
65. http://www.media.utah.edu/.
66. http://www.westminstercollege.edu/
67. See Robert B. Barr and John Tagg, "From Teaching to Learning—A New Paradigm for Undergraduate Education," *Change*, November–December 1995, 13–25.
68. http://www.westminstercollege.edu.
69. http://bx.businessweek.com.
70. Hawkins, *Between Harvard and America*, 177.

Chapter 4: Pioneer Academy

1. http://query.nytimes.com.
2. Doctrine and Covenants (Salt Lake City: Church of Jesus Christ of Latter-day Saints, 1995), 170. (D&C88:79.
3. David Lester Crowder, *The Spirit of Ricks: A History of Ricks College* (Rexburg, ID: Ricks College, 1997), 2.

4. Ibid., 3.
5. Ibid., 3–4.
6. Many of religion courses offered by Ricks Academy and now by BYU-Idaho are analogous to Bible study classes, though they also include studies of other faiths and current social issues.
7. http://www.lib.byui.edu.
8. Crowder, *Spirit of Ricks,* 4–5.
9. Ibid., 7–8, 9–10, 14, 19, 20.
10. Ibid., 23–25, 39–40, 44.
11. Ibid., 25–26, 40, 44.
12. Ibid., 26.
13. Ibid., 39, 43.
14. Harvard did not adopt the Carnegie Unit, or credit hour, the generally accepted measure of educational attainment, notwithstanding its having been championed by Eliot as the standard for secondary schools. See Jessica M. Shedd, *The History of the Student Credit Hour,* New Directions for Higher Education, no. 122 (Summer 2003). http://virtual.parkland.edu. The credit hour is based on time spent per week in the classroom; for example, a three-credit course typically meets three times per week for one hour (really fifty minutes plus a ten-minute break). Generally, 120 credit hours are required to obtain a bachelor's degree.
15. Crowder, *Spirit of Ricks,* 36, 40, 41.
16. Ibid., 24, 28, 34, 37, 44.
17. Ibid., 35–36.
18. Ibid., 45.

Chapter 5: Revitalizing Harvard College

1. See Henry Aaron Yeomans, *Lawrence Lowell: 1856–1943* (Cambridge, MA: Harvard University Press, 1948), 6–12.
2. Ibid., 39–40.
3. Ibid., 44–46.
4. Andrew Schlesinger, *Veritas: Harvard College and the American Experience* (Chicago: Ivan R. Dee, 2005), 151.
5. http://www.gocrimson.com.
6. Nathan Marsh Pusey, *Lawrence Lowell and His Revolution* (Cambridge, MA: Harvard University Press, 1980), 8–9.

7. Hugh Hawkins, *Between Harvard and America: The Educational Leadership of Charles W. Eliot* (New York: Oxford University Press, 1972), 274.
8. Frederick Rudolph, *Curriculum: A History of the American Undergraduate Course of Study Since 1636* (San Francisco: Wiley, 1977), 12.
9. Samuel Eliot Morison, *Three Centuries of Harvard, 1636–1936* (Cambridge, MA: Belknap Press of Harvard University, 2001), 441.
10. Hawkins, *Between Harvard and America*, 277. One study found that "the average student each week spent twelve hours in class and thirteen hours at his desk." Rudolph, *Curriculum,* 232.
11. Derek Bok, *Our Underachieving Colleges* (Princeton, NJ: Princeton University Press, 2007), 16.
12. Harry R. Lewis, *Excellence Without a Soul: How a Great University Forgot Education* (New York: Public Affairs, 2006), 39; Rudolph, *Curriculum,* 233.
13. Rudolph, *Curriculum,* 227.
14. *Harvard Alumni Bulletin* XVII, no. 1 (September 30, 1914): 393.
15. Morton Keller, *Making Harvard Modern* (New York: Oxford University Press, 2001), 14.
16. A Lawrence Lowell, Inaugural Address, October 6, 1909, in A. Lawrence Lowell, *At War with Academic Traditions in America* (New York: Greenwood, 1970). http://hul.harvard.edu.
17. In 1907, Harvard's governing board had demanded that Eliot reign in spending (Lewis, *Excellence,* 39). In 1909, Lowell's first year as president, the university ran a budget deficit. http://pds.lib.harvard.edu.
18. Hawkins, *Between Harvard and America*, 279.
19. Ibid., 92.
20. http://www.thecrimson.com/.
21. Hawkins, *Between Harvard and America*, 279–280.
22. Harvard Annual Report, 1908–1909, in Lowell, *At War,* 245.
23. http://www.thecrimson.com/.
24. http://www.boston.com/news/education/higher.
25. Morison, *Three Centuries,* 476–477.
26. Pusey, *Lawrence Lowell,* 33–34.
27. Ibid., 34
28. Lowell, Inaugural Address, in Lowell, *At War,* 39–40.

29. Lowell was intrigued by the challenge of striking such Aristotelian balances among contradictory or "conjugate" principles, many of which he explored in *Conflicts of Principle* (Cambridge, MA: Harvard University Press, 1932). He treated the tensions between "general" and "professional" education, and between "cultural" and "vocational" aims in pages 115–121.
30. See Lewis, *Excellence,* 48; Lowell, Inaugural Address, in Lowell, *At War*. http://hul.harvard.edu/huarc/lowell_inaug.html through n. xxi.
31. Lewis, 48–49.
32. Ibid., 48.
33. http://hul.harvard.edu/huarc/lowell_inaug.html through n. xxi.
34. Ibid.; also, Lewis, *Excellence,* 50.
35. Lewis, *Excellence,* 49–50.
36. http://hul.harvard.edu/ through xxi.
37. See Clayton M. Christensen, Jerome H. Grossman, and Jason Hwang, *The Innovator's Prescription: A Disruptive Solution for Health Care* (New York: McGraw-Hill, 2008), 20–22.
38. Ibid., 22–23.
39. Pusey, *Lawrence Lowell,* 23, 29.
40. Lewis, *Excellence,* 50.
41. A. Lawrence Lowell, "Degrees, Prizes, and Honors," *Harvard Teachers Record* (June 1934), in Lowell, *At War*, 232.
42. A. Lawrence Lowell, Harvard Annual Report, 1908–1909, in Lowell, *At War*, 238.
43. Morison, *Three Centuries,* 445.
44. Lewis, *Excellence,* 113–114.
45. Lowell, "Degrees, Prizes, and Honors," Lowell, *At War,* 237.
46. Morison, *Three Centuries,* 449.
47. Lewis, *Excellence,* 107.
48. Ibid., 108.
49. Ibid., 132–138.
50. Morison, *Three Centuries,* 451.
51. Lowell, Harvard Annual Report, 1916–1917, in *At War*, 268.
52. Ibid., 270.
53. Ibid., 271.
54. http://www.aaup.org.

Chapter 6: Struggling College

1. A. B. Christensen is not a close relative of Clayton Christensen.
2. http://www.lib.byui.edu.
3. David Lester Crowder, *The Spirit of Ricks: A History of Ricks College* (Rexburg, ID: Ricks College, 1997), 59.
4. Ibid., 53–54, 56, 63, 70.
5. Ibid., 54, 62.
6. George S. Romney was an uncle of George W. Romney, the father of former Massachusetts governor Mitt Romney.
7. http://www.lib.byui.edu.
8. Crowder, *Spirit of Ricks,* 64–65, 71–73, 98–99.
9. Ibid., 64, 78, 99.
10. See http://www.byui.edu.
11. http://www.wm.edu.
12. http://www.virginia.edu.
13. http://www.students.haverford.edu.
14. http://www.haverford.edu/studentlife/.
15. Crowder, *Spirit of Ricks*, 76, 79, 81, 86.
16. Ibid., 93, 125.
17. http://www.lib.byui.edu.
18. Crowder, *Spirit of Ricks,* 104.
19. Ibid., 89, 101–103, 104–105, 109–110.
20. Ibid., 112.
21. Ibid., 115–116.
22. Ibid., 115, 118.
23. Ibid., 115, 119.
24. Ibid., 115–116, 120, 123, 126–127, 129–130.
25. Ibid., 118, 122–124.
26. Ibid., 133–134.
27. Ibid., 136, 140.
28. Ibid., 142–146.
29. Ibid., 154.
30. J. Reuben Clark Jr., *The Charted Course of the Church in Education* (repr. Intellectual Reserve, 1994), 7, 10.
31. Henry J. Eyring, *Mormon Scientist: The Life and Faith of Henry Eyring* (Salt Lake City: Deseret, 2009), 49–50, 51; the phrase "The way, the truth, the life" comes from John 14:16.

32. http://www.bunker.org.
33. Crowder, *Spirit of Ricks,* 144, 148, 159.

Chapter 7: The Drive for Excellence

1. http://www.thecrimson.com.
2. James B. Conant, *My Several Lives: Memoirs of a Social Inventor* (New York: Harper & Row, 1970), 3, 6.
3. *Biographical Memoirs of Fellows of the Royal Society* 25 (November 1979), 209.
4. Morton Keller, *Making Harvard Modern* (New York: Oxford University Press, 2001), 22.
5. Conant, *My Several Lives*, 90.
6. Keller, *Making Harvard Modern*, 23.
7. Samuel Eliot Morison, *Three Centuries of Harvard, 1636–1936* (Cambridge, MA: Belknap Press of Harvard University, 2001), 486.
8. Ibid., 480.
9. Ibid., 460.
10. Andrew Schlesinger, *Veritas: Harvard College and the American Experience* (Chicago: Ivan R. Dee, 2005), 174.
11. Morison, *Three Centuries,* 460.
12. Keller, *Making Harvard Modern*, 13–14.
13. Harry R. Lewis, *Excellence Without a Soul: How a Great University Forgot Education* (New York: Public Affairs, 2006), 52.
14. Morison, *Three Centuries,* 461.
15. Ibid., 487.
16. Keller, *Making Harvard Modern*, 68.
17. Ibid., 69–70.
18. In 1940, the American Association of University Professors established a seven-year limit. Arthur M. Cohen, *The Shaping of American Higher Education: Emergence and Growth of the Contemporary System* (San Francisco: Jossey-Bass, 1998), 131.
19. Keller, *Making Harvard Modern*, 65–66.
20. Ibid., 70.
21. Ibid., 42, 45.
22. Henry Rosovsky, *The University: An Owner's Manual* (New York: W.W. Norton, 1990), 32.

23. *Biographical Memoirs of Fellows of the Royal Society*, 216.
24. Keller, *Making Harvard Modern*, 100–101.
25. Ibid., 46.
26. Ibid.
27. Ibid., 34, 40.
28. Morison, *Three Centuries,* 488; in Conant's day, a "scholarship" was a grant of financial aid, not a reward for superior academic or athletic performance.
29. http://pds.lib.harvard.edu.
30. Conant, *My Several Lives*, 128.
31. http://news.harvard.edu/gazette.
32. See Nicholas Lemann, *The Big Test: The Secret History of American Meritocracy* (New York: Farrar, Strauss & Giroux, 1999), 28–29 and Conant, *My Several Lives*, 419–420.
33. Conant, *My Several Lives*, 131, 134, 417–418.
34. Lemann, *The Big Test*, 33–34.
35. Ibid., 32, 86, 113.
36. http://www.nytimes.com.
37. http://www.admissions.college.harvard.edu.
38. http://www.time.com.
39. http://www.pbs.org.
40. Keller, *Making Harvard Modern*, 154.
41. Ibid.
42. Ibid., 34.
43. Morrision, *Three Centuries,* 459.
44. http://pubs.acs.org.
45. Ibid.
46. Keller, *Making Harvard Modern*, 162.
47. Ibid., 163–164.
48. Ibid., 99.
49. Lewis, *Excellence,* 51.
50. Harvard University, *General Education in a Free Society* (Cambridge, MA: Harvard University Press, 1945), 51, in Lewis, *Excellence,* 53.
51. Lewis, *Excellence,* 53.
52. Keller, *Making Harvard Modern*, 44.
53. Ibid., 54.

54. Nathan Marsh Pusey, *Lawrence Lowell and His Revolution* (Cambridge, MA: Harvard University Press, 1980), 29.
55. Harvard, *General Education*, 196; Final Report, 8. http://www.fas .harvard.edu.
56. Harvard, *General Education*, 217, in Lewis, *Excellence*, 54.
57. Keller, *Making Harvard Modern*, 44.
58. See Lewis, *Excellence*, 56.
59. Keller, *Making Harvard Modern*, 45; Lewis, 54.
60. Louis Menand, *The Marketplace of Ideas: Reform and Resistance in the American University* (New York: W.W. Norton, 2010), 43.
61. "Gentlemen and Gen Ed," *Harvard Crimson*, February 24, 1971. http://www.thecrimson.com, in Lewis, *Excellence*, 54.
62. Harvard, *General Education*, xiii.
63. Ibid., 7.
64. Ibid., 11–13.
65. Ibid., 12–13.
66. Ibid., 22.
67. Ibid., 12–13, 28, 101.
68. Ibid., 107–109, 124, 126–132.
69. Ibid., 138–143, 159–160, 162–166, 168.
70. Ibid., 155.
71. See Cohen, *Shaping of American Higher Education*, 138.
72. http://www.gocrimson.com/sports.
73. http://www.varsityclub.harvard.edu.
74. Lewis, *Excellence*, 237.
75. Keller, *Making Harvard Modern*, 41.
76. Ibid.
77. http://www.varsityclub.harvard.edu; Schlesinger, *Veritas*, 147.
78. Lewis, *Excellence*, 241.
79. 1932–1933 Report of the President of Harvard, 16. http://pds.lib.hardvard.edu.
80. Keller, *Making Harvard Modern*, 476.
81. Morison, *Three Centuries*, 415.
82. Keller, *Making Harvard Modern*, 163.
83. See Cohen, *Shaping of American Higher Education*, 135–136.
84. http://www.time.com.

85. Rosovsky, *University*, 21.
86. Ibid.
87. National Center for Education Statistics, Enrollment in Postsecondary Institutions, Fall 2004; Graduation Rates, 1998 & 2001 Cohorts; and Financial Statistics, Fiscal Year 2004, Table 5. http://nces.ed.gov.
88. Private institutions devote nearly twice as much effort to advising as their public counterparts. See Wesley R. Habley, *The Status of Academic Advising: Findings From the ACT Sixth National Survey* (Manhattan, KS: National Academic Advising Association, 2004).

Chapter 8: Four-Year Aspirations in Rexburg

1. David Lester Crowder, *The Spirit of Ricks: A History of Ricks College* (Rexburg, ID: Ricks College, 1997), 174–175, 178–179.
2. Though BYU-Idaho and its sister institutions welcome students who are not members of the Church of Jesus Christ of Latter-day Saints, those student pay twice the tuition rate. The rationale for this price differential is that more than half of BYU-Idaho's operating and capital costs are paid for by the tithes of the church; the pricing strategy is analogous to that of state institutions that set a higher tuition rate for nonresidents.
3. Crowder, *Spirit of Ricks*, 181–182, 184.
4. Ibid., 188, 192–194, 196–199.
5. Ibid., 200.
6. Ibid., 189.
7. Ibid., 201, 205–206.
8. James B. Conant, *Shaping Educational Policy* (New York: McGraw-Hill, 1964), 15, quoted in John Aubrey Douglass, *The California Idea and American Higher Education* (Stanford, CA: Stanford University Press, 2000), 265.
9. Conant, *Shaping Educational Policy*, 50–52, 55–56. The tendency toward imitation was noted at roughly the same time by Harvard sociologist David Riesman in *Constraint and Variety in American Education* (New York: Doubleday Anchor, 1958). Riesman and his colleague Christopher Jencks described the development and explored the implications of the traditional university model in their 1968 book, *The Academic Revolution* (New Brunswick, NJ: Transaction, 2001).
10. Crowder, *Spirit of Ricks*, 213–214.

11. Ibid, 220.
12. Ibid., 217.
13. Douglass, *California Ideal,* 314–315.
14. Crowder, *Spirit of Ricks*, 221–222.
15. Ibid., 231–237, 258–259, 262–263.
16. Ibid., 261–262, 265, 267–273, 286.
17. Ibid., 274–275.

Chapter 9: Harvard's Growing Power and Profile

1. Morton Keller, *Making Harvard Modern* (New York: Oxford University Press, 2001), 175.
2. Ibid.
3. Ibid., 178.
4. Ibid., 178–180.
5. Ibid., 180.
6. Ibid., 181.
7. Ibid., 182.
8. Tuition went from $400 to $800 under Conant and from $800 to $2,600 under Pusey. Samuel Eliot Morison, *Three Centuries of Harvard, 1636–1936* (Cambridge, MA: Belknap Press of Harvard University, 2001), 460; http://www.thecrimson.com.
9. Keller, *Making Harvard Modern,* 293–296.
10. Ibid., 193–198, 211–214.
11. Ibid., 210.
12. Ibid., 184, 297.
13. Ibid., 185
14. Ibid., 191.
15. Ibid., 151–152, 192–193. The power of departments over faculty appointments, curriculum, and scholarship had been growing since Eliot's time. See Arthur M. Cohen, *The Shaping of American Higher Education: Emergence and Growth of the Contemporary System* (San Francisco: Jossey-Bass, 1998), 135–136, and Christopher Jencks and David Riesman, *The Academic Revolution* (New Brunswick, NJ: Transaction, 2001), 14–16.
16. Keller, *Making Harvard Modern,* 274.
17. Carnegie Foundation, *Flight from Teaching* (New York: Carnegie Foundation, 1964).

18. Ibid., 230.
19. Oliver Fulton and Martin Trow, "Research Activity in American Higher Education," *Sociology of Education* 47, no. 1 (Winter 1974), 55.
20. Ibid., 54.
21. Ibid., 239.
22. Hermann Hesse, *Magister Ludi,* trans. Mervyn Savill (New York: Henry Holt & Company, 1949), 326.
23. Keller, *Making Harvard Modern,* 304.
24. Ibid., 290–291, 293, 297, 304.
25. Ibid., 290, 291, 301, 305.
26. Ibid., 295–297, 325; Harry R. Lewis, *Excellence Without a Soul: How a Great University Forgot Education* (New York: Public Affairs, 2006), 110.
27. Keller, *Making Harvard Modern,* 278, 324.
28. Ibid., 300.
29. Ibid., 313–314.
30. Ibid., 314; http://www.thecrimson.com.
31. Keller, *Making Harvard Modern,* 316–317, 320–322.

Chapter 10: Staying Rooted

1. Paul Harvey, quoted in David Lester Crowder, *The Spirit of Ricks: A History of Ricks College* (Rexburg, ID: Ricks College, 1997).
2. Crowder, *Spirit of Ricks,* 273, 290.
3. Ibid., 295, 301.
4. Ibid., 298, 301–302, 308.
5. *Line upon Line: The Autobiography of Alan Clark* (Self-published), 130.
6. http://www.nytimes.com.
7. Spencer E. Ante, *Creative Capital: Georges Doriot and the Birth of Venture Capital* (Boston: Harvard Business Press, 2008), 47.
8. C. Roland Christensen is not related to Clayton Christensen.
9. See C. Roland Christensen, "Every Student Teaches and Every Teacher Learns: The Reciprocal Gift of Discussion Teaching," in *Education for Judgment: The Artistry of Discussion Leadership,* ed. C. Roland Christensen, David A. Garvin, and Ann Sweet (Boston: Harvard Business School Press, 1991), 99–119.
10. Christensen, "Every Student Teaches," 100.
11. http://www.news.harvard.edu.
12. Christensen, "Every Student Teaches," 99, 109, 116, 117.

13. Eyring journal, 1973, p. 74.
14. Crowder, *Spirit of Ricks*, 311, 318.
15. Ibid., 329–330.
16. http://matdl.org.
17. Crowder, *Spirit of Ricks*, 324–323.
18. http://www.byui.edu.
19. Crowder, *Spirit of Ricks*, 361, 378, 382.
20. Ibid., 399–400; Robert Worrell, *History of Ricks College and Brigham Young University-Idaho: The Bednar Years* (1997–2004) (unpublished manuscript), 9.
21. Crowder, *Spirit of Ricks*, 401.
22. Ibid., 401; Worrell, *History of Ricks College,* 3, 6.
23. Crowder, *Spirit of Ricks*, 401, Worrell, *History of Ricks College,* 10.

Part III: Ripe for Disruption

1. Hermann Hesse, *The Glass Bead Game*, trans. Richard and Clara Winston (New York: Henry Holt, 1990), 275–276.

Chapter 11: The Weight of the DNA

1. Morton Keller, *Making Harvard Modern* (New York: Oxford University Press, 2001), 341–343.
2. Henry Rosovsky, *The University: An Owner's Manual* (New York: W.W. Norton, 1990), 22; Keller, *Making Harvard Modern,* 325–326, 344–335; Andrew Schlesinger, *Veritas: Harvard College and the American Experience* (Chicago: Ivan R. Dee, 2005), 243.
3. Keller, *Making Harvard Modern,* 344, 362, 366.
4. Ibid., 384, 469–470; Rosovsky, *University*, 113–130.
5. Rosovsky, *University,* 126; Harry R. Lewis, *Excellence Without a Soul: How a Great University Forgot Education* (New York: Public Affairs, 2006), 57; Keller, *Making Harvard Modern,* 346.
6. Lewis, *Excellence,* 58; Keller, *Making Harvard Modern,* 346, 470–471.
7. Keller, *Making Harvard Modern,* 344–345, 349–350, 467.
8. http://www.president.harvard.edu.
9. Keller, *Making Harvard Modern,* 346, 356.
10. Ibid., 346.
11. Ibid., 388–390, 419, 432, 434.
12. Ibid., 386.

13. Ibid., 362, 365; Annual Report of the President, 1988–1989, 36–37. http://pds.lib.harvard.edu.
14. Alan David Bloom, *The Closing of the American Mind: How Higher Education Has Failed Democracy and Impoverished the Souls of Today's Students* (New York: Simon & Schuster, 1987).
15. Annual Report of the President, 1988–1989, 3.
16. Ibid., 27–29; Keller, *Making Harvard Modern,* 397, 410.
17. See Keller, *Making Harvard Modern,* 390.
18. Annual Report of the President, 1989–1990, 14–17.
19. Ibid., 19, 30–31.
20. Keller, *Making Harvard Modern,* 379–380.
21. Annual Report of the President, 1989–1990, 10–12.
22. Keller, *Making Harvard Modern,* 353.
23. Ibid., 437–438.
24. Hermann Hesse, *The Glass Bead Game*, trans. Richard and Clara Winston (New York: Henry Holt, 1990), 349–350.
25. Derek Bok, *Higher Learning,* 4th ed. (Cambridge, MA: Harvard University Press, 1988), 35–36.
26. Nathan M. Pusey, "A Faith for These Times," in *The Age of the Scholar* (Cambridge, MA: Belknap Press, 1963), 3–6.
27. Louis Menand notes of this period, "The stars were the people who talked about the failures and omissions in their own fields." *The Marketplace of Ideas Reform and Resistance in the American University* (New York: W.W. Norton, 2010), 86.
28. William Chace has written persuasively of the challenge facing English departments. With regard to a 2009 curriculum proposal at Harvard he has said: "Under the proposal, there would be no one book, or family of books, that every English major at Harvard would have read by the time he or she graduates. The direction to which Harvard would lead its students in this 'clean slate' or 'trickle down' experiment is to suspend literary history, thrusting into the hands of undergraduates the job of cobbling together intellectual coherence for themselves. [Harvard Shakespeare scholar Stephen] Greenblatt puts it this way: students should craft their own literary 'journeys.' The professors might have little idea of where those journeys might lead, or how their paths might become errant. There will be no common destination.

As Harvard goes, so often go the nation's other colleges and universities. Those who once strove to give order to the curriculum will have learned, from Harvard, that terms like *core knowledge* and *foundational experience* only trigger acrimony, turf protection, and faculty mutinies. No one has the stomach anymore to refight the Western culture wars. Let the students find their own way to knowledge." http://www.theamericanscholar.org.

29. http://www.thecrimson.com; http://www.provost.harvard.edu/institutional_research, 27. These are nominal dollars, not adjusted for the considerable inflation of that period.
30. Annual Report of the President, 1988–1989, 19, 34.
31. Ibid., 37.

Chapter 12: Even at Harvard

1. Morton Keller, *Making Harvard Modern* (New York: Oxford University Press, 2001), 372.
2. Final Report, 7. http://www.fas.harvard.edu.
3. Derek Bok, *Our Underachieving Colleges: A Candid Look at How Much Students Learn and Why They Should Be Learning More* (Princeton, NJ: Princeton University Press, 2006), and Harry R. Lewis, *Excellence Without a Soul: How a Great University Forgot Education* (New York: Public Affairs, 2006).
4. Final Report., 11, 13.
5. http://www.seasholes.com; http://www.ucop.edu.
6. Drew Faust, 2008 commencement speech. http://www.president.harvard.edu.
7. Ibid.
8. http://www.forbes.com.
9. Ibid.; http://www.president.harvard.edu.
10. http://www.yaledailynews.com; http://planning.fas.harvard.edu.
11. http://www.president.harvard.edu; http://www.boston.com.
12. http://www.president.harvard.edu.
13. Ibid.
14. Faust, 2008 commencement speech.
15. http://www.president.harvard.edu.
16. http://www.thecrimson.com.
17. http://cdn.wds.harvard.edu.

Chapter 13: Vulnerable Institutions

1. William W. Chace, *One Hundred Semesters* (Princeton, NJ: Princeton University Press, 2006), 49.
2. Morton Keller, *Making Harvard Modern* (New York: Oxford University Press, 2001), 178; http://www.universityofcalifornia.edu.
3. http://www.nytimes.com.
4. Clark Kerr, *The Uses of the University* (Cambridge, MA: Harvard University Press, 2001), 78.
5. http://www.time.com; http://www.admissions.umich.edu; http://ro.umich.edu.
6. See Nicholas Lemann, *The Big Test: The Secret History of American Meritocracy* (New York: Farrar, Strauss & Giroux, 1999), 131–136.
7. Ibid., 133.
8. http://classifications.carnegiefoundation.org.
9. http://www.businessweek.com bschools/content/dec2009, _4.
10. See Christopher J. Lucas, *American Higher Education* (New York: St. Martin's, 1994), 259–260, and Chace, *One Hundred Semesters*, 30.
11. http://classifications.carnegiefoundation.org.
12. See http://www.aftface.org/storage/face/documents, 10.
13. Henry Rosovsky, *The University: An Owner's Manual* (New York: W.W. Norton, 1990), 36.
14. Gaye Tuchman describes the role of upwardly ambitious academic administrators at a state university in *Wannabe U.* (Chicago: University of Chicago Press, 2009).
15. See, e.g., Arthur M. Cohen, *The Shaping of American Higher Education: Emergence and Growth of the Contemporary System* (San Francisco: Jossey-Bass, 1998), 107–108; 149–151; Lucas, *American Higher Education,* 177; Frederick Rudolph, *Curriculum: A History of the American Undergraduate Course of Study Since 1636* (San Francisco: Wiley, 1977), 226–227; Christopher Jencks and David Riesman, *The Academic Revolution* (New Brunswick, NJ: Transaction, 2001), 13–14, 24–25, 27, 514–515; Ernest L. Boyer, *Scholarship Reconsidered: The Priorities of the Professoriate* (Princeton, NJ: Carnegie Foundation for the Advancement of Teaching, 1990), 53–55.
16. Lucas, *American Higher Education,* 195; for a description of the process and mechanisms in California, see Lemann, *The Big Test,* 130–131.

17. Alexander C. McCormick and Chun-Mei Zhao, "Rethinking and Reframing the Carnegie Classification," *Change* 37, no. 5 (September–October 2005): 50–57.
18. See http://www.knightcommission.org.
19. See Cohen, *Shaping of American Higher Education,* 137.
20. "Will Higher Education Be the Next Bubble to Burst?," *Chronicle of Higher Education*, May 2, 2009. http://chronicle.com.The cost of university activities are not the only reason for tuition increases; others may include decreasing state support and increasing financial aid provided by the university to needy students.
21. National Center for Education Statistics, Enrollment in Postsecondary Institutions, Fall 2004; Graduation Rates, 1998 and 2001 Cohorts; and Financial Statistics, Fiscal Year 2004, Tables 5 and 6. http://nces.ed.gov.
22. National Center for Education Statistics, 1992 National Adult Literacy Survey and 2003 National Assessment of Adult Literacy, cited in U.S. Department of Education, *A Test of Leadership: Charting the Future of U.S. Higher Education* (Washington, DC: U.S. Department of Education, Education Publications Center, 2006), 13.
23. http://asufoundation.org.
24. http://oaa.osu.edu; http://oaa.osu.edu/irp/publisher_surveys, 6.
25. http://newamericanuniversity.asu.edu, 5; http://www.time.com.
26. http://www.mindingthecampus.com.

Chapter 14: Disruptive Competition

1. http://www.acenet.edu/e-newsletters/, 1–2.
2. Ibid., 3
3. Judith S. Eaton, *Distance Learning: Academic and Political Challenges for Higher Education* (Washington, DC: Council for Higher Accreditation, 2001), 12.
4. Edward Chancellor, *Devil Take the Hindmost: A History of Financial Speculation* (New York, Plume, 1999), 257; for greater detail on Milken's assessment of the bond markets in the early 1970s, see Connie Bruck, *The Predator's Ball* (New York: Penguin, 1989), 23–40.
5. For a summary of Milken's long-term impact on the financial markets, see http://www.economist.com. This article credits Milken and his colleagues with the "democratization of credit."

6. http://en.wikipedia.org.
7. http://www.census.gov.
8. http://www.wgu.edu.
9. Michael Leavitt, former governor of Utah and U.S. Secretary of Health and Human Services. Interview with the authors, January 2, 2011.
10. http://www.wgu.edu/; http://www.wgu.edu.tuition_financial_aid
11. Though demonstrations of learning outcomes are akin to investment rates of return, they are not equivalent. Risk-weighted rates of return allow precise comparisons among investments of vastly different types. By contrast, the difficulty of quantifying many important outcomes of higher education, such as creativity and judgment, makes similar comparisons of degree providers impossible, even when cognitive learning outcomes are known.
12. http://www.geteducated.com.
13. Assuming a compensation package including medical and retirement benefits of $100,000, a tenured university professor teaching five courses per year receives $20,000 per course, absent external funding. An online adjunct professor is likely to receive roughly one-tenth that amount. That gap can be closed if the tenured professor teaches classes of average size greater than the thirty or more typical of the online offerings of for-profit educators.
14. BYU-Idaho pays $825 per credit hour.
15. http://www.ed.gov/rschstat/eval/tech/evidence-based-practices/finalreport.pdf, xiv.
16. The overhead costs can be substantially less than two times the direct instructional costs for established universities offering online degrees.
17. http://www.trends-collegeboard.com.
18. Ibid.
19. http://www.sloan-c.org/publications; in Clayton Christensen, Michael Horn, and Curtis Johnson, *Disrupting Class: How Disruptive Innovation Will Change the Way the World Learns* (New York: McGraw-Hill, 2008). Christensen et al. have estimated that by 2019 one-half of high school courses will be delivered online. 98.
20. http://www.devryinc.com/investor-relations/annual-report/index.jsp, 88, 98.

21. Most of the DeVry campuses that have been in existence long enough to report six-year graduation rates graduate or transfer to other institutions between one-quarter and one-third of their first-time bachelor's degree-seeking students, compared with a national average of more than 60 percent. See http://nces.ed.gov/collegenavigator.
22. Byron G. August, Adam Cota, Kartick Jayaram, and Martha C. A. Laboissiére, *Winning by Degrees: The Strategy of Highly Productive Higher-Education Institutions* (n.p.: McKinsey & Company), 11. http://www.mckinsey.com.
23. http://www.insidehighered.com.
24. http://www.businessweek.com.
25. http://www.mindingthecampus.com.

Part IV: A New Kind of University

1. Hermann Hesse, *The Glass Bead Game*, trans. Richard and Clara Winston (New York: Henry Holt, 1990), 444.

Chapter 15: A Unique University Design

1. Robert Worrell, *History of Ricks College and Brigham Young University-Idaho: The Bednar Years* (1997–2004) (unpublished manuscript), 2, 32, 48.
2. Ibid., 8, 48–49.
3. Ibid., 3, 7, 14, 84, 225, 461.
4. Ibid., 63, 118–121, 216, 218, 226.
5. Ibid., 14, 46.
6. Ibid., 44–46, 107.
7. Ibid., 46–47, 108, 125.
8. Ibid., 112, 116, 131.
9. Ibid., 81–83, 134.
10. Ibid., 231–232.
11. Byron G. August, Adam Cota, Kartick Jayaram, and Martha C. A. Laboissiére, *Winning by Degrees: The Strategy of Highly Productive Higher-Education Institutions* (n.p.: McKinsey & Company), 43. http://www.mckinsey.com.
12. The exception to this finding was non–BYU students who attended classes at a Church Institute of Religion for four years while attending

another university or college; they experienced outcomes similar to those of BYU students.

13. Worrell, *History of Ricks College,* 85.
14. Undergraduate mentored research is a growing phenomenon recognized by federal research funding agencies. See, e.g., http://www.nsf.gov.
15. Henry B. Eyring, *A Steady, Upward Course*, Brigham Young University-Idaho, September 18, 2001. http://www.byui.edu.
16. Ibid., 10.
17. Ibid., 9–10.
18. http://www.byui.edu. By June 2001, fifty majors were planned for rollout over the next five years. Worrell, *History of Ricks College,* 460.
19. Worrell, *History of Ricks College,* 45, 260, 283.
20. http://webdocs.registrar.fas.harvard.edu.
21. Task Force on Education, *Preliminary Report* (October 2006), 3. http://www.fas.harvard.edu.

Chapter 16: Getting Started

1. See Robert Worrell, *History of Ricks College and Brigham Young University-Idaho: The Bednar Years* (1997–2004) (unpublished manuscript), 629.
2. The concept of a heavyweight team is described in detail Clayton Christensen, Michael Horn, and Curtis Johnson, *Disrupting Class: How Disruptive Innovation Will Change the Way the World Learns* (New York: McGraw-Hill, 2008), 204.
3. Clayton M. Christensen, *The Innovator's Dilemma* (New York: Harper-Collins, 2003).
4. See http://www.byui.edu.
5. See Worrell, *History of Ricks College,* 581–582.
6. http://www.byui.edu; Worrell, *History of Ricks College,* 119.
7. Worrell, *History of Ricks College,* 255.
8. http://www.knightcommissionmedia.org. A recent NCAA study showed athletic expenses growing three times faster than those of total university operations. http://www.ncaa.org.
9. http://www.byui.edu.
10. Worrell, *History of Ricks College,* 385.
11. *Idaho Falls Post Register*, June 22, 2000, D1.
12. http://www.hofstrachronicle.com.

13. http://www.usatoday.com/sports/college/.
14. Worrell, *History of Ricks College,* 265.
15. Ibid., 274.
16. Ibid., 284.
17. Ibid., 285.
18. BYU-Idaho internal data.
19. Worrell, *History of Ricks College,* 409, 582, 632.
20. http://www.byui.edu. The internship program was ably led by Guy Hollingsworth, an Army Reserve colonel and Ph.D. who would later spend a year creating educational programs for the Iraqi military.
21. See David Bednar's comments in Worrell, *History of Ricks College,* 462.
22. Worrell, *History of Ricks College,* 582–584, 607, 623, 633.

Chapter 17: Raising Quality

1. Harvard Business School Dean to Step Down, Move On, *Harvard University Gazette*, June 9, 2005, http://www.news.harvard.edu.
2. Neil Rudenstine, 1999 commencement speech.http://www.president .harvard.edu.
3. "Harvard Business School Dean to Step Down."
4. http://www.byui.edu.
5. Ibid.
6. Ibid.
7. Robert Worrell, *History of Ricks College and Brigham Young University-Idaho: The Bednar Years* (1997–2004) (unpublished manuscript), 633.
8. This calendar was the brainchild of Clark's academic vice president, Max Checketts, who brought unique insights to the task. Originally hired at Ricks College to start a dairy program in the 1980s, he had risen through the administrative ranks while working on a Ph.D. that included a doctoral minor in statistics. Checketts's gift for numerical analysis and his experience with dairy production timetables helped him see an innovative solution to the problem of serving more students while also providing an adequate summer vacation for the faculty.
9. The naming system was created by associate academic vice president Rhonda Seamons, who had played a leading role in the university's initial accreditation process.
10. See http://www.byui.edu.

11. http://www.eric.ed.gov/PDFS/ED101652.pdf, 45 and 49); this study did not account for potential savings from spreading the fixed expense of the health care and retirement benefits of faculty and other university employees.
12. http://www.lao.ca.gov/sections/higher_ed/.
13. http://www.lao.ca.gov/analysis_2006/education/.
14. See http://www.byui.edu.
15. This assessment was offered by Ross Baron, a professor of religion, ethics, and logic.
16. The full list of Learning Model principles can be found at http://www.byui.edu.
17. http://www.hbs.edu.
18. C. Roland Christensen, "Premises and Practices of Discussion Teaching," in *Education for Judgment: The Artistry of Discussion Leadership* , ed. C. Roland Christensen, David A. Garvin, and Ann Sweet (Boston: Harvard Business School Press, 1991), 16.
19. See Abby J. Hansen, "Establishing a Teaching/Learning Contract," in *Education for Judgment*, 123–135.
20. Christensen, "Premises and Practices," 31.
21. See Worrell, *History of Ricks College,* 203–204, 491–498.
22. See http://www.byui.edu.
23. Michael Bassis of Utah's Westminster College has articulated the possibilities created by the combination of new learning and information retrieval technologies: The learning paradigm changes the traditional roles and relationships that have defined higher education for so long. Since technology can provide students with access to more and better learning resources than they could ever get from a lecture, faculty can let go of the full weight of being the "subject matter expert." Freed from the burden of being the sole source of subject-specific information, they can function as learning guides, facilitators, and mentors, placing more emphasis on helping students master those critical intellectual skills and attributes that transcend academic disciplines. And once released from the responsibility to deliver all of the content, faculty can work effectively with more students, thus reducing the cost of the learning experience and increasing its quality. See http://www.businessweek.com.
24. See http://www.byui.edu.

25. Maryellen Weiner, *Making Learner-Centered Teaching Work* (San Francisco, CA: Jossey-Bass, forthcoming).
26. Derek Bok, 1971–1972 President's Report, 15–16, http://pds.lib .harvard.edu.
27. Worrell, *History of Ricks College,* 496.
28. See http://www.byui.edu/Foundations.
29. See Bok, 109–145, 146–171, 225–254.
30. Ibid., 123.
31. Rob Eaton, "A Case for Student Participation," *Perspective* 6, no. 2 Autumn 2006: 25. http://www.byui.edu.
32. Ibid.
33. Bok, 49, emphasis in original.
34. This team member, Humanities and Philosophy Department Chair Vaughan Stephenson, became a highly rated instructor of the BYU-Idaho American Foundations course.
35. The leader of the Pakistan, or "Global Hotspot," course team was former corporate attorney and then-religion professor Rob Eaton. His teammates included Theron Josephson (geographer), Alan Walburger (economist), and Brian Felt (Russian linguist).
36. Though BYU-Idaho negotiated transfer arrangements with the schools to which most of its students transfer—BYU and the Idaho and Utah public universities—the uniqueness of some Foundations courses made them nontransferrable except as part of an associate's degree, leading the university to caution students planning to transfer before the end of the sophomore year against taking those courses.
37. Therese Huston, *Teaching What You Don't Know* (Cambridge, MA: Harvard University Press, 2009).
38. http://www.byui.edu.
39. Release time means an exemption from normal teaching duties.
40. BYU-Idaho Faculty Association internal survey data, 2009.

Chapter 18: Lowering Cost

1. http://www.byui.edu.
2. See http://www.byui.edu; as in the case of admission to BYU-Idaho, the Grant Scholars program is open to all students, regardless of religious affiliation, so long as they commit to living by the universities code of conduct.
3. Statement of Alan Young, leader of online course development at BYU-Idaho.

4. See http://www2.ed.gov/rschstat/.
5. The importance tailoring curriculum to differing learning styles is explored in Clayton Christensen, Michael Horn, and Curtis Johnson, *Disrupting Class: How Disruptive Innovation Will Change the Way the World Learns* (New York: McGraw-Hill, 2008).
6. Christensen et al., *Disrupting Class*, 81.
7. Shoshana Zuboff, *In the Age of the Smart Machine: The Future of Work and Power* (New York: Basic Books, 1989).
8. *Online Learning: Extending the BYU-Idaho Experience,* 72. http://www.byui.edu.
9. See "Peer Instruction: From Harvard to the Two-Year College," *American Journal of Physics* 76, no. 11 (November 2008): 1066–1069.
10. http://www.learner.org.
11. "Peer Instruction."
12. http://www.nytimes.com.
13. Eric Mazur, *Peer Instruction: A User's Manual* (Redwood City, CA: Benjamin Cummings, 1996).
14. http://www.bedu.com.
15. *Online Learning,* 71–72.
16. http://www.ed.gov.
17. Byron G. August, Adam Cota, Kartick Jayaram, and Martha C. A. Laboissiére, *Winning by Degrees: The Strategy of Highly Productive Higher-Education Institutions* (n.p.: McKinsey & Company). http://www.mckinsey.com.
18. http://www.riosalado.edu; August et al., *Winning by Degrees*, 16–17.
19. David Peck, "Participants in an Academic Community," *Perspective* 9, no. 2 (2009): 88–89. http://www.byui.edu.
20. *Online Learning,* 69–70.
21. Ibid, 69–70.
22. BYU-Idaho internal data; the reasons for a tighter distribution of quality outcomes in online courses are well articulated by Todd Gilman, "Combating Myths About Distance Education," February 22, 2010 http://chronicle.com.
23. Clayton M. Christensen, *The Innovator's Dilemma* (New York: Harper-Collins, 2003).
24. The one-third value assumes a full-time faculty teaching load of thirteen three-credit courses per year, the BYU-Idaho standard. The low market

rate for online instruction raises the questions of whether and how the wages of online and full-time face-to-face instructors will converge. Greater use of online instruction should cause online wages to rise, assuming a fixed pool of qualified instructors. However, that pool is truly global and thus very large; it is also likely to grow, via increasing education participation rates in less-developed countries. As a consequence, downward pressure on full-time faculty salaries seems likely, along with a decrease in the proportion of full-time opportunities, an already established trend. See http://www.aftface.org.

25. The authors thank Rob Eaton for this metaphor.
26. The typical college student in the United States takes at least one semester longer to graduate than the eight required. http://nces.ed.gov.
27. See http://webdocs.registrar.fas.harvard.edu.
28. National Center for Education Statistics, Enrollment in Postsecondary Institutions, Fall 2004; Graduation Rates, 1998 & 2001 Cohorts; and Financial Statistics, Fiscal Year 2004, Table 5. http://nces.ed.gov.
29. Louis Menand, *The Marketplace of Ideas: Reform and Resistance in the American University* (New York: W.W. Norton, 2010), 53.
30. Arthur M. Cohen, *The Shaping of American Higher Education: Emergence and Growth of the Contemporary System* (San Francisco: Jossey-Bass, 1998), 108.
31. http://www.byui.edu.
32. National Center for Education Statistics, Enrollment in Postsecondary Institutions, Fall 2004; Graduation Rates, 1998 & 2001 Cohorts; and Financial Statistics, Fiscal Year 2004, Table 6. http://nces.ed.gov
33. See Kim B. Clark and Carlyss Y. Baldwin, *Design Rules, Vol I: The Power of Modularity* (Cambridge, MA: MIT Press, 2000).
34. The slogan was coined by Associate Academic Vice President Bruce Kusch, a former Silicon Valley marketing executive.
35. http://www.byui.edu.
36. Robert S. Kaplan and Davis P. Norton, "The Balanced Scorecard—Measures That Drive Performance," *Harvard Business Review* 70, no. 1 (January–February 1992): 71–79.
37. Ibid.
38. BYU-Idaho's institutional report card can be accessed at http://www.byui.edu.

Chapter 19: Serving More Students

1. http://www.byui.edu.
2. Robert Worrell, *History of Ricks College and Brigham Young University-Idaho: The Bednar Years* (1997–2004) (unpublished manuscript), 489.
3. Kaoru Ishikawa's principles and practices of quality control are explored in his book *What Is Total Quality Control? The Japanese Way* (Englewood Cliffs, NJ: Prentice Hall, 1985).
4. For a detailed presentation of the BYU-Idaho fishbone, see Henry O. Eyring, "Unexploited Efficiencies in Higher Education,"*Contemporary Issues in Education Research*, 4, no. 7 (2011).
5. The task fell to Ric Page, a thirty-year veteran who knew every nook and cranny of the campus.
6. The work of enlisting and coordinating the efforts of these volunteers, as well as recruiting the students, fell to J. D. Griffith. His background in organizing summer youth camps (before the campus was filled with college students in summer by the year-round calendar) made him well suited to the task.
7. See chaps. 5 and 6 of Clayton M. Christensen, *The Innovator's Dilemma* (New York: HarperCollins, 2003).
8. For a description of the effect of organizational structure on innovation in education, see chap. 9, "Giving Schools the Right Structure to Innovate," in Clayton Christensen, Michael Horn, and Curtis Johnson, *Disrupting Class: How Disruptive Innovation Will Change the Way the World Learns* (New York: McGraw-Hill, 2008).
9. http://pef.lds.org/pef.
10. Ibid.
11. These are full-time equivalent figures, assuming a fifteen-hour credit load in each of two semesters, including BYU-Idaho's spring semester.
12. These are constant 2010 dollars.

Part V: Genetic Reengineering

1. Hermann Hesse, *The Glass Bead Game*, trans. Richard and Clara Winston (New York: Henry Holt, 1990), 444.

Chapter 20: New Models

1. http://www.snhu.edu.
2. Ibid.

3. http://www.businessweek.com.
4. Theodore Levitt, "Marketing Myopia," *Harvard Business Review* 38 (July–August 1960): 45–46.
5. Theodore Levitt, *The Marketing Imagination* (New York: Free Press, 1983), 48.
6. Jonathan Cole, *The Great American University: Its Rise to Preeminence, Its Indispensable National Role, Why It Must Be Protected* (New York: Public Affairs, 2010).
7. http://www.nsf.gov.
8. http://www.tco.utah.edu.
9. http://www.tco.utah.edu/vip.html.
10. http://www.deseretnews.com. Eleven of the 109 companies had failed, and eight were operating outside of Utah.
11. See http://infolab.stanford.edu.
12. Allen Peskin, *Garfield* (Kent, OH: Kent State University Press, 1978), 34.
13. http://www.umich.edu/pres.
14. http://www.ecornell.com.
15. http://www.cornellsun.com.
16. http://www.aftface.org.
17. The trend toward hybridization, or blended learning, is well documented. See, e.g., I. Elaine Allen, Jeff Seaman, and Richard Garrett, *Blending In: The Extent and Promise of Blended Education in the United States Sloan* (Needham, MA: Sloan Consortium, 2007); Anthony G. Picciano and Charles D. Dziuban, *Blended Learning: Research Perspectives* (Needham, MA: Sloan Consortium, 2007).
18. A Lawrence Lowell, Inaugural Address, October 6, 1909, in A. Lawrence Lowell, *At War with Academic Traditions in America* (New York: Greenwood, 1970). http://hul.harvard.edu.
19. U.S. Census Bureau, *A Half-Century of Learning: Historical Census Statistics on Educational Attainment in the United States, 1940 to 2000,* Table 2. http://www.census.gov.
20. See http://nces.ed.gov.
21. The earning power of a college degree has held steady (see U.S. Department of Education, National Center for Education Statistics, *The Condition of Education 2008* (NCES 2008–031), Table 20-1,

http://nces.ed.gov), but as the cost has increased faster than inflation, the relative value has decreased.

22. See Ernest L. Boyer, *Scholarship Reconsidered: The Priorities of the Professoriate* (Princeton, NJ: Carnegie Foundation for the Advancement of Teaching, 1990), xii, 33.
23. Micahel E. Porter, "What Is Strategy?," *Harvard Business Review* 74, no. 6 (November–December 1996). http://www.ipocongress.ru.
24. http://www.universitybusiness.com.
25. http://president.babson.edu.
26. http://www3.babson.edu.

Chapter 21: Students and Subjects

1. Byron G. August, Adam Cota, Kartick Jayaram, and Martha C. A. Laboissiére, *Winning by Degrees: The Strategy of Highly Productive Higher-Education Institutions* (n.p., McKinsey & Company), 51. http://www.mckinsey.com.
2. http://www.completecollege.org.
3. August et al., *Winning by Degrees*, 51.
4. The future of digitally empowered constituents that awaits universities and all service providers is described by Jeff Jarvis in *What Would Google Do?* (New York: HarperCollins), 2009. Jarvis suggests that the insensitivity of the multiversity to undergraduate students described by Clark Kerr will not be tolerated indefinitely: "Anyone can use the internet to undercut you—to craigslist you. If you make your living telling people what they can't do because you control resources or relationships, if you work in a closed marketplace where information and choice are controlled and value is obscured, then your days are numbered." 74.
5. http://www.achievingthedream.org.
6. August et al., *Winning by Degrees*, 10, 11, 43. The $56,289 amount is the institution's cost of delivering a degree, inclusive of costs incurred to educate the fraction of students who do not graduate.
7. See http://www.valenciacc.edu.
8. August et al., *Winning by Degrees*, 34–35.
9. Ibid., 49.
10. Ibid., 57.

11. See http://chronicle.com/article/Disappearing-Disciplines; also, http://chronicle.com/ blog/Campus-Cuts.
12. http://www.businessweek.com.
13. One way to avoid these outcomes is grow student enrollments.
14. August et al., *Winning by Degrees*, 11, 36.
15. Derek Bok, *Our Underachieving Colleges*, 38.
16. Ibid.
17. Stanley Fish, *Save the World on Your Own Time* (New York: Oxford University Press, 2008), makes this argument pointedly.
18. Ibid., 65.
19. C. Roland Christensen, "Premises and Practices of Discussion Teaching," in *Education for Judgment: The Artistry of Discussion Leadership* , ed. C. Roland Christensen, David A. Garvin, and Ann Sweet (Boston: Harvard Business School Press, 1991), 117, 118.

Chapter 22: Scholarship

1. Addresses at the Inauguration of Charles William Eliot as President of Harvard College, Tuesday, October 19, 1869, in Samuel Eliot Morison, *Development of Harvard University Since the Inauguration of President Eliot 1869–1929* (Cambridge, MA: Harvard University Press, 1930), p. 29.
2. Ibid., 30.
3. See Ernest L. Boyer, *Scholarship Reconsidered: The Priorities of the Professoriate* (Princeton, NJ: Carnegie Foundation for the Advancement of Teaching, 1990), 15; William W. Chace, *One Hundred Semesters* (Princeton, NJ: Princeton University Press, 2006), 134.
4. See Derek Bok, 340; also, Boyer, *Scholarship Reconsidered*, 37–40.
5. Annual Report of the President, 1988–1989, 14. The most demanding research universities measure not just the number of publications but also the frequency of citation by other scholars; they also seek evaluation of tenure and promotion candidates by domain experts.
6. Ibid., 14–15.
7. *Biographical Memoirs of Fellows of the Royal Society* 25 (November 1979): 211.
8. Ibid., 229–231.
9. *Governments and Parties in Continental Europe* 1, vii.

10. Ibid.
11. Ibid., vi–vii.
12. For a compelling account of a Stanford English professor's experience with similar research constraints, see Chace, *One Hundred Semesters*, chap. 16, "Tenure and Its Discontents," and chap. 16, "The English Department in Disarray."
13. For two descriptions of this dynamic, see http://www.nytimes.com and http://www.lewrockwell.com.
14. See Chace, *One Hundred Semesters,* 57; also, Henry Rosovsky, *The University: An Owner's Manual* (New York: W.W. Norton, 1990), 138–147.
15. http://www.aftface.org.
16. http://journals.aomonline.org.
17. Clark Gilbert and his HBS colleague Joseph L. Bower have written about the general tendency of operating procedures to drive organizational behavior and strategy in their book *From Resource Allocation to Strategy* (New York: Oxford University Press), 2005.
18. Annual Report of the President, 1988–1989, 15.
19. The scholarship of application has also been termed the scholarship of engagement, in recognition of a potential two-way flow—scholars engaged in sharing theories with practitioners can learn in the process. See R. Eugene Rice and Mary Deane Sorcinelli, "Can the Tenure Process Be Improved?" in Richard P. Chait, ed., *The Questions of Tenure* (Cambridge, MA: Harvard University Press, 2005), 110–113.
20. Boyer, *Scholarship Reconsidered*, 16–25.
21. http://www.mindingthecampus.com/.
22. Ibid., 27.
23. Boyer, *Scholarship Reconsidered*, 28, 35.
24. For examples of customization in addition to those that follow in the text, see Rice and Sorcinelli, "Can the Tenure Process Be Improved?," 107–116.
25. For a more detailed description of the scholarship of both Michael Porter and Clayton Christensen, see http://www.innosight.com.
26. http://www.library.hbs.edu.
27. http://www.carnegiefoundation.org.
28. Ibid.

29. http://www.nytimes.com. The fourfold definition of scholarship proposed in *Scholarship Reconsidered* has had less impact on rank and tenure criteria than Ernest Boyer might have hoped. Emphasis on teaching has increased at some institutions, but discovery research generally remains predominant. See Boyer, *Faculty Priorities Reconsidered*, cited in http://www.insidehighered.com.
30. Louis Menand, *The Marketplace of Ideas: Reform and Resistance in the American University* (New York: W.W. Norton, 2010), 121.
31. Boyer and his colleagues proposed "creativity contracts" reflecting different mixes of scholarship types at different points of a faculty member's career. Boyer, *Scholarship Reconsidered*, 48
32. See, e.g., Thomas J. Peters and Robert H. Waterman, *In Search of Excellence: Lessons from America's Best-Run Companies* (New York: Harper Paperbacks, 2004), 244, 249, 252, 261; Jeffery Pfeffer, *Competitive Advantage Through People: Unleashing the Power of the Work Force* (Cambridge, MA: Harvard University Press, 1996), 31–33; Peter Drucker, *Management: Tasks, Responsibilities, Practices* (New York: Harper Paperbacks, 1993), 246–265, 285–288.
33. The analogy is not exact: though partners in law and business consulting firms often specialize, they do so to a lesser degree than university professors, making them more easily deployable to new types of work as the need arises.
34. Jim Collins, *Good to Great: Why Some Companies Make the Leap . . . and Others Don't* (New York: HarperCollins, 2001), 114.
35. See Rosovsky, *University,* 179.
36. See, e.g., Chait, *Questions of Tenure,* 101–106.
37. Robert Worrell, *History of Ricks College and Brigham Young University-Idaho: The Bednar Years* (1997–2004) (unpublished manuscript), 232 (emphasis added).
38. This view is supported by the finding that, in 1989, 70 percent of professors reported feeling loyal to their discipline, but only 40 percent had similar feelings for their institution. Boyer, *Faculty Priorities Reconsidered*, 56, cited in Menand, *Marketplace of Ideas*, 122. That same study showed that tenure does not correlate with a decline in faculty productivity. See Richard P. Chait, "The Future of Academic Tenure," *AGB Priorities*, no. 3 (Spring 1995): 8.

39. As in the case of students, BYU-Idaho employees must commit to abiding by the University's code of honor, regardless of their religious affiliation.
40. http://www.aaup.org.
41. Ibid.
42. Ibid.; Cathy R. Trower, "What Is Current Policy?," 57, in Chait, *Questions of Tenure*.
43. Trower, "What Is Current Policy?," 53–54, 63.
44. See Benjamin, "Implications of Tenure."
45. In this respect tenure makes university professors more powerful than employees of the typical corporation, though not necessarily more so than partners in a professional corporation or members of an organized union.
46. Chait, *Questions of Tenure,* 312.
47. Hugh Hawkins, *Between Harvard and America: The Educational Leadership of Charles W. Eliot* (New York: Oxford University Press, 1972), 77.

Chapter 23: New DNA

1. http://www.jimcollins.com.
2. http://uvu.edu.
3. http://www.time.com.
4. See http://www2.ed.gov
5. http://president.asu.edu.

Chapter 24: Change and the Indispensable University

1. Henry Aaron Yeomans, *Lawrence Lowell: 1856–1943* (Cambridge, MA: Harvard University Press, 1948), 183.
2. http://www.news.harvard.edu.
3. Louis Menand deftly describes the scholar's urge to be relevant: "Mainly, we want to feel we are in a real fight, a fight not with each other and our schools, which is the fight that outsiders seem to be encouraging us to have, but with the forces that make and remake the world most human beings live in . . . . It is important for research and teaching to be relevant, for the university to engage with the public culture and to design its investigative paradigms with actual social and cultural life in view." *The Marketplace of Ideas: Reform and Resistance in the American University* (New York: W.W. Norton, 2010), 124–125, 158.

4. Addresses at the Inauguration of Charles William Eliot as President of Harvard College, Tuesday, October 19, 1869, in Samuel Eliot Morison, *Development of Harvard University Since the Inauguration of President Eliot 1869–1929* (Cambridge, MA: Harvard University Press, 1930), 31, 33.
5. Ibid. 30.
6. "What Is Strategy?," *Harvard Business Review* (November–December 1996).
7. Yeomans, *Lawrence Lowell*, 46.

The Authors

Clayton M. Christensen is the Robert and Jane Cizik Professor of Business Administration at the Harvard Business School and is widely regarded as one of the world's foremost experts on innovation and growth. He is the author or coauthor of ten books, including *Disrupting Class* and the *New York Times* bestsellers *The Innovator's Dilemma* and *The Innovator's Solution*.

* * *

Henry J. Eyring has served as an administrator at Brigham Young University (BYU)-Idaho since 2006. He holds degrees in geology, business administration, and law, all from Brigham Young University in Provo, Utah. He is the author of two other books, *Mormon Scientist: The Life and Faith of Henry Eyring* and *Major Decisions: Taking Charge of Your College Education*.

Innosight Institute

Innosight Institute is a not-for-profit, nonpartisan think tank whose mission is to apply Harvard Business School professor Clayton M. Christensen's theories of disruptive innovation to develop and promote solutions to the most vexing problems in the social sector. It authors a variety of publications—from books to white papers to policy briefs and case studies—in which it applies these theories. Using this work, its staff members speak around the country to educate key stakeholders—from policymakers to CEOs—on how to create positive change.

With existing practices that have focused largely on transforming K–12 education and health care, Insight Institute will apply the royalties from this book in launching its practice in higher education. The intellectual basis for this practice will stem from this exciting book as well as Innosight Institute's recent publication, "Disrupting College: How Disruptive Innovation Can Deliver Quality and Affordability to Postsecondary Education," which it published with the Center for American Progress in February 2011.

INDEX

Page references followed by *fig* indicate an illustrated figure; followed by *t* indicate a table.

C

H

M

N

O

Q

R

U

V

W